Contents

Foreword

Bed & Breakfast has suddenly become the fashionable way to travel. The secret has escaped & thousands of people are discovering for themselves that it is possible to combine high quality accommodation with friendly, personal attention at very reasonable prices. The New York Times said about us that "...after an unannounced inspection of rooms booked through The Worldwide Bed & Breakfast Association it is clear that the standards of comfort & cleanliness are exemplary ...at least as good as in a five star hotel & in most cases, better, reflecting the difference between sensitive hosts taking pride in their homes & itinerant hotel staff doing as little as they can get away with..."

Discerning travellers are turning away from the impersonal hotels with the expensive little refridgerators & microwave breakfasts in each room. How much nicer to have a real English breakfast to begin the day, enough to keep you going until evening. Many of our houses will provide dinner too - often the hostess will be a Cordon Bleu cook & the price will be within your range. We try to provide the best accommodation possible within a wide range of prices, some as little as £15.00 per person per night, whilst others will be up to £60.00 per person per night. The choice is yours, but you can be certain that each will be the best available in that particular area of the country at that price.

Our inspectors are out & about visiting our homes to ensure that standards are maintained. We encourage everyone to use the recommendations & complaints page at the back of the book. Let us know your opinion of the accommodation or inform us of any delightful homes you may have come across & would like to recommend for future inclusion.

In order to avoid the classification trap, which we feel is invidious, we encourage you to read about each home, what they offer & their respective price range, so that you find the one that best suits your expectations. Our hosts in turn offer hospitality in their own unique style, so each home naturally retains its individuality & interest. We have found this to be a very successful recipe which often leads to lasting friendships.

Bed & Breakfast really is a marvellous way to travel, meeting a delightful cross section of fellow travellers with whom to exchange information & maybe the address of ...that lovely little place which was discovered by chance and which serves the most delicious dinner or... the best route to take to a particular farmhouse but make sure you get there by 5 o'clock so that you're in time to watch the evening milking...

This is the fun & real pleasure that is part of Bed & Breakfasting. Once you've tried it you will be a dedicated Best Bed & Breakfaster.

How to use this Guide

To get the full benefits of staying at our Bed & Breakfast homes it is important to appreciate how they differ from hotels, so both hosts & guests know what to expect.

Arrival & Departure

These times are more important to a family than to hotel desk clerks, so your time of arrival (E.T.A.) is vital information when making a reservation either with the home directly or with one of our agencies. This becomes even more important to your reception if you intend travelling overnight & will be arriving in the early morning. So please have this information & your flight number ready when you book your rooms. **At most B & Bs the usual check-in time is 6 P.M. & you will be expected to check out by 10 A.M. on the morning of departure.** These arrangements do vary from home to home. The secret to an enjoyable visit is to let your hosts know as much about your plans as possible & they will do their best to meet your requirements.

Other personal requests

There are a few other details that you should let your hosts know when planning your Bed & Breakfast trip that will make everyone much happier during your visit. Do you smoke? Would you prefer to be in a non-smoking home? Do you suffer from any allergies? Some families have cats, dogs, birds & other pets in the house....Can you make it up a flight of stairs? Would you prefer the ground floor? Do you have any special dietary requirements? Will you be staying for dinner?

Do you prefer a private bathroom or are you prepared to share facilities? Do you prefer a shower instead of a bath? The ages of any children travelling.

In all these cases let your host know what you need & the details can be arranged before you arrive rather than presenting a problem when you are shown to your rooms.

Prices

The prices quoted throughout the guide are the *minimum* per person per night for two sharing. Single occupancy usually attracts a supplement. Prices will increase during busy seasons. You should always confirm the prevailing rate when you make a reservation.

Facilities

The bathroom & toilet facilities affect the prices. Sharing is the cheapest, private is a little more costly & en-suite carries a premium.

Descriptions

Rooms are described as follows: Single:1 bed (often quite small). Double:1large bed (sometimes King or Queensize).

Twin: 2 separate single beds.

Four-poster: a King or Queen size bed with a canopy above supported by four corner posts.

Bathrooms and toilets are described as follows;

Shared: these facilities are shared with some other guests or perhaps the hosts.

Private: for your use only, however they may occasionally be in an adjacent room.

En-suite: private facilities within your bedroom suite.

Making a Reservation

Once you have chosen where you want to stay, have all the following information ready & your reservation will go smoothly without having to run & find more travel documents or ask someone else what they think you should do. Here is a brief check list of what you will probably be asked & examples to illustrate answers:

Dates & number of nights...August 14-19(6 nights).

Estimated time of arrival at the home ...7 P.M.(evening) & flight number.

Type & number of rooms...1 Double & 2 Single.

Toilet & Bathroom facilities...1 Double en-suite) & 2 singles (shared)

Smoking or Non-smoking?

Any allergies?

Special dietary requests?

Children in the party & their ages?

Any other preferences... Is a shower preferred to a bath?

Maximum budget per person per night based on all the above details.

The London Reservation Agency

There is a minimum two night consecutive stay at our London homes.

Reservations for London homes can only be made through one of our Worldwide Bed & Breakfast Agencies. They can be contacted by 'phone, fax, e-mail or on-line from our website at http://www.bestbandb.co.uk.

All reservations must be confirmed with advance payments which are non-refundable in the event of cancellation. You simply pay the balance due after you arrive at the home. The advance payment can be made with major credit & charge cards or by cheque. Cash is the preferred method of paying the balance & always in pounds sterling.

The advance payments confirm each night of your visit, **not just the first one**.

When arriving at a later date or departing at an earlier date than those confirmed, the guest will be liable to pay only the appropriate proportion of the stated balance that is due. For example, staying three nights out of four booked means paying 3/4 of the stated balance due. The advance payment is non-refundable. A minimum of 2 nights will always apply.

Outside London

We encourage you to make use of the information in this guide & contact the homes directly. The hosts may require varying amounts of advance payments & may or may not accept credit & charge cards. Remember, many B&Bs are small, family-run establishments and are unable to accept payment by credit card. The confirmed prices shall be those prevailing on the dates required... as previously mentioned,*the prices shown in this guide are the **minimum** & will increase during the busy seasons.*

Alterations

If you wish to alter or change a previously confirmed booking through one of the agencies there will be a further fee of £15 per alteration.

Cancellations

All advance payments for London are non-refundable.

All booking fees outside London are non-refundable.

Notice of cancellation must be given as soon as possible & the following suggested rates shall apply outside London only;

30 - 49 days notice - 80% refund.

10-29 days notice -50% refund.

0 - 9 days notice - No refund.

The Worldwide Bed & Breakfast Agencies reserve the right to alter your accommodation should it be necessary & will inform you of any alteration as soon as possible.

London Reservation Agency

We offer an outstanding selection of accommodation in London. As with all our accommodation each one has been personally inspected so you can be sure of the highest standards. We offer an immensely wide range of accommodation. We have a type, style and location to suit everyone. From city apartments close to shops, museums and galleries to spacious homes in leafy residential suburbs near the river, parks and restaurants. No matter what your reason for visiting London we can accommodate you. Whether on business or vacation the Best Bed & Breakfast provides great accommodation together with a fast, efficient reservation service. Our helpful staff are always happy to advise you on all your accommodation requirements. We are located in London, we know the city and all our hosts. We know how to provide an enjoyable, affordable, hassle free trip. There are plenty of ways to contact us. To make a reservation simply do one of the following;

Website: http://www.bestbandb.co.uk

Worldwide call Tel: +44 (0)20 8742 9123 (24Hrs.)

North America call Toll Free: 011 800 852 26320

Australia call Toll Free: 0011 800 852 26320

E-mail: bestbandb@atlas.co.uk

Fax: +44 (0)20 8749 7084

The Discount Offer

This offer is made to people who have bought this book & wish to make reservations for Bed & Breakfast in London through our London Reservation Agency. The offer only applies to a minimum stay of three consecutive nights at one of our London homes between the following dates; January 7. 2004 to April 1. 2004 then from September 15. 2004 to December 1. 2004. Only one discount per booking is allowed. Call the reservation office to make your booking in the normal way & tell the clerk that you have bought the book & wish to have the discount. After a couple of questions the discount will be deducted from the advance payment required to confirm the reservation.

Regions

To assist tourists with information during their travels, counties have been grouped together under Regional Tourist Boards that co-ordinate the various efforts of each county.

The British Tourist Authority has designated these areas in consultation with the English, Scottish & Wales Tourist Boards & we have largely adopted these areas for use in this guide

Counties are listed alphabetically throughout our guide & then have a sub-heading indicating which Tourist Region they belong to.

ENGLAND

Cumbria
County of Cumbria

Northumbria.
Counties of Cleveland, Durham, Northumberland, Tyne & Wear.

North West
Counties of Cheshire, Greater Manchester, Lancashire, Merseyside, High Peaks of Derbyshire.

Yorkshire & Humberside
Counties of North Yorkshire, South Yorkshire, West Yorkshire, Humberside.

Heart of England
Counties of Gloucestershire, Herefordshire & Worcestershire, Shropshire, Staffordshire, Warwickshire, West Midlands.

East Midlands
Counties of Derbyshire, Leicestershire, Nottinghamshire, Rutland, Lincolnshire & Northamptonshire,

East Anglia
Counties of Cambridgeshire, Essex, Norfolk, Suffolk.

West Country
Counties of Cornwall, Devon, Dorset (parts of), Somerset, Wiltshire, Isles of Scilly.

Southern
Counties of Hampshire, Dorset (East & North), Isle of Wight.

South East
Counties of East Sussex, Kent, Surrey, West Sussex.

SCOTLAND

The subdivisions of Scottish Regions in this guide differ slightly from the current Marketing Regions of the Scottish Tourist Board.

The Borders, Dumfries & Galloway
Districts & counties of Scottish Borders, Dumfries & Galloway.

Lothian & Strathclyde
City of Edinburgh, Forth Valley, East Lothian, Kirkaldy, St. Andrews & North-East Fife, Greater Glasgow, Clyde Valley, Ayrshire & Clyde Coast, Burns Country.

Argyll & The Isles
Districts & counties of Oban & Mull, Mid Argyll, Kintyre & Islay, Dunoon, Cowal, Rothesay & Isle of Bute, Isle of Arran.

Perthshire, Loch Lommond & The Trossachs.
Districts & counties of Perthshire, Loch Lomond, Stirling & Trossachs.

The Grampians
Districts & counties of Banff & Buchan, Moray, Gordon, Angus, City of Aberdeen, Kincardine & Deeside, City of Dundee.

The Highlands & Islands
Districts & counties of Shetland, Orkney, Caithness, Sutherland, Ross & Cromarty, Western Isles, South West Ross & Isle of Skye, Inverness, Loch Ness & Nairn, Aviemore & Spey Valley, Fort William & Lochaber.

WALES

The regions are defined as follows:
North Wales
Counties of Anglesey, Conwy, Denbighshire, Flintshire & Gwynedd.

Mid Wales
Counties of Ceredigion & Powys.

South Wales
Counties of Carmarthenshire, Glamorgan, Monmouthshire, Newport, Pembrokeshire & Swansea.

The photographs appearing in the Introductions & Gazeteers are by courtesy of the appropriate Tourist Board for each county or W.W.B.B.A.

Counties map

Each county has been assigned a page number where a more detailed map can be found. These maps include principal towns, major roads & the location of each Bed & Breakfast establishment.

SCOTLAND
339

1 INVERCLYDE
2 DUNBARTON & CLYDEBANK
3 RENFREWSHIRE
4 EAST RENFREWSHIRE
5 GLASGOW
6 EAST DUNBARTONSHIRE

7 NORTH LANARKSHIRE
8 FALKIRK
9 CLACKMANNAN
10 WEST LOTHIAN
11 EDINBURGH
12 MID LOTHAIN

OUTER HEBRIDES
WESTERN ISLES
INNER HEBRIDES
HIGHLANDS
MORAY
ABERDEENSHIRE
ABERDEEN
PERTHSHIRE & KINROSS
ANGUS
DUNDEE
ARGYLL & BUTE
STIRLING
FIFE
EAST LOTHIAN
NORTH AYRSHIRE
SOUTH LANARKSHIRE
BORDERS
EAST AYRSHIRE
SOUTH AYRSHIRE
DUMFRIES & GALLOWAY
NORTHUMBERLAND

North Sea

TYNE AND WEAR
211
CUMBRIA
76
DURHAM
CLEVELAND
YORKSHIRE
313 HUMBERSIDE

LANCASHIRE
50

Irish Sea

MANCHESTER
MERSEYSIDE

ENGLAND

FLINTSHIRE
DENBIGHSHIRE
ANGLESEY
CONWY
CHESHIRE
50
DERBYSHIRE
96
LINCOLNSHIRE
191 198
NOTTINGHAM-SHIRE,
GWYNEDD
WREXHAM
STAFFORD-SHIRE
LEICESTERSHIRE & RUTLAND
NORFOLK
204

WALES
373

SHROP-SHIRE
229
CEREDIGION
POWYS
WARWICK-SHIRE
287
CAMBRIDGE-SHIRE & NORTHAMPTON-SHIRE
42
SUFFOLK
260

CARMARTHENSHIRE
HEREFORD & WORCESTER
170
BEDFORDSHIRE, BERKSHIRE, BUCKINGHAMSHIRE & HERTFORDSHIRE
31
ESSEX
143

PEMBROKESHIRE
MONMOUTH-SHIRE
GLOUCESTER-SHIRE
139
OXFORD-SHIRE
219

SWANSEA
NEWPORT
CARDIFF
LONDON
15

1 BRIDGEND
2 RHONDA CYNON TAFF
3 MERTHYR TYDFIL
4 CAERPHILLY
5 BLAENAU GWENT
6 TORFAEN

NEATH & PORT TALBOT
VALE OF GLAMORGAN
WILTSHIRE
304
SURREY
266
KENT
178

SOMERSET
239
HAMPSHIRE
169
SUSSEX
272

128
DEVON
105
DORSET

60
CORNWALL

English Channel

9

General Information

To help overseas visitors with planning their trip to Britain, we have compiled the next few pages explaining the basic requirements & customs you will find here.

Before you arrive

Documents you will have to obtain before you arrive;
Valid passports & visas. Citizens of Commonwealth countries or the U.S.A. do not need visas to enter the U.K.
Bring your local Driving Licence.

Medical Insurance

This is strongly recommended although visitors will be able to receive free emergency treatment. If you have to stay in hospital in the U.K. you will be asked to pay unless you are a citizen of European Community.

Restrictions on arrival

Immigration procedures can be lengthy & bothersome, be prepared for questions like:
a) where are you staying in the U.K.?
b) do you have a round trip ticket?
c) how long do you intend to stay?
d) how much money are you bringing in?
e) do you have a credit card?
Do not bring any animals with you as they are subject to 6 months quarantine & there are severe penalties for bringing in pets without appropriate licences. Do not bring any firearms, prohibited drugs or carry these things for anyone else. If you are in doubt about items in your possession, declare them by entering the Red Channel at Customs & seek the advice of an officer.

After you have arrived

You can bring in as much currency as you like. You can change your own currency or travellers cheques at many places at varying rates.

Airports tend to be the most expensive places to change money & the 'Bureau de Change" are often closed at nights. So bring enough Sterling to last you at least 2 or 3 days. Banks often charge commission for changing money. Most Cashcard machines (or A.T.M.'s) will dispense local currency using your charge card, if they are affiliated systems, & don't charge commissions to your account. Major credit cards/charge cards are widely accepted & you may only need to carry small amounts of cash for "pocket money".

Driving

Don't forget to drive on the Left... especially the first time you get into a car... at the airport car hire parking lot... or from the front of a railway station... or straight after breakfast... old habits are hard to shake off. If you need to know the rules, get a copy of the Highway Code. You must wear a seat belt & so must any other front seat passenger. The speed limits are clearly shown in most areas - generally 30 mph. in residential areas (48 kph) & 70 mph on motorways (113 kph.). Traffic lights are at the side of the road & not hanging overhead. Car hire is relatively expensive in the U.K. & it is often a good idea to arrange this before you arrive. Mileage charges, V.A.T. (Sales Tax) & insurance are usually charged extra & you will need to be over 21 to hire a car in the U.K. Petrol (gas) is also relatively expensive & you may find petrol stations hard to find or closed at night in rural areas... so fill up often. Driving in London is not a recommended experience for newcomers & parking is also a very complex arrangement which can become a nightmare if the car gets "clamped" (immobilised) or towed away.

General Information

Buses & Coaches

If you are not driving & only want to travel 5-10 miles there are good bus services within most towns & cities, however, rural routes have seriously declined over the last few years. There are regular & fast coach services between the major towns which are very popular - so book ahead to be sure of a seat.

Trains

There is an extensive railway system throughout the U.K. which serves the major towns on a fast & frequent basis. These services are relatively expensive & like most railway systems are subject to delays.

Tubes (Subways)

London is the only city with an extensive subway system although some other towns do have "Metro" trains of linked under & overground systems.

The "tube" is a very popular means of getting around London, but it can get very crowded & unpleasant at "rush hours". It is often the preferred way to get into London from Heathrow Airport in the early morning, when there are long delays on the roads that hold up both buses & taxis with increasingly expensive rides into the city centre, £40 is not unusual for this cab fare, compared with a few pounds on the "tube". The "tube" in London is operated by London Transport which also operates the London bus service ... the famous red buses. They sell tickets which allow you to travel all over London on tubes, buses & trains at very good rates, called Travelcards... a transfer system. Ask your local travel agent about these & other travel passes throughout the U.K.

Telephones

When calling the U.K. from abroad always drop the 0 from the area code.

In the U.K. the only free calls are the operator - 100 and emergencies - 999. You may use your calling card to call home which is billed to your account or call collect, ask the operator to "reverse charge" the call. The famous red telephone kiosks are slowly being replaced with glass booths. The internet can now be accessed from some public phone booths. Phonecards are becoming more popular as the number of boxes that only accept these cards increases. Cards can be bought at Post Offices & many newsagents & shops.

Doctors/Chemists

All local police stations have lists of chemists & doctors should you need one, at night, for instance.

Voltage

The standard voltage throughout the country is 240v AC.50Hz. If you bring small electrical appliances with you, a converter will be required.

Tipping

Is not obligatory anywhere but a general guide if you wish to leave a tip for service is between 10%-15%.

Pubs

Most open between 11 a.m. & 11 p.m. and often longer, every day.
You must be over 18 years old to buy & drink alcohol in pubs .
Do not drink and drive. Penalties for being over the legally permitted limit of alcohol are quite severe.

Motorway map

Approximate driving time

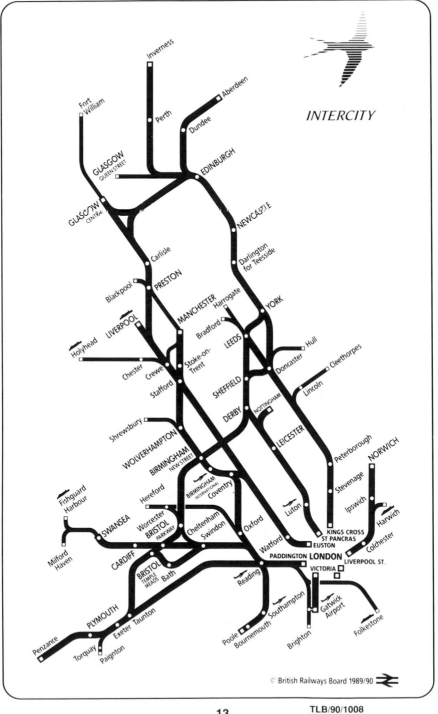

INTERCITY

© British Railways Board 1989/90

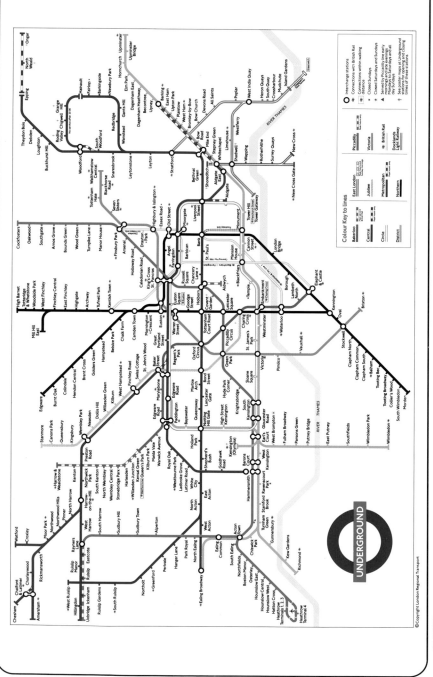

UNDERGROUND

© Copyright London Regional Transport

91/1258

LONDON MAP

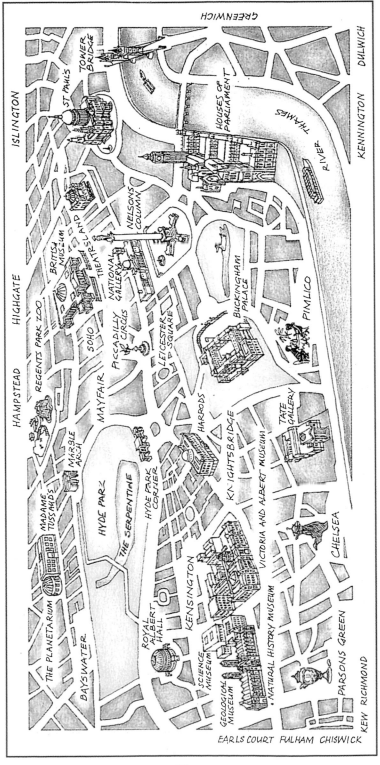

	rate £ from - to per person	children taken	evening meals	animals taken
Home No. 01 London Tel: +44 (0)20-8742-9123 Fax: +44 (0)20-8749-7084 U.S., Canada call: Toll Free 011-800-852-26320 Australia call: Toll Free 0011-800-852-26320 E-mail: bestbandb@atlas.co.uk	Nearest Tube: Putney Bridge An attractive Victorian terraced house, situated in a quiet residential street, yet only 3 mins' walk from the station. 1 spacious double-bedded room with an en-suite bathroom & a twin-bedded room with a private bathroom. Each room is tastefully furnished & has a T.V. & hairdryer. Breakfast is served in the very pleasant dining room. Many good pubs, restaurants & shops locally. An excellent location from which to explore London. Parking by arrangement. Children over 12.	£31.00 to £50.00 (no smoking)	Y	N	N
Home No. 06 London Tel: +44 (0)20-8742-9123 Fax: +44 (0)20-8749-7084 U.S., Canada call: Toll Free 011-800-852-26320 Australia call: Toll Free 0011-800-852-26320 E-mail: bestbandb@atlas.co.uk	Nearest Tube: East Putney A Victorian terraced house with a traditional family atmosphere & set in a quiet residential street. The friendly hosts offer 1 comfortable twin-bedded room with T.V., overlooking the rear garden, & with an adjacent private bathroom. A large Continental or Full English breakfast is served. Putney is a lovely area with many good shops & restaurants. Transport facilities are excellent & provide easy access to central London.	£26.00 to £40.00	Y	N	N
Home No. 07 London Tel: +44 (0)20-8742-9123 Fax +44 (0)20-8749-7084 U.S., Canada call: Toll Free 011-800-852-26320 Australia call: Toll Free 0011-800-852-26320 E-mail: bestbandb@atlas.co.uk	Nearest Tube: Fulham Broadway Set in the heart of Fulham, this is an attractive Victorian maisonette which is elegantly furnished throughout with antiques. The charming host, who is very well-travelled & has an in-depth knowledge of London, offers 2 beautifully furnished double-bedded rooms. Each with tea/coffee-making facilities & an en-suite or private bathroom. In summer, breakfast can be taken in the delightful garden. Only 8 mins' walk from the tube this is an ideal base for exploring London. Many good restaurants & antique shops close by.	£37.00 to £50.00	N	N	N
Home No. 08 London Tel: +44 (0)20-8742-9123 Fax: +44 (0)20-8749-7084 U.S., Canada call: Toll Free 011-800-852-26320 Australia call: Toll Free 0011-800-852-26320 E-mail: bestbandb@atlas.co.uk	Nearest Tube: Maida Vale An attractive Victorian maisonette very well situated only 3 mins' walk from the tube. Offering 1 spacious & comfortably furnished twin-bedded room with T.V., tea/coffee-making facilities & an en-suite shower room. Breakfast is served in the pleasant dining area looking out onto the pretty garden. Good local pubs & restaurants. An excellent location providing easy access to many attractions; with a direct tube link to Piccadilly Circus & the Embankment. Also, Paddington Station for the Heathrow Express.	£32.00 to £50.00 (no smoking)	N	N	N
Home No. 12 London Tel: +44 (0)20-8742-9123 Fax: +44 (0)20-8749-7084 U.S., Canada call: Toll Free 011-800-852-26320 Australia call: Toll Free 0011-800-852-26320 E-mail: bestbandb@atlas.co.uk	Nearest Tube: Parsons Green Set in a quiet residential street, yet only 5 mins' walk from the station, this is a delightful Victorian terraced house. It has been beautifully decorated & is furnished throughout with antiques. The charming hosts offer 1 attractive King-size double/twin-bedded room with T.V., tea/coffee-making facilities & an en-suite shower room. Breakfast is taken in the elegant dining room which overlooks the garden. A number of interesting antique shops & good restaurants just a short walk away.	£40.00 to £78.00 (no smoking)	N	N	N

Home No. 17. London.

London

The column headers (rotated): rate £ from - to per person | children taken | evening meals | animals taken

	Description	rate £ from - to per person	children taken	evening meals	animals taken
Home No. 14 London Tel: +44 (0)20-8742-9123 Fax: +44 (0)20-8749-7084 U.S., Canada call: Toll Free 011-800-852-26320 Australia call: Toll Free 0011-800-852-26320 E-mail: bestbandb@atlas.co.uk	Nearest Tube: Marble Arch Situated in the heart of central London, yet in a surprisingly quiet location, this modern townhouse is the perfect place from which to explore this vibrant city. The charming host offers 3 spacious & attractively furnished double, family or twin-bedded rooms , each has en-suite facilities, T.V. & tea/coffee, etc. Close by are a variety of cafes, bars & restaurants. Hyde Park, the exclusive boutiques of Knightsbridge & Mayfair & a host of attractions are all within easy reach.	£37.00 to £62.00	Y	N	N
Home No. 17 London Tel: +44 (0)20-8742-9123 Fax: +44 (0)20-8749-7084 U.S., Canada call: Toll Free 011-800-852-26320 Australia call: Toll Free 0011-800-852-26320 E-mail: bestbandb@atlas.co.uk	Nearest Tube: Richmond Situated in an excellent 17th-century terrace, this is an outstanding home, elegantly furnished throughout with antiques. 3 guest rooms: 1 double 4-poster, 1 twin-bedded room & a triple with a 4-poster & a single bed. Each has a private bath-room. 2 of the bedrooms have French doors leading onto an Italiante garden, the triple room commands views of the Thames. Historic Richmond with its many shops & riverside restaurants is a short walk. Easy access to central London.	£45.00 to £88.00 see PHOTO over p. 17	N	N	N
Home No. 18 London Tel: +44 (0)20-8742-9123 Fax: +44 (0)20-8749-7084 U.S., Canada call: Toll Free 011-800-852-26320 Australia call: Toll Free 0011-800-852-26320 E-mail: bestbandb@atlas.co.uk	Nearest Tube: High St. Ken. A beautiful house, furnished with many interesting paintings & situated in the heart of Kensington. The charming host offers 1 light & airy, twin-bedded room with a private bathroom. Also another, equally attractive twin-bedded room, which is ideal for a third or fourth member of the party. Each bedroom is well-furnished & a T.V. is available. Only a short walk from the High Street with its many shops & restaurants & within easy reach of Kensington Palace & gardens, Knightsbridge & the museums. Children over 12.	£32.00 to £50.00	Y	N	N
Home No. 19 London Tel: +44 (0)20-8742-9123 Fax: +44 (0)20-8749-7084 U.S., Canada call: Toll Free 011-800-852-26320 Australia call: Toll Free 0011-800-852-26320 E-mail: bestbandb@atlas.co.uk	Nearest Tube: Parsons Green Located in the quiet Parsons Green area of Fulham. This superb house offers accommodation in 1 king-size double-bedded room with private facilities & 2 doubles which share a bathroom. Each room is beautifully decorated & very comfortably furnished. This is a delightful home & the ideal base for visitors to London. Many of the attractions including Buckingham Palace & Knightsbridge are only 15 mins away by tube.	£31.00 to £60.00	N	N	N
Home No. 21 London Tel: +44 (0)20-8742-9123 Fax: +44 (0)20-8749-7084 U.S., Canada call: Toll Free 011-800-852-26320 Australia call: Toll Free 0011-800-852-26320 E-mail: bestbandb@atlas.co.uk	Nearest Tube: Hammersmith A charming Victorian terraced house, where the welcoming hosts offer 1 spacious, attractive & comfortably furnished king-size double/twin room with sitting area & a private bathroom & 1 equally attractive twin-bedded room with private shower room. Each with T.V., tea/coffee & hairdryer. Breakfast is served in the dining room. A delightful family home set in a quiet street, yet only 8 mins walk from Hammersmith with its many restaurants etc. Excellent transport facilities provide easy access to Heathrow & central London.	£32.00 to £50.00	Y	N	N

London

Visit our website: www.bestbandb.co.uk

Column headers (diagonal): rate £ from - to per person | children taken | evening meals | animals taken

---

Home No. 24 London
Tel: +44 (0)20-8742-9123
Fax: +44 (0)20-8749-7084
U.S., Canada call:
Toll Free 011-800-852-26320
Australia call:
Toll Free 0011-800-852-26320
E-mail: bestbandb@atlas.co.uk

Nearest Tube: Parsons Green
An elegantly furnished Victorian terraced house, situated in a quiet street yet only 5 mins walk from all transport facilities. Offering 1 delightful double-bedded room which overlooks the rear garden & an equally attractive king-size double/twin-bedded room. Each has a private bathroom, is beautifully decorated & has every comfort. There are 2 small dogs. Parsons Green is an ideal base from which to explore the delights of London & has many excellent restaurants & antique shops.

rate £ from - to per person	children taken	evening meals	animals taken
£35.00 to £60.00	N	N	N

Home No. 31 London
Tel: +44 (0)20-8742-9123
Fax: +44 (0)20-8749-7084
U.S., Canada call:
Toll Free 011-800-852-26320
Australia call:
Toll Free 0011-800-852-26320
E-mail: bestbandb@atlas.co.uk

Nearest Tube: Parsons Green
A charming Victorian terraced house, situated only minutes from many excellent shops & restaurants in Fulham. The welcoming host has elegantly furnished this property throughout. Accommodation is in 1 attractive double-bedded room. It is very comfortable & has a good private bathroom. There is also a cosy single room for a third member of the party. A large Continental breakfast is served. Situated only a short walk from the station, this is an excellent base from which to explore London. Children over 12.

rate £ from - to per person	children taken	evening meals	animals taken
£30.00 to £50.00	Y	N	N

Home No. 35 London
Tel: +44 (0)20-8742-9123
Fax: +44 (0)20-8749-7084
U.S., Canada call:
Toll Free 011-800-852-26320
Australia call:
Toll Free 0011-800-852-26320
E-mail: bestbandb@atlas.co.uk

Nearest Tube: Fulham Broadway
Located in the cosmopolitan area of Fulham, this modern townhouse is set in a quiet street & yet is only 5 mins walk from the tube, providing easy access to central London. The friendly host offers 1 twin-bedded room with a private bathroom. Also, 1 double room is available for another member of the party. Each room is tastefully furnished & well-appointed with T.V. & tea/coffee-making facilities. A large Continental breakfast is served. A variety of local restaurants offer a wide choice of international cuisine. Children over 12.

rate £ from - to per person	children taken	evening meals	animals taken
£29.00 to £50.00	Y	N	N

Home No. 38 London
Tel: +44 (0)20-8742-9123
Fax: +44 (0)20-8749-7084
U.S., Canada call:
Toll Free 011-800-852-26320
Australia call:
Toll Free 0011-800-852-26320
E-mail: bestbandb@atlas.co.uk

Nearest Tube: Earls Court
A lovely apartment situated on the top floor of a Victorian mansion block (with lift access) & only 3 mins walk from Earls Court station. The charming host offers 1 spacious & attractively furnished double bedded room with an en-suite bathroom & T.V. Breakfast is served in the attractive dining area. Easy access to Knightsbridge, South Kensington & the museums & Heathrow. Many good local restaurants.

rate £ from - to per person	children taken	evening meals	animals taken
£30.00 to £50.00	Y	N	N

Home No. 39 London
Tel: +44 (0)20-8742-9123
Fax: +44 (0)20-8749-7084
U.S., Canada call:
Toll Free 011-800-852-26320
Australia call:
Toll Free 0011-800-852-26320
E-mail: bestbandb@atlas.co.uk

Nearest Tube: Earls Court
A superb home, designer decorated & furnished to the highest standard with antiques throughout. 2 double & 1 twin bedded rooms. Each beautiful bedroom is large & airy with a lovely bathroom en-suite, T.V. & tea/coffee facilities. A large dining room. A delightful garden where breakfast can be served if the weather is good. Guests have their own private entrance. Only 10 mins to Harrods. Children over 12 years. Parking.

rate £ from - to per person	children taken	evening meals	animals taken
£49.00 to £80.00	Y	N	N

see PHOTO over p. 20

see PHOTO over p. 20

Home No. 39. London.

London

Visit our website: www.bestbandb.co.uk

		rate £ from - to per person	children taken	evening meals	animals taken
Home No. 40 London Tel: +44 (0)20-8742-9123 Fax: +44 (0)20-8749-7084 U.S., Canada call: Toll Free 011-800-852-26320 Australia call: Toll Free 0011-800-852-26320 E-mail: bestbandb@atlas.co.uk	Nearest Tube: Gunnersbury A large Victorian residence, with garden, only minutes from the tube station, with easy access to Heathrow, central London, Richmond & beautiful Kew Gardens. The charming host offers 2 spacious guest rooms suitable for doubles or twins & ideal for families. Each room has an en-suite bathroom, T.V., tea/coffee-making facilities & is decorated in natural tones with stripped pine. Children are especially welcome.	£29.00 to £54.00	Y	N	N
Home No. 43 London Tel: +44 (0)20-8742-9123 Fax: +44 (0)20-8749-7084 U.S., Canada call: Toll Free 011-800-852-26320 Australia call: Toll Free 0011-800-852-26320 E-mail: bestbandb@atlas.co.uk	Nearest Tube: Earls Court This is a traditional London mews house set in a quiet location, yet only 5 mins walk from the tube. The charming host offers 1 comfortably furnished double-bedded room with T.V., tea/coffee facilities & fridge. The private bathroom is adjacent. A Continental breakfast is served. There is a good selection of restaurants nearby. A great location within easy reach of many attractions. Also, easy access to Heathrow & Gatwick Airports.	£45.00 to £70.00	N	N	N
Home No. 44 London Tel: +44 (0)20-8742-9123 Fax: +44 (0)20-8749-7084 U.S., Canada call: Toll Free 011-800-852-26320 Australia call: Toll Free 0011-800-852-26320 E-mail: bestbandb@atlas.co.uk	Nearest Tube: Richmond Situated in the heart of delightful Richmond this really is the perfect location for a relaxing break in London. The charming host, who is an interior designer has refurbished this Victorian home & offers 1 gorgeous double-bedded room which has a superb private bathroom adjacent. Delicious Continental breakfasts are served in the lovely kitchen/diner which overlooks a pretty plantsmans garden. Richmond abounds with fashionable shops & restaurants. Within easy reach of several stately homes. Transport facilities are excellent & Waterloo is 15 mins by train.	£37.00 to £50.00	N	N	N
Home No. 48 London Tel: +44 (0)20-8742-9123 Fax: +44 (0)20-8749-7084 U.S., Canada call: Toll Free 011-800-852-26320 Australia call: Toll Free 0011-800-852-26320 E-mail: bestbandb@atlas.co.uk	Nearest Tube: Parsons Green A beautifully decorated, very stylish late Victorian house, situated in leafy Parsons Green & only 20 mins. from Harrods by tube. Accommodation is in 2 double/twin-bedded rooms & 1 single room, all are en-suite & have T.V. & tea/coffee-making facilities. Each room is furnished to the highest standards of comfort. A country house breakfast is served. Good local pubs & restaurants.	£41.00 to £60.00	N	N	N
Home No. 49 London Tel: +44 (0)20-8742-9123 Fax: +44 (0)20-8749-7084 U.S., Canada call: Toll Free 011-800-852-26320 Australia call: Toll Free 0011-800-852-26320 E-mail: bestbandb@atlas.co.uk	Nearest Tube: Parsons Green A lovely Victorian terraced house, which has been tastefully refurbished throughout. The charming & well-travelled hosts offer 1 spacious king-size double/twin-bedded room with an en-suite bathroom & 1 comfortable double-bedded room with a private shower room adjacent. T.V. & tea/coffee-making facilities are available. There are many cafes, restaurants & bars close by & being only 5 mins walk from the tube station; this stylish home is a perfect spot from which to explore London.	£37.00 to £52.00	Y	N	N

London
Visit our website: www.bestbandb.co.uk

	rate £ from - to per person	children taken	evening meals	animals taken
Home No. 50 London Tel: +44 (0)20-8742-9123 Fax: +44 (0)20-8749-7084 U.S., Canada call: Toll Free 011-800-852-26320 Australia call: Toll Free 0011-800-852-26320 E-mail: bestbandb@atlas.co.uk Nearest Tube: Parsons Green. This is a delightful Victorian terraced house which has been beautifully decorated & furnished throughout. The lovely hosts offer 1 very comfortable king-size double-bedded room & 1 attractive single-bedded room. Each room has a T.V. & bottled water etc. & an excellent private bathroom. There are a variety of good bars, bistros & restaurants nearby. Located only 5 mins' walk from the tube station, this is a perfect spot from which to explore London. A charming home.	£37.00 to £57.00	N	N	N
Home No. 51 London Tel: +44 (0)20-8742-9123 Fax: +44 (0)20-8749-7084 U.S., Canada call: Toll Free 011-800-852-26320 Australia call: Toll Free 0011-800-852-26320 E-mail: bestbandb@atlas.co.uk Nearest Tube: Holland Park. Set in a quiet, secluded street, this is a modern mews house with an original brick kiln which has been converted into an elegant dining room. Only a few minutes walk from fashionable restaurants, antique shops, Portobello Market & beautiful Holland Park. It has been attractively furnished throughout by the host who is an interior designer. 1 delightful & spacious en-suite double-bedded room which is well-appointed with T.V. etc. Easy access to many of London's attractions.	£37.00 to £60.00	N	N	N
Home No. 52 London Tel: +44 (0)20-8742-9123 Fax: +44 (0)20-8749-7084 U.S., Canada call: Toll Free 011-800-852-26320 Australia call: Toll Free 0011-800-852-26320 E-mail: bestbandb@atlas.co.uk Nearest Tube: South Kensington. Located in Chelsea, in a quiet residential street yet, only a short walk from many fashionable shops & restaurants. A charming Victorian terraced house which has been attractively decorated throughout with many interesting prints & artifacts. The friendly hosts offer 1 spacious double-bedded room & an equally comfortable twin-bedded room. Each has an en-suite shower room, T.V. & tea/coffee-making facilities. A delightful home with easy access to the museums at South Kensington, Knightsbridge & Harrods.	£34.00 to £50.00	Y	N	N
Home No. 56 London Tel: +44 (0)20-8742-9123 Fax: +44 (0)20-8749-7084 U.S., Canada call: Toll Free 011-800-852-26320 Australia call: Toll Free 0011-800-852-26320 E-mail: bestbandb@atlas.co.uk Nearest Tube: Hammersmith. A lovely house, pleasantly situated in leafy Brook Green mid-way between Hammersmith & Kensington. Offering a spacious & comfortably furnished double bedded room with private bathroom & tea/coffee making facilities which overlooks the rear garden. A pretty lounge with T.V. is often available & in which, guests may choose to relax. An ideal base, with good access to Heathrow & central London.	£32.00 to £50.00	Y	N	N
Home No. 59 London Tel: +44 (0)20-8742-9123 Fax: +44 (0)20-8749-7084 U.S., Canada call: Toll Free 011-800-852-26320 Australia call: Toll Free 0011-800-852-26320 E-mail: bestbandb@atlas.co.uk Nearest Tube: Fulham Broadway. Situated in Fulham, with many good restaurants, pubs & antique shops nearby. This is a charming Victorian house, standing in a quiet street. The delightful hosts offer 1 spacious King-size double/twin-bedded room with an exquisite marble en-suite bathroom & another lovely, light & airy twin-bedded room with a beautiful private bathroom adjacent. Each bedroom is well-furnished & has colour T.V., hairdryer & tea/coffee-making facilities. Very good access to central London & the sights by bus or tube.	£31.00 to £62.00	Y	N	N

London

Column headers (rotated): rate £ from - to per person | children taken | evening meals | animals taken

Home	Description	rate £ from - to per person	children taken	evening meals	animals taken
Home No. 60 London **Tel: +44 (0)20-8742-9123** **Fax: +44 (0)20-8749-7084** **U.S., Canada call:** Toll Free **011-800-852-26320** **Australia call:** Toll Free **0011-800-852-26320** E-mail: **bestbandb@atlas.co.uk**	Nearest Tube: High St. Ken. A beautifully appointed home located in a quiet cul-de-sac, close to Kensington Palace. A lift will take you to the 2nd floor accommodation. A delightful, spacious double room with brass bed, T.V., tea/coffee-making facilities & biscuits are also provided. A delicious varied breakfast is also served. Knightsbridge, Kensington & Hyde Park are all just a short walk from here.	£37.00 to £60.00 (non-smoking)	N	N	N
Home No. 61 London **Tel: +44 (0)20-8742-9123** **Fax: +44 (0)20-8749-7084** **U.S., Canada call:** Toll Free **011-800-852-26320** **Australia call:** Toll Free **0011-800-852-26320** E-mail: **bestbandb@atlas.co.uk**	Nearest Tube: Holland Park A lovely apartment situated on the 7th floor of an Edwardian mansion block with lift access. Offering 1 spacious & attractive double bedded room with a private bathroom, T.V. & a small balcony with rooftop views. A large Continental breakfast is served. The charming host has an extensive knowledge of London & is happy to give advice on what to see & do. Easy access to central London & the sights, beautiful Holland Park, Kensington High Street & many good shops & restaurants. Heathrow Airbus stops nearby.	£33.00 to £50.00	N	N	N
Home No. 63 London **Tel: +44 (0)20-8742-9123** **Fax: +44 (0)20-8749-7084** **U.S., Canada call:** Toll Free **011-800-852-26320** **Australia call:** Toll Free **0011-800-852-26320** E-mail: **bestbandb@atlas.co.uk**	Nearest Tube: Sloane Square An attractive 2-storey penthouse apartment with prize-winning roof garden, situated in the heart of fashionable Chelsea & only minutes from the River Thames & the trendy shops & restaurants of the King's Road. The delightful host, who is an artist, is always happy to advise guests on what to see & do. 1 comfortable en-suite double-bedded room. A Continental breakfast is served in the attractive dining room which is adorned with many of the hosts interesting pictures.	£33.00 to £50.00	N	N	N
Home No. 64 London **Tel: +44 (0)20-8742-9123** **Fax: +44 (0)20-8749-7084** **U.S., Canada call:** Toll Free **011-800-852-26320** **Australia call:** Toll Free **0011-800-852-26320** E-mail: **bestbandb@atlas.co.uk**	Nearest Tube: Camden Town A unique timber & glass house (designed by the host who is an architect), only a short walk from the station, the market & many excellent shops & restaurants. 1 attractive double-bedded room with T.V. & tea/coffee facilities & an equally attractive single room for a third member of the party. Each room is light & airy, comfortable & modern in design. A private bathroom. A full English or large Breakfast is served in the lovely open-plan kitchen/dining area which overlooks the garden. Easy access to the West End & theatreland.	£40.00 to £58.00 (non-smoking)	Y	N	N
Home No. 65 London **Tel: +44 (0)20-8742-9123** **Fax: +44 (0)20-8749-7084** **U.S., Canada call:** Toll Free **011-800-852-26320** **Australia call:** Toll Free **0011-800-852-26320** E-mail: **bestbandb@atlas.co.uk**	Nearest Tube: Baker Street An elegant Georgian townhouse, only moments from Baker Street, Regent's Park & Mayfair. It is pleasantly furnished throughout. A selection of charming guest rooms including double, single & triple rooms. Each bedroom is spacious, attractively decorated, & has an en-suite/private bathroom, T.V. & 'phone. An elegant lounge where tea/coffee is available. A large Continental breakfast is served. A delightful home in a marvellous location only minutes from the West End.	£54.00 to £85.00 (non-smoking)	N	N	N

London

Visit our website: www.bestbandb.co.uk

		rate £ from - to per person	children taken	evening meals	animals taken

Home No. 66 London
Tel: +44 (0)20-8742-9123
Fax: +44 (0)20-8749-7084
U.S., Canada call:
Toll Free 011-800-852-26320
Australia call:
Toll Free 0011-800-852-26320
E-mail: bestbandb@atlas.co.uk

Nearest Tube: Earls Court
A spacious apartment located at garden level offering contemporary accommodation in 1 double bedded room with en-suite facilities, T.V. , fridge & 'phone. The friendly host (a fashion designer) has tastefully furnished & pleasantly decorated this apartment with many interesting paintings. Guests may relax in the garden which is accessible from their room. Situated only a few minutes walk from the tube station, this home is within easy reach of museums, galleries & theatres.

£32.00 to £50.00 — N | N | N (No smoking)

Home No. 69 London
Tel: +44 (0)20-8742-9123
Fax: +44 (0)20-8749-7084
U.S., Canada call:
Toll Free 011-800-852-26320
Australia call:
Toll Free 0011-800-852-26320
E-mail: bestbandb@atlas.co.uk

Nearest Tube: South Kensington
A super home from which to explore London, situated only a very short walk from the Natural History & Science Museums & the station. An attractively furnished apartment, located on the 1st floor of an Edwardian conversion, where the friendly host offers 1 light & airy King-size double/twin-bedded room with full en-suite bathroom & T.V. A Continental breakfast is served. A good location with many restaurants etc.

£32.00 to £50.00 — N | N | N (No smoking)

Home No. 72 London
Tel: +44 (0)20-8742-9123
Fax: +44 (0)20-8749-7084
U.S., Canada call:
Toll Free 011-800-852-26320
Australia call:
Toll Free 0011-800-852-26320
E-mail: bestbandb@atlas.co.uk

Nearest Tube: Baker Street
A traditional 4-storey Georgian townhouse in a marvellous location, only a short walk from Madame Tussauds, the Sherlock Holmes museum, Lord's Cricket Ground & Regents Park.   The charming hosts, who are artists, offer 2 spacious & comfortably furnished double-bedded rooms (1 with low-beamed ceilings), each with an en-suite bathroom, T.V., tea/coffee-making facilities & views towards Regents Park. An ideal base from which to explore London on foot; the West End, theatreland & Piccadilly are only 10 mins away.

£37.00 to £60.00 — Y | N | N

Home No. 76 London
Tel: +44 (0)20-8742-9123
Fax: +44 (0)20-8749-7084
U.S., Canada call:
Toll Free 011-800-852-26320
Australia call:
Toll Free 0011-800-852-26320
E-mail: bestbandb@atlas.co.uk

Nearest Tube: Earls Court
One king-size double or twin-bedded room with very large en-suite bath & separate shower & 1 king-size double with adjacent private bath & shower. Each room has a colour T.V. & clock/radio & has been beautifully decorated & furnished by this most helpful host. This charming Victorian house is very close to all the best places for shopping, museums, sight-seeing & within walking distance of many excellent restaurants. Easy access to Gatwick & Heathrow Airports.

£30.00 to £62.00 — N | N | N (No smoking)

Home No. 77 London
Tel: +44 (0)20-8742-9123
Fax: +44 (0)20-8749-7084
U.S., Canada call:
Toll Free 011-800-852-26320
Australia call:
Toll Free 0011-800-852-26320
E-mail: bestbandb@atlas.co.uk

Nearest Tube:Clapham Jt.(B.R.)
A large Edwardian house built for Earl Spencer backing onto a private park. Breakfast may be served in the dining room or large conservatory. There is 1 double en-suite room, 1 family room ensuite, 1 twin bedded room with private facilities, also, 1 double room with shared bathroom. Plenty of car parking space. There are two cats & a friendly dog. A charming & most friendly host. Smoking permitted on the ground floor.

£32.00 to £50.00 — N | N | N

see PHOTO over
p. 25

Home No. 77 .   London.

London

Visit our website: www.bestbandb.co.uk

	rate £ from - to per person	children taken	evening meals	animals taken

Home No. 78 London
Tel: +44 (0)20-8742-9123
Fax: +44 (0)20-8749-7084
U.S., Canada call:
Toll Free 011-800-852-26320
Australia call:
Toll Free 0011-800-852-26320
E-mail: bestbandb@atlas.co.uk

Nearest Tube: Parsons Green
An impressive Victorian house with pretty garden in a fashionable area facing a park with a public tennis court. Easy access to central London & excellent shops & restaurants nearby. The charming host is a well-travelled author, with 1 cat. 2 bedrooms, each with a double bed, completely private facilities, T.V. & hairdryer. A full English breakfast is served. Charming guest sitting room (rare in a private home).

£33.00 to £50.00 — N N N

Home No. 79 London
Tel: +44 (0)20-8742-9123
Fax: +44 (0)20-8749-7084
U.S., Canada call:
Toll Free 011-800-852-26320
Australia call:
Toll Free 0011-800-852-26320
E-mail: bestbandb@atlas.co.uk

Nearest Tube: East Putney
An elegant Victorian house with a pretty garden located in the residential area of Putney. The charming hosts offer 2 stylishly decorated guest rooms, located on the 3rd floor. An attractive & spacious twin room with a lovely private bathroom & one large, sunny double bedroom with shower room en-suite. Each room has colour T.V. & tea/coffee-making facilities. Only 25 minutes to central London by tube or 35 mins' to Windsor by train. There are many excellent local restaurants.

£32.00 to £50.00 — Y N N

Home No. 83 London
Tel: +44 (0)20-8742-9123
Fax: +44 (0)20-8749-7084
U.S., Canada call:
Toll Free 011-800-852-26320
Australia call:
Toll Free 0011-800-852-26320
E-mail: bestbandb@atlas.co.uk

Nearest Tube: Stamford Brook
A spacious Edwardian house set in a quiet street only 4 mins' walk from the station. The charming hosts offer 1 spacious & beautifully decorated Queen-size double-bedded room with Victorian-style brass bedstead, fridge, T.V./video, trouser press, tea/coffee-making facilities & an excellent bathroom en-suite. Breakfast is served in the conservatory overlooking the garden. Only 7 mins' walk from the River Thames with its variety of riverside pubs. Easy access to central London & Heathrow Airport. Children over 8.

£31.00 to £50.00 — Y N N

Home No. 85 London
Tel: +44 (0)20-8742-9123
Fax: +44 (0)20-8749-7084
U.S., Canada call:
Toll Free 011-800-852-26320
Australia call:
Toll Free 0011-800-852-26320
E-mail: bestbandb@atlas.co.uk

Nearest Tube: Fulham Broadway
Situated in the heart of Fulham, this is a delightful 3 storey Victorian house conveniently located only 3 mins' walk from the tube. The very friendly hosts offer 1 double-bedded room with an en-suite bathroom & another double-bedded room with a shower room en-suite. Each bedroom is beautifully decorated & very comfortable. T.V. & tea/coffeee facilities are available. There are many famous bars, bistros & restaurants in Fulham Broadway. Heathrow Airport & Londons' many attractions are easily accessible by tube.

£32.00 to £50.00 — N N N

Home No. 88 London
Tel: +44 (0)20-8742-9123
Fax: +44 (0)20-8749-7084
U.S., Canada call:
Toll Free 011-800-852-26320
Australia call:
Toll Free 0011-800-852-26320
E-mail: bestbandb@atlas.co.uk

Nearest Tube: Sloane Square
This is an elegantly furnished apartment situated less than 10 mins' walk from the tube. The friendly hosts offer 1 twin-bedded room with an adjacent private bathroom. Breakfast is served in the elegant dining room. Situated in the heart of Chelsea within easy reach of the fashionable shops & restaurants in the King's Road. The museums at South Kensington are a short distance away by bus or tube.

£36.00 to £60.00 — N N N

Beds:Berks:Bucks:Herts.

Bedfordshire
(Thames & Chilterns)

The county of Bedfordshire is an area of great natural beauty from the Dunstable Downs in the south to the great River Ouse in the north, along with many country parks & historic houses & gardens.

Two famous wildlife parks are to be found, at Woburn &Whipsnade. The Woburn Wild Animal Kingdom is Britain's largest drive-through safari park, with entrance to an exciting leisure park all included in one admission ticket.

Whipsnade Zoo came into existence in the 1930's as a country retreat for the animals of London Zoo, but is now very much a zoo in its own right & renowned for conservation work.

Woburn Abbey, home of the Dukes of Bedford for three centuries, is often described as one of England's finest showplaces. Rebuilt in the 8th century the Abbey houses an important art collection & is surrounded by a magnificent 3,000 acre deer park.

John Bunyan drew on local Bedfordshire features when writing the Pilgrims Progress, & the ruins of Houghton House, his "House Beautiful" still remain.

Buckinghamshire
(Thames & Chilterns)

Buckinghamshire can be divided into two distinct geographical regions: The high Chilterns with their majestic beechwoods & the Vale of Aylesbury chosen by many over the centuries as a beautiful & accessible place to build their historical homes.

The beechwoods of the Chilterns to the south of the county are crisscrossed with quiet lanes & footpaths., Ancient towns & villages like Amersham & Chesham lie tucked away in the

Rose gardens. St.Albans. Herts.

folds of the hills & a prehistoric track; the Ichnield Way winds on its 85 mile journey through the countryside.

The Rothschild family chose the Vale of Aylesbury to create several impressive homes, & Waddesdon House & Ascott House are both open to the public. Benjamin Disraeli lived at Hughenden Manor, & Florence Nightingale, "the Lady with the Lamp", at Claydon House. Sir Francis Dashwood, the 18th century eccentric founded the bizarre Hellfire Club, which met in the man-made caves near West Wycombe House.

Berkshire
(Thames & Chilterns)

Berkshire is a compact county but one of great variety & beauty.

In the East is Windsor where the largest inhabited castle in the world stands in its majestic hilltop setting. Nine centuries of English monarchy have lived here, & it is home to the present Queen. The surrounding parkland, enormous yards, vast interior & splendour of the State Apartments make a trip to Windsor Castle an unforgettable experience.

To the West are the gently rolling Berkshire Downs where many a champion racehorse has been trained.

Beds:Berks:Bucks:Herts.

To the north of the county, the River Thames dominates the landscape - an opportunity for a river-bank stroll & a drink at a country pub.

In the south is the Kennet & Avon Canal, a peaceful waterway with horse-drawn barges.

Historically, Berkshire has occupied an important place due to its strategic position commanding roads to & from Oxford & the north, & Bath & the west. Roundheads & Cavaliers clashed twice near Newbury during the 17th century English Civil Wars. Their battles are colourfully recreated by historic societies like the Sealed Knot.

The Tudor period brought great wealth from wool-weaving. Merchants built wonderful houses & some built churches but curiously, there is no cathedral in Berkshire.

Hertfordshire
(Thames & Chilterns)

Old & new exist side by side in Hertfordshire. This attractive county includes historic sites, like the unique Roman theatre in St. Albans, as well as new additions to the landscape such as England's first Garden City at Letchworth.

The countryside varies from the chalk hills & rolling downlands of the Chilterns to rivers, lakes, canals & pretty villages. The county remains largely rural despite many large towns & cities. The Grand Union Canal, built at the end of the 18th century to link the Midlands to London, passes through some glorious scenery, particularly at Cassiobury Park in Watford.

Verulamium was a newly-built town of the Roman Empire. It was the first name of Alban, himself a Roman, who became the first Christian to be martyred for his faith in England. The great Abbey church was built by the Normans around his original church, & it was re-established under the Rule of St. Benedict & named St. Albans some 600 years after his death.

Windsor Castle.

Beds:Berks:Bucks:Herts.

Bedfordshire
Gazeteer
Area of outstanding natural beauty.
Dunstable Downs, Ivinghoe Beacon

Historic Houses
Woburn Abbey - house & gardens, extensive art collection, deer park, antiques centre.

Other Things to see & do
Bedford Butterfly Park - set in 10 acres of wild flower hay meadows. A global conservation park.
The Glenn Miller Museum - Bedford
Old Warden - the village houses a collection of working vintage planes. Fying displays each month from April to October.
Shuttleworth Collection - a unique collection of historic aircraft spanning 100 years of flight
Woburn Safari Park
Whipsnade Zoo-Whipsnade

Berkshire Gazeteer
Areas of outstanding natural beauty.
North West Downs.

Historic Houses & Castles
Windsor Castle - Royal Residence at Windsor
State apartments, house, historic treasures. The Cloisters, Windsor Chapel. Mediaeval house.
Basildon Park - Nr. Pangbourne
Overlooking the Thames. 18th century Bath stone building, massive portico & linked pavilions. Painted ceiling in Octagon Room, gilded pier glasses. Garden & wooded walks.
Cliveden - Nr. Taplow
Once the home of Nancy Astor.

Churches
Lambourn (St. Michael & All Saints)
Norman with 15th century chapel. 16th century brasses, glass & tombs.
Padworth (St. John the Baptist)
12th century Norman with plastered exterior, remains of wall paintings, 18th century monuments.

Warfield (St. Michael & All Angels)
14th century decorated style. 15th century wood screen & loft.

Museums
Newbury Museum - Newbury
Natural History & Archaeology -
Paleolithic to Saxon & Mediaeval times
Household Cavalry Museum - Windsor

Other Things to see & do
Racing - at Newbury, Ascot & Windsor
Highlight of the racing year is the Royal Meeting at Ascot each June, attended by the Queen & other members of the Royal Family.
Antiques - Hungerford is a famous centre for antiques.

Buckinghamshire
Gazeteer
Area of outstanding natural beauty.
Burnham Beeches - 70 acres of unspoilt woodlands, inspiration to poet
Thomas Gray.

Historic Houses
Waddesdon Manor & Ascott House - homes of the Rothschilds.
Chalfont St. Giles - cottage home of great English poet John Milton.
Old Jordans & the Meeting House - 17th century buildings associated with William Penn, the founder of Pennsylvania & with the Society of Friends, often called the Quakers.

Things to see & do
Buckinghamshire Railway Centre - at Quainton
Vintage steam train rides & largest private railway collection in Britain.
Chalfont Shire Horse Centre - home of the gentle giants of the horse world.

Beds:Berks:Bucks:Herts.

Hertfordshire
Gazeteer
Areas of outstanding natural beauty.
Parts of the Chilterns.

Historic Houses & Castles
Hatfield House - Hatfield
Home of the Marquess of Salisbury.
Jacobean House & Tudor Palace -
childhood home of Queen Elizabeth I.
Knebworth House - Knebworth
Family home of the Lyttons. 16th century
house transformed into Victorian High
Gothic. Furniture, portraits. Formal
gardens & unique Gertrude Jekyll herb
garden.
Shaw's Corner - Ayot St. Lawrence
Home of George Bernard Shaw.

Cathedrals & Churches
St. Albans Cathedral - St. Albans
9th century foundation, murals, painted
roof over choir, 15th century reredos,
stone rood screen.

Stanstead St. Abbots (St. James)12th
century nave, 13th century chancel, 15th
century tower & porch, 16th century
North chapel, 18th century box pews
& 3-decker pulpit.
Watford (St. Mary)
13 - 15th century. Essex chapel.
Tuscan arcade. Morryson tombs.

Museums
**Rhodes Memorial Museum &
Commonwealth Centre** - at Bishop
Stortford
Zoological Museum - Tring
Gardens
Gardens of the Rose - Chiswell Green
Nr. St Albans
Showgrounds of the Royal National Rose
Society
Capel Manor
Extensive grounds of horticultural college.
Many fine trees, including the largest
copper beech in the country.

Bledlow Village; Bucks.

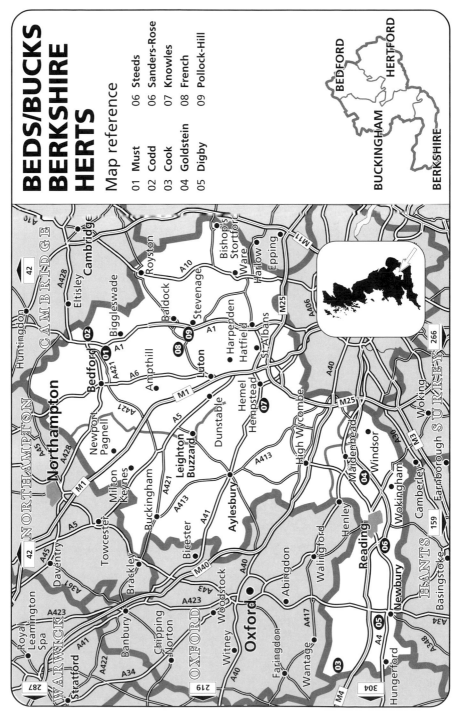

BEDS/BUCKS
BERKSHIRE
HERTS

Map reference

01 Must
02 Codd
03 Cook
04 Goldstein
05 Digby
06 Steeds
06 Sanders-Rose
07 Knowles
08 French
09 Pollock-Hill

BEDFORD
HERTFORD
BUCKINGHAM
BERKSHIRE

Bedfordshire & Berkshire

Church Farm

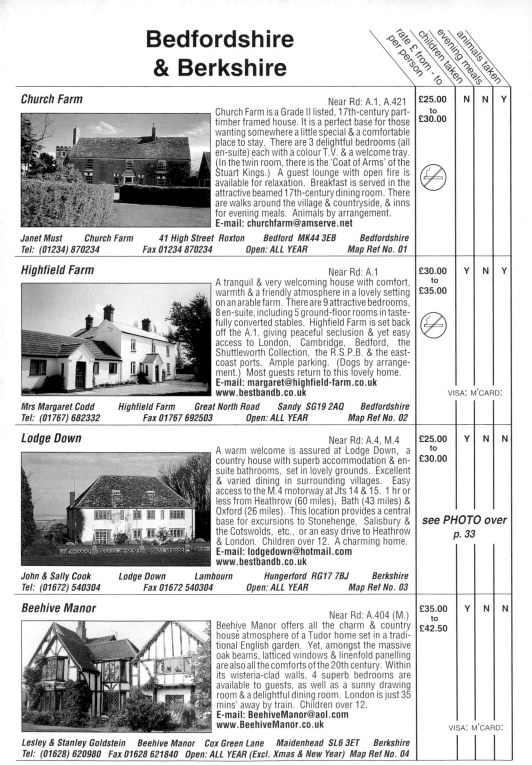

Near Rd: A.1, A.421

Church Farm is a Grade II listed, 17th-century part-timber framed house. It is a perfect base for those wanting somewhere a little special & a comfortable place to stay. There are 3 delightful bedrooms (all en-suite) each with a colour T.V. & a welcome tray. (In the twin room, there is the 'Coat of Arms' of the Stuart Kings.) A guest lounge with open fire is available for relaxation. Breakfast is served in the attractive beamed 17th-century dining room. There are walks around the village & countryside, & inns for evening meals. Animals by arrangement.
E-mail: churchfarm@amserve.net

£25.00 to £30.00	N N Y	

Janet Must   Church Farm   41 High Street Roxton   Bedford MK44 3EB   Bedfordshire
Tel: (01234) 870234   Fax 01234 870234   Open: ALL YEAR   Map Ref No. 01

Highfield Farm

Near Rd: A.1

A tranquil & very welcoming house with comfort, warmth & a friendly atmosphere in a lovely setting on an arable farm. There are 9 attractive bedrooms, 8 en-suite, including 5 ground-floor rooms in taste-fully converted stables. Highfield Farm is set back off the A.1, giving peaceful seclusion & yet easy access to London, Cambridge, Bedford, the Shuttleworth Collection, the R.S.P.B. & the east-coast ports. Ample parking. (Dogs by arrange-ment.) Most guests return to this lovely home.
E-mail: margaret@highfield-farm.co.uk
www.bestbandb.co.uk

£30.00 to £35.00   Y N Y

VISA: M'CARD:

Mrs Margaret Codd   Highfield Farm   Great North Road   Sandy SG19 2AQ   Bedfordshire
Tel: (01767) 682332   Fax 01767 692503   Open: ALL YEAR   Map Ref No. 02

Lodge Down

Near Rd: A.4, M.4

A warm welcome is assured at Lodge Down, a country house with superb accommodation & en-suite bathrooms, set in lovely grounds. Excellent & varied dining in surrounding villages. Easy access to the M.4 motorway at Jts 14 & 15. 1 hr or less from Heathrow (60 miles), Bath (43 miles) & Oxford (26 miles). This location provides a central base for excursions to Stonehenge, Salisbury & the Cotswolds, etc., or an easy drive to Heathrow & London. Children over 12. A charming home.
E-mail: lodgedown@hotmail.com
www.bestbandb.co.uk

£25.00 to £30.00   Y N N

see PHOTO over p. 33

John & Sally Cook   Lodge Down   Lambourn   Hungerford RG17 7BJ   Berkshire
Tel: (01672) 540304   Fax 01672 540304   Open: ALL YEAR   Map Ref No. 03

Beehive Manor

Near Rd: A.404 (M.)

Beehive Manor offers all the charm & country house atmosphere of a Tudor home set in a traditional English garden. Yet, amongst the massive oak beams, latticed windows & linenfold panelling are also all the comforts of the 20th century. Within its wisteria-clad walls, 4 superb bedrooms are available to guests, as well as a sunny drawing room & a delightful dining room. London is just 35 mins' away by train. Children over 12.
E-mail: BeehiveManor@aol.com
www.BeehiveManor.co.uk

£35.00 to £42.50   Y N N

VISA: M'CARD:

Lesley & Stanley Goldstein   Beehive Manor   Cox Green Lane   Maidenhead SL6 3ET   Berkshire
Tel: (01628) 620980 Fax 01628 621840   Open: ALL YEAR (Excl. Xmas & New Year) Map Ref No. 04

Lodge Down. Lambourn.

Berkshire
& Hertfordshire

Rookwood Farmhouse

Near Rd: A.4, A.34

This charming & comfortable former farmhouse combines ease of access with rural views & a large garden. The guest bedrooms are in a newly converted coach house which is traditionally furnished & yet affords all modern facilities. In winter, there is a welcoming log fire in the guests' sitting room, while in summer, breakfast is served in the conservatory overlooking the swimming pool. Rookwood House is an ideal base for touring & it is a perfect spot for a relaxing break.
www.bestbandb.co.uk

| £35.00 to £35.00 | Y | N | N |

VISA: M'CARD:

Mrs Charlotte Digby   Rookwood Farmhouse   Stockcross   Newbury RG20 8JX   Berkshire
Tel: (01488) 608676   Fax 01488 657961   Open: ALL YEAR   Map Ref No. 05

Highwoods

Near Rd: A.4, M.4

A friendly & relaxing atmosphere at this fine Victorian country house set in 4 acres of attractive grounds, with unspoilt, far-reaching views. There are 3 spacious, comfortable, attractively furnished rooms (1 en-suite) all with colour T.V. etc. Guests are welcome to use the garden & hard tennis court. Also, there is a gallery specialising in English watercolours & prints. Easy access to London, Heathrow Airport, Windsor, Oxford & Bath. Non-smokers are preferred.
E-mail: janesteeds@aol.com
www.bestbandb.co.uk

| £28.00 to £35.00 | Y | N | N |

Mrs J. Steeds   Highwoods   Reading Road   Burghfield Common   Reading RG7 3BG   Berkshire
Tel: (0118) 9832320   Fax 0118 9831070   Open: ALL YEAR (Excl. Xmas & New Year)   Map Ref No. 06

The Old Manor

Near Rd: A.4

A beautiful country house in 10 acres of secluded grounds yet a mere 2 miles from Junction 12 on the M.4. Very large, elegant, beamed en-suite bedrooms. The west suite has a 4-poster bed & jacuzzi bath. The east suite has a bath, separate shower & dressing room. Evening meals are of a very high standard & include wine. A beautiful drawing room is available, & the dining room & morning room are furnished with elegance. Relaxation, hospitality & quality are the keynotes at The Old Manor.
E-mail: rags-r@theoldmanor.fsbusiness.co.uk
www.bestbandb.co.uk

| £35.00 to £35.00 | N | Y | N |

Mrs R. Sanders-Rose   The Old Manor   Whitehouse Green   Sulhamstead   Reading RG7 4EA   Berks.
Tel: (0118) 9832423   Fax 0118 9836262   Open: All Year (Excl. Xmas & New Year)   Map Ref No. 06

Broadway Farm

Near Rd: A.4251

A warm welcome is guaranteed at Broadway, a working arable farm with its own fishing lake. There are 3 comfortable en-suite rooms in a converted building adjacent to the farmhouse. Each has tea/coffee-making facilities & colour T.V.. Everything for the leisure or business guest: the relaxation of farm life in an attractive rural setting, yet easy access to London, airports, motorways & mainline rail services. Single supplement.
E-mail: aknowles@broadway.nildram.co.uk
www.bestbandb.co.uk

| £27.00 to £30.00 | Y | N | N |

VISA: M'CARD:

Mrs Alison Knowles   Broadway Farm   Berkhamsted HP4 2RR   Hertfordshire
Tel: (01442) 866541   Fax 01442 866541   Open: ALL YEAR (Excl. Xmas)   Map Ref No. 07

Little Offley.   Great Offley.

	rate £ from - to per person	children taken	evening meals	animals taken

Little Offley House

Near Rd: A.505

A Grade II listed 17th-century house with extensive gardens surrounded by farmland. Set in a very quiet location, it offers 3 double/twin bedrooms with en-suite/private facilities & a drawing room. Dinner can be provided for a min. of 4 people. A restaurant & 2 pubs serving good food are in the village, 2 miles away. Ideal for executive meetings or conferences (max. 10 people). A car can be left if flying from Luton Airport. London 30 mins' by train. Cambridge 1 hour. Children over 12.
E-mail: info@little-offley.co.uk
www.little-offley.co.uk

£37.50 to £37.50	Y	Y	N

see PHOTO over
p. 35

VISA: M'CARD:

Lady Rosemary French   **Little Offley House**   **Great Offley**   **Hitchin SG5 3BU**   **Hertfordshire**
Tel: (01462) 768243   Fax 01462 768243   **Open: ALL YEAR (Excl. Xmas)**   Map Ref No. 08

Homewood

Near Rd: A.1 M

Homewood is a classic blend of comfort & style: an Edwardian country house which is also a well-equipped family home. It has been used as a location for period drama by the B.B.C., & is often sought out by admirers of its designer, the distinguished architect Edwin Lutyens. You will be treated as a member of the family, or your privacy will be respected - whichever you prefer. 2 lovely bedrooms, each with an en-suite/private bathroom. Also, a family suite. Animals by arrangement.
E-mail: bookings@homewood-bb.co.uk
www.homewood-bb.co.uk

£35.00 to £45.00	Y	N	Y

see PHOTO over
p. 37

Samantha Pollock-Hill   **Homewood**   **Park Lane**   **Old Knebworth**   **Stevenage SG3 6PP**   **Hertfordshire**
Tel: (01438) 812105   Fax 01438 812572   **Open: ALL YEAR (Excl. Xmas)**   Map Ref No. 09

WORLDWIDE BED & BREAKFAST ASSOCIATION

When booking your accommodation please mention
The Best Bed & Breakfast

Homewood. Knebworth.

Cambridge & Northants

Cambridgeshire
(East Anglia)

A county very different from any other, this is flat, mysterious, low-lying Fenland crisscrossed by a network of waterways both natural & man-made.

The Fens were once waterlogged, misty marshes but today the rich black peat is drained & grows carrots, sugar beet, celery & the best asparagus in the world.

Drive north across the Fens & slowly you become aware of a great presence dominating the horizon. Ely cathedral, the "ship of the Fens", sails closer. The cathedral is a masterpiece with its graceful form & delicate tracery towers. Begun before the Domesday Book was written, it took the work of a full century before it was ready to have the timbered roof raised up. Norman stonemasons worked with great skill & the majestic nave is glorious in its simplicity. Their work was crowned by the addition of the Octagon in the 14th century. Despite the ravages of the Reformation, the lovely Lady Chapel survives as one of the finest examples of decorated architecture in Britain with its exquisitely fine stone carving.

To the south, the Fens give way to rolling chalk hills & fields of barley, wheat & rye, & Cambridge. Punts gliding through the broad river, between smooth, lawned banks, under willow trees, past college buildings as extravagant as wedding cakes. The names of the colleges resound through the ages - Peterhouse, Corpus Christi, Kings, Queens, Trinity, Emmanuel. A city of learning & progress, & a city of great tradition where cows graze in open spaces, just 500 yards from the market square.

Northamptonshire
(East Midlands)

Northamptonshire has many features to attract & interest the visitor, from the town of Brackley in the south with its charming buildings of mellow stone, to ancient Rockingham Forest in the north. There are lovely churches, splendid historic houses & peaceful waterways.

The Waterways Museum at Stoke Bruerne makes a popular outing, with boat trips available on the Grand Union Canal beside the museum. Horseracing at Towcester & motor-racing at Silverstone draws the crowds, but there are quieter pleasures in visits to Canons Ashby, or to Sulgrave Manor, home of George Washington's ancestors.

In the pleasantly wooded Rockingham Forest area are delightful villages, one of which is Ashton with its thatched cottages, the scene of the World Conker Championships each October. Mary Queen of Scots was executed at Fotheringay, in the castle of which only the mound remains.

Rockingham Castle has a solid Norman gateway & an Elizabethan hall; Deene Park has family connections with the Earl of Cardigan who led the Charge of the Light Brigade & Kirby Hall is a dramatic Elizabethan ruin.

The county is noted for its parish churches, with fine Saxon examples at Brixworth & at Earl's Barton, as well as the round Church of the Holy Sepulchre in the county town itself.

Northampton has a fine tradition of shoemaking, so it is hardly surprising that boots & shoes & other leathergoods take pride of place in the town';s museums. The town has one of the country's biggest market squares, an historic Royal Theatre & a mighty Wurlitzer Organ to dance to at Turner's Musical Merry-go-round ! !

Cambridge & Northants

Cambridgeshire Gazeteer

Areas of outstanding natural beauty
The Nene Valley

Historic Houses & Castles

Anglesy Abbey - Nr. Cambridge
Origins in the reign of Henry I. Was redesigned into Elizabethan Manor by Fokes family. Houses the Fairhaven collection of Art treasures - stands in 100 acres of Ground.

Hinchingbrooke House - Huntingdon
13th century nunnery converted mid-16th century into Tudor house. Later additions in 17th & 19th centuries.

King's School - Ely
12th & 14th centuries - original stonework & vaulting in the undercroft, original timbering 14th century gateway & monastic barn.

Kimbolton Castle - Kimbolton
Tudor Manor house - has associations with Katherine of Aragon. Remodelled by Vanbrugh 1700's - gatehouse by Robert Adam.

Longthorphe Tower - Nr. Peterborough
13th & 14th century fortification - rare wall paintings.

Peckover House - Wisbech
18th century domestic architecture - charming Victorian garden.

University of Cambridge Colleges

Peterhouse -	1284
Clare	1320
Pembroke	1347
Gonville & Caius	1348
Trinity Hall -	1350
Corpus Christi -	1352
King's	1441
Queen's -	1448
St. Catherine's -	1473
Jesus	1496
Christ's -	1505
St. John's	1511
Magadalene	1542
Trinity-	1546
Emmanuel	1584
Sidney Sussex -	1596
Downing	1800

Wimpole Hall - Nr. Cambridge
18th & 19th century - beautiful staterooms - aristocratic house.

Cathedrals & Churches

Alconbury (St. Peter & St. Paul)
13th century chancel & 15th century roof. Broach spire.

Babraham (St. Peter)
13th century tower - 17th century monument.

Ely Cathedral
Rich arcading - west front incomplete. Remarkable interior with Octagon - unique in Gothic architecture.

Great Paxton (Holy Trinity)
12th century.

Harlton (Blessed Virgin Mary)
Perpendicular - decorated transition. 17th century monuments

Hildersham (Holy Trinity)
13th century - effigies, brasses & glass.

Lanwade (St. Nicholas)
15th century - mediaeval fittings

Peterborough Cathedral
Great Norman church fine example - little altered. Painted wooden roof to   nave - remarkable west front - Galilee Porch & spires later additions.

Ramsey (St. Thomas of Canterbury)
12th century arcades - perpendicular nave. Late Norman chancel with Angevin vault.

St. Neots (St. Mary)
15th century

Sutton (St. Andrew)
14th century

Trumpington (St. Mary & St. Nicholas)
14th century. Framed brass of 1289 of Sir Roger de Trumpington.

Westley Waterless (St. Mary the Less)
Decorated. 14th century brass of Sir John & Lady Creke.

Wimpole (St. Andrew)
14th century rebuilt 1749 - splendid heraldic glass.

Yaxley (St. Peter)
15th century chancel screen, wall paintings, fine steeple.

Museums & Galleries

Cromwell Museum - Huntingdon
Exhibiting portraits, documents, etc. of the Cromwellian period.

Fitzwilliam Museum - Cambridge
Gallery of masters, old & modern, ceramics, applied arts, prints & drawing, mediaeval manuscripts, music & art library.

Cambridge & Northants

Scott Polar Research Institute - Cambridge
Relics of expeditions & the equipment used. Current scientific work in Arctic & Antarctic.

University Archives - Cambridge
13th century manuscripts, Charters, Statutes, Royal letters & mandates. Wide variety of records of the University.

University Museum of Archaeology & Anthropology - Cambridge
Collections illustrative of Stone Age in Europe, Africa & Asia.
Britain prehistoric to mediaeval times. Prehistoric America.

Ethnographic material from South-east Asia, Africa & America.

University Museum of Classical Archaeology - Cambridge
Casts of Greek & Roman Sculpture - representative collection.

Whipple Museum of the History of Science - Cambridge16th, 17th & 18th century scientific instruments - historic collection.

Other Things to see & do

Nene Valley Railway
Steam railway with locomotives & carriages from many countries.

Caius College; Cambridge.

40

Cambridge & Northants

Northamptonshire
Gazeteer
Historic Houses & Castles

Althorp - Nr. Northampton
Family home of the Princess of Wales, with fine pictures & porcelain.
Boughton House - Nr. Kettering
Furniture, tapestries & pictures in late 17th century building modelled on Versailles, in beautiful parkland.
Canons Ashby House - Nr. Daventry
Small 16th century manor house with gardens & church.
Deene Park - Nr. Corby
Family home for over 4 centuries, surrounded by park, extensive gardens & lake.
Holdenby House - Nr. Northampton
Gardens include part of Elizabethan garden, with original entrance arches, terraces & ponds. Falconry centre. Rare breeds.
Kirby Hall - Nr. Corby
Large Elizabethan mansion with fine gardens.
Lamport Hall - Nr. Northampton
17th & 18th century house with paintings, furniture & china. One of the first garden rockeries in Britain. Programme of concerts & other special events.
Rockingham Castle - Rockingham, Nr. Market Harborough
Norman gateway & walls surrounding mainly Elizabethan house, with pictures & Rockingham china. Extensive gardens with 16th century yew hedge.
Rushton Triangular Lodge - Nr. Kettering
Symbolic of the Trinity, with 3 sides, 3 floors, trefoil windows.
Sulgrave Manor - Nr. Banbury
Early English Manor, home of George Washington's ancestors.

Museums

Abington Museum - Northampton
Domestic & social life collections in former manor house.
Museum of Leathercraft - Northampton
History of leather use, with Queen Victoria's saddle, & Samuel Pepys' wallet.

Waterways Museum - Stoke Bruerne Nr. Towcester
200 years of canal & waterway life, displayed beside the Grand Union Canal.

Cathedrals & Churches

Brixworth Church - Nr. Northampton
One of the finest Anglo-Saxon churches in the country, mostly 7th century.
Earls Barton Church - Nr. Northampton
Fine Anglo-Saxon tower & Norman arch & arcading.
Church of the Holy Sepulchre - Northampton
Largest & best preserved of four remaining round churches in England, dating from 1100.

Other Things to see & do

Billing Aquadrome - Nr. Northampton
Boating, fishing, swimming & amusements.
Wicksteed Park - Kettering
Large playground & variety of amusements for families.
Lilford Park - Nr. Oundle
Birds & farm animals in parkland setting where many special events are held.

Rushton Triangular Lodge.

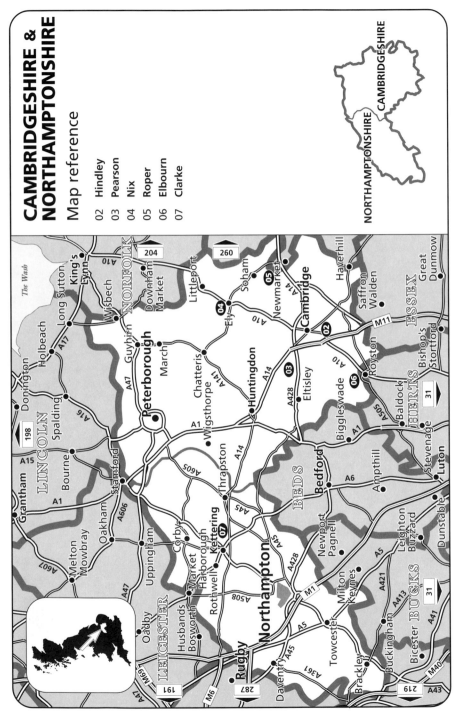

CAMBRIDGESHIRE & NORTHAMPTONSHIRE

Map reference

02 Hindley
03 Pearson
04 Nix
05 Roper
06 Elbourn
07 Clarke

NORTHAMPTONSHIRE

CAMBRIDGESHIRE

Cambridgeshire

| £25.00 to £34.00 | Y | N | N |

(No Smoking)

Purlins

Near Rd: A.10

Lovely, individually designed family home, with 2 acres of parkland, situated in a quiet, pretty village on the Cam, 4 miles south of Cambridge. An ideal centre for Colleges, Audley End House, the Imperial War Museum & bird watching. There are 3 well-appointed double bedrooms (2 ground-floor), all with en-suite bathrooms, colour T.V. & tea/coffee-making facilities. Varied breakfasts (special diets by arrangement). Restaurants nearby. Children over 8 welcome. Single supplement.
E-mail: dgallh@ndirect.co.uk
www.bestbandb.co.uk

Olga & David Hindley   Purlins   12 High Street   Little Shelford   Cambridge CD2 5ES   Cambridgeshire
Tel. (01223) 842043   Fax (01223) 842643   Open: FEB - Mid DEC   Map Ref No. 02

| £37.50 to £57.50 | Y | N | N |

(No Smoking)

VISA: M'CARD: AMEX:

The Grange Manor House

Near Rd: A.14

The Grange Manor House is an amazing Victorian establishment, a mere 10 minute drive from historic Cambridge city centre. There are 3 beautiful & spacious rooms; the Blue, Green & Yellow rooms are open to both business people & vacationers. Unsurpassed, mature gardens set in over 3 acres (with tennis court & swimming pool) are surrounded by farmland. Full English, smoked salmon, continental etc. breakfasts are available & there are restaurants & pubs nearby. Children over 13.
E-mail: gr@ngemanor.com
www.grangemanor.com

May-Britt Pearson The Grange Manor House   Robin's Lane   Lolworth   Cambridge CB3 8HL   Cambs.
Tel: (01954) 781298   Fax 01954 781298   Open: ALL YEAR   Map Ref No. 03

| £25.00 to £27.00 | Y | N | N |

(No Smoking)

VISA: M'CARD:

Hill House Farm

Near Rd: A.142, A.10

A warm welcome awaits you at this spacious Victorian farmhouse, situated in the quiet village of Coveney, 3 miles from the historic cathedral city of Ely. Open views of the surrounding countryside & easy access to Cambridge, Newmarket & Huntingdon. Ideal for touring Cambridgeshire, Norfolk & Suffolk. Wicken Fen & Welney wildfowl refuge are nearby. 3 tastefully furnished bedrooms, 1 twin & 2 double en-suite rooms, 1 ground floor. All have their own entrance, T.V. etc. Children over 12. Single supplement.
E-mail: hill_house@madasafish.com

Mrs Hilary Nix   Hill House Farm   9 Main Street   Coveney   Ely CB6 2DJ   Cambridgeshire
Tel: (01353) 778369   Fax 01353 778369   Open: ALL YEAR   Map Ref No. 04

| £30.00 to £50.00 | Y | N | Y |

(No Smoking)

Queensberry

Near Rd: A.14, A.142

A delightful Georgian home, featured in many T.V. travel programmes, set in large grounds with croquet lawn & parking. Ideally situated for touring East Anglia, Cambridge, Ely Cathedral, Newmarket, Bury St. Edmunds, & many National Trust properties. Equine tours can be arranged. 2 attractive bedrooms, 1 with en-suite facilities in the house & 3 bedrooms in a cottage in the grounds. Fordham is the 1st village off the A.14 on the Newmarket to Ely A.142 road. Good local restaurants. Children & animals by arrangement.
E-mail: queensberry@queensberry196.demon.co.uk

Jan & Malcolm Roper   Queensberry   196 Carter Street   Fordham CB7 5JU   Cambridgeshire
Tel: (01638) 720916   Fax 01638 720233   Open: ALL YEAR   Map Ref No. 05

Cambridgeshire & Northamptonshire

Chiswick House

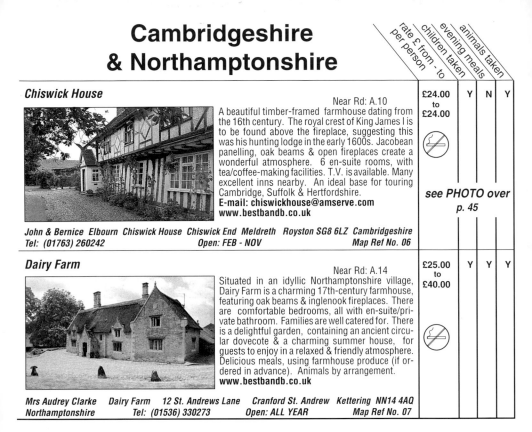

Near Rd: A.10

A beautiful timber-framed farmhouse dating from the 16th century. The royal crest of King James I is to be found above the fireplace, suggesting this was his hunting lodge in the early 1600s. Jacobean panelling, oak beams & open fireplaces create a wonderful atmosphere. 6 en-suite rooms, with tea/coffee-making facilities. T.V. is available. Many excellent inns nearby. An ideal base for touring Cambridge, Suffolk & Hertfordshire.
E-mail: chiswickhouse@amserve.com
www.bestbandb.co.uk

| £24.00 to £24.00 | Y | N | Y |

see PHOTO over
p. 45

John & Bernice Elbourn Chiswick House Chiswick End Meldreth Royston SG8 6LZ Cambridgeshire
Tel: (01763) 260242   Open: FEB - NOV   Map Ref No. 06

Dairy Farm

Near Rd: A.14

Situated in an idyllic Northamptonshire village, Dairy Farm is a charming 17th-century farmhouse, featuring oak beams & inglenook fireplaces. There are comfortable bedrooms, all with en-suite/private bathroom. Families are well catered for. There is a delightful garden, containing an ancient circular dovecote & a charming summer house, for guests to enjoy in a relaxed & friendly atmosphere. Delicious meals, using farmhouse produce (if ordered in advance). Animals by arrangement.
www.bestbandb.co.uk

| £25.00 to £40.00 | Y | Y | Y |

Mrs Audrey Clarke Dairy Farm   12 St. Andrews Lane   Cranford St. Andrew Kettering NN14 4AQ
Northamptonshire   Tel: (01536) 330273   Open: ALL YEAR   Map Ref No. 07

WORLDWIDE BED & BREAKFAST ASSOCIATION

All the establishments mentioned in this guide are members of
The Worldwide Bed & Breakfast Association

Chiswick House. Royston

Cheshire & Lancashire

Cheshire
(North West)

Cheshire is located between the Peak District & the mountains of North Wales & is easily accessible from three major motorways. It has much to attract long visits but is also an ideal stopping-off point for travellers to the Lake District & Scotland, or to North Wales or Ireland. There is good access eastwards to York & the east coast & to the south to Stratford-upon-Avon & to London.

Cheshire can boast seven magnificent stately homes, the most visited zoo outside London, four of Europe's largest garden centres & many popular venues which feature distinctive Cheshire themes such as silk, salt, cheese, antiques & country crafts.

The Cheshire plain with Chester, its fine county town, & its pretty villages, rises up to Alderley Edge in the east from where there are panoramic views, & then climbs dramatically to meet the heights of the Peaks.

To the west is the coastline of the Wirral Peninsula with miles of sandy beaches & dunes &, of course, Liverpool.

The countryside shelters very beautiful houses. Little Moreton Hall near Congleton, is one of the most perfect imaginable. It is a black & white "magpie" house & not one of its walls is perpendicular, yet it has withstood time & weather for nearly four centuries, standing on the waterside gazing at its own reflection.

Tatton Hall is large & imposing & is splendidly furnished with many fine objects on display. The park & gardens are a delight & especially renowned for the azaleas & rhododendrons. In complete contrast is the enormous radio telescope at Jodrell Bank where visitors can be introduced to planetary astronomy in the planetarium.

Chester is a joy; a walk through its streets is like walking through living history. The old city is encircled by city walls enclosing arcaded streets with handsome black & white galleried buildings that blend well with modern life. There are many excellent shops along these "Rows". Chester Cathedral is a fine building of monastic foundation, with a peaceful cloister & outstanding wood carving in the choir stalls. Boat rides can be taken along the River Dee which flows through the city.

Manchester has first rate shopping, restaurants, sporting facilities, theatres & many museums ranging from an excellent costume museum to the fascinating Museum of Science & Industry.

Little Moreton Hall.

Liverpool grew from a tiny fishing village on the northern shores of the Mersey River, receiving its charter from King John in 1207. Commercial & slave trading with the West Indies led to massive expansion in the 17th & 18th centuries. The Liverpool of today owes much to the introduction of the steam ship in the mid 1900s, which enabled thousands of Irish to emigrate when the potatoe famine was at its height in Ireland. This is a city with a reputation for patronage of art, music & sport.

Cheshire & Lancashire

Lancashire
(North West)

Lancashire can prove a surprisingly beautiful county. Despite its industrial history of cotton production, there is magnificent scenery & there are many fine towns & villages. Connections with the Crown & the clashes of the Houses of Lancaster & York have left a rich heritage of buildings with a variety of architecture. There are old stone cottages & farmhouses, as well as manor houses from many centuries.

For lovers of the countryside, Lancashire has the sweeping hills of Bowland, the lovely Ribble Valley, the moors of Rossendale & one mountain, mysterious Pendle Hill.

The Royal Forest of Bowland is a forest without trees, which has provided rich hunting grounds over the centuries. An old windswept pass runs over the heights of Salter Fell & High Cross Fell from Slaidburn, where the Inn, the "Hark to Bounty", was named after the noisiest hound in the squire's pack & used to be the courtroom where strict forest laws were enforced.

Further south, the Trough of Bowland provides an easier route through the hills, & here is the beautiful village of Abbeystead in Wynesdale where monks once farmed the land. The church has stained glass windows portraying shepherds & their flocks & there are pegs in the porch where shepherds hung their crooks.

Below the dramatic hills of Bowland, the green valley of the Ribble climbs from Preston to the Yorkshire Dales. Hangridge Fell, where the tales of witches are almost as numerous as those of Pendle Hill, lies at the beginning of the valley.

Pendle Hill can be reached from the pretty village of Downham which has Tudor, Jacobean & Georgian houses, village stocks & an old inn. Old Pendle rises abruptly to 1831 feet & is a strange land formation. It is shrouded in legend & stories of witchcraft.

Between Pendle Hill & the moors of Rossendale are the textile towns of Nelson, Colne, Burnley, Accrington & Blackburn. The textile industry was well established in Tudor times & the towns grew up as markets for the trading of the cloth woven in the Piece Halls.

The moors which descend to the very edges of the textile towns are wild & beautiful & have many prehistoric tumuli & earthworks. Through the towns & the countryside, winds the Liverpool & Leeds canal, providing an excellent towpath route to see the area.

Lancaster is an historic city boasting the largest castle in England, dating back to Norman times.

Lancashire's coastal resorts are legendary, & Blackpool is Queen of them all with her miles of illuminations & millions of visitors.

Downham Village.

Cheshire & Lancashire

Lancashire Gazeteer

Areas of outstanding natural beauty.
The Forest of Bowland, Parts of Arnside & Silverdale.

Historic Houses & Castles

Rufford Old Hall - Rufford
15th century screen in half-timbered hall of note. Collection of relics of Lancashire life.
Chingle Hall - Nr. Preston
13th century - small manor house with moat. Rose gardens. Haunted!
Astley Hall - Chorley
Elizabethan house reconstructed in 17th century. Houses pictures, tapestries, pottery & furniture.
Gawthorpe Hall - Padiham
17th century manor house with 19th century restoration. Moulded ceilings & some fine panelling. A collection of lace & embroidery.
Bramall Hall - Bramall
Fine example of half-timbered (black & white) manor house built in 14th century & added to in Elizabethan times. .
Lancaster Castle - Lancaster
Largest of English castles - dates back to Norman era.
Astley Hall - Chorley
16th century half-timbered grouped around central court. Rebuilt in the Jacobean manner with long gallery. Unique furniture.
Hoghton Tower - Nr. Preston
16th century - fortified hill-top mansion - magnificent banquet hall. Dramatic building - walled gardens & rose gardens.
Thurnham Hall - Lancaster
13th century origins. 16th century additions & 19th century facade. Beautiful plasterwork of Elizabethan period. Jacobean staircase.

Cathedrals & Churches

Lancaster (St. Mary)
15th century with 18th century tower. Restored chapel - fine stalls.
Whalley (St. Mary)
13th century with 15th century tower, clerestory & aisle windows. Fine wood carving of 15th century canopied stalls.
Halsall (St. Cuthbert)
14th century chancel, 15th century perpendicular spire. 14th century tomb. Original doors, brasses & effigies. 19th century restoration.
Tarleton (St. Mary)
18th century, part 19th century.
Great Mitton (All Hallows)
15th century rood screen, 16th century font cover, 17th century pulpit.

Museums & Galleries

Blackburn Museum - Blackburn
Extensive collections relating to local history archeology, ceramics, geology & natural history. One of the finest collection of coins & fine collection of mediaeval illuminated manuscripts & early printed books.
Bury Museum & Art Gallery - Bury
Houses fine Victorian oil & watercolours. Turner, Constable, Landseer, de Wint.
City Gallery - Manchester
Pre-Raphaelites, Old Masters, Impressionists, modern painters all represented in this fine gallery; also silver & pottery collections.
Higher Mill Museum - Helmshaw
One of the oldest wool textile finishing mills left in Lancashire. Spinning wheels, Hargreave's Spinning Jenny, several of Arkwrights machines, 20 foot water wheel.
Townley Hall Art Gallery & Museum, & Museum of Local Crafts & Industries - Burnley.

Cheshire Gazeteer

Area of outstanding natural beauty
Part of the Peaks National Park
Addington Hall - Macclesfield
15th century Elizabethan Black & White half timbered house.
Bishop Lloyd's House - Chester
17th century half timbered house (restored). Fine carvings. Has associations with Yale University & New Haven, USA.
Chorley Old Hall - Alderley Edge
14th century hall with 16th century Elizabethan wing.
Forfold Hall - Nantwich
17th century Jacobean country house, with fine panelling.

Cheshire & Lancashire

Gawsworth Hall - Macclesfield
Fine Tudor Half timbered Manor House.
Tilting ground. Pictures, furniture,
sculptures, etc.
Lyme Park - Disley
Elizabethan with Palladian exterior by
Leoni. Gibbons carvings. Beautiful park
with herd of red deer.
Peover Hall - Over Peover, Knutsford
16th century- stables of Tudor period;
has the famous magpie ceiling.
Tatton Park - Knutsford
Beautifully decorated & furnished
Georgian House with a fine collection of
glass, china & paintings including Van
Dyke & Canaletto. Landscaping by
Humphrey Repton.
Little Moreton Hall - Nr. Congleton
15th century timbered, moated house
with 16th century wall-paintings.

Cathedrals & Churches

Acton (St. Mary)
13th century with stone seating around
walls. 17th century effigies.
Bunbury (St. Boniface)
14th century collegiate church -
alabaster effigy.
Congleton (St. Peter)
18th century - box pews, brass
candelabrum, 18th century glass.
Chester Cathedral - Chester
Subjected to restoration by Victorians -
14th century choir stalls.
Malpas (St. Oswalds)
15th century - fine screens, some old
stalls, two family chapels.
Mobberley (St. Wilfred)
Mediaeval - 15th century rood screen,
wall paintings, very old glass.
Shotwick (St. Michael)
Twin nave - box pews, 14th century
quatre - foil lights, 3 deck pulpit.
Winwick (St. Oswald)
14th century - splendid roof. Pugin
chancel.
Wrenbury (St. Margaret)
16th century - west gallery, monuments
& hatchments. Box pews.
Liverpool Cathedral - the Anglican
Cathedral was completed in 1980 after
76 years of work. It is of massive
proportions, the largest in the U.K. with
much delicate detailed work.

Museums & Galleries

Grosvenor Museum - Chester
Art, folk history, natural history, Roman
antiquities including a special display of
information about the Roman army.
Chester Heritage Centre - Chester
Interesting exhibition of the architectural
heritage of Chester.
Cheshire Military Museum - Chester
The three local Regiments are
commemorated here.
King Charles Tower - Chester
Chester at the time of the Civil War
illustrated by dioramas.
Museum & Art Gallery - Warrington
Anthropology, geology, ethnology, botany
& natural history. Pottery, porcelain,
glass, collection of early English
watercolours.
West Park Museum & Art Gallery -
Macclesfield
Egyptian collection, oil paintings,
watercolours, sketches by Landseer &
Tunnicliffe.
Norton Priory Museum - Runcorn
Remains of excavated mediaeval priory.
Also wildlife display.
Quarry Bank Mill - Styal
The Mill is a fine example of industrial
building & houses an exhibition of the
cotton industry: the various offices retain
their original furnishing, & the turbine
room has the transmission systems &
two turbines of 1903.
Nether Alderley Mill - Nether Alderley
15th century corn mill which was still
used in 1929. Now restored.
The Albert Dock & Maritime Museum
- Liverpool
Housing the Liverpool Tate Gallery, the
Tate of the North.
Walker Art Gallery - Liverpool
Jodrell Bank - radio telescope &
planetarium.

Historic Monuments

Chester Castle - Chester
Huge square tower remaining.
Roman Amphitheatre - Chester
12th legion site - half excavated.
Beeston Castle - Beeston
Remains of a 13th century fort.
Sandbach Crosses - Sandbach
Carved stone crosses date from the 9th C.

CHESHIRE & LANCASHIRE

Map reference

02 **Ikin**	06 **Sobey**	08 **M. Smith**
03 **Ahooie**	07 **Rothwell**	09 **J. Smith**
04 **Rayner**	08 **Townend**	
05 **Taylor**		

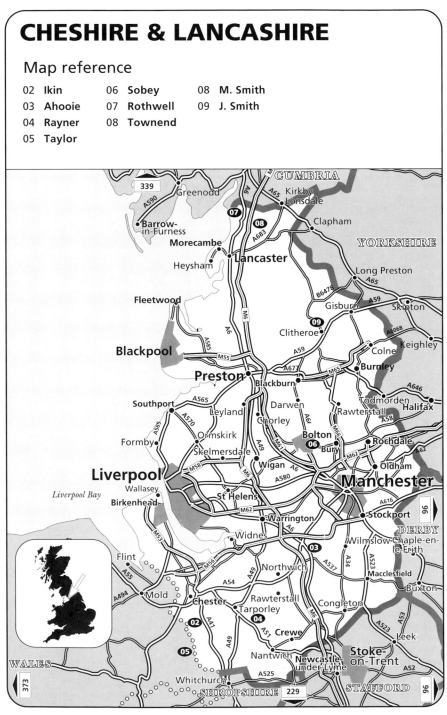

The Manor. Worthenbury.

	rate £ from - to per person	children taken	evening meals	animals taken

Golborne Manor

Near Rd: A.41

| £29.00 to £35.00 | Y | Y | Y |

Golborne Manor is an elegant 19th-century country residence with glorious views, renovated to a high standard & set in 3 1/2 acres of gardens & grounds. Beautifully decorated with spacious en-suite bedrooms. Farmhouse breakfasts. Evening meals (available Mon-Fri) by arrangement. Piano & croquet set available for guests' use. Car park. Easy access for motorways. 10 mins' drive south from Chester on the A.41, turning right a few yards after D.P. Motors (on the left). Animals by arrangement.
E-mail: ann.ikin@golbornemanor.co.uk
www.golbornemanor.co.uk

Mrs Ann Ikin   Golborne Manor   Platts Lane   Hatton Heath   Nr. Chester CH3 9AN   Cheshire
Tel: (01829) 770310   Fax 01829 770370   Open: ALL YEAR   Map Ref No. 02

Longview Hotel

Near Rd: A.50

| £37.75 to £68.75 | Y | Y | Y |

Set in this pleasant Cheshire market town overlooking the common is this lovely, friendly hotel, furnished with many antiques that reflect the elegance of this Victorian building. Care has been taken to retain its character, while also providing all comforts for the discerning traveller. All of the 26 en-suite bedrooms are prettily decorated, giving them that cared-for feeling which is echoed throughout the hotel. You are assured of a warm friendly welcome as soon as you step into reception.
E-mail: enquiries@longviewhotel.com
www.longviewhotel.com

VISA: M'CARD: AMEX:

Mr & Mrs Ahooie   Longview Hotel   51 & 55 Manchester Road   Knutsford WA16 0LX   Cheshire
Tel: (01565) 632119 Fax 01565 652402 Open: ALL YEAR (Excl. Xmas & New Year) Map Ref No. 03

Hill House Farm B & B

Near Rd: A.49, A.51

| £30.00 to £35.00 | Y | N | Y |

Hill House Farm is a Victorian former farmhouse situated in the middle of the beautiful Cheshire countryside & offers spacious accommodation with comfortable bedrooms & a guests' drawing room with open log fire. The house is set in an acre of attractive gardens overlooking a further 12 acres of horse paddocks. Hill House Farm is an ideal base for local attractions such as Oulton Park (2 miles), Beeston Castle (5 miles), Nantwich (10 miles) & the city of Chester (12 miles).
E-mail: rayner@hillhousefarm.fsnet.co.uk
www.hillhousefarm.info

Mrs Catherine Rayner Hill House Farm B & B The Hall Lane Rushton Tarporley CW6 9AU Cheshire
Tel: (01829) 732238   Fax 01829 733929   Open: ALL YEAR   Map Ref No. 04

The Manor

Near Rd: A.525, A.41

| £30.00 to £38.00 | Y | Y | N |

Surrounded by rolling Cheshire Plains, Welsh Marches & National Trust properties, Worthenbury Manor makes the ideal setting for a relaxing break. In this fully restored Grade II listed building with oak panelling & 4-poster beds, you can indulge yourself with dinner, prepared by a qualified chef using fresh local produce. Guaranteed to be an experience you will want to repeat again & again. An elegant home, situated 2 miles from Bangor on Dee & 4 miles from Malpas. Children over 10. (Restricted smoking areas.)
www.bestbandb.co.uk

see PHOTO over
p. 51

Ian Taylor   The Manor   Worthenbury   Wrexham LL13 0AW   Cheshire
Tel: (01948) 770342   Fax 01948 770711   Open: FEB - NOV   Map Ref No. 05

The Bower. Yealand Conyers.

	rate £ from - to per person	children taken	evening meals	animals taken

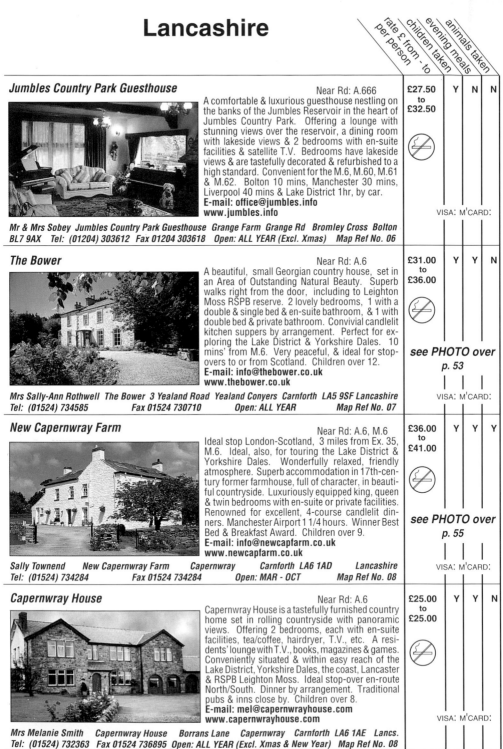

Jumbles Country Park Guesthouse

Near Rd: A.666

£27.50 to £32.50 — Y — N — N

A comfortable & luxurious guesthouse nestling on the banks of the Jumbles Reservoir in the heart of Jumbles Country Park. Offering a lounge with stunning views over the reservoir, a dining room with lakeside views & 2 bedrooms with en-suite facilities & satellite T.V. Bedrooms have lakeside views & are tastefully decorated & refurbished to a high standard. Convenient for the M.6, M.60, M.61 & M.62. Bolton 10 mins, Manchester 30 mins, Liverpool 40 mins & Lake District 1hr, by car.
E-mail: office@jumbles.info
www.jumbles.info

VISA: M'CARD:

Mr & Mrs Sobey Jumbles Country Park Guesthouse Grange Farm Grange Rd Bromley Cross Bolton BL7 9AX   Tel: (01204) 303612 Fax 01204 303618   Open: ALL YEAR (Excl. Xmas)   Map Ref No. 06

The Bower

Near Rd: A.6

£31.00 to £36.00 — Y — Y — N

A beautiful, small Georgian country house, set in an Area of Outstanding Natural Beauty. Superb walks right from the door, including to Leighton Moss RSPB reserve. 2 lovely bedrooms, 1 with a double & single bed & en-suite bathroom, & 1 with double bed & private bathroom. Convivial candlelit kitchen suppers by arrangement. Perfect for exploring the Lake District & Yorkshire Dales. 10 mins' from M.6. Very peaceful, & ideal for stopovers to or from Scotland. Children over 12.
E-mail: info@thebower.co.uk
www.thebower.co.uk

see PHOTO over
p. 53

VISA: M'CARD:

Mrs Sally-Ann Rothwell The Bower 3 Yealand Road Yealand Conyers Carnforth LA5 9SF Lancashire
Tel: (01524) 734585   Fax 01524 730710   Open: ALL YEAR   Map Ref No. 07

New Capernwray Farm

Near Rd: A.6, M.6

£36.00 to £41.00 — Y — Y — Y

Ideal stop London-Scotland, 3 miles from Ex. 35, M.6. Ideal, also, for touring the Lake District & Yorkshire Dales. Wonderfully relaxed, friendly atmosphere. Superb accommodation in 17th-century former farmhouse, full of character, in beautiful countryside. Luxuriously equipped king, queen & twin bedrooms with en-suite or private facilities. Renowned for excellent, 4-course candlelit dinners. Manchester Airport 1 1/4 hours. Winner Best Bed & Breakfast Award. Children over 9.
E-mail: info@newcapfarm.co.uk
www.newcapfarm.co.uk

see PHOTO over
p. 55

VISA: M'CARD:

Sally Townend   New Capernwray Farm   Capernwray   Carnforth LA6 1AD   Lancashire
Tel: (01524) 734284   Fax 01524 734284   Open: MAR - OCT   Map Ref No. 08

Capernwray House

Near Rd: A.6

£25.00 to £25.00 — Y — Y — N

Capernwray House is a tastefully furnished country home set in rolling countryside with panoramic views. Offering 2 bedrooms, each with en-suite facilities, tea/coffee, hairdryer, T.V., etc. A residents' lounge with T.V., books, magazines & games. Conveniently situated & within easy reach of the Lake District, Yorkshire Dales, the coast, Lancaster & RSPB Leighton Moss. Ideal stop-over en-route North/South. Dinner by arrangement. Traditional pubs & inns close by. Children over 8.
E-mail: mel@capernwrayhouse.com
www.capernwrayhouse.com

VISA: M'CARD:

Mrs Melanie Smith   Capernwray House   Borrans Lane   Capernwray   Carnforth LA6 1AE Lancs.
Tel: (01524) 732363 Fax 01524 736895 Open: ALL YEAR (Excl. Xmas & New Year) Map Ref No. 08

New Capernwray Farm. Carnforth.

	rate £ from - to per person	children taken	evening meals	animals taken
Peter Barn Country House Near Rd: A.59	£26.00 to £28.00	Y	N	N

Nestling on the edge of the Forest of Bowland, & surrounded by a beautiful garden with stream & ponds, is the award-winning Peter Barn. Superb accommodation, oak beams & log fires in the 1st floor sitting room with panoramic views of the glorious Ribble Valley. All 3 bedrooms are most attractive, each has an en-suite or private bathroom & tea/coffee-making facilities. The home-made marmalade is delicious. Good walking & exploring - Browsholme Hall, Whalley Abbey...or just relaxing. Children over 12.
E-mail: jean@peterbarn.co.uk

Jean Smith   Peter Barn Country House   Cross Lane Waddington Clitheroe BB7 3JH   Lancashire
Tel: (01200) 428585   Open: ALL YEAR (Excl. Xmas & New Year)   Map Ref No. 09

All the establishments mentioned in this guide are members of
The Worldwide Bed & Breakfast Association

When booking your accommodation please mention
The Best Bed & Breakfast

Cornwall

Cornwall
(West Country)

Cornwall is an ancient Celtic land, a narrow granite peninsula with a magnificent coastline of over 300 miles & wild stretches of moorland.

The north coast, washed by Atlantic breakers, has firm golden sands & soaring cliffs. The magnificent beaches at Bude offer excellent surfing & a few miles to the south you can visit the picturesque harbour at Boscastle & the cliff-top castle at Tintagel with its legends of King Arthur. Newquay, with its beaches stretching for over seven miles, sheltered coves & modern hotels & shops, is the premier resort on Cornwall's Atlantic coast. St. Ives, another surfing resort, has great charm which has attracted artists for so long & is an ideal place from which to explore the Land's End peninsula.

The south coast is a complete contrast - wooded estuaries, sheltered coves, little fishing ports, & popular resorts. Penzance, with its warmth & vivid colours, is an all-the-year-round resort & has wonderful views across the bay to St. Michael's Mount. Here are excellent facilities for sailing & deep-sea fishing, as there are at Falmouth & Fowey with their superb harbours. Mevagissey, Polperro & Looe are fine examples of traditional Cornish fishing villages.

In the far west of Cornwall, you can hear about a fascinating legend: the lost land of Lyonesse - a whole country that was drowned by the sea. The legend goes that the waters cover a rich & fertile country, which had 140 parish churches. The Anglo-Saxon Chronicle records two great storms within a hundred years, which drowned many towns & innumerate people. Submerged forests are known to lie around these coasts - & in Mount's Bay beech trees have been found with the nuts still hanging on the branches, so suddenly were they swamped.

Today, St Michael's Mount & the Isles of Scilly are said to be all that remains of the vanished land. St. Michael's Mount, with its tiny fishing village & dramatic castle, can be visited on foot at low tide or by boat at high water. The Isles of Scilly, 28 miles beyond Land's End, have five inhabited islands, including Tresco with its sub-tropical gardens. Day trips to the numerous uninhabited islands are a special feature of a Scilly holiday.

Inland Cornwall also has its attractions. To the east of Bodmin, the county town, are the open uplands of Bodmin Moor, with the county's highest peaks at Rough Tor & Brown Willy. "Jamaica Inn", immortalised in the novel by Daphne du Maurier, stands on the lonely road across the moor, & "Frenchman's Creek" is on a hidden inlet of the Helford River.

There is a seemingly endless number & variety of Cornish villages in estuaries, wooded, pastoral or moorland settings, & here customs & traditions are maintained. In Helston the famous "Fleury Dance" is still performed, & at the ancient port of Padstow, May Day celebrating involves decorating the houses with green boughs & parading the Hobby Horse through the street to the tune of St. George's Song.

Helford Creek

57

Cornwall

Cornwall Gazeteer

Areas of outstanding natural beauty.
Almost the entire county.

Historic Houses & Castles

Anthony House - Torpoint
18th century - beautiful & quite unspoiled Queen Anne house, excellent panelling & fine period furnishings.

Cotehele House - Calstock
15th & 16th century house, still contains the original furniture, tapestry, armour, etc.

Ebbingford Manor - Bude
12th century Cornish manor house, with walled garden.

Godolphin House - Helston
Tudor - 17th century colonnaded front.

Lanhydrock - Bodmin
17th century - splendid plaster ceilings, picture gallery with family portraits 17th/20th centuries.

Mount Edgcumbe House - Plymouth
Tudor style mansion - restored after destruction in 1949. Hepplewhite furniture & portrait by Joshua Reynolds.

St. Michael's Mount - Penzance
Mediaeval castle & 17th century with 18th & 19th century additions.

Pencarrow House & Gardens - Bodmin
18th century Georgian Mansion - collection of paintings, china & furniture - mile long drive through fine woodlands & gardens.

Old Post Office - Tintagel
14th century manor house in miniature - large hall used as Post Office for a period, hence the name.

Trewithen - Probus Nr. Truro
Early Georgian house with lovely gardens.

Trerice - St. Newlyn East
16th century Elizabethan house, small with elaborate facade. Excellent fireplaces, plaster ceilings, miniature gallery & minstrels' gallery.

Cathedral & Churches

Altarnun (St. Nonna)
15th century, Norman font, 16th century bench ends, fine rood screen.

Bisland (St. Protus & St. Hyacinth)
15th century granite tower - carved wagon roofs, slate floor. Georgian wine - glass pulpit, fine screen.

Kilkhampton (St. James)
16th century with fine Norman doorway, arcades & wagon roofs.

Laneast (St. Michael or St. Sedwell)
13th century, 15th century enlargement, 16th century pulpit, some painted glass.

Lanteglos-by-Fowley (St. Willow)
14th century, refashioned 15th century, 13th century font, 15th century brasses & altar tomb, 16th century bench ends.

Launcells (St. Andrew)
Interior unrestored - old plaster & ancient roofs remaining, fine Norman font with 17th century cover, box pews, pulpit, reredos, 3 sided alter rails.

Probus (St. Probus & St. Gren)
16th century tower, splendid arcades, three great East windows.

St. Keverne (St. Keverne)
Fine tower & spire. Wall painting in 15th century interior.

St. Neot (St. Neot)
Decorated tower - 16th century exterior, buttressed & double-aisled. Many windows of mediaeval glass renewed in 19th century.

Museums & Galleries

Museum of Witchcraft - Boscastle
Relating to witches, implements & customs.

Military Museum - Bodmin
History of Duke of Cornwall's Light Infantry.

Public Library & Museum - Cambourne
Collections of mineralogy, archaeology, local antiquities & history.

Cornish Museum - East Looe
Collection of relics relating to witchcraft customs & superstitions. Folk life & culture of district.

Helston Borough Museum - Helston
Folk life & culture of area around Lizard.

Museum of Nautical Art - Penzance
Exhibition of salvaged gold & silver treasures from underwater wreck of 1700's.

Museum of Smuggling - Polperro
Activities of smugglers, past & present.

Cornwall

Penlee House Museum - Penlee, Penzance
Archaeology & local history & tin mining exhibits.
Barbara Hepworth Museum - St. Ives
Sculpture, letters, documents, photographs, etc., exhibited in house where Barbara Hepworth lived.
Old Mariners Church - St. Ives
St. Ives Society of Artists hold exhibitions here.
County Museum & Art Gallery - Truro
Ceramics, art local history & antiquities, Cornish mineralogy.

Historic Monuments

Cromwell's Castle - Tresco (Scilly Isles)
17th century castle.
King Charles' Fort - Tresco (Scilly Isles)
16th century fort.
Old Blockhouse - Tresco (Scilly Isles)
16th century coastal battery.
Harry's Wall - St. Mary's (Scilly Isles)
Tudor Coastal battery
Ballowall Barrow - St. Just
Prehistoric barrow.
Pendennis Castle - Falmouth
Fort from time of Henry VII.

Restormel Castle - Lostwithiel
13th century ruins.
St. Mawes Castle - St. Mawes
16th century fortified castle.
Tintagel Castle - Tintagel
Mediaeval ruin on wild coast, King Arthur's legendary castle.

Things to see & do

Camel trail - Padstow to Bodmin
12 miles of recreation path along scenic route, suitable for walkers, cyclists & horse-riders.
Tresco Abbey Gardens - Tresco
Collection of sub-tropical flora
Trethorne Leisure Farm - Launceston
Visitors are encouraged to feed & stroke the farm animals
Seal sanctuary - Gweek Nr. Helston
Seals, exhibition hall, nature walk, aquarium, seal hospital, donkey paddock.
Dobwalls Theme Park - Nr. Liskeard
2 miles of scenically dramatic miniature railway based on the American railroad.
Padstow tropical bird gardens - Padstow
Mynack Theatre - Porthcurno

Lands End.

CORNWALL
Map reference

01	Knight	15	Tuckett
02	Tremayne	16	Studley
03	Gough	17	Epperson
04	Otway-R.	18	Nancarrow
05	Sleep	19	Martin
06	Griffin	20	Semmens
07	Rowe	21	Rundle
08	Rosier	22	Heasman
09	Mackenzie	23	Poole
10	Woodley	24	Vichniakov
11	Taylor	25	Barstow
12	Wilson	26	A. Tremayne
13	Edwards	27	Dymond
14	Wooldridge		

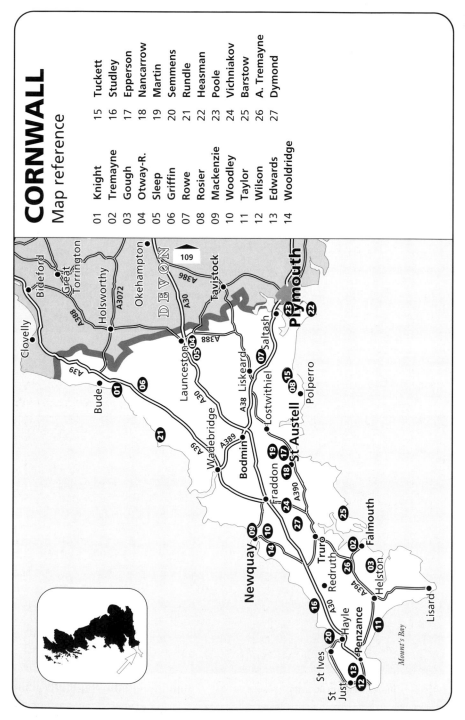

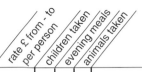
Cornwall

£30.00 to £35.00   N Y N

Manor Farm

Near Rd: A.39

A really super 11th-century manor house, retaining all its former charm & elegance. Mentioned in the 1086 Domesday book, it belonged to the Earl of Mortain, half-brother to William the Conqueror. Delightfully located in a beautiful & secluded position, & surrounded by both attractive gardens & 40 acres of farmland. Guest rooms have private facilities. Dining at Manor Farm is considered the highlight of the day. Only 1 mile from the beach. Non-smokers only. West Country winner of the Best Bed & Breakfast award.

Mrs Muriel Knight   **Manor Farm**   Crackington Haven EX23 0JW   *Cornwall*
Tel: (01840) 230304   *Open: ALL YEAR (Excl. Xmas Day)*   Map Ref No. 01

£30.00 to £35.00   Y Y N
VISA: M'CARD:

'The Home' Country House Hotel

Near Rd: A.39

A quiet & charming country house, with views over Maenporth & Falmouth Bay. Accommodation is in 18 comfortable rooms, 16 with a private/en-suite bath/shower. All have tea/coffee-making facilities. A colour-T.V. lounge & bar are available, & guests may relax in the beautiful sheltered garden. A golf course & boating facilities nearby. A friendly host, who prepares delicious meals using local produce. Special diets provided for by arrangement. Children over 6 years welcome.
www.bestbandb.co.uk

T. P. Tremayne   **'The Home' Country House Hotel**   Penjerrick   Budock Water   Falmouth TR11 5EE
Tel: (01326) 250427   Fax 01326 250143   *Open: APR - OCT*   Map Ref No. 02

£30.00 to £30.00   Y Y N

Calamansac Vean

Near Rd: A.39

Situated beside the Helford River, Calamansac Vean is set in a secluded south-facing garden beside the water's edge. The guest bedrooms, 1 twin & 1 single with private facilities, have lovely views across the river to Frenchman's Creek. A delicious full English breakfast with homemade bread & preserves is served. Evening meals by arrangement. In the neighbourhood there is a wide choice of good pubs & restaurants, also facilities for sailing, riding & golf. Children over 7.
www.bestbandb.co.uk

Julia & David Gough   **Calamansac Vean**   Port Navas   Falmouth TR11 5RN   *Cornwall*
Tel: (01326) 340264   *Open: ALL YEAR*   Map Ref No. 03

£35.00 to £35.00   Y Y Y

Hornacott

Near Rd: A.30

Hornacott nestles in the River Inny Valley with sloping gardens & a stream surrounded by fields. Offering a spacious suite of rooms in a wing of the house, with a private sitting room, bedroom & en-suite bathroom & an additional single room for an accompanying family member/friend. Guests really enjoy the space, comfort & privacy amidst peaceful surroundings & the visitors book is a testament to happy guests, many of whom return again. Evening meals & animals by arrangement.
E-mail: otwayruthven@btinternet.com

Jos & Mary-Anne Otway-Ruthven   **Hornacott**   South Petherwin   Launceston PL15 7LH
Tel: (01566) 782461   Fax 01566 782461   *Open: ALL YEAR (Excl. Xmas)*   Map Ref No. 04

Cornwall

Trevadlock Farm

Near Rd: A.30

Trevadlock Farm is a character farmhouse situated 1 1/2 miles off the A.30 on the edge of Bodmin Moor, offering magnificent views & a relaxing atmosphere. Ideally placed for touring Cornwall & Devon north/south coasts, Eden Project (1/2 hr), & many National Trust properties nearby. Pretty, spacious en-suite bedrooms with tea/coffee-making facilities, T.V. & hairdryer. Enjoy a special break (just 4 hours from London.)

E-mail: trevadlock@farming.co.uk
www.trevadlock.co.uk

| £24.00 to £27.00 | Y | N | N |

VISA: M'CARD:

| Mrs Barbara Sleep | Trevadlock Farm | Trevadlock | Launceston PL15 7PW | Cornwall |
| Tel: (01566) 782239 | Fax 01566 782239 | Open: FEB - NOV | Map Ref No. 05 |

Wheatley Farm

Near Rd: A.39

You will be made very welcome at this spacious farmhouse, built by the Duke of Bedford in 1871, which stands in landscaped gardens on a working family farm in the peaceful countryside. Excellent base for exploring Cornwall/Devon & within easy reach of the Eden Project. Beautiful accommodation, en-suite bedrooms, 1 with romantic 4-poster; each with T.V. & tea/coffee-making facilities. Luxury indoor heated pool, spa & sauna. Splendid food using local produce. Log fires. Children over 7.

E-mail: valerie@wheatleyfrm.com
www.wheatleyfrm.com

| £26.00 to £28.00 | Y | Y | N |

VISA: M'CARD:

| Mrs Valerie Griffin | Wheatley Farm | Maxworthy | Launceston PL15 8LY | Cornwall |
| Tel: (01566) 781232 | Fax 01566 781232 | Open: FEB - NOV | Map Ref No. 06 |

Tregondale Farm

Near Rd: A.390, A.38

Relax in style in this charming, elegant farmhouse, beautifully set in an original walled garden. 3 delightful bedrooms, 2 en-suite & 1 with private bathroom, all with T.V., radio & tea/coffee-making facilities. Log fires for chilly evenings. Home produce a speciality. Play tennis, explore the woodland trail with its abundance of wild flowers & birds, through a 200-acre mixed farm. Find pedigree cattle, lambs in spring. Cycling, fishing from the pond. Information for walkers. Children over 2.

E-mail: tregondale@connectfree.co.uk
www.tregondalefarm.co.uk

| £25.00 to £28.00 | Y | Y | N |

VISA: M'CARD: AMEX:

| Stephanie Rowe | Tregondale Farm | Menheniot | Liskeard PL14 3RG | Cornwall |
| Tel: (01579) 342407 | Fax 01579 342407 | Open: ALL YEAR | Map Ref No. 07 |

Allhays

Near Rd: A.387

Allhays is a spacious family house built in the late 1930s, set in its own peaceful gardens with breathtaking views over the wild & romantic remoteness of Talland Bay. Ideal for walking the coastal path. Many National Trust properties are nearby, as well as the Lost Gardens of Heligan & the Eden Project. Very comfortable freshly refurbished accommodation. Parking. Extensive breakfasts with home-baked breads, free range & organic produce.

E-mail: info@allhays.co.uk
www.allhays.co.uk

| £30.00 to £45.00 | N | N | N |

VISA: M'CARD: AMEX:

| Mr & Mrs Rosier | Allhays | Talland | Looe PL13 2JB | Cornwall |
| Tel: (01503) 273188/272434 | Open: ALL YEAR (Excl. Xmas & New Year) | Map Ref No. 08 |

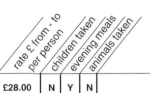

Column headers (diagonal): rate £ from - to per person | children taken | evening meals | animals taken

---

£28.00 to £35.00 — N | Y | N

VISA: M'CARD:

Trenance Lodge Hotel & Restaurant

Near Rd: A.3075

An attractive house standing in its own grounds, overlooking the lakes & gardens of Trenance Valley, leading to the Gannel Estuary. The restaurant has a reputation for serving the finest fresh local food in elegant surroundings. Adjoining the restaurant is a spacious, relaxing bar lounge. Accommodation is in 5 comfortable bedrooms, en-suite, with T.V., radio & tea/coffee facilities. An excellent base for touring, with a warm welcome assured.
E-mail: info@trenance-lodge.co.uk
www.trenance-lodge.co.uk

Mac & Jennie Mackenzie Trenance Lodge Hotel & Restaurant 83 Trenance Road Newquay TR7 2HW
Tel: (01637) 876702   Fax 01637 878772   Open: ALL YEAR   Map Ref No. 09

£25.00 to £28.00 — Y | N | N

(no smoking symbol)

VISA: M'CARD:

Degembris Farmhouse

Near Rd: A.3058

The original manor house of Degembris was built in the 16th century & is now used as a barn. The present-day house, surrounded by attractive gardens, was built a mere 200 years ago, & its slate-hung exterior blends well with the rolling countryside. 5 bedrooms, 3 en-suite, each prettily decorated, with dried flowers & stripped pine enhancing the country atmosphere. Hearty breakfasts are served. Centrally situated in superb countryside, yet close to the sea, this is the perfect holiday base.
E-mail: kathy@degembris.co.uk
www.degembris.co.uk

Kathy Woodley   Degembris Farmhouse   St. Newlyn East   Newquay TR8 5HY   Cornwall
Tel: (01872) 510555   Fax 01872 510230   Open: ALL YEAR   Map Ref No. 10

£32.50 to £40.00 — N | N | N

(smoking symbol)

see PHOTO over p. 64

VISA: M'CARD: AMEX:

Ednovean Farm

Near Rd: A.394

A small farm nestling above the peaceful village of Perranuthnoe, with glorious views towards St. Michael's Mount & Mounts Bay. A stunning 17th-century barn, lovingly renovated, with elegant, country style en suite bedrooms, some with private terraces or four-poster beds. All with little luxuries to spoil you. Stroll to the village, cliff-top walks, secluded coves or just enjoy the view. The perfect spot for a relaxing break.
E-mail: info@ednoveanfarm.co.uk
www.ednoveanfarm.co.uk

Mrs Christine Taylor   Ednovean Farm   Perranuthnoe   Nr. Penzance TR20 9LZ   Cornwall
Tel: (01736) 711883   Fax 01736 710480   Open: ALL YEAR (Excl. Xmas)   Map Ref No. 11

£24.00 to £26.00 — Y | Y | N

VISA: M'CARD:

Boscean Country Hotel

Near Rd: A.3071

The Boscean Country Hotel is set in 3 acres of walled gardens in an Area of Outstanding Natural Beauty overlooking the sea & countryside. There is a wealth of oak pannelling in the downstairs rooms & a grand oak staircase. (Much of the wood is from HMS Camperdown.) All 12 en-suite bedrooms are attractively furnished & have tea/coffee facilities. T.V. lounge, well-stocked bar & residents dining room. The Boscean has an established reputation for excellent home-cooking. Children over 7.
E-mail: boscean@aol.com
www.bosceancountryhotel.co.uk

Dennis & Linda Wilson   Boscean Country Hotel   Bosweddon Road St. Just   Penzance TR19 7QP
Tel: (01736) 788748   Fax 01736 788748   Open: ALL YEAR   Map Ref No. 12

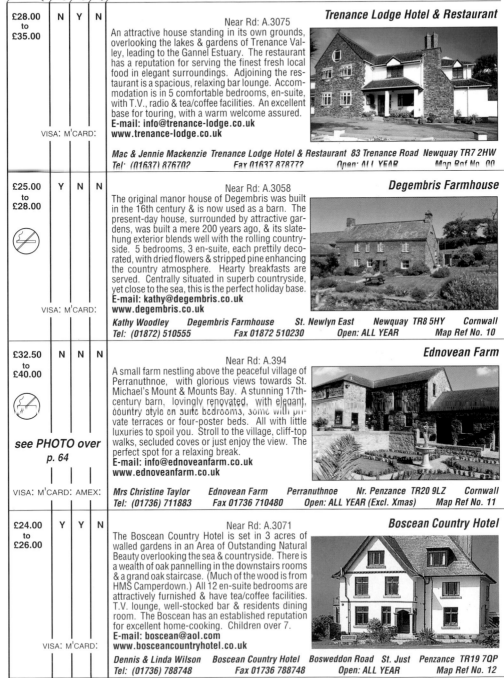

Ednovean Farm   Perranuthnoe.

Trenderway Farm. Pelynt.

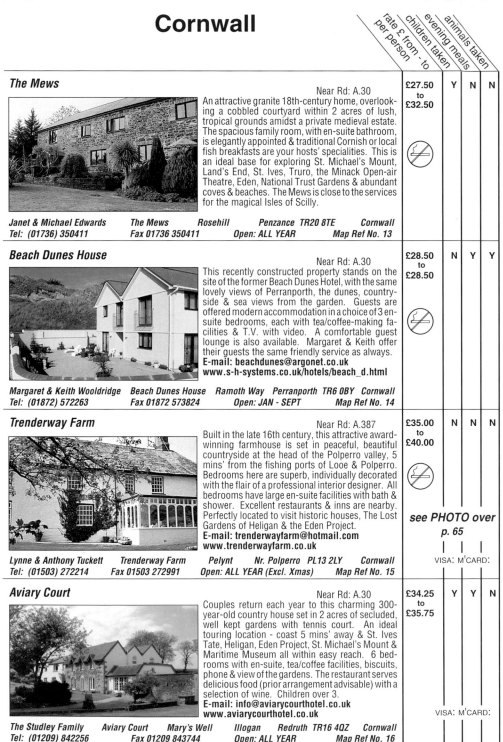

	rate £ from - to per person	children taken	evening meals	animals taken

The Mews

Near Rd: A.30

An attractive granite 18th-century home, overlooking a cobbled courtyard within 2 acres of lush, tropical grounds amidst a private medieval estate. The spacious family room, with en-suite bathroom, is elegantly appointed & traditional Cornish or local fish breakfasts are your hosts' specialities. This is an ideal base for exploring St. Michael's Mount, Land's End, St. Ives, Truro, the Minack Open-air Theatre, Eden, National Trust Gardens & abundant coves & beaches. The Mews is close to the services for the magical Isles of Scilly.

£27.50 to £32.50 — Y — N — N

Janet & Michael Edwards   The Mews   Rosehill   Penzance TR20 8TE   Cornwall
Tel: (01736) 350411   Fax 01736 350411   Open: ALL YEAR   Map Ref No. 13

Beach Dunes House

Near Rd: A.30

This recently constructed property stands on the site of the former Beach Dunes Hotel, with the same lovely views of Perranporth, the dunes, countryside & sea views from the garden. Guests are offered modern accommodation in a choice of 3 en-suite bedrooms, each with tea/coffee-making facilities & T.V. with video. A comfortable guest lounge is also available. Margaret & Keith offer their guests the same friendly service as always.
E-mail: beachdunes@argonet.co.uk
www.s-h-systems.co.uk/hotels/beach_d.html

£28.50 to £28.50 — N — Y — Y

Margaret & Keith Wooldridge   Beach Dunes House   Ramoth Way   Perranporth TR6 0BY   Cornwall
Tel: (01872) 572263   Fax 01872 573824   Open: JAN - SEPT   Map Ref No. 14

Trenderway Farm

Near Rd: A.387

Built in the late 16th century, this attractive award-winning farmhouse is set in peaceful, beautiful countryside at the head of the Polperro valley, 5 mins' from the fishing ports of Looe & Polperro. Bedrooms here are superb, individually decorated with the flair of a professional interior designer. All bedrooms have large en-suite facilities with bath & shower. Excellent restaurants & inns are nearby. Perfectly located to visit historic houses, The Lost Gardens of Heligan & the Eden Project.
E-mail: trenderwayfarm@hotmail.com
www.trenderwayfarm.co.uk

£35.00 to £40.00 — N — N — N

see PHOTO over
p. 65

VISA: M'CARD:

Lynne & Anthony Tuckett   Trenderway Farm   Pelynt   Nr. Polperro PL13 2LY   Cornwall
Tel: (01503) 272214   Fax 01503 272991   Open: ALL YEAR (Excl. Xmas)   Map Ref No. 15

Aviary Court

Near Rd: A.30

Couples return each year to this charming 300-year-old country house set in 2 acres of secluded, well kept gardens with tennis court. An ideal touring location - coast 5 mins' away & St. Ives Tate, Heligan, Eden Project, St. Michael's Mount & Maritime Museum all within easy reach. 6 bedrooms with en-suite, tea/coffee facilities, biscuits, phone & view of the gardens. The restaurant serves delicious food (prior arrangement advisable) with a selection of wine. Children over 3.
E-mail: info@aviarycourthotel.co.uk
www.aviarycourthotel.co.uk

£34.25 to £35.75 — Y — Y — N

VISA: M'CARD:

The Studley Family   Aviary Court   Mary's Well   Illogan   Redruth TR16 4QZ   Cornwall
Tel: (01209) 842256   Fax 01209 843744   Open: ALL YEAR   Map Ref No. 16

Nanscawen House. St. Blazey.

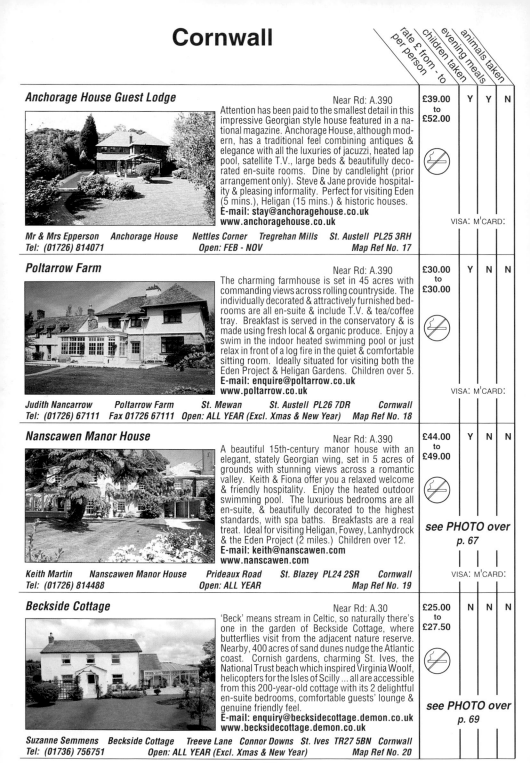

	rate £ from - to per person	children taken	evening meals	animals taken

Anchorage House Guest Lodge

Near Rd: A.390

Attention has been paid to the smallest detail in this impressive Georgian style house featured in a national magazine. Anchorage House, although modern, has a traditional feel combining antiques & elegance with all the luxuries of jacuzzi, heated lap pool, satellite T.V., large beds & beautifully decorated en-suite rooms. Dine by candlelight (prior arrangement only). Steve & Jane provide hospitality & pleasing informality. Perfect for visiting Eden (5 mins.), Heligan (15 mins.) & historic houses.
E-mail: stay@anchoragehouse.co.uk
www.anchoragehouse.co.uk

£39.00 to £52.00 — Y Y N

VISA: M'CARD:

Mr & Mrs Epperson   Anchorage House   Nettles Corner   Tregrehan Mills   St. Austell PL25 3RH
Tel: (01726) 814071   Open: FEB - NOV   Map Ref No. 17

Poltarrow Farm

Near Rd: A.390

The charming farmhouse is set in 45 acres with commanding views across rolling countryside. The individually decorated & attractively furnished bedrooms are all en-suite & include T.V. & tea/coffee tray. Breakfast is served in the conservatory & is made using fresh local & organic produce. Enjoy a swim in the indoor heated swimming pool or just relax in front of a log fire in the quiet & comfortable sitting room. Ideally situated for visiting both the Eden Project & Heligan Gardens. Children over 5.
E-mail: enquire@poltarrow.co.uk
www.poltarrow.co.uk

£30.00 to £30.00 — Y N N

VISA: M'CARD:

Judith Nancarrow   Poltarrow Farm   St. Mewan   St. Austell PL26 7DR   Cornwall
Tel: (01726) 67111   Fax 01726 67111   Open: ALL YEAR (Excl. Xmas & New Year)   Map Ref No. 18

Nanscawen Manor House

Near Rd: A.390

A beautiful 15th-century manor house with an elegant, stately Georgian wing, set in 5 acres of grounds with stunning views across a romantic valley. Keith & Fiona offer you a relaxed welcome & friendly hospitality. Enjoy the heated outdoor swimming pool. The luxurious bedrooms are all en-suite, & beautifully decorated to the highest standards, with spa baths. Breakfasts are a real treat. Ideal for visiting Heligan, Fowey, Lanhydrock & the Eden Project (2 miles.) Children over 12.
E-mail: keith@nanscawen.com
www.nanscawen.com

£44.00 to £49.00 — Y N N

see PHOTO over p. 67

VISA: M'CARD:

Keith Martin   Nanscawen Manor House   Prideaux Road   St. Blazey PL24 2SR   Cornwall
Tel: (01726) 814488   Open: ALL YEAR   Map Ref No. 19

Beckside Cottage

Near Rd: A.30

'Beck' means stream in Celtic, so naturally there's one in the garden of Beckside Cottage, where butterflies visit from the adjacent nature reserve. Nearby, 400 acres of sand dunes nudge the Atlantic coast. Cornish gardens, charming St. Ives, the National Trust beach which inspired Virginia Woolf, helicopters for the Isles of Scilly ... all are accessible from this 200-year-old cottage with its 2 delightful en-suite bedrooms, comfortable guests' lounge & genuine friendly feel.
E-mail: enquiry@becksidecottage.demon.co.uk
www.becksidecottage.demon.co.uk

£25.00 to £27.50 — N N N

see PHOTO over p. 69

Suzanne Semmens   Beckside Cottage   Treeve Lane   Connor Downs   St. Ives TR27 5BN   Cornwall
Tel: (01736) 756751   Open: ALL YEAR (Excl. Xmas & New Year)   Map Ref No. 20

Beckside Cottage.   Connor Down.

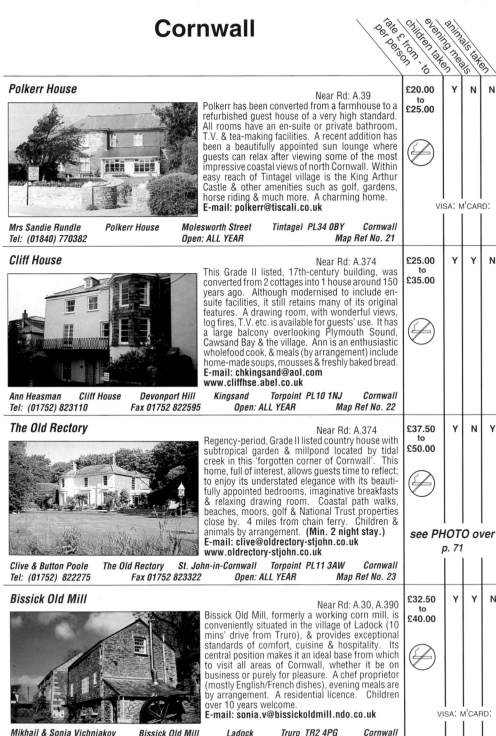

	rate £ from - to per person	children taken	evening meals	animals taken

Polkerr House

Near Rd: A.39

Polkerr has been converted from a farmhouse to a refurbished guest house of a very high standard. All rooms have an en-suite or private bathroom, T.V. & tea-making facilities. A recent addition has been a beautifully appointed sun lounge where guests can relax after viewing some of the most impressive coastal views of north Cornwall. Within easy reach of Tintagel village is the King Arthur Castle & other amenities such as golf, gardens, horse riding & much more. A charming home.
E-mail: polkerr@tiscali.co.uk

£20.00 to £25.00 — Y N N

VISA: M'CARD:

| Mrs Sandie Rundle | Polkerr House | Molesworth Street | Tintagel PL34 0BY | Cornwall |
| Tel: (01840) 770382 | | Open: ALL YEAR | | Map Ref No. 21 |

Cliff House

Near Rd: A.374

This Grade II listed, 17th-century building, was converted from 2 cottages into 1 house around 150 years ago. Although modernised to include en-suite facilities, it still retains many of its original features. A drawing room, with wonderful views, log fires, T.V. etc. is available for guests' use. It has a large balcony overlooking Plymouth Sound, Cawsand Bay & the village. Ann is an enthusiastic wholefood cook, & meals (by arrangement) include home-made soups, mousses & freshly baked bread.
E-mail: chkingsand@aol.com
www.cliffhse.abel.co.uk

£25.00 to £35.00 — Y Y N

| Ann Heasman | Cliff House | Devonport Hill | Kingsand | Torpoint PL10 1NJ | Cornwall |
| Tel: (01752) 823110 | Fax 01752 822595 | | Open: ALL YEAR | | Map Ref No. 22 |

The Old Rectory

Near Rd: A.374

Regency-period, Grade II listed country house with subtropical garden & millpond located by tidal creek in this 'forgotten corner of Cornwall'. This home, full of interest, allows guests time to reflect; to enjoy its understated elegance with its beautifully appointed bedrooms, imaginative breakfasts & relaxing drawing room. Coastal path walks, beaches, moors, golf & National Trust properties close by. 4 miles from chain ferry. Children & animals by arrangement. **(Min. 2 night stay.)**
E-mail: clive@oldrectory-stjohn.co.uk
www.oldrectory-stjohn.co.uk

£37.50 to £50.00 — Y N Y

see PHOTO over p. 71

| Clive & Button Poole | The Old Rectory | St. John-in-Cornwall | Torpoint PL11 3AW | Cornwall |
| Tel: (01752) 822275 | Fax 01752 823322 | | Open: ALL YEAR | | Map Ref No. 23 |

Bissick Old Mill

Near Rd: A.30, A.390

Bissick Old Mill, formerly a working corn mill, is conveniently situated in the village of Ladock (10 mins' drive from Truro), & provides exceptional standards of comfort, cuisine & hospitality. Its central position makes it an ideal base from which to visit all areas of Cornwall, whether it be on business or purely for pleasure. A chef proprietor (mostly English/French dishes), evening meals are by arrangement. A residential licence. Children over 10 years welcome.
E-mail: sonia.v@bissickoldmill.ndo.co.uk

£32.50 to £40.00 — Y Y N

VISA: M'CARD:

| Mikhail & Sonia Vichniakov | Bissick Old Mill | Ladock | Truro TR2 4PG | Cornwall |
| Tel: (01726) 882557 | Fax 01726 884057 | | Open: FEB - NOV | | Map Ref No. 24 |

The Old Rectory. St. John-in-Cornwall.

Cornwall

Crugsillick Manor

Near Rd: A.3078

A hidden treasure of the Roseland Peninsula, one of Cornwall's loveliest areas - meandering lanes, unspoilt fishing villages & sheltered coves. This beautiful Grade II listed Queen Anne manor house, offers peace & comfort. Stroll down the smugglers' path below the house to glorious beaches & spectacular coastline, visit historic houses, the Eden Project & Falmouth's Maritime Museum. Dine on freshly caught seafood & home-grown vegetables. Children 12+. Animals by arrangement.
E-mail: barstow@adtel.co.uk
www.adtel.co.uk

| £42.00 to £49.00 | Y | Y | Y |

VISA: M'CARD:

Oliver & Rosemary Barstow   Crugsillick Manor   Ruan High Lanes   Truro TR2 5LJ   Cornwall
Tel: (01872) 501214   Fax 01872 501228   Open: ALL YEAR   Map Ref No. 25

Apple Tree Cottage

Near Rd: A.390

Apple Tree Cottage, set amid rolling countryside with delightful gardens & river, is furnished with country antiques & has a warm, welcoming atmosphere. The large lounge has a log fire, & traditional farmhouse breakfasts, cooked on the Aga, are taken in the sunlit dining room. The attractive bedrooms have pine double beds, tea/coffee facilities, washbasins & lovely views. Several National Trust gardens & the famous Trebah Gardens on the Helford River are close by. Children over 10.
E-mail: appletreecottage@talk21.com
www.cornwall-online.co.uk

| £25.00 to £28.00 | Y | N | Y |

Ann Tremayne   Apple Tree Cottage   Laity Moor   Ponsanooth   Truro TR3 7HR   Cornwall
Tel: (01872) 865047   Open: ALL YEAR (Excl. Xmas)   Map Ref No. 26

Trevispian-Vean Farm Guest House

Near Rd: A.39

A delightful farmhouse, dating back over 300 years, offering a very warm welcome & good accommodation in 5 comfortably furnished en-suite guest rooms. Only 7 miles from the coast, & surrounded by beautiful, tranquil countryside, it is a perfect base for everyone. Families will enjoy it here, as children can look around the farm, & there are plenty of places to visit & things to do. There's even a donkey for the children. For garden lovers, the Eden Project & the Lost Gardens of Heligan are within easy reach. Dinner by arrangement.
www.guesthousestruro.com

| £20.00 to £25.00 | Y | N | N |

Nick & Jacqui Dymond   Trevispian-Vean Farm Guest House   St. Erme   Truro TR4 9AT   Cornwall
Tel: (01872) 279514   Open: ALL YEAR   Map Ref No. 27

Visit our website at:
http://www.bestbandb.co.uk

Cumbria

Cumbria

The Lake District National Park is deservedly famous for its magnificent scenery. Here, England's highest mountains & rugged fells surround shimmering lakes & green valleys. But there is more to Cumbria than the beauty of the Lake District. It also has a splendid coastline, easily accessible from the main lakeland centres, as well as a border region where the Pennines, the backbone of England, reach their highest point, towering over the Eden valley.

Formation of the dramatic Lakeland scenery began in the Caledonian period when earth movements raised & folded the already ancient rocks, submerging the whole mass underseas & covering it with limestone. During the ice age great glaciers ground out the lake beds & dales of todays landscape. There is tremendous variety, from the craggy outcrops of the Borrowdale Volcanics with Skiddaw at 3054 feet, to the gentle dales, the open moorlands & the lakes themselves. Each lake is distinctive, some with steep mountain sides sliding straight to the water's edge, others more open with sloping wooded hillsides. Ellerwater, the enchanting "lake of swans" is surrounded by reed & willows at the foot of Langdale. The charm of Ullswater inspired Wordsworth's famous poem "Daffodils". Whilst many lakes are deliberately left undisturbed for those seeking peace, there are others - notably Windermere - where a variety of water sports can be enjoyed. The changeable weather of the mountainous region can produce a sudden transformation in the character of a tranquil lake, raising choppy waves across the darkened surface to break along the shoreline. It is all part of the fascination of Lakeland.

Fell walking is the best way to appreciate the full beauty of the area. There are gentle walks along the dales, & the tops of the ridges are accessible to walkers with suitable footwear & an eye to the weather.

Ponytrekking is another popular way to explore the countryside & there are many centres catering even for inexperienced riders.

There are steamboats on lakes such as Coniston & Ullswater, where you can appreciate the scenery. On Windermere there are a variety of boats for hire, & facilities for water-skiing.

Traditional crafts & skills are on display widely. Craft centres at Keswick, Ambleside & Grasmere, & the annual exhibition of the Guild of Lakeland Craftsmen held in Windermere from mid-July to early September represent the widest variety of craft artistry.

Fairs & festivals flourish in Lakeland. The famous Appleby Horse Fair, held in June is the largest fair of its kind in the world & attracts a huge gypsy gathering. Traditional agriculture shows, sheep dog trials & local sporting events abound. The Grasmere Sports, held each August include gruelling fell races, Cumberland & Westmoreland wrestling, hound trails & pole-leaping.

The traditional custom of "rush-bearing" when the earth floors of the churches were strewn with rushes still survives as a procession in Ambleside & Grasmere & many other villages in the summer months

The coast of Cumbria stretches from the estuaries of Grange-over-Sands & Burrow-in-Furness by way of the beautiful beaches between Bootle & Cardurnock, to the mouth of the Solway Firth. The coastal areas, especially the estuaries, are excellent for bird-watching. The sand dunes north of the Esk are famous for the colony of black-headed gulls which can be visited by arrangement, & the colony of seabirds at St. Bees Head is the largest in Britain.

Cumbria

Cumbria
Gazeteer

Area of outstanding natural beauty.
The Lake District National Park.

House & Castles

Carlisle Castle - Carlisle
12th century. Massive Norman keep - half-moon battery - ramparts, portcullis & gatehouse.
Brough Castle - Kirby Stephen
13th century - on site of Roman Station between York & Carlisle.
Dacre Castle - Penrith
14th century - massive pele tower.
Sizergh Castle - Kendal
14th century - pele tower - 15th century great hall. English & French furniture, silver & china - Jacobean relics. 18th century gardens.
Belle Island - Boweness-on-Windermere
18th century - interior by Adams Brothers, portraits by Romney.
Swarthmoor Hall - Ulverston
Elizabethan house, mullioned windows, oak staircase, panelled rooms. Home of George Fox - birthplace of Quakerism - belongs to Society of Friends.
Lorton Hall - Cockermouth
15th century pele tower, priest holes, oak panelling, Jacobean furniture.
Muncaster Castle - Ravenglass
14th century with 15th & 19th century additions - site of Roman tower.
Rusland Hall - Ulveston
Georgian mansion with period panelling, sculpture, furniture, paintings.
Levens Hall - Kendal
Elizabethan - very fine panelling & plasterwork - famous topiary garden.
Hill Top - Sawrey
17th century farmhouse home of Beatrix Potter - contains her furniture, china & some of original drawings for her children's books.
Dove Cottage - Town End, Grasmere
William Wordsworth's cottage - still contains his furnishing & his personal effects as in his lifetime.
Brantwood
The Coniston home of John Ruskin, said to be the most beautifully situated house in the Lake District. Exhibition, gardens, bookshops & tearooms.

Cathedrals & Churches

Carlisle Cathedral - Carlisle
1130. 15th century choir stalls with painted backs - carved misericords, 16th century screen, painted roof.
Cartmel Priory (St. Mary Virgin)
15th century stalls, 17th century screen, large east window, curious central tower.
Lanercost Priory (St. Mary Magdalene)
12th century - Augustinian - north aisle now forms Parish church.
Greystoke (St. Andrew)
14th/15th century. 19th century misericords. Lovely glass in chancel.
Brougham (St. Wilfred)
15th century carved altarpiece.
Furness Abbey
12th century monastery beautiful setting.
Shap Abbey
12th century with 16th century tower.

Museums & Galleries

Abbot Hall - Kendal
18th century, Georgian house with period furniture, porcelain, silver, pictures, etc. Also contains modern galleries with contemporary paintings, sculptures & ceramics. Changing exhibitions on show.
Carlisle Museum & Art Gallery - Carlisle
Archaeological & natural history collections. National centre of studies of Roman Britain. Art gallery principally exhibiting paintings & porcelain.
Hawkshead Courthouse - Kendal
Exhibition of domestic & working life housed in mediaeval building.
Helena Thompson Museum - Workington
displays Victorian family life & objects of the period.
Lakeland Motor Museum - Holker Hall - Grange-over-Sands
Exhibits cars, bicycles, tricycles, motor cycles, etc., & model cars.
Millom Folk Museum - St. George's Road, Millom
Reconstructions of drift in iron ore mine, miner's cottage kitchen, blacksmith's forge & agricultural relics.
Ravenglass Railway Museum - Ravenglass
History of railways relics, models, etc.

Cumbria

Wordsworth Museum - Town End, Grasmere
Personal effects, first editions, manuscripts, & general exhibits from the time of William Wordsworth.
Border Regiment Museum - The Castle, Carlisle.
Collection of uniforms, weapons, trophies, documents, medals from 1702, to the present time.
Whitehaven Museum - Whitehaven
History & development of area show in geology, paleontology, archaeology, natural history, etc. Interesting maritime past.
Fitz Park Museum & Art Gallery - Keswick.

Collection of manuscripts - Wordsworth, Walpole, Coleridge, Southey.
The Beatrix Potter Gallery - Hawkshead

Things to see & do

Fell Walking - there is good walking throughout Cumbria, but check weather reports, clothing & footwear before tackling the heights.
Pony-trekking - opportunities for novice & experienced riders.
Watersports - Windermere is the ideal centre for sailing, waterskiing, windsurfing, scuba-diving.
Golf - championship course to the north at Silloth.

Grasmere.

CUMBRIA

Map reference

02 Kirby	17 R. Jones
03 Clark	17 Coy
04 Hempstead	18 Jameison
05 Stobbart	19 Lowe
06 Duff	20 Reynolds
07 McKenzie	20 Davidson
08 Sisson	21 White
09 Lawler	22 Clowes
10 Thompson	23 Holcroft
11 Pettit	23 Drinkall
12 Cervetti	23 Thomas
14 Kaye	24 Blaney
15 Midwinter	
16 Miller	

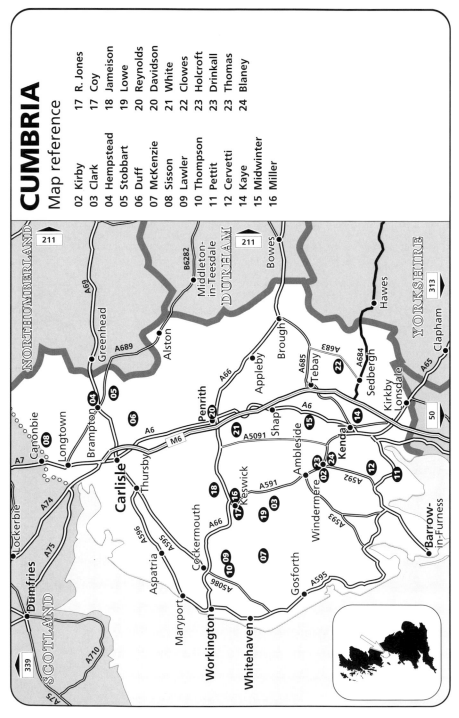

Courtyard Cottages.   Brampton.

Cumbria

Buckle Yeat

Near Rd: A.590

Buckle Yeat is famous for its connections with Beatrix Potter. Although over 200 years old, it has been sympathetically & tastefully refurbished. There is a large lounge with log fire & an attractive dining room which also serves morning coffee & afternoon teas. There are 6 comfortable en-suite bedrooms. Many good local pubs & restaurants offer excellent meals. Buckle Yeat is in an ideal position for touring Lakeland, with walks, fishing & birdwatching all nearby. Animals by arrangement.
E-mail: info@buckle-yeat.co.uk
www.buckle-yeat.co.uk

| £30.00 to £32.50 | Y | N | Y |

VISA: M'CARD: AMEX:

Robert & Helen Kirby   Buckle Yeat   Nr. Sawrey   Hawkshead   Ambleside LA22 0LF   Cumbria
Tel: (015394) 36446/36538   Open: ALL YEAR   Map Ref No. 02

Banerigg Guest House

Near Rd: A.591

Delightfully situated overlooking Grasmere Lake is this small, friendly guest house. The informal hospitality & relaxing atmosphere make this a super base for a holiday. All 6 comfortable rooms have modern amenities. A pleasant lounge with a cosy log fire. A delicious & plentiful breakfast is served. Ideally located for fell walking, sailing, canoeing & fishing. Angela & Martin ensure that guests have a memorable Lakeland holiday.
E-mail: banerigg2001@hotmail.com
www.baneriggguesthouse.co.uk

| £26.00 to £30.00 | Y | N | N |

Angela & Martin Clark Banerigg Guest House Lake Road Grasmere Ambleside LA22 9PW Cumbria
Tel: (015394) 35204   Open: ALL YEAR   Map Ref No. 03

Courtyard Cottages

Near Rd: A.69

You won't be staying in someone else's home but in 1 of 2 comfortable double-bedded en-suite bedrooms in the lovely courtyard cottage of a Victorian mansion standing in 3 acres of grounds. Stone steps lead to the upper accommodation, providing total independence & privacy. Breakfast is served in your room. Relax & enjoy the tranquillity or venture out to Hadrian's Wall, the lakes & Scottish borders, or just stay as a stop-over & be pampered as you travel north or south. (M.6 10 mins.)
E-mail: janet@warrenbank.demon.co.uk
www.bed-breakfast-cumbria.com

| £40.00 to £45.00 | N | N | N |

see PHOTO over
p. 77

Janet Hempstead   Courtyard Cottages   Warren Bank, Station Road   Brampton CA8 1EX   Cumbria
Tel: (016977) 41818 Fax 016977 41398 Open: ALL YEAR (Excl. Xmas & New Year) Map Ref No. 04

Hullerbank

Near Rd: A.69

Attractive pink-washed Georgian style farmhouse dated 1635-1751 standing in its own grounds, near the picturesque village of Talkin, 2 1/2 miles from Brampton. Superb walking country & central for Hadrian's Wall, the Lake District & the Borders. A friendly, relaxed atmosphere awaits. 3 bedrooms with private facilities, tea/coffee & T.V. & a sitting room with inglenook fireplace & separate dining room where excellent breakfasts are served. 2 inns with restaurant facilities nearby. Children over 12.
E-mail: info@hullerbank.freeserve.co.uk
www.hullerbankbnb.co.uk

| £24.00 to £25.00 | Y | N | N |

VISA: M'CARD:

Sheila Stobbart   Hullerbank   Talkin   Brampton CA8 1LB   Cumbria
Tel: (016977) 46668   Fax 016977 46668   Open: FEB - DEC   Map Ref No. 05

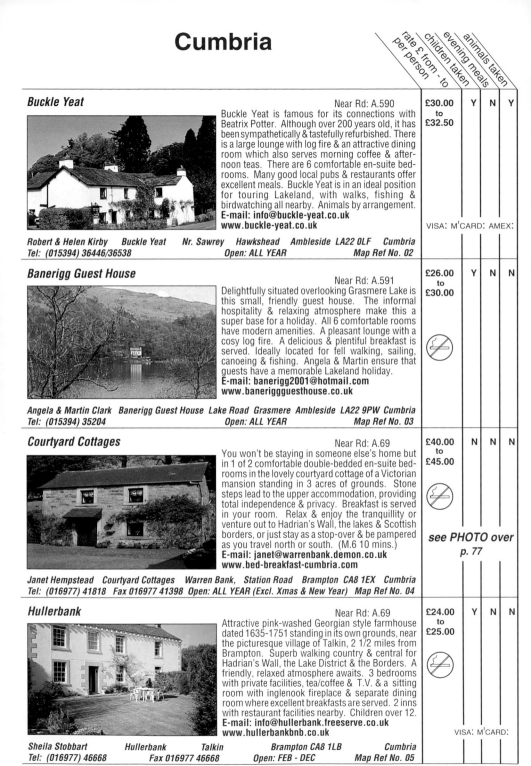

Wood House.   Buttermere .

	rate £ from - to per person	children taken	evening meals	animals taken

Cumrew House

Near Rd: A.6

Built in 1753, the house has a classic Georgian facade built from mellow Eden sandstone. Many original features remain, including the ornate ceiling in the dining room. Find the secret door to the billiard room, draw a chair up to the fire, play tennis, or settle on the terrace for a sun-downer. Bedrooms & bathrooms are large & freshly painted. Delicious breakfasts made from only the finest local produce. Shooting, fishing, golf, sailing or riding can be arranged. Babies & children over 8.
E-mail: rabduff@aol.com
www.countrysport-lodge.com

£35.00 to £35.00 — Y Y Y

Roddy & Isabel Duff   Cumrew House   Cumrew   Brampton CA8 9DD   Cumbria
Tel: (01768) 896115   Fax 01768 896117   Open: ALL YEAR (Excl. Easter & Xmas)   Map Ref No. 06

Wood House

Near Rd: A.66

The view overlooking Wood House was chosen by J.M.W. Turner for his famous painting of Buttermere in 1798. A visitor describing the interior has written, "The furnishings & decor are serene & beautiful though completely unpretentious. The bedrooms reach similarly high standards & enjoy lovely views." Food is freshly prepared from carefully selected ingredients. Woodalls (Royal Warranty) supply the house with their renowned meat products. Judy's home-baked bread is delicious.
E-mail: woodhouse.guest@virgin.net
www.wdhse.co.uk

£32.00 to £40.00 — N Y N

see PHOTO over p. 79

Michael & Judy McKenzie   Wood House   Buttermere CA13 9XA   Cumbria
Tel: (017687) 70208   Fax 017687 70241   Open: FEB - NOV   Map Ref No. 07

Bessiestown Farm Country Guesthouse

Near Rd: A.7

A multi-award-winning country guest house, overlooking the Scottish borders, where a friendly, relaxing atmosphere is assured. 6 pretty, en-suite rooms with radio, T.V. & tea/coffee-making facilities. Delightfully decorated public rooms & conservatory. Also, ground-floor accommodation in extremely comfortable courtyard cottages. Delicious home-cooking. Residential drinks licence. Guests may use the indoor heated swimming pool. Stop-off to/from Scotland & N. Ireland.
E-mail: info@bessiestown.co.uk
www.bessiestown.co.uk

£27.00 to £37.00 — Y Y N

VISA: M'CARD:

Margaret Sisson   Bessiestown Farm Country Guesthouse   Catlowdy   Longtown   Carlisle CA6 5QP
Tel: (01228) 577219/577019   Fax 01228 577219/577019   Open: ALL YEAR   Map Ref No. 08

Winder Hall Country House

Near Rd: A.66

This historic manor house has grounds to the River Cocker in possibly the most peaceful valley in the National Park, ideal for the Northern & Western Lakes. Ann & Nick provide 7 luxurious rooms with superb views, 2 with special 4-posters. Guests appreciate the attentive service, the wide breakfast choice & the 4-course dinner featuring local produce. Residential licence. Complimentary membership to a local gym & spa with swimming pool. Short breaks available.
E-mail: stay@winderhall.co.uk
www.winderhall.co.uk

£45.00 to £50.00 — Y Y N

see PHOTO over p. 81

VISA: M'CARD:

Ann & Nick Lawler   Winder Hall Country House   Low Lorton   Cockermouth CA13 9UP   Cumbria
Tel: 01900 85107   Fax 01900 85479   Open: ALL YEAR   Map Ref No. 09

Winder Hall. Low Lorton.

	rate £ from - to per person	children taken	evening meals	animals taken

New House Farm

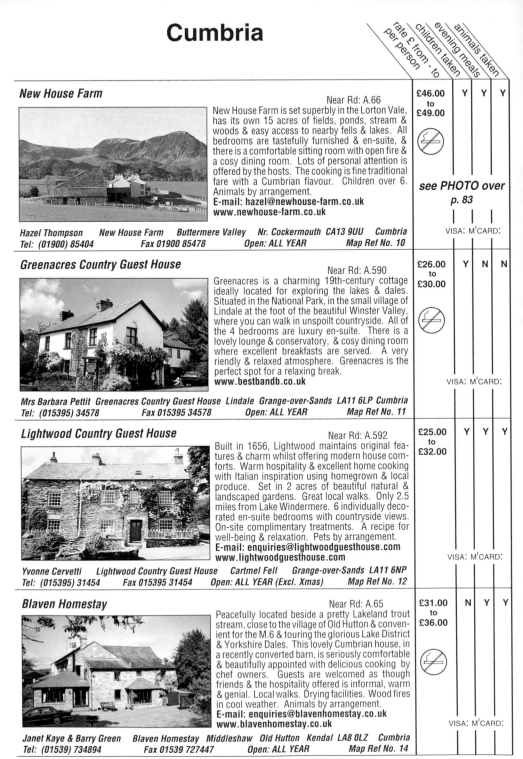

Near Rd: A.66

New House Farm is set superbly in the Lorton Vale, has its own 15 acres of fields, ponds, stream & woods & easy access to nearby fells & lakes. All bedrooms are tastefully furnished & en-suite, & there is a comfortable sitting room with open fire & a cosy dining room. Lots of personal attention is offered by the hosts. The cooking is fine traditional fare with a Cumbrian flavour. Children over 6. Animals by arrangement.

E-mail: hazel@newhouse-farm.co.uk
www.newhouse-farm.co.uk

£46.00 to £49.00 — Y Y Y

see PHOTO over p. 83

VISA: M'CARD:

Hazel Thompson   New House Farm   Buttermere Valley   Nr. Cockermouth CA13 9UU   Cumbria
Tel: (01900) 85404   Fax 01900 85478   Open: ALL YEAR   Map Ref No. 10

Greenacres Country Guest House

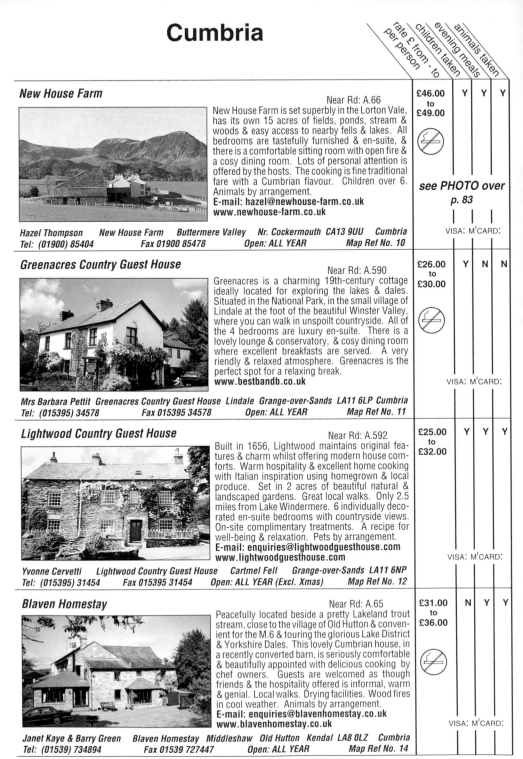

Near Rd: A.590

Greenacres is a charming 19th-century cottage ideally located for exploring the lakes & dales. Situated in the National Park, in the small village of Lindale at the foot of the beautiful Winster Valley, where you can walk in unspoilt countryside. All of the 4 bedrooms are luxury en-suite. There is a lovely lounge & conservatory, & cosy dining room where excellent breakfasts are served. A very friendly & relaxed atmosphere. Greenacres is the perfect spot for a relaxing break.

www.bestbandb.co.uk

£26.00 to £30.00 — Y N N

VISA: M'CARD:

Mrs Barbara Pettit Greenacres Country Guest House Lindale Grange-over-Sands LA11 6LP Cumbria
Tel: (015395) 34578   Fax 015395 34578   Open: ALL YEAR   Map Ref No. 11

Lightwood Country Guest House

Near Rd: A.592

Built in 1656, Lightwood maintains original features & charm whilst offering modern house comforts. Warm hospitality & excellent home cooking with Italian inspiration using homegrown & local produce. Set in 2 acres of beautiful natural & landscaped gardens. Great local walks. Only 2.5 miles from Lake Windermere. 6 individually decorated en-suite bedrooms with countryside views. On-site complimentary treatments. A recipe for well-being & relaxation. Pets by arrangement.

E-mail: enquiries@lightwoodguesthouse.com
www.lightwoodguesthouse.com

£25.00 to £32.00 — Y Y Y

VISA: M'CARD:

Yvonne Cervetti   Lightwood Country Guest House   Cartmel Fell   Grange-over-Sands LA11 6NP
Tel: (015395) 31454   Fax 015395 31454   Open: ALL YEAR (Excl. Xmas)   Map Ref No. 12

Blaven Homestay

Near Rd: A.65

Peacefully located beside a pretty Lakeland trout stream, close to the village of Old Hutton & convenient for the M.6 & touring the glorious Lake District & Yorkshire Dales. This lovely Cumbrian house, in a recently converted barn, is seriously comfortable & beautifully appointed with delicious cooking by chef owners. Guests are welcomed as though friends & the hospitality offered is informal, warm & genial. Local walks. Drying facilities. Wood fires in cool weather. Animals by arrangement.

E-mail: enquiries@blavenhomestay.co.uk
www.blavenhomestay.co.uk

£31.00 to £36.00 — N Y Y

VISA: M'CARD:

Janet Kaye & Barry Green   Blaven Homestay Middleshaw Old Hutton Kendal LA8 0LZ   Cumbria
Tel: (01539) 734894   Fax 01539 727447   Open: ALL YEAR   Map Ref No. 14

New House Farm. Lorton.

The Grange Country House Hotel. Keswick

Column headers (rotated):
- rate £ from - to per person
- children taken
- evening meals taken
- animals taken

£25.00 to £31.00 | Y Y Y

VISA: M'CARD:

Low Jock Scar

Near Rd: A.6

A charming country guest house. A relaxing & friendly atmosphere with genuine warmth. In an idyllic setting with 6 acres of garden & woodland, it is a peaceful base from which to explore the Lakes & Yorkshire Dales. There are 5 comfortable bedrooms (3 en-suite, 2 on the ground floor) & a lounge well stocked with books & maps. Excellent freshly prepared dinners by arrangement - vegetarians catered for. Licensed. Single supplement. Children over 12. Animals by arrangement.

E-mail: ljs@avmail.co.uk
www.SmoothHound.co.uk/hotels/lowjocks

Philip & Alison Midwinter   Low Jock Scar   Selside   Kendal LA8 9LE   Cumbria
Tel: (01539) 823259   Fax 01539 823259   Open: Mid MAR - NOV   Map Ref No. 15

£32.50 to £41.00 | Y N N

see PHOTO over p. 84

VISA: M'CARD:

The Grange Country House

Near Rd: A.591

Grange Country House is situated in its own grounds, with excellent parking, overlooking Keswick-on-Derwentwater & the surrounding mountains. Lovely bedrooms with those extra touches together with comfort, care, quality furnishings & relaxed hospitality make this award-winning home a perfect holiday base. The exceptional breakfast menu will give you an ideal start to your day in Lakeland. Somewhere special for lovers of the countryside. Children over 7.

E-mail: info@grangekeswick.com
www.grangekeswick.com

Duncan & Jane Miller   The Grange Country House   Manor Brow   Keswick CA12 4BA   Cumbria
Tel: 017687 72500   Open: MAR - NOV   Map Ref No. 16

£23.00 to £28.00 | Y N N

see PHOTO over p. 86

VISA: M'CARD:

Greystones Hotel

Near Rd: A.591

Greystones enjoys an enviable position overlooking the grounds of St. John's Church, & has excellent fell views. It is just a short walk to the market square & Lake Derwentwater. There are 8 delightful en-suite rooms, each with T.V., hot drinks tray & a folder of suggested walks & tours. Private parking. An excellent base for a relaxing break. Children over 10 welcome. A charming base from which to explore the Lakes & the surrounding area.

E-mail: greystones@keslakes.freeserve.co.uk
www.greystones.tv

Robert & Janet Jones   Greystones Hotel   Ambleside Road   Keswick CA12 4DP   Cumbria
Tel: (017687) 73108   Open: JAN - NOV   Map Ref No. 17

£27.00 to £29.00 | Y N Y

VISA: M'CARD:

Scales Farm Country Guest House

Near Rd: A.66

Stunning open views & a warm friendly welcome await you at Scales Farm, a traditional 17th-century fells farmhouse sensitively modernised to provide accommodation of the highest standard. All bedrooms are en-suite, centrally heated, with tea/coffee-making facilities, colour T.V. & fridges. Separate entrance from private car park allows guests access to rooms & traditional lounge. Lakeland Inn/Restaurant next door. A lovely base for touring or walking.

E-mail: scales@scalesfarm.com
www.scalesfarm.com

Alan & Angela Jameison   Scales Farm Country Guest House   Scales   Threlkeld   Keswick CA12 4SY
Tel: (017687) 79660   Fax 017687 79510   Open: ALL YEAR (Excl. Xmas)   Map Ref No. 18

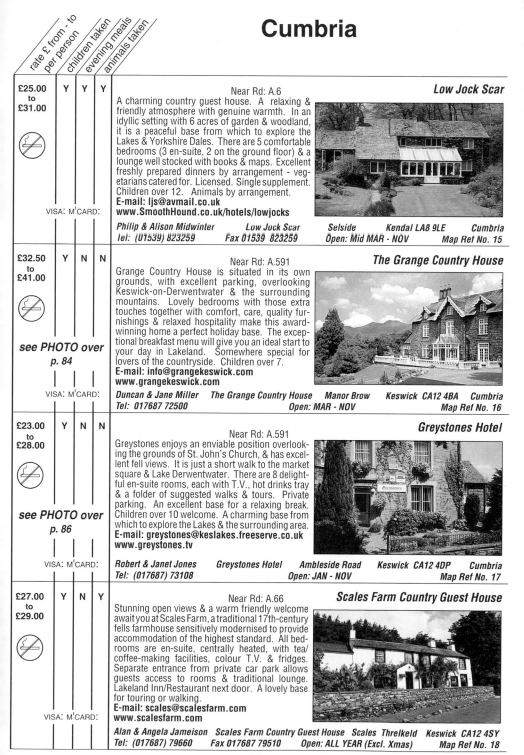

Greystones. Keswick.

rate £ from - to per person	children taken	evening meals	animals taken		

| £45.00 to £55.00 | Y | Y | N | Near Rd: A.591 | **Dale Head Hall Lakeside Hotel** |

see PHOTO over p. 88

VISA: M'CARD: AMEX:

Lose yourself in the ancient woodlands & mature gardens of an Elizabethan country manor, set serenely on the shores of Lake Thirlmere. Delicious dinners prepared by mother & daughter, using fresh produce from the Victorian kitchen garden, served with fine wines in the oak-beamed dining room. 12 individually decorated bedrooms, some with 4-posters, each with bath/shower rooms. Together with the lounge & bar, there are unspoilt views across lawns, lakes & fells.
E-mail: onthelakeside@daleheadhall.info
www.daleheadhall.info

Alan & Shirley Lowe   Dale Head Hall Lakeside Hotel   Lake Thirlmere   Keswick CA12 4TN   Cumbria
Tel: (017687) 72478   Fax 017687 71070   Open: FEB - DEC   Map Ref No. 19

| £38.00 to £44.00 | Y | Y | N | Near Rd: A.66 | **Lairbeck Hotel** |

VISA: M'CARD:

Featured on television's 'Wish You Were Here?' holiday programme, Lairbeck Hotel is only 10 mins' walk from Keswick town centre, in a secluded location with superb mountain views. Here you can treat yourself to traditional, award-winning dining & hospitality in a friendly informal atmosphere & relax in front of cosy log fires. All 14 bedrooms are en-suite & individually decorated. Single & ground-floor rooms available. Spacious parking. Children over 5.
E-mail: bbb@lairbeckhotel-keswick.co.uk
www.lairbeckhotel-keswick.co.uk

Roger & Irene Coy   Lairbeck Hotel   Vicarage Hill   Keswick CA12 5QB   Cumbria
Tel: (017687) 73373   Fax 017687 73144   Open: MAR - DEC   Map Ref No. 17

| £23.00 to £30.00 | Y | N | N | Near Rd: A.6 | **Brandelhow Guest House** |

Brandelhow is a very pleasant Victorian house situated in the lovely market town of Penrith. Accommodation is in 5 tastefully decorated & furnished, bright & comfortable rooms, including 3 en-suite rooms, & all with modern amenities, central heating, colour T.V. & tea/coffee-making facilities. Penrith is an ideal base for touring the Lake District & enjoying the usual outdoor sporting activities. A warm & friendly welcome is assured.
E-mail: enquiries@brandelhowguesthouse.co.uk
www.brandelhowguesthouse.co.uk

Martyn & Melanie Reynolds   Brandelhow Guest House   1 Portland Place   Penrith CA11 7QN
Tel: (01768) 864470   Open: ALL YEAR   Map Ref No. 20

| £20.00 to £25.00 | Y | N | Y | Near Rd: A.6 | **Glendale Guest House** |

VISA: M'CARD:

Julie & Mike invite you to enjoy a relaxing break in their family-run guest house. All of the rooms are designed to provide comfortable accommodation for your stay. A delicious full English or vegetarian breakfast is served, although special diets can be catered for on request. Glendale is in a good central location for exploring the Lake District, Eden Valley, Hadrian's Wall & for visiting southern Scotland. Children & pets are welcome.
E-mail: glendale@lineone.net
www.glendaleguesthouse.net

Julie & Mike Davidson   Glendale Guest House   4 Portland Place   Penrith CA11 7QN   Cumbria
Tel: (01768) 862579   Fax 01768 867934   Open: ALL YEAR   Map Ref No. 20

Dale Head Hall.   Lake Thirlmere.

Cumbria

rate £ from - to per person | *children taken* | *evening meals taken* | *animals taken*

Beckfoot Country House

| £25.00 to £45.00 | Y | N | Y |

Near Rd: A.66

A fine old residence featuring a half-panelled hall, staircase & attractive panelled dining room. Set in 3 acres of grounds in the delightful Lake District, it is a quiet, peaceful retreat for a holiday base, & is within easy reach of the many pleasure spots in the area. Offering 7 rooms, all with private shower/bathroom & tea/coffee-making facilities. A dining room, drawing & reading room. Beckfoot Country House is a delightful base for a touring holiday.
E-mail: info@beckfoot.co.uk
www.beckfoot.co.uk

VISA: M'CARD: AMEX:

Lesley White   Beckfoot Country House   Helton   Nr. Penrith   CA10 2QD   Cumbria
Tel: (01931) 713241   Fax 01931 713391   Open: MAR - NOV   Map Ref No. 21

The Cross Keys Temperance Inn

| £35.00 to £35.00 | Y | Y | N |

(no smoking)

Near Rd: A.683

For those looking for an inn full of character situated in one of the most magnificent of Dales settings, the Cross Keys offers excellent food & accommodation. The restaurant provides wonderful home-produced food with a wide choice to suit all tastes, and although a Temperance Inn guests are invited to bring along the drink of their choice. The bedrooms, recently totally refurbished, offer full en-suite facilities. A delightful home.
E-mail: clowes@freeuk.com
www.cautleyspout.co.uk

VISA: M'CARD:

Alan & Chris Clowes   The Cross Keys Temperance Inn   Cautley   Sedbergh   LA10 5NE   Cumbria
Tel: (015396) 20284   Fax 015396 21966   Open: ALL YEAR   Map Ref No. 22

Lynwood Guest House

| £17.00 to £26.00 | Y | N | N |

(no smoking)

Near Rd: A.591

A Victorian Lakeland stone house built in 1865, offering 9 charming bedrooms, each with en-suite bathrooms, colour T.V. & tea/coffee-making facilities etc. Guests may relax in the T.V. lounge available throughout the day. Centrally located, only 150 yards from village shops & restaurants, & only 5 mins' from the bus & railway station. The host is a Lakeland tour guide, & is happy to assist in planning your stay. Children over 5.
E-mail: enquires@lynwood-guest-house.co.uk
www.lynwood-guest-house.co.uk

Frances & Brian Holcroft   Lynwood Guest House   Broad Street   Windermere LA23 2AB   Cumbria
Tel: (015394) 42550   Fax 015394 42550   Open: ALL YEAR   Map Ref No. 23

Fir Trees

| £36.00 to £42.00 | Y | N | N |

(no smoking)

see PHOTO over
p. 90

Near Rd: A.591

Situated mid-way between Windermere village & the lake, & built in the traditional Lakeland style, Fir Trees offers delightful accommodation of exceptional quality & charm. The dining room has been extensively refurbished, as have the 8 en-suite bedrooms, which are beautifully appointed offering T.V., video, tea/coffee & bath robes. A full English breakfast is served using the best of local produce with vegetarians catered for. Parking. Also, guests have free use of a local leisure club.
E-mail: enquiries@fir-trees.com
www.fir-trees.com

VISA: M'CARD:

Mr & Mrs Drinkall   Fir Trees   Lake Road   Windermere LA23 2EQ   Cumbria
Tel: (015394) 42272   Fax 015394 42512   Open: ALL YEAR   Map Ref No. 23

Fir Trees. Windermere.

Cumbria

rate £ from - to per person	children taken	evening meals	animals taken		
£20.00 to £40.00	Y	N	N		**Rosemount**

Near Rd: A.591

Rosemount is an attractive Victorian house half-way between Windermere & the lake. There are family, twin & single rooms, as well as ground-floor rooms & 2 lovely 4-posters. All rooms (except one) are en-suite with T.V. & tea/coffee-making facilities & hairdryers. An excellent breakfast of local produce is served. Rosemount is the perfect base for a relaxing break & affords first-class accommodation.
E-mail: enquiries@lakedistrictguesthouse.com
www.lakedistrictguesthouse.com

VISA: M'CARD: AMEX:

Steve Thomas   Rosemount   Lake Road   Windermere LA23 2EQ   Cumbria
Tel: (015394) 43739   Fax 015394 48978   Open: ALL YEAR   Map Ref No. 23

£27.00 to £40.00	Y	Y	Y		**The Fairfield**

Near Rd: A.592

Fairfield is a small friendly, family-run B & B in a 200-year-old house, set in its own grounds with a large beautiful garden & terrace. Close to the waterfront & with its own car park, 200 metres from the shops, pubs & restaurant & waterfront of Bowness. An ideal base for exploring the area. 10 en-suite bedrooms with modern facilities. Bar & free internet access are available. Generous break-fasts are a speciality. Evening meals are available during the low season. Animals by arrangement.
E-mail: info@the-fairfield.co.uk
www.the-fairfield.co.uk

see PHOTO over p. 92

VISA: M'CARD: AMEX:

Tony & Liz Blaney   The Fairfield   Brantfell Road   Bowness-on-Windermere   Windermere LA23 3AE
Tel: (015394) 46565   Fax 015394 46565   Open: ALL YEAR   Map Ref No. 24

WORLDWIDE BED & BREAKFAST ASSOCIATION

Visit our website at:
http://www.bestbandb.co.uk

The Fairfield. Bowness-on-Windermere.

Derbyshire & Staffordshire

Derbyshire
(East Midlands)

A county with everything but the sea, this was Lord Byron's opinion of Derbyshire, & the special beauty of the Peak District was recognised by its designation as Britain's first National Park.

Purple heather moors surround craggy limestone outcrops & green hills drop to sheltered meadows or to deep gorges & tumbling rivers.

Derbyshire's lovely dales have delightful names too - Dove Dale, Monk's Dale, Raven's Dale, Water-cum-Jolly-Dale, & they are perfect for walking. The more adventurous can take up the challenge of the Pennine Way, a 270 mile pathway from Edale to the Scottish border.

The grit rock faces offer good climbing, particularly at High Tor above the River Derwent, & underground there are extensive & spectacular caverns. There are show caves at the Heights of Abraham, which you reach by cable-car, & at Castleton, source of the rare Blue John mineral, & at Pole's Cavern in Buxton where there are remarkable stalactites & stalagmites.

Buxton's splendid Crescent reflects the town's spa heritage, & the Opera House is host to an International Festival each summer.

The waters at Matlock too were prized for their curative properties & a great Hydro was built there in the last century, to give treatment to the hundreds of people who came to "take the waters".

Bakewell is a lovely small town with a fascinating market, some fine buildings & the genuine Bakewell Pudding, (known elsewhere as Bakewell tart).

Well-dressing is a custom carried on throughout the summer in the villages & towns. It is a thanksgiving for the water, that predates the arrival of Christianity in Britain. Flower-petals, leaves, moss & bark are pressed in

Haddon Hall; Derby.

Derbyshire & Staffordshire

intricate designs into frames of wet clay & erected over the wells, where they stay damp & fresh for days.

The mining of lead & the prosperity of the farms brought great wealth to the landowning families who were able to employ the finest of architects & craftsmen to design & build their great houses. Haddon Hall is a perfectly preserved 12th century manor house with with terraced gardens of roses & old-fashioned flowers. 17th century Chatsworth, the "Palace of the Peak", houses a splendid collection of paintings, drawings, furniture & books, & stands in gardens with elaborate fountains.

Staffordshire
(Heart of England)

Staffordshire is a contrast of town & county. Miles of moorland & dramatic landscapes lie to the north of the country, & to the south is the Vale of Trent & the greenery of Cannock Chase. But the name of Staffordshire invokes that of the Potteries, the area around Stoke-on-Trent where the world-renowned ceramics are made.

The factories that produce the Royal Doulton, Minton, Spode & Coalport china will arrange tours for visitors, & there is a purpose-built visitor centre at Barlaston displaying the famous Wedgwood tradition.

The Gladstone Pottery Museum is set in a huge Victorian potbank, & the award-winning City museum in Stoke-on-Trent has a remarkable ceramics collection.

There is lovely scenery to be found where the moorlands of Staffordshire meet the crags & valleys of the Peak District National Park. From the wild & windy valleys of The Roaches (from the French 'roche') you can look across the county to Cheshire & Wales. Drivers can take high moorland roads that are marked out as scenic routes.

The valleys of the Dove & Manifold are beautiful limestone dales & ideal for walking or for cycling. Sir Izzak Walton, author of 'The Compleat Angler', drew his inspiration, & his trout, from the waters here.

The valley of the River Churnet is both pretty & peaceful, being largely inaccessible to cars. The Caldon Canal, with its colourful narrowboats, follows the course of the river & there are canalside pubs, picnic areas, boat rides & woodland trails to enjoy. The river runs through the grounds of mock-Gothic Alton Towers, now a leisure park.

The Vale of Trent is largely rural with small market towns, villages, river & canals.

Cannock Chase covers 20 square miles of heath & woodland & is the home of the largest herd of fallow deer in England. Shugborough Hall stands in the Chase. The ancestral home of Lord Lichfeld, it also houses the Staffordshire County Museum & a farm for rare breeds including the famous Tamworth Pig.

Burton-on-Trent is known as the home of the British brewery industry & there are two museums in the town devoted to the history of beer.

Lichfield is a small & picturesque city with a cathedral which dates from the 12th century & has three graceful spires known as the 'Ladies of the Vale'. Dr. Samuel Johnson was born in the city & his house is now a museum dedicated to his life & work.

One of the Vale's villages retains its mediaeval tradition by performing the Abbot's Bromley Horn Dance every September.

Derbyshire & Staffordshire

Derbyshire

Gazeteer

Areas of outstanding natural beauty.
Peak National Park. The Dales.

Houses & Castles

Chatsworth - Bakewell
17th century, built for 1st. Duke of
Devonshire. Furniture, paintings &
drawings, books, etc. Fine gardens &
parklands.
Haddon Hall - Bakewell
Mediaeval manor house - complete.
Terraced rose gardens.
Hardwick Hall - Nr. Chesterfield
16th century - said to be more glass than
wall. Fine furniture, tapestries &
furnishings. Herb garden.
Kedlestone Hall - Derby
18th century - built on site of 12th century
Manor house. Work of Robert Adam - has
world famous marble hall. Old Master
paintings. 11th century church nearby.
Melbourne Hall - Nr. Derby
12th century origins - restored by Sir John
Coke. Fine collection of pictures & works
of art. Magnificent gardens & famous
wrought iron pagoda
Sudbury Hall - Sudbury
Has examples of work of the greatest
craftsmen of the period-Grinling
Gibbons,Pierce and Laguerre.
Winster Market House   Nr. Matlock
17th century stone built market house.

Cathedrals & Churches

Chesterfield (St. Mary & All Saints)
13th & 14th centuries.
4 chapels, polygonal apse, mediaeval
screens, Jacobean pulpit.
Derby (All Saints)
Perpendicular tower - classical style - 17th
century plate, 18th century screen.
Melbourne (St. Michael & St. Mary)
Norman with two west towers & crossing
tower.
Splendid plate, 18th century screen.
Normbury (St. Mary & St. Barloke)
14th century - perpendicular tower.
Wood carving & brasses.
Wirksworth (St. Mary)
13th century, restored & enlarged.

Staffordshire

Gazeteer

Houses & Castles

Ancient High House - Stafford
16th century - largest timber-framed town
house in England.
Shugborough - Nr. Stafford
Ancestral home of the Earl of Lichfield.
Mansion house, paintings, silver,
ceramics, furniture. County Museum.
Rare Breeds Farm.
Moseley Old Hall - Nr. Wolverhampton
Elizabethan house formerly half-timbered.
Stafford Castle
Large & well-preserved Norman castle in
grounds with castle trail.
Tamworth Castle
Norman motte & bailey castle with later
additions. Museum.

Cathedrals & Churches

Croxden Abbey
12th century foundation Cistercian abbey.
Ruins of 13th century church.
Ingestre (St. Mary the Virgin)
A rare Wren church built in1676.
Lichfield Cathedral
Unique triple-spired 12th century cathedral.
Tamworth (St. Editha's)
Founded 963, rebuilt 14th century. Unusual
double spiral staircase.
Tutbury (St. Mary's)
Norman church with impressive West front.

Museums & Galleries

City Museum & Art Gallery - Stoke-on-
Trent
Modern award-winning museum.
Ceramics, decorative arts, etc.
Dr. Johnson Birthplace Museum -
Lichfield
Gladstone Pottery Museum - Longton
Izaak Walton Cottage & Museum -
Shallowfield, Nr. Stafford
**National Brewery Museum & the Bass
Museum of Brewing**-both in Stoke-on-
Trent
Stafford Art Gallery & Craft Shop -
Stafford
Major gallery for the visual arts & centre
for quality craftsmanship.

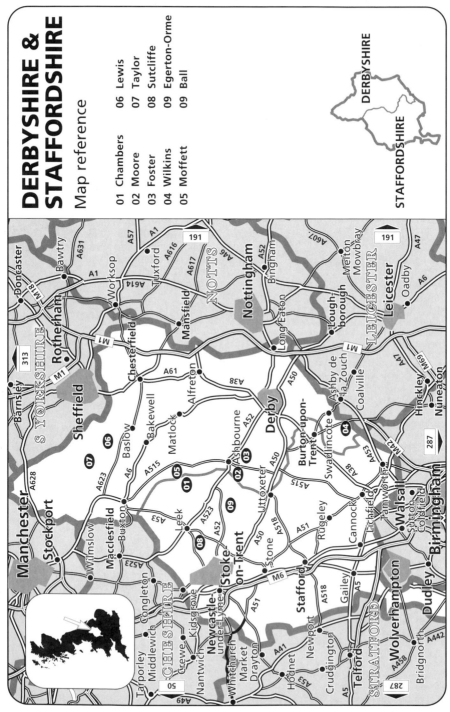

DERBYSHIRE & STAFFORDSHIRE

Map reference

01 Chambers
02 Moore
03 Foster
04 Wilkins
05 Moffett
06 Lewis
07 Taylor
08 Sutcliffe
09 Egerton-Orme
09 Ball

rate £ from - to per person	children taken	evening meals	animals taken

---

£30.00 to £40.00 — Y Y N

VISA: M'CARD:

Near Rd: A.515

Stanshope Hall

Stanshope Hall, with its informal feel but with every comfort, stands in splendid isolation among the dry stone walls of the southern Peak District. Walks from the door lead to verdant Dovedale or the undiscovered seclusion of the Manifold Valley. The attractive en-suite rooms have hand-painted walls & frescos in the bathrooms. Candle-lit dinners (by arrangement) are prepared using uncomplicated but imaginative recipes with local & garden produce. A charming home.
E-mail: naomi@stanshope.demon.co.uk
www.stanshope.net

Naomi Chambers & Nicholas Lourie   Stanshope Hall   Stanshope   Ashbourne DE6 2AD   Derbyshire
Tel: (01335) 310278   Fax 01335 310127   Open: ALL YEAR (Excl. Xmas)   Map Ref No. 01

£26.00 to £28.00 — Y N N

Near Rd: A.515

Rose Cottage

A mid-Victorian house in 6 acres, Rose Cottage is a family home in quiet, unspoilt, beautiful & peaceful countryside. Bedrooms have panoramic views over Dove Valley towards Weaver Hills (George Eliot's 'Adam Bede' country). Ideal for visiting Dales, walking, country houses (Chatsworth, Haddon Hall etc.), potteries & Alton Towers (9 miles). Comfortable double rooms, private bathrooms, 1 en-suite, T.V., tea-making facilities in rooms. Children over 12 years.
E-mail: pjmoore@beeb.net
www.rosecottageashbourne.co.uk

Mrs Cynthia Moore   Rose Cottage   Snelston   Ashbourne DE6 2DL   Derbyshire
Tel: (01335) 324230   Fax 01335 324651   Open: ALL YEAR   Map Ref No. 02

£25.00 to £28.00 — Y N N

Near Rd: A.52

Shirley Hall

Shirley Hall is a lovely, peaceful old farmhouse, just to the south of Ashbourne, close to the village of Shirley. In the centre of rolling pastureland enjoy the tranquillity of this part-moated, timbered farmhouse, surrounded by a large lawned garden. 3 attractive bedrooms with en-suite bathrooms, T.V. & tea/coffee facilities. The full English breakfast with homemade bread & preserves is renowned. The village pub is excellent for evening meals. Coarse-fishing is available. Woodland walks.
E-mail: sylviafoster@shirleyhallfarm.com
www.shirleyhallfarm.com

Mrs Sylvia Foster   Shirley Hall   Shirley   Ashbourne DE6 3AS   Derbyshire
Tel: (01335) 360346   Fax 01335 360346   Open: ALL YEAR   Map Ref No. 03

£33.00 to £35.00 — Y Y N

Near Rd: A.444

The Old Hall

A particularly peaceful Grade II listed manor house set in 18 acres of gardens & woodland, overlooking a lake. The house, dating from 1644, incorporates part of a medieval monastery & despite all modern conveniences retains its unique character, original features & panelling. 3 bedrooms with en-suite/private bathrooms, T.V. etc. Traditional English food is served by arrangement. Convenient for Lichfield, Shugborough, Calke Abbey, Kedleston, Castle Donington & the N.E.C.. Children over 14.
E-mail: clemencywilkins@hotmail.com

Mrs Clemency Wilkins   The Old Hall   Netherseal   Swadlincote   Ashby de la Zouche DE12 8DF
Tel: (01283) 760258   Fax 01283 762991   Open: ALL YEAR   Map Ref No. 04

Biggin Hall. Biggin by Hartington.

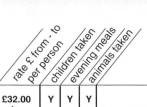
rate £ from - to per person	children taken	evening meals taken	animals taken		

Biggin Hall

£32.00 to £53.00 — Y / Y / Y

see PHOTO over p. 98

VISA: M'CARD: AMEX:

Near Rd: A.515

A delightful 17th-century old hall, Grade II listed, completely restored & keeping all the character of its origins, with massive oak beams. 19 bedrooms, all charmingly furnished, 1 with a 4-poster bed, all with en-suite facilities & modern amenities. Guests have the choice of 2 sitting rooms, 1 with a log fire, 1 with T.V. & library, & there is a lovely garden. The house is beautifully furnished, with many antiques. Non-smoking areas. Children 12 & over. Animals by arrangement.
E-mail: enquiries@bigginhall.co.uk
www.bigginhall.co.uk

James Moffett   Biggin Hall   Biggin-by-Hartington   Buxton SK17 0DH   Derbyshire
Tel: (01298) 84451   Fax 01298 84681   Open: ALL YEAR   Map Ref No. 05

Delf View House

£25.00 to £42.00 — Y / N / N

(non-smoking)

Near Rd: A.623

Beautiful & tranquil accommodation in an elegant listed Georgian country house in historic Eyam village in the magnificent Peak National Park. Guests are warmly welcomed in the drawing room, delightfully furnished with antiques & pictures. 3 bedrooms, 1 en-suite, include a Sheraton 4-poster & 18th-century French twin beds. Sumptuous breakfasts served in the oak-beamed dining room. Restaurants nearby. Ideal for visiting Chatsworth, Haddon & Eyam Hall. Children over 12.
E-mail: lewis@delfviewhouse.co.uk
www.delfviewhouse.co.uk

David & Meirlys Lewis   Delf View House   Church Street   Eyam S32 5QH   Derbyshire
Tel: (01433) 631533   Fax 01433 630030   Open: ALL YEAR   Map Ref No. 06

Underleigh House

£32.00 to £34.50 — Y / N / N

(non-smoking)

see PHOTO over p. 100

VISA: M'CARD:

Near Rd: A.6187

Set in an idyllic & peaceful location amidst glorious scenery, this extended cottage & barn conversion (dating from 1873) is the perfect base for exploring the Peak District. Underleigh is in the heart of magnificent walking country & offers 6 en-suite rooms is furnished to a high standard with many thoughtful extras included. Delicious breakfasts in the flagstoned dining hall feature local & homemade specialities. The beamed lounge with log fire is the perfect place to relax. Children over 12.
E-mail: underleigh.house@btinternet.com
www.underleighhouse.co.uk

Philip & Vivienne Taylor Underleigh House   Off Edale Road   Hope   Hope Valley S33 6RF Derbys.
Tel: (01433) 621372 Fax 01433 621324 Open: ALL YEAR (Excl. Xmas & New Year) Map Ref No. 07

Choir Cottage & Choir House

£29.50 to £32.50 — Y / N / N

(non-smoking)

Near Rd: A.520

This 17th-century stone cottage, once a resting place for ostlers, now provides beautifully appointed bedrooms, with full en-suite facilities, central heating, colour T.V., tea/coffee tray & telephone. The Pine Room & Rose Room have 4-poster beds, & 1 is suitable as a family suite. Quiet location convenient for the Peak District, potteries & Alton Towers. Excellent food & careful attention to detail is assured.
E-mail: enquiries@choircottage.co.uk
www.choircottage.co.uk

Mr & Mrs Sutcliffe Choir Cottage & Choir House Ostlers Lane Cheddleton Leek ST13 7HS Staffs.
Tel: (01538) 360561   Open: ALL YEAR   Map Ref No. 08

Underleigh House. Hope.

rate £ from - to per person	children taken	evening meals	animals taken		

£37.50 to £40.00	Y	N	Y	**Bank House**

Near Rd: A.50, A.52

A handsome house, overlooking the picturesque Churnet Valley. This elegantly furnished home provides superb en-suite/private accommodation. All rooms are extremely well-equipped. The aim at Bank House is to create a relaxed & friendly 'house party' ambience for guests, & the facilities are all that one might expect from a friend's country house that has all the comforts of a quality hotel. Wonderful centre for touring this region. Animals by arrangement. Single supplement.
E-mail: john.orme@dial.pipex.com
www.SmoothHound.co.uk/hotels/bank.html

VISA: M'CARD:

Mrs M. Egerton-Orme   Bank House   Farley Road   Oakamoor   Stoke-on-Trent ST10 3BD   Staffs.
Tel: (01538) 702810   Fax 01538 702810   Open: ALL YEAR (Excl. Xmas & New Year)   Map Ref No. 09

£25.00 to £27.00	Y	N	N	**Manor House Farm**

Near Rd: A.50

A beautiful Grade II listed farmhouse, set amid rolling hills & rivers. Accommodation is in 3 attractive bedrooms, all with 4-poster beds & an en-suite bathroom. (1 can be used as a twin.) Tastefully furnished with antiques & retaining traditional features including an oak-panelled breakfast room. Guests may relax in the extensive gardens with grass tennis court & Victorian summer house. Ideal for visiting Alton Towers, the Peak District or the potteries.
E-mail: cm_ball@yahoo.co.uk
www.4posteraccom.com

VISA: M'CARD:

C. M. Ball   Manor House Farm   Quixhill Lane   Prestwood   Denstone   Uttoxeter ST14 5DD   Staffs.
Tel: (01889) 590415   Fax 01335 342198   Open: ALL YEAR   Map Ref No. 09

WORLDWIDE BED & BREAKFAST ASSOCIATION

All the establishments mentioned in this guide are members of The Worldwide Bed & Breakfast Association

Devon

Devon
(West Country)

Here is a county of tremendous variety. Two glorious & contrasting coastlines with miles of sandy beaches, sheltered coves & rugged cliffs. There are friendly resorts & quiet villages of cob & thatch, two historic cities, & a host of country towns & tiny hamlets as well as the wild open spaces of two national parks.

From the grandeur of Hartland Point east to Foreland Point where Exmoor reaches the sea, the north Devon coast is incomparable. At Westward Ho!, Croyde & Woolacombe the rolling surf washes the golden beaches & out to sea stands beautiful Lundy Island, ideal for bird watching, climbing & walking. The tiny village of Clovelly with its cobbled street tumbles down the cliffside to the sea. Ilfracombe is a friendly resort town & the twin towns of Lynton & Lynmouth are joined by a cliff railway.

The south coast is a colourful mixture of soaring red sandstone cliffs dropping to sheltered sandy coves & the palm trees of the English Riviera. This is one of England's great holiday coasts with a string of popular resorts; Seaton, Sidmouth, Budleigh Salterton, Exmouth, Dawlish, Teignmouth & the trio of Torquay, Paignton & Brixham that make up Torbay. To the south, beyond Berry Head are Dartmouth, rich in navy tradition, & Salcombe, a premiere sailing centre in the deep inlet of the Kingsbridge estuary. Plymouth is a happy blend of holiday resort, tourist centre, historic & modern city, & the meeting-point for the wonderful old sailing vessels for the Tall Ships Race.

Inland the magnificent wilderness of Dartmoor National Park offers miles of sweeping moorland, granite tors, clear streams & wooded valleys, ancient stone circles & clapper bridges. The tors, as the Dartmoor peaks, are called are easily climbed & the views from the tops are superb. Widecombe-in-the-Moor, with its imposing church tower, & much photographed Buckland-in-the-Moor are only two of Dartmoor's lovely villages.

The Exmoor National Park straddles the Devon/Somerset border. It is a land of wild heather moorland above deep wooded valleys & sparkling streams, the home of red deer, soaring buzzards & of legendary Lorna Doone from R.D. Blackmore's novel. The south west peninsula coastal path follows the whole of the Exmoor coastline affording dramatic scenery & spectacular views, notably from Countisbury Hill.

The seafaring traditions of Devon are well-known. Sir Walter Raleigh set sail from Plymouth to Carolina in 1584; Sir Francis Drake began his circumnavigation of the world at Plymouth in the "Golden Hind" & fought the Spanish Armada off Plymouth Sound. The Pilgrim Fathers sailed from here & it was to here that Sir Francis Chichester returned having sailed around the world in 1967.

Exeter's maritime tradition is commemorated in an excellent museum located in converted riverside warehouses but the city's chief glory is the magnificent 13th century cathedral of St. Mary & St. Peter, built in an unusual decorated Gothic style, with its west front covered in statues.

The River Dart near Dittisham.

Devon

Devon
Gazeteer

Areas of outstanding natural beauty.
North, South, East Devon.

Houses & Castles

Arlington Court - Barnstaple
Regency house, collection of shell, pewter & model ships.

Bickleigh Castle - Nr. Tiverton
Thatched Jacobean wing. Great Hall & armoury. Early Norman chapel, gardens & moat.

Buckland Abbey - Nr. Plymouth
13th century Cistercian monastery - 16th century alterations. Home of Drake - contains his relics & folk gallery.

Bradley Manor - Newton Abbot
15th century Manor house with perpendicular chapel.

Cadhay - Ottery St. Mary
16th century Elizabethan Manor house.

Castle Drogo - Nr.Chagford
Designed by Lutyens - built of granite, standing over 900 feet above the gorge of the Teign river.

Chambercombe Manor - Illfracombe
14th-15th century Manor house.

Castle Hill - Nr. Barnstaple
18th century Palladian mansion - fine furniture of period, pictures, porcelain & tapestries.

Hayes Barton - Nr. Otterton
10th century plaster & thatch house. Birthplace of Walter Raleigh.

Oldway - Paignton
19th century house having rooms designed to be replicas of rooms at the Palace of Versailles.

Powederham Castle - Nr. Exeter
14th century mediaeval castle much damaged in Civil War. Altered in 18th & 19th centuries. Fine music room by Wyatt.

Saltram House - Plymouth
Some remnants of Tudor house built into George II house, with two rooms by Robert Adam. Excellent plasterwork & woodwork.

Shute Barton - Nr. Axminster
14th century battlemented Manor house with Tudor & Elizabethan additions.

Tiverton Castle - Nr. Tiverton
Fortress of Henry I. Chapel of St. Francis. Gallery of Joan of Arc.

Torre Abbey Mansion - Torquay
Abbey ruins, tithe barn. Mansion house with paintings & furniture.

Cathedrals & Churches

Atherington (St. Mary)
Perpendicular style - mediaeval effigies & glass, original rood loft. Fine screens, 15th century bench ends.

Ashton (St. John the Baptist)
15th century - mediaeval screens, glass & wall paintings. Elizabethan pulpit with canopy, 17th century altar railing.

Bere Ferrers (St. Andrew)
14th century rebuilding - 14th century glass, 16th century benches, Norman font.

Bridford (St. Thomas a Becket)
Perpendicular style - mediaeval glass & woodwork. Excellent rood screen c.1530.

Cullompton (St. Andrew)
15th century perpendicular - Jacobean west gallery - fan tracery in roof, exterior carvings.

Exeter Cathedral
13th century decorated - Norman towers. Interior tierceron ribbed vault (Gothic) carved corbels & bosses, moulded piers & arches. Original pulpitum c.1320. Choir stalls with earliest misericords in England c.1260.

Haccombe (St. Blaize)
13th century effigies, 14th century glass, 17th century brasses, 19th century screen pulpit & reredos.

Kentisbeare (St. Mary)
Perpendicular style - checkered tower. 16th century rood screen.

Ottery St. Mary (St. Mary)
13th century, 14th century clock, fan vaulted roof, tomb with canopy, minstrel's gallery, gilded wooded eagle. 18th century pulpit.

Parracombe (St. Petrock)
Unrestored Georgian - 16th century benches, mostly perpendicular, early English chancel.

Sutcombe (St. Andrew)
15th century - some part Norman. 16th century bench ends, restored rood screen, mediaeval glass & floor tiles.

Swimbrige (St. James)
14th century tower & spire - mediaeval stone pulpit, 15th century rood screen, font cover of Renaissance period.

Devon

Tawstock (St. Peter)
14th century, Italian plasterwork ceiling, mediaeval glass, Renaissance memorial pew, Bath monument.
Buckfast Abbey
Living Benedictine monastery, built on mediaeval foundation. Famous for works of art in church, modern stained glass, tonic wine & bee-keeping.

Museums & Galleries

Bideford Museum - Bideford
Geology, maps, prints, shipwright's tools, North Devon pottery.
Burton Art Gallery - Bideford
Hubert Coop collection of paintings etc.
Butterwalk Museum - Dartmouth
17th century row of half timbered buildings, nautical museum. 140 model ships.
Newcomen Engine House - Nr.
Butterwalk Museum
Original Newcomen atmospheric/pressure steam engine c.1725.
Royal Albert Memorial Museum Art Gallery - Exeter
Collections of English watercolours, paintings, glass & ceramics, local silver, natural history & anthropology.
Rougemont House Museum - Exeter
Collections of archaeology & local history. Costume & lace collection
Guildhall - Exeter
Mediaeval structure with Tudor frontage - City regalia & silver.
Exeter Maritime Museum - Exeter
Largest collection in the world of working boats, afloat, ashore & under cover.
The Steam & Countryside Museum - Exmouth
Very large working layout - hundreds of exhibits.
Including Victorian farmhouse - farmyard pets for children.
Shebbear - North Devon
Alcott Farm Museum with unique collections of agricultural implements & photographs, etc.
The Elizabethan House - Totnes
Period costumes & furnishings, tools, toys, domestic articles, etc.
The Elizabethan House - Plymouth
16th century house with period furnishings.

City Museum & Art Gallery - Plymouth
Collections of pictures & porcelain, English & Italian drawing. Reynolds' family portraits, early printed books, ship models.
Cookworthy Museum - Kingsbridge
Story of china clay. Local history, shipbuilding tools, rural life.
Honiton & Allhallows Public Museum - Honiton
Collection of Honiton lace, implements etc. Complete Devon Kitchen.
Lyn & Exmoor Museum - Lynton
Life & history of Exmoor.
Torquay & Natural History Society Museum - Torquay
Collection illustrating Kent's Cavern & other caves - natural history & folkculture.

Historic Monuments

Okehampton Castle - Okehampton
11th -14th century chapel, keep & hall.
Totnes Castle - Totnes
13th - 14th century ruins of Castle.
Blackbury Castle - Southleigh
Hill fort - well preserved.
Dartmouth Castle - Dartmouth
15th century castle - coastal defence.
Lydford Castle - Lydford
12th century stone keep built upon site of Saxon fortress town.
Hound Tor - Manaton
Ruins of mediaeval hamlet.

Other things to see & do

The Big Sheep - Abbotsham
Sheep-milking parlour, with gallery, dairy & production rooms. Exhibition & play area.
Dartington Crystal - Torrington
Watch skilled craftworkers make lead crystalware. Glass centre & exhibition.
Dartmoor Wildlife Park - Sparkwell Nr. Plymouth
Over 100 species, including tigers, lions, bears, deer, birds of prey & waterfowl.
The Devon Guild of Craftsmen - Riverside Mill, Bovey Tracey
Series of quality exhibitions throughout the year.
Paignton Zoological & Botanical Gardens - Paignton
Third largest zoo in England. Botanical gardens, tropical house, "The Ark" family activity centre.

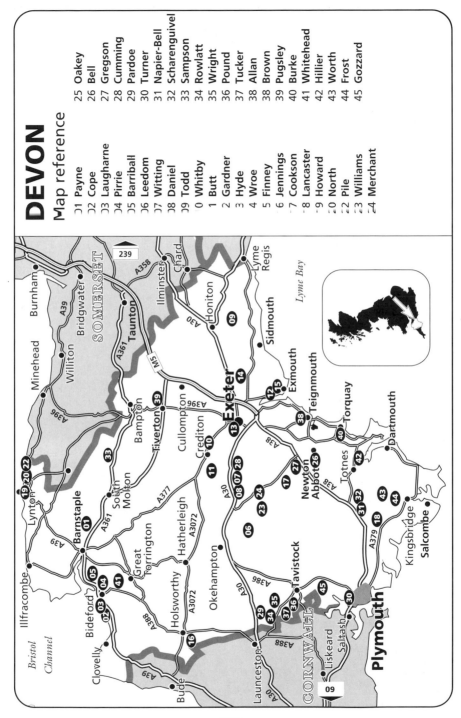

DEVON
Map reference

01 Payne
02 Cope
03 Laugharne
04 Pirrie
05 Barriball
06 Leedom
07 Witting
08 Daniel
09 Todd
10 Whitby
11 Butt
12 Gardner
13 Hyde
14 Wroe
15 Finney
16 Jennings
17 Cookson
18 Lancaster
19 Howard
20 North
21 Pile
22 Williams
23 Williams
24 Merchant

25 Oakey
26 Bell
27 Gregson
28 Cumming
29 Pardoe
30 Turner
31 Napier-Bell
32 Scharenguivel
33 Sampson
34 Rowlatt
35 Wright
36 Pound
37 Tucker
38 Allan
38 Brown
39 Pugsley
40 Burke
41 Whitehead
42 Hillier
43 Worth
44 Frost
45 Gozzard

	rate £ from - to per person	children taken	evening meals	animals taken

Huxtable Farm

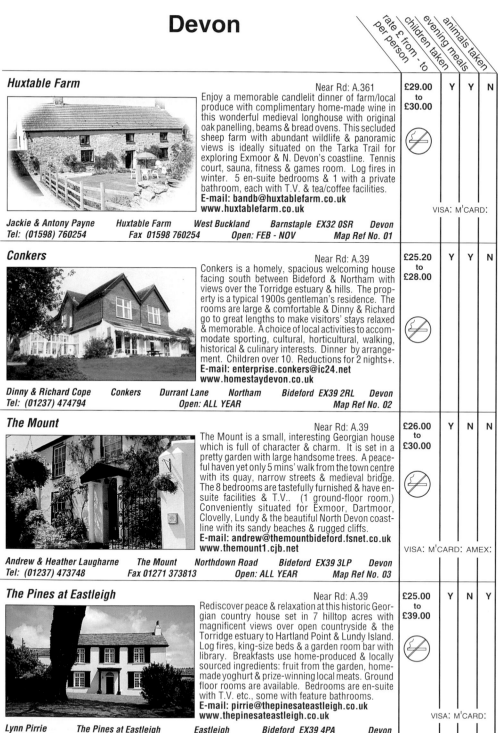

Near Rd: A.361

Enjoy a memorable candlelit dinner of farm/local produce with complimentary home-made wine in this wonderful medieval longhouse with original oak panelling, beams & bread ovens. This secluded sheep farm with abundant wildlife & panoramic views is ideally situated on the Tarka Trail for exploring Exmoor & N. Devon's coastline. Tennis court, sauna, fitness & games room. Log fires in winter. 5 en-suite bedrooms & 1 with a private bathroom, each with T.V. & tea/coffee facilities.

E-mail: bandb@huxtablefarm.co.uk
www.huxtablefarm.co.uk

£29.00 to £30.00 — Y — Y — N

VISA: M'CARD:

Jackie & Antony Payne   Huxtable Farm   West Buckland   Barnstaple EX32 0SR   Devon
Tel: (01598) 760254   Fax 01598 760254   Open: FEB - NOV   Map Ref No. 01

Conkers

Near Rd: A.39

Conkers is a homely, spacious welcoming house facing south between Bideford & Northam with views over the Torridge estuary & hills. The property is a typical 1900s gentleman's residence. The rooms are large & comfortable & Dinny & Richard go to great lengths to make visitors' stays relaxed & memorable. A choice of local activities to accommodate sporting, cultural, horticultural, walking, historical & culinary interests. Dinner by arrangement. Children over 10. Reductions for 2 nights+.

E-mail: enterprise.conkers@ic24.net
www.homestaydevon.co.uk

£25.20 to £28.00 — Y — Y — N

Dinny & Richard Cope   Conkers   Durrant Lane   Northam   Bideford EX39 2RL   Devon
Tel: (01237) 474794   Open: ALL YEAR   Map Ref No. 02

The Mount

Near Rd: A.39

The Mount is a small, interesting Georgian house which is full of character & charm. It is set in a pretty garden with large handsome trees. A peaceful haven yet only 5 mins' walk from the town centre with its quay, narrow streets & medieval bridge. The 8 bedrooms are tastefully furnished & have en-suite facilities & T.V.. (1 ground-floor room.) Conveniently situated for Exmoor, Dartmoor, Clovelly, Lundy & the beautiful North Devon coastline with its sandy beaches & rugged cliffs.

E-mail: andrew@themountbideford.fsnet.co.uk
www.themount1.cjb.net

£26.00 to £30.00 — Y — N — N

VISA: M'CARD: AMEX:

Andrew & Heather Laugharne   The Mount   Northdown Road   Bideford EX39 3LP   Devon
Tel: (01237) 473748   Fax 01271 373813   Open: ALL YEAR   Map Ref No. 03

The Pines at Eastleigh

Near Rd: A.39

Rediscover peace & relaxation at this historic Georgian country house set in 7 hilltop acres with magnificent views over open countryside & the Torridge estuary to Hartland Point & Lundy Island. Log fires, king-size beds & a garden room bar with library. Breakfasts use home-produced & locally sourced ingredients: fruit from the garden, home-made yoghurt & prize-winning local meats. Ground floor rooms are available. Bedrooms are en-suite with T.V. etc., some with feature bathrooms.

E-mail: pirrie@thepinesateastleigh.co.uk
www.thepinesateastleigh.co.uk

£25.00 to £39.00 — Y — N — Y

VISA: M'CARD:

Lynn Pirrie   The Pines at Eastleigh   Eastleigh   Bideford EX39 4PA   Devon
Tel: (01271) 860561   Open: ALL YEAR   Map Ref No. 04

rate £ from - to per person	children taken	evening meals	animals taken

---

£40.00 to £45.00

Y | N | N

(no smoking symbol)

Horwood House

Near Rd: A.39

This impressive Grade II listed Georgian manor house is set on the edge of a pretty hamlet. Handy for the coast & shopping centres, Horwood is also within easy reach of many National Trust properties & the gardens at RHS Rosemoor. Surrounded by 40 acres of its own organic farmland, the house offers the highest quality B & B in 2 lovely guest rooms with en-suite facilities. Horwood House is the perfect place to enjoy Devon life at its best. Children over 12.
www.bestbandb.co.uk

Gill Barriball   Horwood House   Horwood   Bideford EX39 4PD   Devon
Tel: (01271) 858201   Fax 01271 858413   Open: ALL YEAR (Excl. Xmas & New Year)   Map Ref No. 05

£32.50 to £35.00

N | Y | N

(no smoking symbol)

Cherryford House

Near Rd: A.30

'Far from the madding crowd' Cherryford House is situated in idyllic surroundings with 'the prettiest of walks' & 'food to die for' according to discerning guests, which is cooked by Graham. If you live to eat & enjoy a dinner party atmosphere (maximum 6 guests) it's a must to stay with the Leedoms in Gidleigh. Accommodation is in 3 delightful double rooms - all with en-suite facilities. Experience bed & breakfast with style at Cherryford House.
E-mail: stay@cherryfordhouse.co.uk
www.cherryfordhouse.co.uk

Pauline Leedom   Cherryford House   Gidleigh   Chagford TQ13 8HS   Devon
Tel: (01647) 433260   Fax 01647 433637   Open: ALL YEAR   Map Ref No. 06

£27.50 to £35.00

Y | N | Y

VISA: M'CARD:

(no smoking symbol)

Easton Court

Near Rd: A.382

Home of 'Brideshead Revisited', Easton Court is a charming Tudor country house, set in 4 acres of grounds within the Dartmoor National Park. The Edwardian wing houses 5 lovely en-suite guest bedrooms, some with 4 poster beds & all with stunning views towards the Teign Gorge. The light & airy guest lounge/breakfast room & access to the delightful gardens completes this luxury accommodation. Easton Court is an ideal base for touring Dartmoor & the West Country. Children over 12.
E-mail: stay@easton.co.uk
www.easton.co.uk

Debra & Paul Witting   Easton Court   Easton Cross   Chagford TQ13 8JL   Devon
Tel: (01647) 433469   Fax 01647 433654   Open: ALL YEAR   Map Ref No.07

£28.00 to £36.00

Y | N | N

(no smoking symbol)

Parford Well

Near Rd: A.382

Parford Well is a comfortable & cosy house, surrounded by its own walled garden, set in the tiny hamlet of Sandy Park in the Dartmoor National Park. It is the ideal place to stay if you want to get away from it all, relax & be well looked after. Accommodation is in 3 charming & attractively furnished bedrooms, each with an en-suite/private bathroom. There are wonderful walks on the doorstep both in the wooded valley of the River Teign & on the open moor. Children over 8.
Email: tim@parfordwell.co.uk
www.parfordwell.co.uk

Tim Daniel   Parford Well   Sandy Park   Chagford TQ13 8JW   Devon
Tel: (01647) 433353   Open: MAR - XMAS   Map Ref No. 08

Devon

	rate £ from - to per person	children taken	evening meals	animals taken

Smallicombe Farm

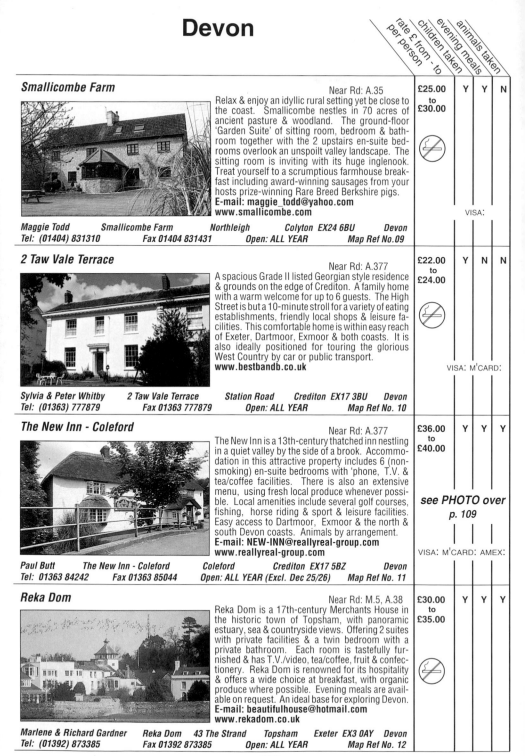

Near Rd: A.35

Relax & enjoy an idyllic rural setting yet be close to the coast. Smallicombe nestles in 70 acres of ancient pasture & woodland. The ground-floor 'Garden Suite' of sitting room, bedroom & bathroom together with the 2 upstairs en-suite bedrooms overlook an unspoilt valley landscape. The sitting room is inviting with its huge inglenook. Treat yourself to a scrumptious farmhouse breakfast including award-winning sausages from your hosts prize-winning Rare Breed Berkshire pigs.

E-mail: maggie_todd@yahoo.com
www.smallicombe.com

£25.00 to £30.00 — Y Y N

VISA:

Maggie Todd   Smallicombe Farm   Northleigh   Colyton EX24 6BU   Devon
Tel: (01404) 831310   Fax 01404 831431   Open: ALL YEAR   Map Ref No.09

2 Taw Vale Terrace

Near Rd: A.377

A spacious Grade II listed Georgian style residence & grounds on the edge of Crediton. A family home with a warm welcome for up to 6 guests. The High Street is but a 10-minute stroll for a variety of eating establishments, friendly local shops & leisure facilities. This comfortable home is within easy reach of Exeter, Dartmoor, Exmoor & both coasts. It is also ideally positioned for touring the glorious West Country by car or public transport.

www.bestbandb.co.uk

£22.00 to £24.00 — Y N N

VISA: M'CARD:

Sylvia & Peter Whitby   2 Taw Vale Terrace   Station Road   Crediton EX17 3BU   Devon
Tel: (01363) 777879   Fax 01363 777879   Open: ALL YEAR   Map Ref No. 10

The New Inn - Coleford

Near Rd: A.377

The New Inn is a 13th-century thatched inn nestling in a quiet valley by the side of a brook. Accommodation in this attractive property includes 6 (non-smoking) en-suite bedrooms with 'phone, T.V. & tea/coffee facilities. There is also an extensive menu, using fresh local produce whenever possible. Local amenities include several golf courses, fishing, horse riding & sport & leisure facilities. Easy access to Dartmoor, Exmoor & the north & south Devon coasts. Animals by arrangement.

E-mail: NEW-INN@reallyreal-group.com
www.reallyreal-group.com

£36.00 to £40.00 — Y Y Y

see PHOTO over
p. 109

VISA: M'CARD: AMEX:

Paul Butt   The New Inn - Coleford   Coleford   Crediton EX17 5BZ   Devon
Tel: 01363 84242   Fax 01363 85044   Open: ALL YEAR (Excl. Dec 25/26)   Map Ref No. 11

Reka Dom

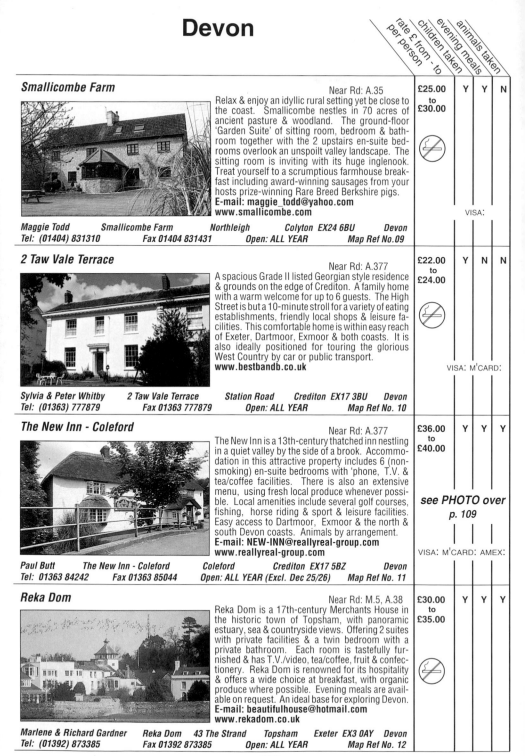

Near Rd: M.5, A.38

Reka Dom is a 17th-century Merchants House in the historic town of Topsham, with panoramic estuary, sea & countryside views. Offering 2 suites with private facilities & a twin bedroom with a private bathroom. Each room is tastefully furnished & has T.V./video, tea/coffee, fruit & confectionery. Reka Dom is renowned for its hospitality & offers a wide choice at breakfast, with organic produce where possible. Evening meals are available on request. An ideal base for exploring Devon.

E-mail: beautifulhouse@hotmail.com
www.rekadom.co.uk

£30.00 to £35.00 — Y Y Y

Marlene & Richard Gardner   Reka Dom   43 The Strand   Topsham   Exeter EX3 0AY   Devon
Tel: (01392) 873385   Fax 01392 873385   Open: ALL YEAR   Map Ref No. 12

The New Inn. Coleford.

	rate £ from - to	children taken	evening meals	animals taken

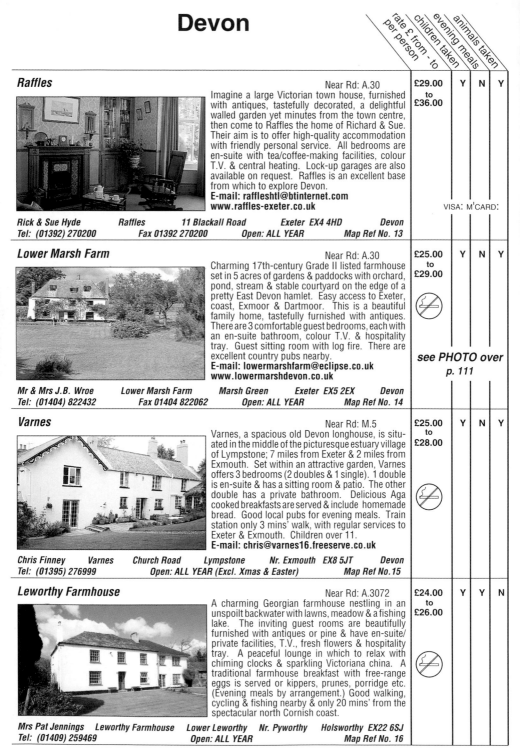

Raffles

Near Rd: A.30

Imagine a large Victorian town house, furnished with antiques, tastefully decorated, a delightful walled garden yet minutes from the town centre, then come to Raffles the home of Richard & Sue. Their aim is to offer high-quality accommodation with friendly personal service. All bedrooms are en-suite with tea/coffee-making facilities, colour T.V. & central heating. Lock-up garages are also available on request. Raffles is an excellent base from which to explore Devon.
E-mail: raffleshtl@btinternet.com
www.raffles-exeter.co.uk

| £29.00 to £36.00 | Y | N | Y |

VISA: M'CARD:

| Rick & Sue Hyde | Raffles | 11 Blackall Road | Exeter EX4 4HD | Devon |
| Tel: (01392) 270200 | Fax 01392 270200 | Open: ALL YEAR | Map Ref No. 13 | |

Lower Marsh Farm

Near Rd: A.30

Charming 17th-century Grade II listed farmhouse set in 5 acres of gardens & paddocks with orchard, pond, stream & stable courtyard on the edge of a pretty East Devon hamlet. Easy access to Exeter, coast, Exmoor & Dartmoor. This is a beautiful family home, tastefully furnished with antiques. There are 3 comfortable guest bedrooms, each with an en-suite bathroom, colour T.V. & hospitality tray. Guest sitting room with log fire. There are excellent country pubs nearby.
E-mail: lowermarshfarm@eclipse.co.uk
www.lowermarshdevon.co.uk

| £25.00 to £29.00 | Y | N | Y |

see PHOTO over
p. 111

| Mr & Mrs J.B. Wroe | Lower Marsh Farm | Marsh Green | Exeter EX5 2EX | Devon |
| Tel: (01404) 822432 | Fax 01404 822062 | Open: ALL YEAR | Map Ref No. 14 | |

Varnes

Near Rd: M.5

Varnes, a spacious old Devon longhouse, is situated in the middle of the picturesque estuary village of Lympstone; 7 miles from Exeter & 2 miles from Exmouth. Set within an attractive garden, Varnes offers 3 bedrooms (2 doubles & 1 single). 1 double is en-suite & has a sitting room & patio. The other double has a private bathroom. Delicious Aga cooked breakfasts are served & include homemade bread. Good local pubs for evening meals. Train station only 3 mins' walk, with regular services to Exeter & Exmouth. Children over 11.
E-mail: chris@varnes16.freeserve.co.uk

| £25.00 to £28.00 | Y | N | Y |

| Chris Finney | Varnes | Church Road | Lympstone | Nr. Exmouth EX8 5JT | Devon |
| Tel: (01395) 276999 | Open: ALL YEAR (Excl. Xmas & Easter) | Map Ref No.15 | | |

Leworthy Farmhouse

Near Rd: A.3072

A charming Georgian farmhouse nestling in an unspoilt backwater with lawns, meadow & a fishing lake. The inviting guest rooms are beautifully furnished with antiques or pine & have en-suite/private facilities, T.V., fresh flowers & hospitality tray. A peaceful lounge in which to relax with chiming clocks & sparkling Victoriana china. A traditional farmhouse breakfast with free-range eggs is served or kippers, prunes, porridge etc. (Evening meals by arrangement.) Good walking, cycling & fishing nearby & only 20 mins' from the spectacular north Cornish coast.

| £24.00 to £26.00 | Y | Y | N |

| Mrs Pat Jennings | Leworthy Farmhouse | Lower Leworthy | Nr. Pyworthy | Holsworthy EX22 6SJ |
| Tel: (01409) 259469 | Open: ALL YEAR | Map Ref No. 16 | | |

Lower Marsh Farm. Marsh Green.

	rate £ from - to per person	children taken	evening meals	animals taken

Bagtor House

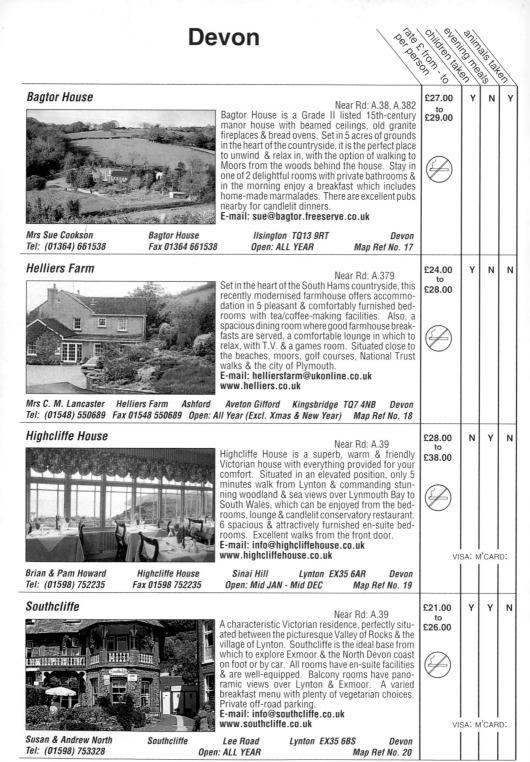

Near Rd: A.38, A.382

Bagtor House is a Grade II listed 15th-century manor house with beamed ceilings, old granite fireplaces & bread ovens. Set in 5 acres of grounds in the heart of the countryside, it is the perfect place to unwind & relax in, with the option of walking to Moors from the woods behind the house. Stay in one of 2 delightful rooms with private bathrooms & in the morning enjoy a breakfast which includes home-made marmalades. There are excellent pubs nearby for candlelit dinners.

E-mail: sue@bagtor.freeserve.co.uk

£27.00 to £29.00 — Y N Y

Mrs Sue Cookson	Bagtor House	Ilsington TQ13 9RT	Devon
Tel: (01364) 661538	Fax 01364 661538	Open: ALL YEAR	Map Ref No. 17

Helliers Farm

Near Rd: A.379

Set in the heart of the South Hams countryside, this recently modernised farmhouse offers accommodation in 5 pleasant & comfortably furnished bedrooms with tea/coffee-making facilities. Also, a spacious dining room where good farmhouse breakfasts are served, a comfortable lounge in which to relax, with T.V. & a games room. Situated close to the beaches, moors, golf courses, National Trust walks & the city of Plymouth.

E-mail: helliersfarm@ukonline.co.uk
www.helliers.co.uk

£24.00 to £28.00 — Y N N

Mrs C. M. Lancaster	Helliers Farm	Ashford	Aveton Gifford	Kingsbridge TQ7 4NB	Devon
Tel: (01548) 550689	Fax 01548 550689	Open: All Year (Excl. Xmas & New Year)			Map Ref No. 18

Highcliffe House

Near Rd: A.39

Highcliffe House is a superb, warm & friendly Victorian house with everything provided for your comfort. Situated in an elevated position, only 5 minutes walk from Lynton & commanding stunning woodland & sea views over Lynmouth Bay to South Wales, which can be enjoyed from the bedrooms, lounge & candlelit conservatory restaurant. 6 spacious & attractively furnished en-suite bedrooms. Excellent walks from the front door.

E-mail: info@highcliffehouse.co.uk
www.highcliffehouse.co.uk

£28.00 to £38.00 — N Y N

VISA: M'CARD:

Brian & Pam Howard	Highcliffe House	Sinai Hill	Lynton EX35 6AR	Devon
Tel: (01598) 752235	Fax 01598 752235	Open: Mid JAN - Mid DEC		Map Ref No. 19

Southcliffe

Near Rd: A.39

A characteristic Victorian residence, perfectly situated between the picturesque Valley of Rocks & the village of Lynton. Southcliffe is the ideal base from which to explore Exmoor & the North Devon coast on foot or by car. All rooms have en-suite facilities & are well-equipped. Balcony rooms have panoramic views over Lynton & Exmoor. A varied breakfast menu with plenty of vegetarian choices. Private off-road parking.

E-mail: info@southcliffe.co.uk
www.southcliffe.co.uk

£21.00 to £26.00 — Y Y N

VISA: M'CARD:

Susan & Andrew North	Southcliffe	Lee Road	Lynton EX35 6BS	Devon
Tel: (01598) 753328		Open: ALL YEAR		Map Ref No. 20

Gate House.   North Bovey.

	rate £ from - to per person	children taken	evening meals	animals taken

Coombe Farm

Near Rd: A.39

Coombe Farm is a 365-acre, hill-sheep farm, with an early-17th-century farmhouse set betwixt Lynmouth & the legendary Doone Valley. The coast path runs through the farm at Desolate. All within the spectacular Exmoor National Park. The bedrooms are 2 doubles, en-suite, 1 twin & 2 family. All have hot-drink facilities, shaver points, & bath & hand towels. Central heating. A lounge with woodburner fire & colour T.V..
E-mail: coombefarm@freeuk.com
www.brendonvalley.co.uk/coombefarm.htm.

£25.00 to £27.00   Y   N   N

VISA: M'CARD:

Susan Pile   Coombe Farm   Countisbury   Lynton EX35 6NF   Devon
Tel: (01598) 741236   Fax 01598 741236   Open: MAR - NOV   Map Ref No. 22

Gate House

Near Rd: A.30, A.38

North Bovey is an historic village set within the Dartmoor National Park. Gate House, near the village green, is a listed 500-year-old thatched medieval longhouse with beamed ceilings, old granite fireplaces & bread oven. An acre of gardens with a swimming pool. The charming bedrooms combine country-style elegance with en-suite/private bathrooms. Lovely walks amidst breathtaking scenery & National Trust properties within easy reach. Animals by arrangement. Children over 15 years.
E-mail: gatehouseondartmoor@talk21.com
www.gatehouseondartmoor.com

£31.00 to £32.00   N   Y   Y

see PHOTO over
p. 113

John & Sheila Williams   Gate House   The Village   North Bovey   Nr. Moretonhampstead TQ13 8RB
Tel: (01647) 440479   Fax 01647 440479   Open: ALL YEAR   Map Ref No. 23

Great Sloncombe Farm

Near Rd: A.382

Great Sloncombe Farm is a listed, granite-&-cob-built, 13th-century farmhouse. Set in a peaceful Dartmoor valley, the rambling house has a magical atmosphere, & is furnished with oak & pine, antique china & interesting old photographs. The 3 warm & pleasant bedrooms are all en-suite, with every facility included. Delicious breakfasts, with home-made bread & plentiful Devonshire suppers, are served. Children over 8 yrs.
E-mail: hmerchant@sloncombe.freeserve.co.uk
www.greatsloncombefarm.co.uk

£25.00 to £27.00   Y   Y   Y

Trudie Merchant   Great Sloncombe Farm   Moretonhampstead TQ13 8QF   Devon
Tel: (01647) 440595   Fax 01647 440595   Open: ALL YEAR   Map Ref No. 24

Visit our website at:
http://www.bestbandb.co.uk

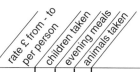

rate £ from - to per person	children taken	evening meals taken	animals taken

---

£22.00 to £22.00

Y | N | N

(non-smoking)

Great Doccombe Farm

Near Rd: A.30

Great Doccombe Farm is situated in the pretty hamlet of Doccombe, within the Dartmoor National Park, on the B.3212 from Exeter. An ideal base for walking in the Teign Valley & nearby moors, with golf, riding & fishing nearby. This lovely 16th-century granite farmhouse is surrounded by gardens & fields. The bedrooms (1 ground-floor) are all en-suite, & have shower, T.V. & tea/coffee-making facilities. A traditional English breakfast is served. A perfect place to relax.
E-mail: david.oakey3@btopenworld.com
www.greatdoccombefarm.co.uk

Gill & David Oakey   *Great Doccombe Farm*   *Doccombe*   *Moretonhampstead TQ13 8SS*   *Devon*
Tel: (01647) 440681   Open: ALL YEAR   Map Ref No. 25

£25.00 to £45.00

Y | Y | Y

VISA: M'CARD: AMEX:

Sampsons Farm Hotel Restaurant

Near Rd: A.38, A.380

Sampsons is a welcoming thatched farmhouse, set in its own grounds in a tiny, sleepy village & yet it is only 5 mins from the A.38 & A.380. There are a wealth of oak beams, log fires, history & tranquillity & a renowned (award-winning) restaurant serving delicious country produce. Pretty en-suite rooms are available in barn conversions. A disabled en-suite room & an apartment for groups & families. Also, charming en-suite rooms in the farmhouse. Lovely river & meadow walks. Dartmoor views.
E-mail: nigel@sampsonsfarm.com
www.sampsonsfarm.com

Nigel Bell   *Sampsons Farm Hotel Restaurant*   *Preston*   *Newton Abbot TQ12 3PP*   *Devon*
Tel: (01626) 354913   Fax 01626 354913   Open: ALL YEAR   Map Ref No. 26

£27.00 to £30.00

Y | Y | N

(non-smoking)

Penpark

Near Rd: A.38

In the Dartmoor National Park, with secluded, beautiful woodland gardens, tennis court & glorious panoramic views, Penpark is an elegant country house, a gem of its period, designed by Clough Williams Ellis of Portmeirion fame. 4 charming rooms: a spacious double/twin with balcony; a single next door & a further double & a garden room with doors opening out into the garden - all with wonderful views; private facilities; tea/coffee & T.V.. Evening meals by arrangement.
E-mail: maddy@penpark.co.uk
www.penpark.co.uk

Mrs Madeleine Gregson   *Penpark*   *Bickington*   *Newton Abbot TQ12 6LH*   *Devon*
Tel: (01626) 821314   Open: ALL YEAR   Map Ref No. 27

£23.00 to £26.00

Y | N | N

(non-smoking)

VISA: M'CARD:

Great Wooston Farm

Near Rd: A.30

Great Wooston Farm was once part of the Manor House Estate owned by Lord Hambledon. Situated high above the Teign Valley in the Dartmoor National Park, with views across the moors. Plenty of walks, golf, fishing & riding nearby. The farmhouse is surrounded by a delightful garden of 1/2 an acre, also barbeque & picnic area. 3 bedrooms, 2 en-suite, 1 with 4-poster bed, 1 with private bathroom. Excellent breakfasts. Also, a guests' lounge for your relaxation. Children over 8.
E-mail: info@greatwoostonfarm.com
www.greatwoostonfarm.com

Mary Cuming   *Great Wooston Farm*   *Moretonhampstead*   *Newton Abbot TQ13 8QA*   *Devon*
Tel/Fax: (01647) 440367   Mobile 07798 670590   Open: ALL YEAR   Map Ref No. 28

Devon

Stowford House

Near Rd: A.30

A warm welcome awaits you at this delightful Georgian country house. Perfectly located for exploring Devon & Cornwall, including Dartmoor, the lovely Tamar Valley & the coast. The world renowned Eden Project & several National Trust properties are nearby. Large bedrooms, the elegant drawing room & garden ensure a relaxing stay. The area offers walking, cycling, golf, riding & sailing. Good food prepared from local produce. Light snacks available on request. Children over 14.
E-mail: alison@stowfordhouse.com
www.stowfordhouse.com

£25.00 to £32.50 | Y | N | N

VISA: M'CARD:

Alison Pardoe   Stowford House   Lewdown   Okehampton EX20 4BZ   Devon
Tel: (01566) 783415   Fax 01566 783109   Open: ALL YEAR (Excl. Xmas)   Map Ref No. 29

Westways

Near Rd: A.38, A.386

Situated approx. 3 1/2 miles from Plymouth city centre, this attractive detached house offers pleasant accommodation in 3 well-furnished (non-smoking) rooms, with tea/coffee-making facilities. Excellent breakfasts are served in the elegant dining room. Guests may choose to relax & plan their excursions in the comfortable sitting room or make use of the small T.V. room. A homely & friendly base both for visitors wishing to make the most of the many attractions in the area, & for touring Devon. Children over 12 years.
E-mail: turner.jd@btopenworld.com

£25.00 to £25.00 | Y | N | N

VISA: M'CARD:

John & Daphne Turner   Westways   706 Budshead Road   Crownhill   Plymouth PL6 5DY   Devon
Tel: (01752) 776617   Fax 01752 776617   Open: ALL YEAR   Map Ref No. 30

Brookdale House

Near Rd: A.38

Brookdale House is a Grade II listed Tudor style house, situated in a peaceful secluded valley with delightful grounds. Offering 6 individually designed bedrooms, with T.V. & tea/coffee-making facilities. Each room is elegantly furnished with antiques in period style. A delicious Aga-cooked breakfast is served using only the finest local ingredients. A charming home, perfect for a relaxing break & an ideal base for exploring Dartmoor or the coastal attractions. Animals by arrangement.
www.brookdale-house.com

£25.00 to £27.50 | Y | N | Y

Mrs Christa Napier-Bell   Brookdale House   North Huish   Nr. South Brent TQ10 9NR   Devon
Tel: (01548) 821661   Fax 01548 821606   Open: ALL YEAR   Map Ref No. 31

Coombe House

Near Rd: A.38

Coombe House is a gracious Georgian residence set in a tranquil & beautiful valley in a designated Area of Outstanding Natural Beauty. 4 en-suite bedrooms & a twin with private bathroom. T.V., hairdryer & tea/coffee tray etc. Elegant dining room & lounge. Enjoy delicious home-cooked food prepared using fresh local produce (by arrangement.) The coast, Dartmoor, Totnes, Salcombe, Plymouth & Exeter are all within easy reach. 4 barn conversions for self-catering. Children over 12.
E-mail: coombehouse@hotmail.com
www.coombehouse.uk.com

£30.00 to £45.00 | Y | Y | N

see PHOTO over
p. 117

Faith & John Scharenguivel   Coombe House   North Huish   South Brent TQ10 9NJ   Devon
Tel: (01548) 821277   Fax 01548 821277   Open: ALL YEAR   Map Ref No. 32

Coombe House.   North Huish.

	rate £ from - to per person	children taken	evening meals	animals taken

Kerscott Farm

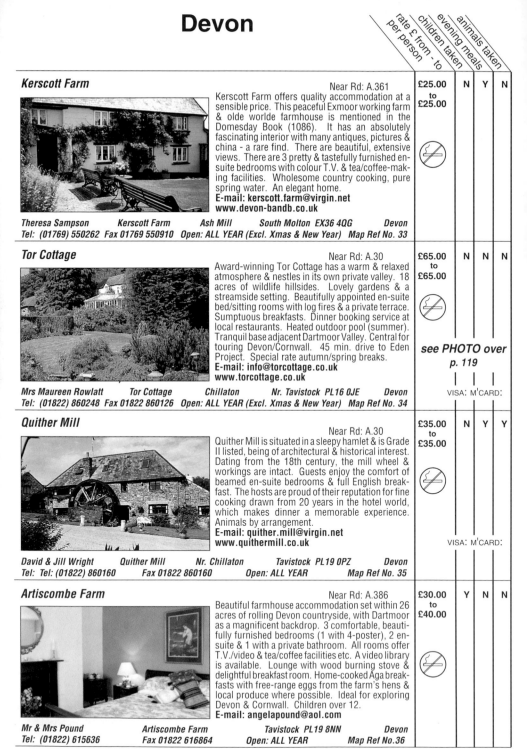

Near Rd: A.361
Kerscott Farm offers quality accommodation at a sensible price. This peaceful Exmoor working farm & olde worlde farmhouse is mentioned in the Domesday Book (1086). It has an absolutely fascinating interior with many antiques, pictures & china - a rare find. There are beautiful, extensive views. There are 3 pretty & tastefully furnished en-suite bedrooms with colour T.V. & tea/coffee-making facilities. Wholesome country cooking, pure spring water. An elegant home.
E-mail: kerscott.farm@virgin.net
www.devon-bandb.co.uk

£25.00 to £25.00 — N | Y | N

Theresa Sampson   Kerscott Farm   Ash Mill   South Molton EX36 4QG   Devon
Tel: (01769) 550262 Fax 01769 550910 Open: ALL YEAR (Excl. Xmas & New Year) Map Ref No. 33

Tor Cottage

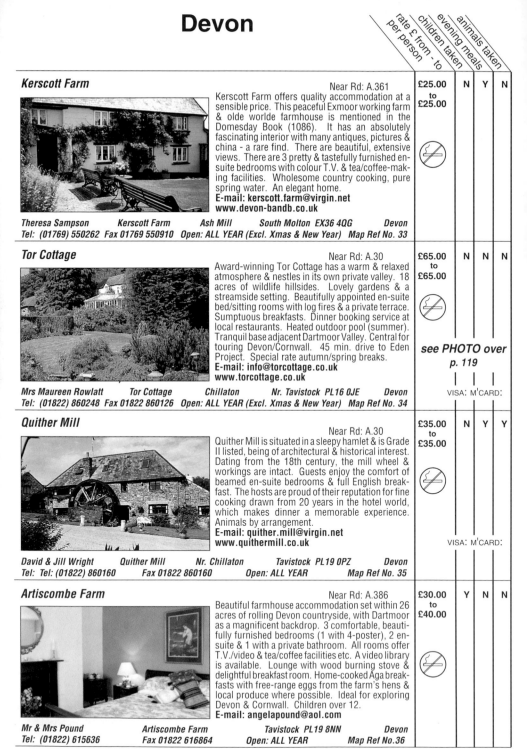

Near Rd: A.30
Award-winning Tor Cottage has a warm & relaxed atmosphere & nestles in its own private valley. 18 acres of wildlife hillsides. Lovely gardens & a streamside setting. Beautifully appointed en-suite bed/sitting rooms with log fires & a private terrace. Sumptuous breakfasts. Dinner booking service at local restaurants. Heated outdoor pool (summer). Tranquil base adjacent Dartmoor Valley. Central for touring Devon/Cornwall. 45 min. drive to Eden Project. Special rate autumn/spring breaks.
E-mail: info@torcottage.co.uk
www.torcottage.co.uk

£65.00 to £65.00 — N | N | N

see PHOTO over
p. 119

VISA: M'CARD:

Mrs Maureen Rowlatt   Tor Cottage   Chillaton   Nr. Tavistock PL16 0JE   Devon
Tel: (01822) 860248 Fax 01822 860126 Open: ALL YEAR (Excl. Xmas & New Year) Map Ref No. 34

Quither Mill

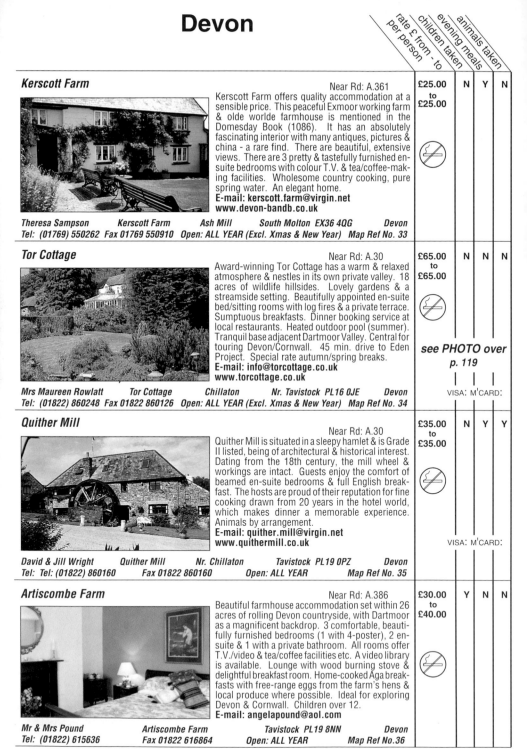

Near Rd: A.30
Quither Mill is situated in a sleepy hamlet & is Grade II listed, being of architectural & historical interest. Dating from the 18th century, the mill wheel & workings are intact. Guests enjoy the comfort of beamed en-suite bedrooms & full English breakfast. The hosts are proud of their reputation for fine cooking drawn from 20 years in the hotel world, which makes dinner a memorable experience. Animals by arrangement.
E-mail: quither.mill@virgin.net
www.quithermill.co.uk

£35.00 to £35.00 — N | Y | Y

VISA: M'CARD:

David & Jill Wright   Quither Mill   Nr. Chillaton   Tavistock PL19 0PZ   Devon
Tel: Tel: (01822) 860160   Fax 01822 860160   Open: ALL YEAR   Map Ref No. 35

Artiscombe Farm

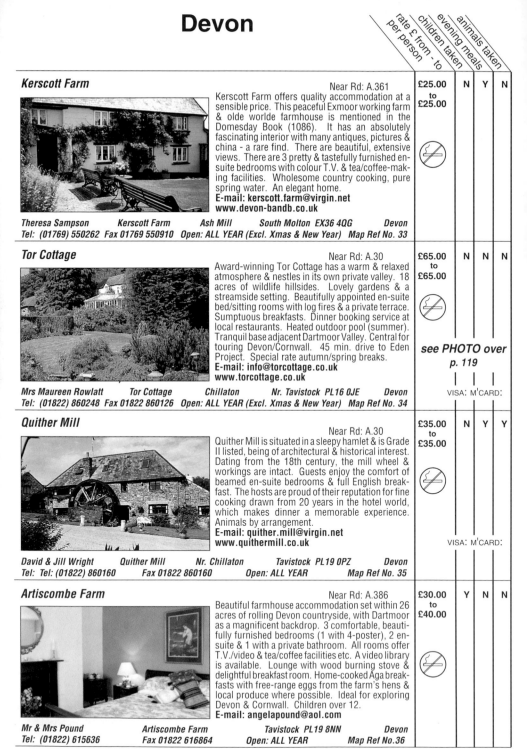

Near Rd: A.386
Beautiful farmhouse accommodation set within 26 acres of rolling Devon countryside, with Dartmoor as a magnificent backdrop. 3 comfortable, beautifully furnished bedrooms (1 with 4-poster), 2 en-suite & 1 with a private bathroom. All rooms offer T.V./video & tea/coffee facilities etc. A video library is available. Lounge with wood burning stove & delightful breakfast room. Home-cooked Aga breakfasts with free-range eggs from the farm's hens & local produce where possible. Ideal for exploring Devon & Cornwall. Children over 12.
E-mail: angelapound@aol.com

£30.00 to £40.00 — Y | N | N

Mr & Mrs Pound   Artiscombe Farm   Tavistock PL19 8NN   Devon
Tel: (01822) 615636   Fax 01822 616864   Open: ALL YEAR   Map Ref No.36

Tor Cottage. Chillaton.

Devon

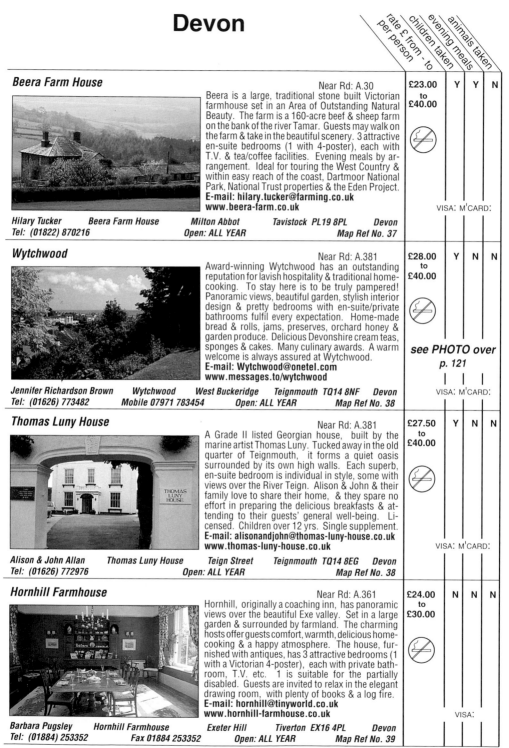

	rate £ from - to	children taken	evening meals	animals taken

Beera Farm House

Near Rd: A.30

Beera is a large, traditional stone built Victorian farmhouse set in an Area of Outstanding Natural Beauty. The farm is a 160-acre beef & sheep farm on the bank of the river Tamar. Guests may walk on the farm & take in the beautiful scenery. 3 attractive en-suite bedrooms (1 with 4-poster), each with T.V. & tea/coffee facilities. Evening meals by arrangement. Ideal for touring the West Country & within easy reach of the coast, Dartmoor National Park, National Trust properties & the Eden Project.
E-mail: hilary.tucker@farming.co.uk
www.beera-farm.co.uk

£23.00 to £40.00 — Y — Y — N

VISA: M'CARD:

Hilary Tucker   Beera Farm House   Milton Abbot   Tavistock PL19 8PL   Devon
Tel: (01822) 870216   Open: ALL YEAR   Map Ref No. 37

Wytchwood

Near Rd: A.381

Award-winning Wytchwood has an outstanding reputation for lavish hospitality & traditional home-cooking. To stay here is to be truly pampered! Panoramic views, beautiful garden, stylish interior design & pretty bedrooms with en-suite/private bathrooms fulfil every expectation. Home-made bread & rolls, jams, preserves, orchard honey & garden produce. Delicious Devonshire cream teas, sponges & cakes. Many culinary awards. A warm welcome is always assured at Wytchwood.
E-mail: Wytchwood@onetel.com
www.messages.to/wytchwood

£28.00 to £40.00 — Y — N — N

see PHOTO over p. 121

VISA: M'CARD:

Jennifer Richardson Brown   Wytchwood   West Buckeridge   Teignmouth TQ14 8NF   Devon
Tel: (01626) 773482   Mobile 07971 783454   Open: ALL YEAR   Map Ref No. 38

Thomas Luny House

Near Rd: A.381

A Grade II listed Georgian house, built by the marine artist Thomas Luny. Tucked away in the old quarter of Teignmouth, it forms a quiet oasis surrounded by its own high walls. Each superb, en-suite bedroom is individual in style, some with views over the River Teign. Alison & John & their family love to share their home, & they spare no effort in preparing the delicious breakfasts & attending to their guests' general well-being. Licensed. Children over 12 yrs. Single supplement.
E-mail: alisonandjohn@thomas-luny-house.co.uk
www.thomas-luny-house.co.uk

£27.50 to £40.00 — Y — N — N

VISA: M'CARD:

Alison & John Allan   Thomas Luny House   Teign Street   Teignmouth TQ14 8EG   Devon
Tel: (01626) 772976   Open: ALL YEAR   Map Ref No. 38

Hornhill Farmhouse

Near Rd: A.361

Hornhill, originally a coaching inn, has panoramic views over the beautiful Exe valley. Set in a large garden & surrounded by farmland. The charming hosts offer guests comfort, warmth, delicious home-cooking & a happy atmosphere. The house, furnished with antiques, has 3 attractive bedrooms (1 with a Victorian 4-poster), each with private bathroom, T.V. etc. 1 is suitable for the partially disabled. Guests are invited to relax in the elegant drawing room, with plenty of books & a log fire.
E-mail: hornhill@tinyworld.co.uk
www.hornhill-farmhouse.co.uk

£24.00 to £30.00 — N — N — N

VISA:

Barbara Pugsley   Hornhill Farmhouse   Exeter Hill   Tiverton EX16 4PL   Devon
Tel: (01884) 253352   Fax 01884 253352   Open: ALL YEAR   Map Ref No. 39

Wytchwood. West Buckeridge.

	rate £ from - to per person	children taken	evening meals	animals taken

Fairmount House Hotel

Near Rd: A.380

Experience somewhere special & feel completely at home in the tranquillity, warmth & informal atmosphere of this small hotel. Offering 8 comfortable en-suite bedrooms, unhurried breakfasts & undisturbed evenings. (2 lower-ground-floor rooms have private doors opening onto the garden.) Torquay boasts a profusion of sub-tropical plants & miles of beaches & sheltered coves. Nestling away from the busy seafront, Fairmount offers quality, comfort & genuine friendly service.
E-mail: fairmounthouse@aol.com

£28.00 to £33.00 — Y Y Y

VISA: M'CARD:

Mr & Mrs Burke   Fairmount House Hotel   Herbert Road   Chelston   Torquay TQ2 6RW   Devon
Tel: (01803) 605446   Fax 01803 605446   Open: ALL YEAR   Map Ref No. 40

Huntshaw Barton

Near Rd: A.39

An historic 14th-century Grade II listed farmhouse, standing in its own grounds & set in stunning countryside. Offering a warm welcome, seclusion, tranquillity & beautiful views. Breakfast & evening meals, fresh from the Aga, are served in the dining room featuring the original inglenook. All bedrooms are en-suite & have T.V. & tea/coffee. Close to RHS Rosemoor, the coast, the Dartington Factory, Torrington (Battle 1646), the Tarka Trail & wooded walks straight from the garden.
E-mail: enquiries@huntshawbarton.com
www.huntshawbarton.com

£25.00 to £28.00 — Y Y Y

Mr & Mrs Stuart Whitehead   Huntshaw Barton   Huntshaw   Torrington EX38 7HH   Devon
Tel: (01805) 625736   Open: ALL YEAR   Map Ref No.41

The Old Forge at Totnes

Near Rd: A.381

Be assured of a warm welcome at this 600-year-old, creeper-clad converted smithy. This family-run hotel offers 10 comfortable, well-equipped bedrooms. A cottage suite is available for families & 2 ground-floor rooms are suitable for semi-disabled guests. A quiet spot, yet only a few mins' walk from the town centre & riverside. Parking. Licensed. Leisure lounge with whirlpool spa. Ideal for touring South Hams, Torbay, Dartmoor & only 1 1/2 hours from the Eden Project.
E-mail: enq@oldforgetotnes.com
www.oldforgetotnes.com

£27.00 to £37.00 — Y N N

VISA: M'CARD: AMEX:

Christine Hillier & David Miller   The Old Forge at Totnes   Seymour Place   Totnes TQ9 5AY   Devon
Tel: (01803) 862174   Fax 01803 865385   Open: ALL YEAR   Map Ref No. 42

Orchard House

Near Rd: A.381

Surrounded by quiet countryside in a beautiful valley between Totnes & Kingsbridge, Orchard House is ideally placed for the nearby South Devon coastline & Dartmoor. It offers 3 wonderfully furnished en-suite bedrooms, each with colour T.V., clock/radio, hairdryer & tea/coffee-making facilities. Also, guests' sitting room with antiques & log fire. In the spacious dining room breakfasts are served on a large platter using local produce & homemade preserves. Large garden & private parking. Children over 3 years.
www.orchard-house-halwell.co.uk

£23.00 to £25.00 — Y N N

see PHOTO over
p. 123

Mrs Helen Worth   Orchard House   Horner   Halwell   Totnes TQ9 7LB   Devon
Tel: (01548) 821448   Open: MAR - OCT   Map Ref No. 43

Orchard House. Horner.

		rate £ from - to per person	children taken	evening meals	animals taken

Lower Grimpstonleigh

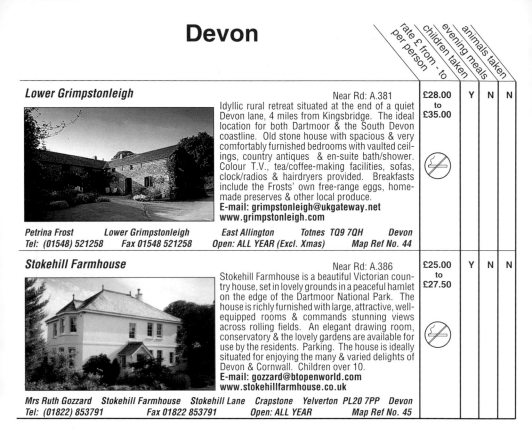

Near Rd: A.381

Idyllic rural retreat situated at the end of a quiet Devon lane, 4 miles from Kingsbridge. The ideal location for both Dartmoor & the South Devon coastline. Old stone house with spacious & very comfortably furnished bedrooms with vaulted ceilings, country antiques & en-suite bath/shower. Colour T.V., tea/coffee-making facilities, sofas, clock/radios & hairdryers provided. Breakfasts include the Frosts' own free-range eggs, homemade preserves & other local produce.
E-mail: grimpstonleigh@ukgateway.net
www.grimpstonleigh.com

£28.00 to £35.00 — Y — N — N

Petrina Frost   Lower Grimpstonleigh
Tel: (01548) 521258   Fax 01548 521258
East Allington   Totnes TQ9 7QH   Devon
Open: ALL YEAR (Excl. Xmas)   Map Ref No. 44

Stokehill Farmhouse

Near Rd: A.386

Stokehill Farmhouse is a beautiful Victorian country house, set in lovely grounds in a peaceful hamlet on the edge of the Dartmoor National Park. The house is richly furnished with large, attractive, well-equipped rooms & commands stunning views across rolling fields. An elegant drawing room, conservatory & the lovely gardens are available for use by the residents. Parking. The house is ideally situated for enjoying the many & varied delights of Devon & Cornwall. Children over 10.
E-mail: gozzard@btopenworld.com
www.stokehillfarmhouse.co.uk

£25.00 to £27.50 — Y — N — N

Mrs Ruth Gozzard   Stokehill Farmhouse   Stokehill Lane   Crapstone   Yelverton PL20 7PP   Devon
Tel: (01822) 853791   Fax 01822 853791   Open: ALL YEAR   Map Ref No. 45

WORLDWIDE BED & BREAKFAST ASSOCIATION

Visit our website at:
http://www.bestbandb.co.uk

Dorset

Dorset
(West Country)

The unspoilt nature of this gem of a county is emphasised by the designation of virtually all of the coast & much of the inland country as an Area of Outstanding Natural Beauty. Along the coast from Christchurch to Lyme Regis there are a fascinating variety of sandy beaches, towering cliffs & single banks, whilst inland is a rich mixture of downland, lonely heaths, fertile valleys, historic houses & lovely villages of thatch & mellow stone buildings.

Thomas Hardy was born here & took the Dorset countryside as a background for many of his novels. Few writers can have stamped their identity on a county more than Hardy on Dorset, forever to be known as the "Hardy Country". Fortunately most of the area that he so lovingly described remains unchanged, including Egdon Heath & the county town of Dorchester, famous as Casterbridge.

In the midst of the rolling chalk hills which stretch along the Storr Valley lies picturesque Cerne Abbas, with its late mediaeval houses & cottages & the ruins of a Benedictine Abbey. At Godmanstone is the tiny thatched "Smiths Arms" claiming to be the smallest pub in England.

The north of the county is pastoral with lovely views over broad Blackmoor Vale. Here is the ancient hilltop town of Shaftesbury, with cobbled Gold Hill, one of the most photographed streets in the country.

Coastal Dorset is spectacular. Poole harbour is an enormous, almost circular bay, an exciting mixture of 20th century activity, ships of many nations & beautiful building of the 15th, 18th & early 19th centuries.

Westwards lies the popular resort of Swanage, where the sandy beach & sheltered bay are excellent for swimming. From here to Weymouth is a marvellous stretch of coast with scenic wonders like Lulworth Cove & the arch of Durdle Door.

Chesil Beach is an extraordinary bank of graded pebbles, as perilous to shipping today as it was 1,000 years ago. It is separated from the mainland by a sheltered lagoon known as the Fleet. From here a range of giant cliffs rises to 617 feet at Golden Gap & stretches westwards to Lyme Regis, beloved by Jane Austen who wrote "Persuasion" whilst living here.

Dorset has many interesting archaeological features. Near Dorchester is Maiden Castle, huge earthwork fortifications on a site first inhabited 6,000 years ago. The Badbury rings wind round a wooded hilltop near Wimborne Minster; legend has it that King Arthur's soul, in the form of a raven, inhabited this "dread" wood. The giant of Cerne Abbas is a figure of a man 180 feet high carved into the chalk hillside. Long associated with fertility there is still speculation about the figures' origins, one theory suggesting it is a Romano-British depiction of Hercules. A Roman amphitheatre can be seen at Dorchester, & today's road still follows the Roman route to Weymouth.

Corfe Castle.

Dorset

Dorset
Gazeteer

Areas of outstanding natural beauty.
The Entire County.

Houses & Castles

Athelthampton
Mediaeval house - one of the finest in all England. Formal gardens.

Barneston Manor - Nr. Church Knowle
13th - 16th century stone built manor house.

Forde Abbey - Nr. Chard
12th century Cistercian monastery - noted Mortlake tapestries.

Manor House - Sandford Orcas
Mansion of Tudor period, furnished with period furniture, antiques, silver, china, glass, paintings.

Hardy's Cottage - Higher Bockampton
Birthplace of Thomas Hardy, author (1840-1928).

Milton Abbey - Nr. Blandford
18th century Georgian house built on original site of 15th century abbey.

Purse Caundle Manor - Purse Caundle
Mediaeval Manor - furnished in style of period.

Parnham House - Beaminster
Tudor Manor - some later work by Nash. Leaded windows & heraldic plasterwork. Home of John Makepeace & the International School for Craftsmen in Wood. House, gardens & workshops.

Sherborne Castle - Sherborne
16th century mansion - continuously occupied by Digby family.

No. 3 Trinity Street - Weymouth
Tudor cottages now converted into one house, furnished 17th century.

Smedmore - Kimmeridge
18th century manor.

Wolfeton House - Dorchester
Mediaeval & Elizabethan Manor. Fine stone work, great stair. 17th century furniture - Jacobean ceilings & fireplaces.

Cathedrals & Churches

Bere Regis (St. John the Baptist)
12th century foundation - enlarged in 13th & 15th centuries.
Timber roof & nave, fine arcades.
16th century seating.

Blandford (St. Peter & St. Paul)
18th century - ashlar - Georgian design. Galleries, pulpit, box pews, font & mayoral seat.

Bradford Abbas (St. Mary)
14th century - parapets & pinnacled tower, panelled roof. 15th century bench ends, stone rood screen. 17th century pulpit.

Cerne Abbas (St. Mary)
13th century - rebuilt 15th & 16th centuries, 14th century wall paintings, 15th century tower, stone screen, pulpit possibly 11th century.

Chalbury (dedication unknown)
13th century origin - 14th century east windows, timber bellcote. Plastered walls, box pews, 3-decker pulpit, west gallery.

Christchurch (Christ Church)
Norman nave - ribbed plaster vaulting - perpendicular spire. Tudor renaissance Salisbury chantry - screen with Tree of Jesse: notable misericord seats.

Milton Abbey (Sts. Mary, Michael, Sampson & Branwaleder)
14th century pulpitum & sedilla, 15th century reredos & canopy, 16th century monument, Milton effigies 1775.

Sherborne (St. Mary)
Largely Norman but some Saxon remains - excellent fan vaulting, of nave & choir. 12th & 13th century effigies - 15th century painted glass.

Studland (St. Nicholas)
12th century - best Norman church in the country. 12th century font, 13th century east windows.

Whitchurch Canonicorum (St. Candida & Holy Cross)
12th & 13th century. 12th century font, relics of patroness in 13th century shrine, 15th century painted glass, 15th century tower.

Wimbourne Minster (St. Cuthberga)
12th century central tower & arcade, otherwise 13th-15th century. Former collegiate church. Georgian glass, some Jacobean stalls & screen. Monuments & famed clock of 14th century.

Yetminster (St. Andrew)
13th century chancel - 15th century rebuilt with embattled parapets. 16th century brasses & seating.

Dorset

Museums & Galleries

Abbey Ruins - Shaftesbury
Relics excavated from Benedictine
Nunnery founded by Alfred the Great.
Russell-Cotes Art Gallery & Museum -
Bournemouth
17th-20th century oil paintings,
watercolours, sculptures, ceramics,
miniatures, etc.
Rothesay Museum - Bournemouth
English porcelain, 17th century furniture,
collection of early Italian paintings, arms &
armour, ethnography, etc.
**Bournemouth Natural Science
Society's Museum**
Archaeology & local natural history.
Brewery Farm Museum - Milton Abbas
Brewing & village bygones from Dorset.
Dorset County Museum - Dorchester
Geology, natural history, pre-history.
Thomas Hardy memorabilia
Philpot Museum - Lyme Regis
Old documents & prints, fossils, lace & old
fire engine.
Guildhall Museum - Poole
Social & civic life of Poole during 18th &
19th centuries displayed in two-storey
Georgian market house.
Scapolen's Court - Poole
14th century house of local merchant

exhibiting local & archaeological history of
town, also industrial archaeology.
Sherborne Museum - Sherborne
Local history & geology - abbey of AD
705, Sherborne missal AD 1400, 18th
century local silk industry.
Gallery 24 - Shaftesbury
Art exhibitions - paintings, pottery, etc.
Red House Museum & Art Gallery -
Christchurch
Natural history & antiques of the region.
Georgian house with herb garden.
Priest's House Museum Wimbourne
Minster
Tudor building in garden exhibiting local
archaeology & history.

Other things to see & do

Abbotsbury Swannery - Abbotsbury
Unique colony of Swans established by
monks in the 14th century. 16th century
duck decoy, reed walk, information centre.
Dorset Rare Breeds Centre - Park Farm,
Gillingham
Poole Potteries - the Quay, Poole
Sea Life Centre - Weymouth
Variety of displays, including Ocean
Tunnel, sharks, living "touch" pools.

West Bay.

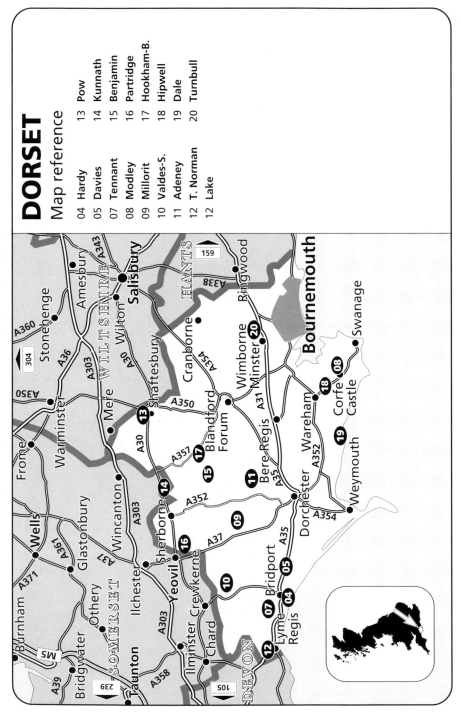

DORSET
Map reference

04	Hardy	13	Pow
05	Davies	14	Kunnath
07	Tennant	15	Benjamin
08	Modley	16	Partridge
09	Millorit	17	Hookham-B.
10	Valdes-S.	18	Hipwell
11	Adeney	19	Dale
12	T. Norman	20	Turnbull
12	Lake		

Dorset

rate £ from - to per person	children taken	evening meals taken	animals taken		

£24.00 to £32.00 — Y N Y

VISA: M'CARD:

Britmead House

Near Rd: A.35

A friendly welcome in a relaxed & comfortable atmosphere. Renowned for good food, a high standard of facilities, personal service & attention to detail. Situated between Bridport, the fishing harbour of West Bay, Chesil Beach & the Dorset Coastal Path. 8 individually decorated en-suite bedrooms, 3 on the ground floor, all with T.V., tea/coffee-making facilities & hairdryer. South-facing lounge & dining room overlook the garden & open countryside beyond. Parking.
E-mail: britmead@talk21.com
www.britmeadhouse.co.uk

Alan Hardy	Britmead House	154 West Bay Road	Bridport DT6 4FG	Dorset
Tel: (01308) 422941		Open: ALL YEAR		Map Ref No. 04

£35.00 to £42.50 — Y Y Y

VISA: M'CARD:

Innsacre Farmhouse

Near Rd: A.35

17th-century farmhouse & barn in a magical & peaceful setting. Hidden midway between Lyme Regis & Dorchester, 3 miles from the sea & National Trust coastal path. South-facing, 10 acres of spinneys, steep hillsides, orchard & lawns in a beautiful setting. A mix of French rustic style, English comfort & a genuine, warm welcome. All rooms en-suite (with T.V. etc.). Cosy sitting-room, log fires, beams & delicious breakfasts. Parking. Licensed. Children over 9. Single supplement.
E-mail: innsacre.farmhouse@btinternet.com
www.innsacre.com

Sydney & Jayne Davies	Innsacre Farmhouse	Shipton Gorge	Bridport DT6 4LJ	Dorset
Tel: (01308) 456137		Open: ALL YEAR (Excl. Xmas & New Year)		Map Ref No. 05

£38.00 to £40.00 — Y N Y

Champ's Land

Near Rd: A.35

Champ's Land is a pretty 17th-century former farmhouse. It is in a beautiful, rural setting, with an attractive walled garden & orchard leading to a stream. It is tastefully decorated throughout with antiques & offers 2 comfortable guest rooms with tea/coffee facilities. Also, a lovely sitting room with T.V. A delicious breakfast is served. Several good pubs & restaurants locally for dinner. Many gardens & historic houses within easy reach. Situated only 1 1/2 miles from the sea. Children over 10. Single supplement. Animals by arrangement.
www.bestbandb.co.uk

Mrs Miranda Tennant	Champ's Land	North Chideock	Bridport DT6 6JZ	Dorset
Tel: (01297) 489314		Open: ALL YEAR (Excl. Xmas & New Year)		Map Ref No. 07

£30.00 to £30.00 — Y Y N

Springbrook Cottage

Near Rd: A.351

Springbrook Cottage is a beautiful house which is set in an acre of garden, lawn & shrubs including mature trees. There is an attractive conservatory in which guests may choose to relax, which boasts lovely views down to the valley beyond. Traditionally furnished with antiques, the property offers attractive accommodation in 2 charming bedrooms. The light & airy rooms are very comfortable. A delicious breakfast is served. Evening meals by prior arrangement. A lovely base from which to explore the beautiful Dorset countryside.
www.bestbandb.co.uk

Mrs Modley	Springbrook Cottage	Springbrook Close	Corfe Castle BH20 5HS	Dorset
Tel: (01929) 480509		Open: ALL YEAR		Map Ref No. 08

Dorset

Brambles

Near Rd: A.37

Set in beautiful, tranquil countryside, Brambles is a pretty thatched cottage offering every comfort, superb views & a friendly welcome. There is a choice of en-suite twin, double or single rooms, all very comfortable & with colour T.V. & tea/coffee-making facilities. Pretty garden available for relaxing in. Full English or Continental breakfast served. Evening meals available by prior arrangement. There are many interesting places to visit & wonderful walks for enthusiasts.
www.bestbandb.co.uk

| £28.00 to £28.00 | Y | Y | N |

see PHOTO over
p. 131

Anita & Andre Millorit   Brambles   Woolcombe   Melbury Bubb   Dorchester DT2 0NJ   Dorset
Tel: (01935) 83672   Open: ALL YEAR (Excl. Xmas & New Year)   Map Ref No. 09

Woodwalls House

Near Rd: A.356, A.37

Woodwalls is a pretty country house set in 12 acres of its own grounds, surrounded by wild flower meadows, woods & fields, creating a haven of peace & tranquillity. 2 light, airy bedrooms, 1 double en-suite & 1 twin with private bathroom, each with colour T.V. & tea/coffee-making facilities are available for guests. A pretty award-winning pub serving excellent food is within easy reach. Your hosts pride themselves on their breakfasts, which include honey from their own bees & home-made marmalade. A delightful home.
www.bestbandb.co.uk

| £35.00 to £35.00 | N | N | N |

Mrs S Valdes-Scott   Woodwalls House   Corscombe   Dorchester DT2 0NT   Dorset
Tel: (01935) 891477   Fax 01935 891477   Open: ALL YEAR (Excl. Xmas)   Map Ref No.10

Whites Dairy House

Near Rd: A.35, A.352

Nestling in the lovely Piddle Valley, a warm welcome awaits guests at the oldest house in the village (1622) with its ancient beams & interesting features. Outside a charming stream runs at the bottom of the garden. The old stables have recently been converted to provide high-quality en-suite rooms, each with T.V., radio & tea/coffee facilities. There are 4 pubs with excellent restaurants within 3 1/2 miles, 1 within easy walking distance. Children over 12. Animals by arrangement.
E-mail: robin.adeney@care4free.net
www.whitesdairyhouse.co.uk

| £27.50 to £35.00 | Y | N | Y |

VISA: M'CARD: AMEX:

Liz & Robin Adeney   Whites Dairy House   High Street   Piddlehinton Dorchester DT2 7TD   Dorset
Tel: (01300) 348386   Open: ALL YEAR (Excl. Xmas & New Year)   Map Ref No. 11

The Red House

Near Rd: A.3052

This distinguished house, set in mature grounds, enjoys spectacular coastal views, & yet is only a short walk to the centre of Lyme Regis. The 3 en-suite bedrooms (1 for family use; 2 are especially spacious) are furnished with every comfort, including tea/coffee makers, T.V., clock-radio, desk, armchairs, a drink refrigerator, central heating & electric heaters. Fresh flowers & magazines are among the little extras. Breakfast can be taken on the garden balcony. Parking. Children over 8.
E-mail: red.house@virgin.net
www.SmoothHound.co.uk/hotels/redhous2.html

| £22.00 to £29.00 | Y | N | N |

VISA: M'CARD:

Tony & Vicky Norman   The Red House   Sidmouth Road   Lyme Regis DT7 3ES   Dorset
Tel: (01297) 442055   Fax 01297 442055   Open: Mid MAR - Early NOV   Map Ref No. 12

Brambles. Woolcombe.

Dorset

rate £ from - to per person
children taken
evening meals
animals taken

Rashwood Lodge

| | £22.00 to £30.00 | Y | N | N |

Near Rd: A.3052

Rashwood Lodge is an unusual octagonal house, located on the western hillside with views over Lyme Bay. Just a short walk away is the coastal footpath & Ware Cliff, famed for its part in 'The French Lieutenant's Woman'. The attractive bedrooms have their own facilities & benefit from their south-facing aspect overlooking a large & colourful garden set in peaceful surroundings. Golf course 1 mile. Rashwood Lodge is a charming home. Children over 4 years welcome.
www.bestbandb.co.uk

Mrs Diana Lake   Rashwood Lodge   Clappentail Lane   Lyme Regis DT7 3LZ   Dorset
Tel: (01297) 445700   Open: FEB - NOV   Map Ref No. 12

Cliff House

| | £30.00 to £35.00 | Y | N | N |

Near Rd: A.30, A.350

Cliff House is a spacious Regency Grade II listed property set in an acre of peaceful mature garden. Within walking distance of the historic Saxon town with magnificent views & the famous Gold Hill. An ideal position for visiting the beautiful surrounding countryside, historic houses, towns & villages with cathedrals & abbeys. Both bedrooms are attractive with en-suite bathrooms. A delicious full English breakfast is served with home-made jams, or choose kippers or haddock for a change. Children over 5.
E-mail: dianaepow@aol.com
www.cliff-house.co.uk

Diana Pow   Cliff House   Breach Lane   Shaftesbury SP7 8LF   Dorset
Tel: (01747) 852548   Mobile 07990 574849   Fax 01747 852548   Open: ALL YEAR   Map Ref No. 13

The Old Vicarage

| | £30.00 to £54.00 | Y | Y | Y |

Near Rd: A.30

The Old Vicarage is a gothic Victorian building, set in 3 1/2 acres of grounds on the edge of a charming village. It is 2 miles from the historic town of Sherborne & affords magnificent views of open country. All of the 6 bedrooms are stylishly decorated & have en-suite facilities. The large lounge is beautifully furnished with antiques. On Friday & Saturday evenings, one of the owners, a highly acclaimed chef, prepares dinner. All inclusive weekend breaks are available. Children over 5.
E-mail: theoldvicarage@milborneport.freeserve.co.uk
www.milborneport.freeserve.co.uk

VISA: M'CARD: AMEX:

Jorgen Kunath & Anthony Ma   The Old Vicarage   Sherborne Road   Milborne Port   Sherborne DT9 5AT
Tel: (01963) 251117   Fax 01963 251515   Open: FEB - DEC   Map Ref No. 14

Munden House

| | £32.50 to £49.00 | Y | N | N |

Near Rd: A.3030

A warm welcome awaits you at Munden House. 6 attractively decorated & tastefully furnished bedrooms & a studio annex. Each room has its own bathroom, T.V., tea/coffee facilities etc. It is located in the picturesque Blackmore Vale on the outskirts of Sherborne with its historic castle, Abbey & Almshouses. Golf & tennis close by. Horse-riding a short drive away. Excellent pubs & restaurants. Reflexology, shiatsu & aromatherapy massage available from visiting therapists.
E-mail: sylvia@mundenhouse.demon.co.uk
www.mundenhouse.demon.co.uk

VISA: M'CARD:

Sylvia & Joe Benjamin   Munden House   Munden Lane   Alweston   Sherborne DT9 5HU   Dorset
Tel: (01963) 23150   Fax 01963 23153   Open: ALL YEAR   Map Ref No. 15

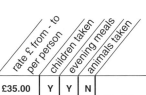

Dorset

rate £ from - to per person	children taken	evening meals taken	animals taken		

Manor Farmhouse

£35.00 to £35.00 — Y | Y | N

(No smoking) VISA: M'CARD:

Near Rd: A.37

This 17th-century farmhouse, with oak panelling, beams & inglenook fireplaces, offers every comfort to the discerning visitor. 3 en-suite bedrooms with modern amenities including T.V. & tea/coffee. Delicious meals served, made from traditional recipes & using fresh local produce. The village is described as the best 17th-century stone-built village in the south of England. An excellent centre for visiting Sherborne, Glastonbury, New Forest & Hardy's Dorset. Children over 12.
E-mail: anneparty@aol.com
www.ann-partridge.co.uk

Mrs Ann Partridge   Manor Farmhouse   High Street   Yetminster   Sherborne DT9 6LF   Dorset
Tel: (01935) 872247   Fax 01935 873017   Open: ALL YEAR   Map Ref No. 16

Stourcastle Lodge

£35.00 to £42.00 — N | Y | N

see PHOTO over p. 134

VISA: M'CARD:

Near Rd: A.357

Stourcastle Lodge is a family-run business, offering a very high standard of accommodation, with personal service & excellent cuisine. A superb breakfast is served in the attractive dining room. All the elegant en-suite bedrooms are south-facing & overlook the delightful garden, which is stocked full of herbaceous & perennial borders. Stourcastle Lodge is a beautiful home, & an ideal base for exploring Dorset & its many attractions.
E-mail: enquiries@stourcastle-lodge.co.uk
www.stourcastle-lodge.co.uk

Jill & Ken Hookham-Bassett   Stourcastle Lodge   Gough's Close   Sturminster Newton DT10 1BU
Tel: (01258) 472320   Fax 01258 473381   Open: ALL YEAR   Map Ref No. 17

Gold Court House

£27.50 to £37.50 — Y | Y | N

Near Rd: A.351

Gold Court House is a charming Georgian house with walled garden on a small square on the south-side of Wareham. It offers 3 light & airy double or twin rooms with private bathrooms & all facilities at hand, at your request. Wareham is ideally situated for exploring the magnificent coastline of South Dorset & the Isle of Purbeck. Anthea & Michael are always pleased to help & advise on the numerous places of interest, sporting activities & where to dine. (Evening meals are available during the winter only.) Children over 10 years.

Anthea & Michael Hipwell   Gold Court House   St. John's Hill   Wareham BH20 4LZ   Dorset
Tel: (01929) 553320 Fax 01929 553320   Open: ALL YEAR (Excl. Xmas & New Year) Map Ref No. 18

Gatton House

£24.00 to £38.00 — Y | N | N

(No smoking) VISA: M'CARD:

Near Rd: A.352

Spectacularly positioned, quiet & comfortable, this small hotel is set amongst the Purbeck Hills, yet only a strolling distance from famous Lulworth Cove. The house has a spacious breakfast room, 8 attractive bedrooms (all en-suite) & a lounge with T.V.. Outside, the terrace provides a perfect venue for morning coffee or afternoon tea. Gatton House is an ideal location for walking or touring Dorset's beauty spots, & it is within easy reach of Bournemouth, Poole, Swanage, Dorchester & Weymouth.
E-mail: avril@gattonhouse.co.uk
www.gattonhouse.co.uk

Mike & Avril Dale   Gatton House   Main Road   West Lulworth   Wareham BH20 5RL   Dorset
Tel: (01929) 400252   Fax 01929 400252   Open: MAR - OCT   Map Ref No. 19

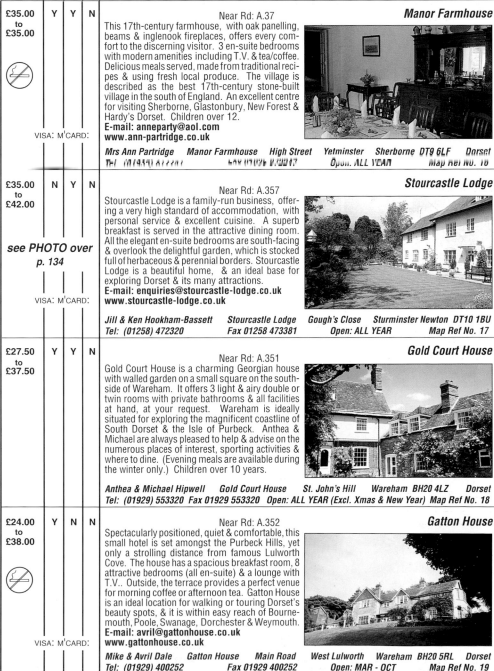

Stourcastle Lodge. Sturminster Newton.

rate £ from - to per person	children taken	evening meals	animals taken	
£23.00 to £26.00	Y	N	N	**Thornhill**

Near Rd: A.31

Visitors are warmly welcomed to this large, thatched family house located in rural surroundings 3 1/2 miles from Wimborne. Large garden. Hard tennis court available. Double, twin & single rooms. 1 private bathroom, & another which may be shared. Sitting room with colour T.V. & coffee/tea-making & laundry facilities. Plenty of good local pubs. Well situated for exploring the coast, New Forest & Salisbury area. Children over 12 years welcome.
E-mail: scturnbull@lineone.net
www.bestbandb.co.uk

John & Sara Turnbull　*Thornhill*　*Holt*　*Wimborne BH21 7DJ*　*Dorset*
Tel: (01202) 889434　Open: ALL YEAR　Map Ref No. 20

All the establishments mentioned in this guide are members of
The Worldwide Bed & Breakfast Association

When booking your accommodation please mention
The Best Bed & Breakfast

Gloucestershire

Gloucestershire
(Heart of England)

The landscape is so varied the people speak not of one Gloucestershire but of three - Cotswold, Vale & Forest. The rounded hills of the Cotswolds sweep & fold in graceful compositions to form a soft & beautiful landscape in which nestle many pretty villages. To the east there are wonderful views of the Vale of Berkeley & Severn, & across to the dark wooded slopes of the Forest of Dean on the Welsh borders.

Hill Forts, ancient trackways & long barrows of neolithic peoples can be explored, & remains of many villas from late Roman times can be seen. A local saying "Scratch Gloucester & find Rome" reveals the lasting influence of the Roman presence. Three major roads mark the path of invasion & settlement. Akeman street leads to London, Ermine street & the Fosse Way to the north east. A stretch of Roman road with its original surface can be seen at Blackpool Bridge in the Forest of Dean, & Cirencester's museum reflects its status as the second most important Roman city in the country.

Offa's Dyke, 80 miles of bank & ditch on the Welsh border was the work of the Anglo-Saxons of Mercia who invaded in the wake of the Romans. Cotswold means "hills of the sheepcotes" in the Anglo-Saxon tongue, & much of the heritage of the area has its roots in the wealth created by the wool industry here.

Fine Norman churches such as those at Tewkesbury & Bishops Cleeve were overshadowed by the development of the perpendicular style of building made possible by the growing prosperity. Handsome 15th century church towers crown many wool towns & villages as at Northleach, Chipping Camden & Cirencester, & Gloucester has a splendid 14th century cathedral. Detailing on church buildings gives recognition to the source of the wealth-cloth-workers shears are depicted on the north west buttresses of Grantham church tower & couchant rams decorate church buttresses at Compton Bedale.

Wool & cloth weaving dominated life here in the 14th & 15th centuries with most families dependent on the industry. The cottage craft of weaving was gradually overtaken by larger looms & water power. A water mill can be seen in the beautiful village of Lower Slaughter & the cottages of Arlington Row in Bibury were a weaving factory.

The Cotswold weaving industry gave way to the growing force of the Lancashire mills but a few centres survive. At Witney you can still buy the locally made blankets for which the town is famous.

From the 16th century the wealthy gentry built parks & mansions. Amongst the most notable are the Jacobean Manor house at Stanway & the contrasting Palladian style mansion at Barnsley Park. Elizabethan timber frame buildings can be seen at Didbrook, Dymock & Deerhurst but houses in the local mellow golden limestone are more common, with Chipping Camden providing excellent examples.

Cheltenham was only a village when, in 1716 a local farmer noticed a flock of pigeons pecking at grains of salt around a saline spring in his fields. He began to bottle & sell the water & in 1784 his son-in-law, Henry Skillicorne, built a pump room & the place received the name of Cheltenham Spa. Physicians published treatises on the healing qualities of the waters, visitors began to flock there & Cheltenham grew in style & elegance.

Gloucestershire

Gloucestershire Gazeteer

Areas of outstanding natural beauty
The Cotswolds, Malvern Hills & the Wye Valley.

Houses & Castles

Ashleworth Court - Ashleworth
15th century limestone Manor house.

Badminton House - Badminton
Built in the reign of Charles II.
Stone newel staircase.

Berkeley Castle - Berkeley
12th century castle - still occupied by the Berkeley family. Magnificent collections of furniture, paintings, tapestries & carved timber work. Lovely terraced gardens & deer park.

Chavenage - Tetbury
Elizabethan Cotswold Manor house, Cromwellian associations.

Clearwell Castle - Nr. Coleford
A Georgian neo-Gothic house said to be oldest in Britain, recently restored.

Court House - Painswick
Cotswold Manor house - has original court room & bedchamber of Charles I. Splendid panelling & antique furniture.

Dodington House - Chipping Sodbury
Perfect 18th century house with superb staircase.   Landscape by Capability Brown.

Horton Court - Horton
Cotswold manor house altered & restored in 19th century.

Kelmscott Manor - Nr. Lechlade
16th century country house - 17th century additions. Examples of work of William Morris, Rosetti & Burne-Jones.

Owlpen Manor - Nr. Dursley
Historic group of traditional Cotswold stone buildings. Tudor Manor house with church, barn, court house & a grist mill. Holds a rare set of 17th century painted cloth wall hangings.

Snowshill Manor - Broadway
Tudor house with 17th century facade. Unique collection of musical instruments & clocks, toys, etc. Formal garden.

Sudeley Castle - Winchcombe
12th century - home of Katherine Parr, is rich in historical associations, contains art treasures & relics of bygone days.

Cathedrals & Churches

Bishops Cleeve (St. Michael & All Saints)
12th century with 17th century gallery. Magnificent Norman west front & south porch. Decorated chancel.   Fine window.

Bledington (St.Leonards)
15th century glass in this perpendicular church, Norman bellcote. Early English east window.

Buckland (St. Michael)
10th century nave arcades. 17th century oak panelling, 15th century glass.

Cirencester (St. John the Baptist)
A magnificent church - remarkable exterior, 3 storey porch, 2 storey oriel windows, traceries & pinnacles. Wine-glass pulpit c.1450. 15th century glass in east window, monuments in Lady chapel.

Gloucester Cathedral
Birthplace of Perpendicular style in 14th century. Fan vaulting, east windows commemorate Battle of Crecy - Norman Chapter House.

Hailes Abbey - Winchcombe
14th century wall paintings, 15th century tiles, glass & screen, 17th century pulpit. Elizabethan benches.

Iron Acton (St. James the Less)
Perpendicular - 15th century memorial cross. 19th century mosaic floors, Laudian alter rails, Jacobean pulpit, effigies.

Newland (All Saints)
13th century, restored 18th century. Pinnacled west tower, effigies.

Prinknash Abbey - Gloucester
14th & 16th century - Benedictine Abbey.

Tewkesbury Abbey - Tewkesbury
Dates back to Norman times, contains Romanesque & Gothic styles. 14th century monuments.

Yate (St. Mary)
Splendid perpendicular tower.

Museums & Galleries

Bishop Hooper's Lodgings - Gloucester
3 Tudor timber frame buildings - museum of domestic life & agriculture in Gloucester since 1500.

Bourton Motor Museum - Bourton-on-the-Water
Collection of cars & motor cycles.

Cheltenham Art Gallery - Cheltenham.

Gloucestershire

Lower Slaughter.

Gallery of Dutch paintings, collection of oils, watercolours, pottery, porcelain, English & Chinese; furniture.
City Wall & Bastion - Gloucester
Roman & mediaeval city defences in an underground exhibition room.
Stroud Museum - Cirencester
Depicts earlier settlements in the area & has a very fine collection of Roman antiquities.

Historic Monuments

Chedworth Roman Villa - Yanworth
Remains of Romano-British villa.
Belas Knap Long Barrow - Charlton Abbots
Neolithic burial ground - three burial chambers with external entrances.
Hailes Abbey - Stanway
Ruins of beautiful mediaeval abbey built by son of King John, 1246.
Witcombe Roman Villa - Nr. Birdlip

Large Roman villa - Hypocaust & mosaic pavements preserved.
Ashleworth Tithe Barn - Ashleworth
15th century tithe barn - 120 feet long - stone built, interesting roof timbering.
Odda's Chapel - Deerhurst
Rare Saxon chapel dating back to 1056.
Hetty Pegler's Tump - UleLong Barrow- fairly complete, chamber is 120 feet long.

Other things to see & do

Cheltenham International Festival of Music & Literature - Annual event.
Cotswolds Farm Park - dozens of rare breeds of farm animals.
The Three Choirs Festival - music festival staged in alternating years at Gloucester, Hereford & Worcester Cathedrals.
Slimbridge - Peter Scott's Wildfowl Trust.

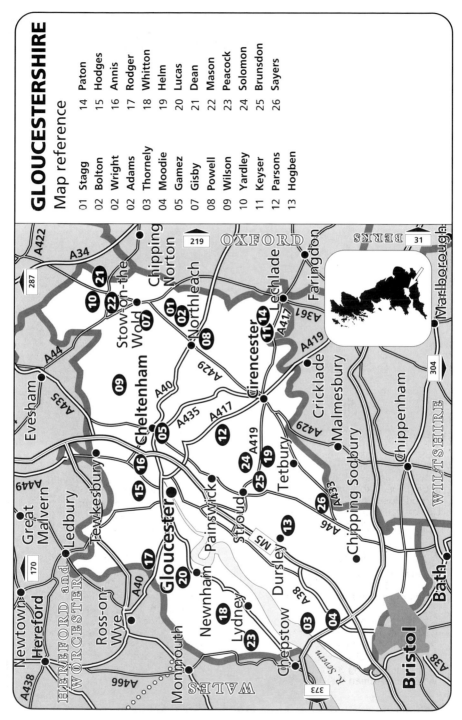

GLOUCESTERSHIRE

Map reference

01	Stagg	14	Paton
02	Bolton	15	Hodges
02	Wright	16	Annis
02	Adams	17	Rodger
03	Thornely	18	Whitton
04	Moodie	19	Helm
05	Gamez	20	Lucas
07	Gisby	21	Dean
08	Powell	22	Mason
09	Wilson	23	Peacock
10	Yardley	24	Solomon
11	Keyser	25	Brunsdon
12	Parsons	26	Sayers
13	Hogben		

Clapton Manor. Clapton on the Hill.

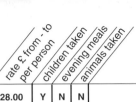

rate £ from - to per person | children taken | evening meals | animals taken

---

| £28.00 to £32.00 | Y | N | N |

🚭

VISA: M'CARD:

Coombe House

Near Rd: A.429

A charming, peaceful house in lovely gardens with 1st floor sun terrace. 5 mins' easy riverside walk from the centre of the village & restaurants. 6 pretty en-suite bedrooms thoughtfully equipped with plenty of welcoming extras. Guests sitting room & attractive dining room where traditional/ continental breakfast is served. Parking. Licensed. Perfect for exploring the Cotswolds, Hidcote Gardens, Sudeley Castle, Oxford, Blenheim, Stratford-upon-Avon & Warwick Castle. Children over 12.
E-mail: coombe.house@virgin.net
www.2staggs.com

Richard & Pat Stagg   Coombe House   Rissington Road   Bourton-on-the-Water GL54 2DT
Tel (01451) 821900   Fax (01451) 810022   Open: FEB - NOV   Map Ref No. 07

| £40.00 to £50.00 | Y | Y | N |

🚭

see PHOTO over p. 140

VISA: M'CARD:

Clapton Manor

Near Rd: A.40, A.429

Clapton Manor dates from the 16th century & stands at the top of a quiet village with stunning views over the Windrush valley. It is an informal, very comfortable & welcoming family home with massive inglenook fireplaces & old oak beams. Guests have the use of a private sitting room with log fire, a dining room with a Tudor fireplace & 2 delightful, light & airy en-suite rooms, 1 of which has a secret door to its bathroom & the other overlooks the garden. Dinner by arrangement.
E-mail: bandb@claptonmanor.co.uk
www.claptonmanor.co.uk

James & Karin Bolton   Clapton Manor   Clapton-on-the-Hill   Bourton-on-the-Water GL54 2LG
Tel: (01451) 810202 Fax 01451 821804 Open: ALL YEAR (Excl. Xmas & New Year) Map Ref No. 02

| £22.00 to £25.00 | Y | N | N |

🚭

Farncombe

Near Rd: A.429

Come & share the peace, tranquillity & superb views of Farncombe, & eat, drink & sleep - smoke-free - 700ft above sea level & only 2 miles from Bourton-on-the-Water. There are 2 attractive doubles with showers, & 1 twin en-suite. A spacious dining room, with tea/coffee-making facilities, & a comfortable T.V. lounge. Tourist information, maps & books, & current menus for your choice when eating out. Numerous walks & drives, with easy access to all attractions & places of interest. Children over 11.
E-mail: JWRIGHTbb@aol.com

Julia Wright   Farncombe   Clapton-on-the-Hill   Bourton-on-the-Water GL54 2LG   Gloucestershire
Tel: (01451) 820120   Mobile 07714 703142   Fax 01451 820120   Open: ALL YEAR   Map Ref No. 02

| £25.00 to £25.00 | Y | N | N |

🚭

Upper Farm

Near Rd: A.40, A.429

For almost 3 decades guests worldwide have recommended & returned to Upper Farm. A beautiful family home offering exceptional accommodation in a 17th-century stone farmhouse; lovingly restored yet retaining a wealth of original charm & character. Bedrooms, all with en-suite/private bathrooms, are tastefully designed with attention to detail. Your hosts take great pride in providing the best & the panoramic views complement the experience. Children over 5 years welcome.
www.bestbandb.co.uk

Helen Adams   Upper Farm   Clapton-on-the-Hill   Bourton-on-the-Water GL54 2LG   Gloucestershire
Tel: (01451) 820453   Fax 01451 810185   Open: FEB - DEC (Excl. Xmas)   Map Ref No. 02

The Elms. Olveston.

rate £ from - to per person	children taken	evening meals	animals taken

Eastcote Cottage

£26.00 to £28.00	Y	N	Y

Near Rd: A.38

Eastcote is a charming 200-year-old stone house located in a lovely rural setting, with splendid views across open countryside. Guests have a choice of 2 comfortable bedrooms with modern amenities. A colour-T.V. lounge is available for guests' use. Conveniently situated for the M.4/M.5 interchange for the Cotswolds, with Bristol, Bath, Cheltenham & the Wye Valley easily accessible. Private parking available.
E-mail: nick@nickthornely.co.uk
www.bestbandb.co.uk

Ann Thornely   Eastcote Cottage   Knapp Road East   Thornbury   Bristol BS35 3UE   Gloucestershire
Tel: (01454) 412105   Fax 01454 201010   Open: ALL YEAR (Excl. Xmas)   Map Ref No. 03

The Elms

£35.00 to £40.00	N	N	Y

Near Rd: A.38

An elegant Grade II listed village house set in attractive 2 acre gardens with comfortable suite & a self-contained cottage. Convenient for Bristol, M.4/M.5 interchange. Great emphasis is placed on immaculate, luxurious standards & green issues. Breakfasts are organic when possible. Allergy sufferers are welcome & the environment is kept as pollutant free as possible. Guests are requested not to use scented products. The owners are great animal & garden lovers. Hard tennis court.
E-mail: b&b@theelmsmoodie.co.uk
www.theelmsmoodie.co.uk

see PHOTO over
p. 142

Mr & Mrs David Moodie   The Elms   Olveston   Bristol BS35 4DR   Gloucestershire
Tel: (01454) 614559   Fax 01454 618607   Open: ALL YEAR   Map Ref No. 04

Georgian House

£37.50 to £42.50	N	N	N

Near Rd: A.40

Take 3 beautiful bedrooms in an elegant Georgian home, set them among the charming terraces of Montpellier, only 5 mins' from the Promenade, add a warm welcome from your hosts, Penny & Alex, & there you have Georgian House. Each en-suite room has T.V. with satellite, 'phone with modem socket, ironing facilities, trouser press & fridge. The delicious English breakfasts include fresh fruit - the perfect combination! Parking available.
E-mail: georgian_house@yahoo.com
www.georgianhouse.net

VISA: M'CARD: AMEX:

Penny & Alex Gamez   Georgian House   77 Montpellier Terrace   Cheltenham GL50 1XA   Glos.
Tel: (01242) 515577   Fax 01242 545929   Open: ALL YEAR (Excl. Xmas & New Year)   Map Ref No. 05

Rectory Farmhouse

£35.00 to £42.50	Y	N	N

Near Rd: A.429

Rectory Farmhouse is an historic 17th-century traditional Cotswold farmhouse located in the quiet hamlet of Lower Swell, which lies about 1 mile to the west of Stow-on-the-Wold. It is elegantly furnished throughout & boasts superb double bedrooms with luxurious en-suite bathrooms, enjoying stunning views over open countryside. All bedrooms are centrally heated & have . Chipping Campden & Bourton-on-the-Water are just a short drive away. Cheltenham, Oxford & Stratford-upon-Avon are all easily accessible. Children over 16.
E-mail: rectory.farmhouse@cw-warwick.co.uk

see PHOTO over
p. 144

Sybil Gisby   Rectory Farmhouse   Lower Swell   NR. Stow-on-the-Wold   Cheltenham GL54 1LH
Tel: (01451) 832351   Open: ALL YEAR   Map Ref No. 07

Rectory Farmhouse.   Lower Swell.

rate £ from - to per person	children taken	evening meals	animals taken

---

£27.50 to £37.50

N N N

(no smoking symbol)

VISA: M'CARD:

Cotteswold House

Near Rd: A.40, A.429

Relax in this 400-year-old Cotswold-stone wealthy wool merchant's home with beamed ceilings, original panelling & Tudor archway. It offers the choice of a luxury private suite or en-suite double or twin rooms - all spacious, elegant & well-equipped. Enjoy traditional English food & a friendly welcome. Cotteswold House is in the centre of this ancient market town of Northleach in the centre of the Cotswolds - an ideal touring base.
E-mail: cotteswoldhouse@aol.com
www.cotteswoldhouse.com

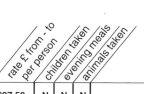

Pauline & Frank Powell   Cotteswold House   Market Place   Northleach   Cheltenham GL54 3EG
Tel: (01451) 860493 Fax 01451 860100   Open: ALL YEAR (Excl. Xmas & New Year)   Map Ref No. 08

£35.00 to £45.00

Y Y Y

(no smoking symbol)

see PHOTO over p. 146

VISA: M'CARD:

Westward

Near Rd: A.40

The Wilson families share this beautiful Grade II listed Georgian house on the scarp of the Cotswolds above Sudeley Castle, sitting within its own 600-acre estate with spectacular views to the Malverns. The heart of the Cotswolds is close, with Broadway, Oxford & Stratford within easy reach. The Wilsons combine good food - Susie trained at Prue Leith's - with elegance & comfort in a relaxed family home. 3 delightful en-suite rooms. Children over 10. Dinner & animals by arrangement.
E-mail: jimw@haldon.co.uk
www.westward-sudeley.co.uk

Mrs Susie Wilson   Westward   Sudeley   Winchcombe   Cheltenham GL54 5JB   Gloucestershire
Tel: (01242) 604372   Fax 01242 604640   Open: ALL YEAR (Excl. Xmas)   Map Ref No. 09

£27.50 to £30.00

Y N N

(no smoking symbol)

VISA: M'CARD:

Nineveh Farm

Near Rd: A.44

This fine Georgian farmhouse, with flagstone floors, beams & antique furnishings, is set in large gardens surrounded by open countryside, close to Mickleton village. Comfortable bedrooms with en-suite/private bath/shower rooms, all have T.V. & tea/coffee tray. Ideally placed for Stratford-upon-Avon & the Cotswolds, Kiftsgate & Hidcote Gardens & other N.T. properties. Warwick Castle, Blenheim Palace, Sudeley Castle & the NEC (40 mins' drive). Children over 8. Single supplement.
E-mail: stay@ninevehfarm.co.uk
www.ninevehfarm.co.uk

Alison & Michael Yardley   Nineveh Farm   Campden Road   Mickleton   Chipping Campden GL55 6PS
Tel: (01386) 438923   Open: ALL YEAR   Map Ref No. 10

£33.00 to £33.00

Y N Y

VISA: M'CARD:

Lady Lamb Farm

Near Rd: A.417

Lady Lamb Farm is a Cotswold-stone farmhouse, surrounded by countryside & situated less than a mile from the small market town of Fairford. 2 attractively furnished guest rooms, each with T.V. & tea/coffee-making facilities. (1 is en-suite.) A swimming pool & tennis court are available. Set on the edge of the Cotswolds, Bath, Oxford & many Cotswold towns, & wonderful gardens are within easy reach. Cotswold Water Park offers a wide range of watersports. Golf, riding & fishing are available nearby. Animals by arrangement.
E-mail: jekeyser1@aol.com

Mrs J. Keyser   Lady Lamb Farm   Meysey Hampton   Cirencester GL7 5LH   Gloucestershire
Tel: (01285) 712206   Fax 01285 712206   Open: ALL YEAR   Map Ref No. 11

Westward. Sudeley.

Column headers (rotated):
- rate £ from - to per person
- children taken
- evening meals taken
- animals taken

£30.00 to £36.00	Y	Y	Y

see PHOTO over p. 148

VISA: M'CARD:

Winstone Glebe

Near Rd: A.417

A small Georgian rectory overlooking a Saxon church in a Domesday-listed village, & enjoying spectacular rural views. Ideal for exploring Cotswold market towns, with their medieval churches, antique shops & rich local history. 3 bedrooms with private/en-suite bathrooms. Being an Area of Outstanding Natural Beauty, there are signposted walks. The more energetic can borrow a bicycle & explore, or just enjoy warm hospitality & good food cooked by Susanna. Single supplement.
E-mail: sparsons@winstoneglebe.com
www.winstoneglebe.com

Shaun & Susanna Parsons   Winstone Glebe   Winstone   Cirencester GL7 7LN   Gloucestershire
Tel. (01285) 821431   Fax 01285 821094   Open: ALL YEAR (Excl. Xmas)   Map Ref No. 12

£30.00 to £30.00	Y	Y	N

(no smoking symbol)

VISA: M'CARD:

The Black Horse

Near Rd: A.38

The Black Horse, a traditionally built Cotswold building, has recently been fully refurbished & now provides a very welcoming atmosphere with a modern interior. 6 comfortably furnished en-suite double rooms with T.V. & tea/coffee-making facilities. Also, a 4-poster honeymoon suite for special occasions. There are 2 restaurants, one specialising in fresh fish. All meals are of the highest quality & are freshly prepared incorporating local produce whenever possible. Berkeley Castle, Slimbridge Wildfowl & Wetlands Trust, Gloucester & Bristol are all within easy reach. Single supplement.

Mr & Mrs E Hogben   The Black Horse   1-3 Barrs Lane   North Nibley   Nr. Dursley GL11 6DT
Tel: (01453) 543777   Fax 01453 546841   Open: ALL YEAR   Map Ref No.13

£20.00 to £35.00	Y	N	Y

(no smoking symbol)

VISA: M'CARD:

Milton Farm

Near Rd: A.417

Milton Farm is an impressive Georgian farmhouse with spacious & distinctive en-suite bedrooms. Situated on the edge of the attractive market town of Fairford, it is a welcoming & ideal base for exploring the Cotswolds. Facilities for business guests & families, special breaks can be arranged for fishermen (fly & course fishing), walkers, cyclists & water sports enthusiasts using the Cotswold Water Park. A working farm with stabling available for horse guests by arrangement.
E-mail:milton@farmersweekly.net
www.milton-farm.co.uk

Suzie Paton   Milton Farm   Fairford GL7 4HZ   Gloucestershire
Tel: (01285) 712205 Fax 01285 711349 Open: ALL YEAR (Excl. Xmas & New Year) Map Ref No.14

£25.00 to £25.00	Y	N	Y

The Old Vicarage

Near Rd: A.38

A Victorian vicarage in 1 3/4 acres of gardens with views towards the Cotswold escarpment & Malvern Hills, & a footpath from a garden gate leading to a riverside pub & the Severn Way. There are 4 delightful rooms (most en-suite) all with T.V., hairdryer, hospitality tray & fridge. An English country house breakfast is served with a log fire burning in the hearth when chilly. A secluded retreat with a relaxed ambience, a short drive from Cheltenham, Gloucester & Tewkesbury.
www.bestbandb.co.uk

Mrs Shirley Hodges   The Old Vicarage   Norton   Gloucester GL2 9LR   Gloucestershire
Tel: (01452) 731214/731818   Fax 01452 739091   Open: ALL YEAR   Map Ref No.15

Winstone Glebe. Winstone.

The Old Farm.   Longhope .

Gloucestershire

Evington Hill Farm

Near Rd: A.38

Crown your Gloucestershire visit at this lovely 16th-century house. Take tea & homemade cake in the sunny conservatory, stay in the antique pine furnished bedrooms with their beautiful new spacious bathrooms. 1 has a 4-poster bed, all have T.V. & hostess tray. The old beamed sitting room with log burning fire is perfect for a relaxing drink. Set in 4 acres with ample parking. Licensed bar. Also, a games room & hard tennis court. 2 holiday cottages available for extended stays.
E-mail: mail@evingtonfarm.freeserve.co.uk
www.evingtonhillfarm.co.uk

£36.00 to £42.00 | Y | N | N

Keith & Joyce Annis   Evington Hill Farm   Tewkesbury Road   The Leigh GL19 4AQ   Gloucestershire
Tel: (01242) 680255   Open: ALL YEAR   Map Ref No. 16

The Old Farm

Near Rd: A.40

Treat yourself to a stay in this charming 16th-century farmhouse with its wealth of beams, fireplaces & character. Relax with afternoon tea in front of the fire or in the sunny garden. All bedrooms are en-suite including 4-poster. Sumptuous breakfasts made from local produce including free-range eggs from your host's hens. Ideal for visiting the Royal Forest of Dean, Cheltenham, Gloucester, & the Cotswolds. Good pubs & restaurants. Children over 12. Animals by arrangement
E-mail: BBB@the-old-farm.co.uk
www.the-old-farm.co.uk

£23.00 to £29.00 | Y | N | Y

see PHOTO over
p. 149

VISA: M'CARD:

Lucy Rodger   The Old Farm   Barrel Lane   Longhope GL17 0LR   Gloucestershire
Tel: (01452) 830252   Fax 01452 830255   Open: ALL YEAR   Map Ref No. 17

Edale House

Near Rd: A.48

Edale House is a fine Georgian residence facing the cricket green in the village of Parkend at the heart of the Royal Forest of Dean. Once the home of local G.P. Bill Tandy, author of 'A Doctor in the Forest', the house has been tastefully restored to provide comfortable en-suite accommodation with every facility for guests. Enjoy delicious & imaginative cuisine prepared by your hosts. Fully licensed. Children over 12. Animals by arrangement.
E-mail: enquiry@edalehouse.co.uk
www.edalehouse.co.uk

£23.00 to £28.50 | Y | Y | Y

VISA: M'CARD: AMEX:

Pat & Brian Whitton   Edale House   Folly Road   Parkend   Nr. Lydney GL15 4JF   Gloucestershire
Tel: (01594) 562835   Fax 01594 564488   Open: ALL YEAR   Map Ref No. 18

Hunters Lodge

Near Rd: A.46, A.419

A friendly and helpful welcome is assured for guests at this beautifully furnished Cotswold stone country house situated adjoining 600 acres of National Trust common land and a golf course. Central heating. All bedrooms have T.V., tea/coffee facilities & en-suite/private bathrooms. A visitors' lounge, with T.V., adjoins a delightful conservatory overlooking the garden. An ideal centre for Bath, Cheltenham, Cirencester & the Cotswolds. Peter is a registered tourist guide. Children over 10.
E-mail: hunterslodge@hotmail.com

£25.00 to £27.00 | Y | N | N

see PHOTO over
p. 151

Margaret & Peter Helm   Hunters Lodge   Dr. Browns Road   Minchinhampton GL6 9BT   Glos.
Tel: (01453) 883588   Fax 01453 731449   Open: ALL YEAR (Excl. Xmas)   Map Ref No. 19

Hunters Lodge. Minchinhampton.

Gunn Mill House. Mitcheldean.

rate £ from - to per person	children taken	evening meals	animals taken

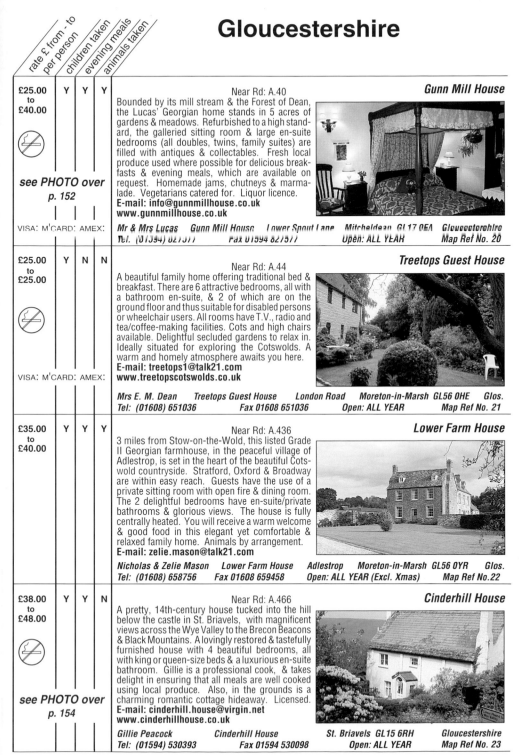

£25.00 to £40.00 Y Y Y

🚭

see PHOTO over p. 152

VISA: M'CARD: AMEX:

Gunn Mill House

Near Rd: A.40

Bounded by its mill stream & the Forest of Dean, the Lucas' Georgian home stands in 5 acres of gardens & meadows. Refurbished to a high standard, the galleried sitting room & large en-suite bedrooms (all doubles, twins, family suites) are filled with antiques & collectables. Fresh local produce used where possible for delicious breakfasts & evening meals, which are available on request. Homemade jams, chutneys & marmalade. Vegetarians catered for. Liquor licence.
E-mail: info@gunnmillhouse.co.uk
www.gunnmillhouse.co.uk

Mr & Mrs Lucas Gunn Mill House Lower Spout Lane Mitcheldean GL17 0EA Gloucestershire
Tel. (01594) 827577 Fax 01594 827577 Open: ALL YEAR Map Ref No. 20

£25.00 to £25.00 Y N N

🚭

VISA: M'CARD: AMEX:

Treetops Guest House

Near Rd: A.44

A beautiful family home offering traditional bed & breakfast. There are 6 attractive bedrooms, all with a bathroom en-suite, & 2 of which are on the ground floor and thus suitable for disabled persons or wheelchair users. All rooms have T.V., radio and tea/coffee-making facilities. Cots and high chairs available. Delightful secluded gardens to relax in. Ideally situated for exploring the Cotswolds. A warm and homely atmosphere awaits you here.
E-mail: treetops1@talk21.com
www.treetopscotswolds.co.uk

Mrs E. M. Dean Treetops Guest House London Road Moreton-in-Marsh GL56 0HE Glos.
Tel: (01608) 651036 Fax 01608 651036 Open: ALL YEAR Map Ref No. 21

£35.00 to £40.00 Y Y Y

Lower Farm House

Near Rd: A.436

3 miles from Stow-on-the-Wold, this listed Grade II Georgian farmhouse, in the peaceful village of Adlestrop, is set in the heart of the beautiful Cotswold countryside. Stratford, Oxford & Broadway are within easy reach. Guests have the use of a private sitting room with open fire & dining room. The 2 delightful bedrooms have en-suite/private bathrooms & glorious views. The house is fully centrally heated. You will receive a warm welcome & good food in this elegant yet comfortable & relaxed family home. Animals by arrangement.
E-mail: zelie.mason@talk21.com

Nicholas & Zelie Mason Lower Farm House Adlestrop Moreton-in-Marsh GL56 0YR Glos.
Tel: (01608) 658756 Fax 01608 659458 Open: ALL YEAR (Excl. Xmas) Map Ref No.22

£38.00 to £48.00 Y Y N

🚭

see PHOTO over p. 154

Cinderhill House

Near Rd: A.466

A pretty, 14th-century house tucked into the hill below the castle in St. Briavels, with magnificent views across the Wye Valley to the Brecon Beacons & Black Mountains. A lovingly restored & tastefully furnished house with 4 beautiful bedrooms, all with king or queen-size beds & a luxurious en-suite bathroom. Gillie is a professional cook, & takes delight in ensuring that all meals are well cooked using local produce. Also, in the grounds is a charming romantic cottage hideaway. Licensed.
E-mail: cinderhill.house@virgin.net
www.cinderhillhouse.co.uk

Gillie Peacock Cinderhill House St. Briavels GL15 6RH Gloucestershire
Tel: (01594) 530393 Fax 01594 530098 Open: ALL YEAR Map Ref No. 23

Cinderhill House. St. Briavels.

rate £ from - to per person	children taken	evening meals	animals taken		

Pretoria Villa

| £25.00 to £25.00 | Y | Y | N |
| 🚭 | | | |

Near Rd: A.419

Enjoy luxurious bed & breakfast in a relaxed family country house set in peaceful secluded gardens. Spacious bedrooms, with en-suite/private facilities. Hospitality trays, hairdryers & bathrobes in all rooms. Guests have their own comfortable lounge & delicious breakfasts are served in the dining room. Evening meals by prior arrangement, although many good eating places nearby. An ideal base from which to explore the Cotswolds. Personal service & your comfort are guaranteed.
E-mail: glynis@gsolomon.freeserve.co.uk

Mrs Glynis Solomon Pretoria Villa Wells Road Eastcombe Stroud GL6 7EE Gloucestershire
Tel: (01162) 770105 Fax 01452 770403 Open: ALL YEAR (Excl. Xmas) Map Ref No. 24

Hope Cottage

| £25.00 to £30.00 | Y | N | N |
| 🚭 | | | |

see PHOTO over p. 156

Near Rd: A.46, A.419

For peace & tranquillity, this charming, undiscovered village 10 miles from Cirencester is unrivalled. Box is in an Area of Outstanding Natural Beauty enjoying glorious Cotswold views. Here you can savour the charm of this delightful country house, set in 3 acres of landscaped gardens & with a heated pool. Lovely en-suite rooms all with king-size bed, settee, T.V. & hospitality tray. Sumptuous English breakfasts. Good local restaurants & pubs. Strategic base for walking & touring.
E-mail: garth.brunsdon@virgin.net

Sheila & Garth Brunsdon Hope Cottage Box Nr. Stroud GL6 9HD Gloucestershire
Tel: (01453) 832076 Open: FEB - NOV Map Ref No. 25

The Old Rectory

| £27.50 to £27.50 | N | N | N |
| 🚭 | | | |

Near Rd: A.433

The Old Rectory (Grade II listed) is a charming home, where a happy & relaxed atmosphere prevails. The friendly hosts offer very comfortable accommodation in 3 attractive bedrooms, each with an en-suite/private bathroom & T.V.. Also, a cosy lounge with T.V. & a pretty garden in which guests may choose to relax. A delicious breakfast is served. The Old Rectory is an ideal base from which to explore this beautiful region & its many attractions. Single supplement.
E-mail: mt@febcentral.com

Marie-Teresa Sayers The Old Rectory Didmarton Tetbury GL9 1DS Gloucestershire
Tel: (01454) 238233 Fax 01454 238909 Open: ALL YEAR (Excl. Xmas & New Year) Map Ref No. 26

Visit our website at:
http://www.bestbandb.co.uk

Hope Cottage. Box.

Hampshire & Isle of Wight

Hampshire
(Southern)

Hampshire is located in the centre of the south coast of England & is blessed with much beautiful & unspoilt countryside. Wide open vistas of rich downland contrast with deep woodlands. Rivers & sparkling streams run through tranquil valleys passing nestling villages. There is a splendid coastline with seaside resorts & harbours, the cathedral city of Winchester & the "jewel" of Hampshire, the Isle of Wight.

The north of the county is known as the Hampshire Borders. Part of this countryside was immortalised by Richard Adams & the rabbits of 'Watership Down'. Beacon Hill is a notable hill-top landmark. From its slopes some of the earliest aeroplane flights were made by De Haviland in 1909. Pleasure trips & tow-path walks can be taken along the restored Basingstoke Canal.

The New Forest is probably the area most frequented by visitors. It is a landscape of great character with thatched cottages, glades & streams & a romantic beauty. There are herds of deer & the New Forest ponies wander at will. To the N.W. of Beaulieu are some of the most idyllic parts of the old forest, with fewer villages & many little streams that flow into the Avon. Lyndhurst, the "capital" of the New Forest offers a range of shops & has a contentious 19th century church constructed in scarlet brickwork banded with yellow, unusual ornamental decoration, & stained glass windows by William Morris.

The Roman city of Winchester became the capital city of Saxon Wessex & is today the capital of Hampshire. It is famous for its beautiful mediaeval cathedral, built during the reign of William the Conquerer & his notorious son Rufus. It contains the great Winchester Bible.

William completed the famous Domesday Book in the city, & Richard Coeur de Lion was crowned in the cathedral in 1194.

Portsmouth & Southampton are major ports & historic maritime cities with a wealth of castles, forts & Naval attractions from battleships to museums.

The channel of the Solent guarded by Martello towers, holds not only Southampton but numerous yachting centres, such as Hamble, Lymington & Bucklers Hard where the ships for Admiral Lord Nelson's fleet were built.

The River Test.

The Isle of Wight

The Isle of Wight lies across the sheltered waters of the Solent, & is easily reached by car or passenger ferry. The chalk stacks of the Needles & the multi-coloured sand at Alum Bay are among the best known of the island's natural attractions & there are many excellent beaches & other bays to enjoy. Cowes is a famous international sailing centre with a large number of yachting events throughout the summer. Ventnor, the most southerly resort is known as the "Madeira of England" & has an exotic botanic garden. Inland is an excellent network of footpaths & trails & many castles, manors & stately homes.

Hampshire & Isle of Wight

Hampshire

Gazeteer

Areas of outstanding natural beauty.
East & South Hampshire, North Wessex
Downs & Chichester Harbour.

Houses & Castles

Avington Park - Winchester
16th century red brick house, enlarged in
17th century by the addition of two wings
& a classical portico. Stateroom, ballroom
with wonderful ceiling. Red drawing room,
library, etc.

Beaulieu Abbey & Palace House -
Beaulieu
12th century Cistercian abbey - the
original gatehouse of abbey converted to
palace house 1538. Houses historic car
museum.

Breamore House - Breamore
16th century Elizabethan Manor House,
tapestries, furniture, paintings. Also
museum.

Jane Austen's Home - Chawston
Personal effects of the famous writer.

Broadlands - Romsey
16th century - park & garden created by
Capability Brown. Home of the Earl
Mountbatten of Burma.

Mottisfont Abbey - Nr. Romsey
12th century Augustinian Priory until
Dissolution. Painting by Rex Whistler
trompe l'oeil in Gothic manner.

Stratfield Saye House - Reading
17th century house presented to the Duke
of Wellington 1817. Now contains his
possessions - also wild fowl sanctuary.

Sandham Memorial Chapel - Sandham,
Nr. Newbury
Paintings by Stanley Spencer cover the
walls.

The Vyne - Sherbourne St. John
16th century red brick chapel with
Renaissance glass & rare linenfold
panelling. Alterations made in 1654 -
classical portico. Palladian staircase
dates form 1760.

West Green House - Hartley Wintney
18th century red brick house set in a
walled garden.

Appuldurcombe House - Wroxall, Isle of
Wight
The only house in the 'Grand Manner' on
the island. Beautiful English baroque east
facade. House now an empty shell
standing in fine park.

Osbourne House - East Cowes, Isle of
Wight
Queen Victoria's seaside residence.

Carisbrooke Castle - Isle of Wight
Oldest parts 12th century, but there was a
wooden castle on the mound before that.
Museum in castle.

Cathedrals & Churches

Winchester Cathedral
Largest Gothic church in Europe. Norman
& perpendicular styles, three sets of
mediaeval paintings, marble font c.1180.
Stalls c.1320 with 60 misericords.
Extensive mediaeval tiled floor.

Breamore (St. Mary) - Breamore
10th century Saxon. Double splayed
windows, stone rood.

East Meon (All Saints)
15th century rebuilding of Norman fabric.
Tournai marble front.

Idsworth (St. Hubert)
16th century chapel - 18th century bell
turret. 14th century paintings in chancel.

Pamber (dedication unknown)
Early English - Norman central tower, 15th
central pews, wooden effigy of knight
c.1270.

Romsey (St. Mary & St. Ethelfleda)
Norman - 13th century effigy of a lady -
Saxon rood & carving of crucifixion, 16th
century painted reredos.

Silchester (St. Mary)
Norman, perpendicular, 14th century effigy
of a lady, 15th century screen, Early
English chancel with painted patterns on
south window splays, Jacobean pulpit with
domed canopy.

Winchester (St. Cross)
12th century. Original chapel to Hospital.
Style changing from Norman at east to
decorated at west. Tiles, glass,
wall painting.

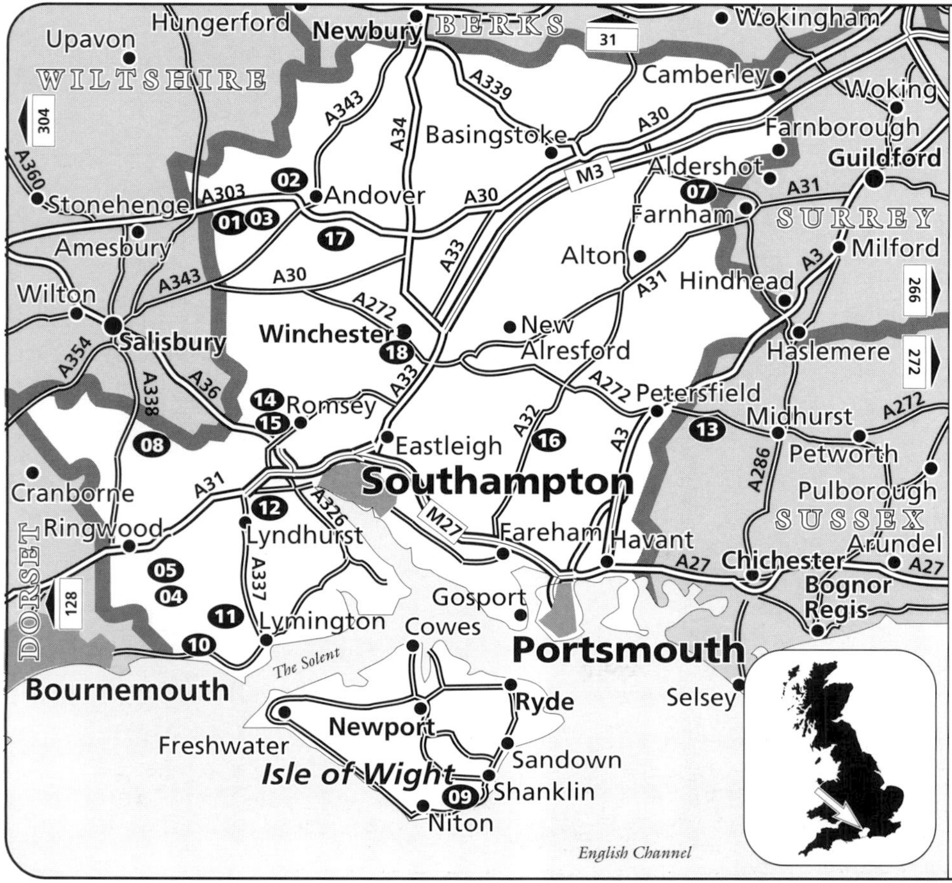

HAMPSHIRE
Map reference

01 Mallam
02 Biddolph
08 Chetwynd-T.
04 Ford
05 Buckley
07 Tose
03 Cadman
09 Pritchett
1C Iles

11 Barnfield
12 Ames
13 Baigent
14 Lightfoot
15 Hughes
16 Taylor
17 Talbot
18 Pollock

English Channel

159

May Cottage.   Thruxton.

rate £ from - to per person	children taken	evening meals taken	animals taken

---

| £30.00 to £30.00 | Y | N | N |

🚭

VISA: M'CARD:

Broadwater

Near Rd: A.303

Broadwater is a 17th-century, listed, thatched cottage situated in a peaceful unspoilt village just off the A.303. It is an ideal base for sightseeing in Hampshire, with easy access to the West Country & London. The cottage offers 2 delightful, double/twin-bedded rooms, both with en-suite facilities. Guests have a private & very comfortable sitting/dining room with a traditional open log fire & a very pretty garden to enjoy. Homemade bread. T.V..
E-mail: broadwater@dmac.co.uk
www.bestbandb.co.uk

Mrs Carolyn Mallam   Broadwater   Amport   Nr. Andover SP11 8AY   Hampshire
Tel: (01264) 772240   Fax 01264 772240   Open: ALL YEAR   Map Ref No. 01

| £30.00 to £40.00 | Y | N | N |

🚭

see PHOTO over p. 160

May Cottage

Near Rd: A.303

May Cottage dates back to 1740 & is situated in the heart of this picturesque tranquil village with Post Office & old inn. A most comfortable home with 2 doubles & 1 twin room with en-suite/private bathrooms. All with colour T.V. & tea trays. Guests' own sitting/dining room with T.V.. An ideal base for visiting ancient cities, stately homes & gardens, yet within easy reach of ports & airports. There are 2 good local inns which offer food. Parking. Children over 5. (Mobile tel. 07768 242166).
E-mail: info@maycottage-thruxton.co.uk
www.maycottage-thruxton.co.uk

Tom & Fiona Biddolph   May Cottage   Thruxton   Nr. Andover SP11 8LZ   Hampshire
Tel: (01264) 771241   Fax 01264 771770   Open: ALL YEAR   Map Ref No. 02

| £30.00 to £30.00 | Y | Y | Y |

🚭

Gunville House

Near Rd: A.303

Gunville House is a charming thatched, beamed family house, dating from the 18th century in a secluded, rural situation, 5 mins' from the A.303. Offering 1 twin bedroom & 1 single, both with en-suite bath & shower, T.V. etc. Ideally situated for Salisbury, Winchester, Stonehenge, Marlborough & many famous Hampshire/Wiltshire attractions. Fly fishing, golf, clay pigeon shooting can all be arranged locally. Good pub within walking distance. Dinner by arrangement. Children over 5.
E-mail: pct@onetel.net.uk
www.gunvillehouse.co.uk

Mrs Sarah Chetwynd-Talbot   Gunville House   Grateley   Andover SP11 8JQ   Hampshire
Tel: (01264) 889206   Fax 01264 889060   Open: ALL YEAR   Map Ref No. 03

| £30.00 to £32.00 | Y | N | Y |

🚭

Holmans

Near Rd: A.35, A.31

Holmans is a charming country house in the heart of the New Forest, set in 4 acres with stabling available for guests' own horses. Superb walking, horse riding & carriage driving, with a golf course nearby. A warm, friendly welcome is assured at this elegant home, which is ideal for a relaxing break. All bedrooms are tastefully furnished & en-suite with tea/coffee-making facilities, radio & hairdryers. Colour T.V. in guests' lounge with adjoining orangery & log fires in winter.
www.bestbandb.co.uk

Robin & Mary Ford   Holmans   Bisterne Close   Burley BH24 4AZ   Hampshire
Tel: (01425) 402307   Fax 01425 402307   Open: ALL YEAR (Excl. Xmas)   Map Ref No. 04

Rudge House. Crondall.

Hampshire

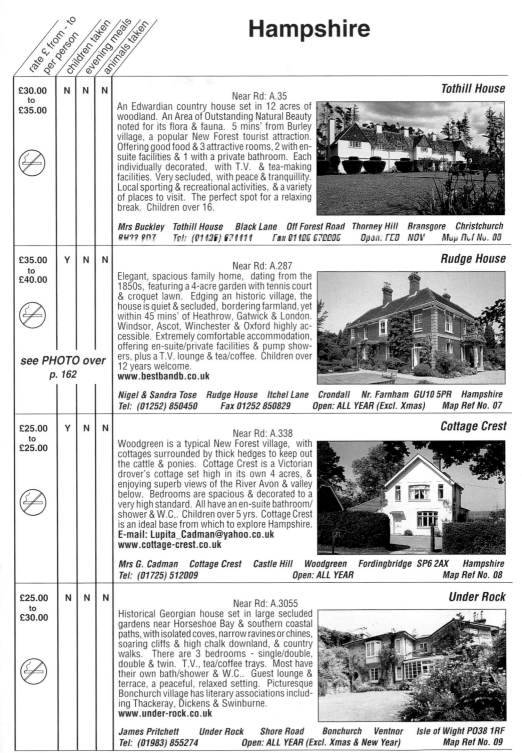

£30.00 to £35.00	N	N	N

Tothill House

Near Rd: A.35

An Edwardian country house set in 12 acres of woodland. An Area of Outstanding Natural Beauty noted for its flora & fauna. 5 mins' from Burley village, a popular New Forest tourist attraction. Offering good food & 3 attractive rooms, 2 with en-suite facilities & 1 with a private bathroom. Each individually decorated, with T.V. & tea-making facilities. Very secluded, with peace & tranquillity. Local sporting & recreational activities, & a variety of places to visit. The perfect spot for a relaxing break. Children over 16.

Mrs Buckley   Tothill House   Black Lane   Off Forest Road   Thorney Hill   Bransgore   Christchurch
BH23 8DZ   Tel: (01425) 671111   Fax 01425 670006   Open: FEB NOV   Map Ref No. 06

£35.00 to £40.00	Y	N	N

see PHOTO over p. 162

Rudge House

Near Rd: A.287

Elegant, spacious family home, dating from the 1850s, featuring a 4-acre garden with tennis court & croquet lawn. Edging an historic village, the house is quiet & secluded, bordering farmland, yet within 45 mins' of Heathrow, Gatwick & London. Windsor, Ascot, Winchester & Oxford highly accessible. Extremely comfortable accommodation, offering en-suite/private facilities & pump showers, plus a T.V. lounge & tea/coffee. Children over 12 years welcome.
www.bestbandb.co.uk

Nigel & Sandra Tose   Rudge House   Itchel Lane   Crondall   Nr. Farnham   GU10 5PR   Hampshire
Tel: (01252) 850450   Fax 01252 850829   Open: ALL YEAR (Excl. Xmas)   Map Ref No. 07

£25.00 to £25.00	Y	N	N

Cottage Crest

Near Rd: A.338

Woodgreen is a typical New Forest village, with cottages surrounded by thick hedges to keep out the cattle & ponies. Cottage Crest is a Victorian drover's cottage set high in its own 4 acres, & enjoying superb views of the River Avon & valley below. Bedrooms are spacious & decorated to a very high standard. All have an en-suite bathroom/shower & W.C.. Children over 5 yrs. Cottage Crest is an ideal base from which to explore Hampshire.
E-mail: Lupita_Cadman@yahoo.co.uk
www.cottage-crest.co.uk

Mrs G. Cadman   Cottage Crest   Castle Hill   Woodgreen   Fordingbridge SP6 2AX   Hampshire
Tel: (01725) 512009   Open: ALL YEAR   Map Ref No. 08

£25.00 to £30.00	N	N	N

Under Rock

Near Rd: A.3055

Historical Georgian house set in large secluded gardens near Horseshoe Bay & southern coastal paths, with isolated coves, narrow ravines or chines, soaring cliffs & high chalk downland, & country walks. There are 3 bedrooms - single/double, double & twin. T.V., tea/coffee trays. Most have their own bath/shower & W.C.. Guest lounge & terrace, a peaceful, relaxed setting. Picturesque Bonchurch village has literary associations including Thackeray, Dickens & Swinburne.
www.under-rock.co.uk

James Pritchett   Under Rock   Shore Road   Bonchurch   Ventnor   Isle of Wight PO38 1RF
Tel: (01983) 855274   Open: ALL YEAR (Excl. Xmas & New Year)   Map Ref No. 09

	rate £ from - to per person	children taken	evening meals	animals taken

Briantcroft

Near Rd: A.337

Enjoy the grace & elegance of this Edwardian house with its spacious & luxurious rooms. Set in peaceful surroundings, at the edge of the New Forest, Briantcroft is 10 mins' walk to the beach. The 4 large bedroom suites are individually themed, with en-suite/private facilities, T.V., 3-seater sofas & a refreshment tray. Breakfast is a gourmet experience with traditional & other tempting choices using fresh & local produce. Full colour brochure/menu on request. Children over 12.

E-mail: florence.iles@lineone.net
www.briantcroft.co.uk

£30.00 to £37.50 — Y N N

VISA: M'CARD:

Florence Iles   Briantcroft   George Road   Milford-on-Sea   Lymington   SO41 0RS   Hampshire
Tel: (01590) 644355   Fax 01590 644185   Open: ALL YEAR   Map Ref No. 10

The Nurse's Cottage

Near Rd: A.337

The former tiny cottage, home of Sway's District Nurses, has been lovingly refurbished by Tony Barnfield & is now one of the New Forest's premier properties. The en-suite bedrooms, situated on the ground floor, feature T.V./video, cd player, 'phone, & much more. The award-winning Garden Room Restaurant (open to the public) offers a seasonally changing dinner menu, with over 60 wines. Ideal touring centre. Reduced rates for 2+ nights. Prices include 3-course dinner. Children over 10.

E-mail: nurses.cottage@lineone.net
www.nursescottage.co.uk

£75.00 to £££ — Y Y Y

VISA: M'CARD: AMEX:

R. A. Barnfield   The Nurse's Cottage   Station Road   Sway   Lymington   SO41 6BA   Hampshire
Tel: (01590) 683402   Fax 01590 683402   Open: ALL YEAR   Map Ref No. 11

Ormonde House Hotel

Near Rd: A.35

Ormonde House is set back from the main road opposite the open forest; ideal for an early morning walk. Lyndhurst village is just 5 mins' walk & Exbury Gardens, the National Motor Museum & Beaulieu 20 mins' drive. The popular licensed restaurant offers freshly prepared dishes. There are 21 pretty en-suite bedrooms & 2 luxury self-contained suites, all with Sky T.V., 'phone & tea-making facilities. Delightful rooms with huge king-size beds & whirlpool baths for that special treat.

E-mail: enquiries@ormondehouse.co.uk
www.ormondehouse.co.uk

£26.00 to £60.00 — Y Y Y

VISA: M'CARD:

Mr. Paul Ames   Ormonde House Hotel   Southampton Road   Lyndhurst   SO43 7BT   Hampshire
Tel: (02380) 282806   Fax 02380 282004   Open: ALL YEAR (Excl. Xmas)   Map Ref No. 12

Trotton Farm

Near Rd: A.272

This charming home, set in 200 acres of farmland, offers comfortable accommodation in 2 twin-bedded rooms & 1 double-bedded room, each with en-suite shower & modern amenities, including tea/coffee-making facilities. Residents' lounge is available throughout the day. Games room & pretty garden for guests' relaxation. Ideally situated for visiting many local, historical & sporting attractions, & 1 hour from Gatwick & Heathrow Airports. Single supplement.

E-mail: baigentfarms@farmersweekly.net

£20.00 to £25.00 — Y N Y

Mrs J. E. Baigent   Trotton Farm   Trotton   Petersfield   GU31 5EN   Hampshire
Tel: (01730) 813618   Fax 01730 816093   Open: ALL YEAR   Map Ref No. 13

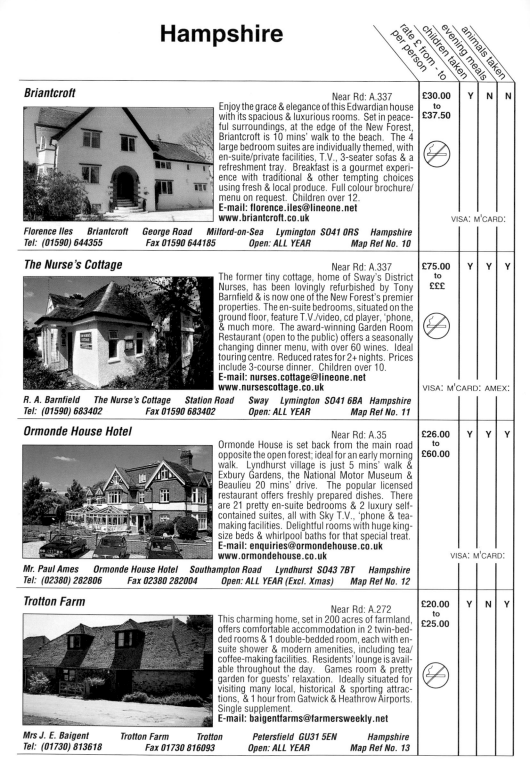

Column headers (rotated): rate £ from - to per person | children taken | evening meals taken | animals taken

Crofton Country B & B

| £25.00 to £27.50 | Y | N | N |

Near Rd: A.27

Nestling in 2 acres of garden, Crofton offers quality accommodation within the tranquil setting of a small hamlet in the beautiful Test Valley. A large family room, a twin room & a single room, all tastefully decorated & each with tea/coffee, T.V. & video, hairdryer & toiletries. Delicious breakfasts are served in the conservatory & a lounge area is also available for guests' use. Located just 4 miles north of Romsey, making Salisbury, Winchester, New Forest & south coast resorts accessible.

E-mail: pauline@croftonbandb.com
www.croftonbandb.com

VISA: M'CARD:

Mrs Pauline Lightfoot   Crofton Country B & B   Kent's Oak   Awbridge   Romsey SO51 0HH
Tel: (01794) 340333   Fax 01794 340333   Open: ALL YEAR (Excl. Xmas & New Year) Map Ref No. 14

Ranvilles Farm House

| £25.00 to £30.00 | Y | N | Y |

Near Rd: A.3090

Ranvilles Farm House dates from the 13th century when Richard De Ranville came from Normandy & settled with his family. Now this Grade II listed house provides a peaceful setting surrounded by 5 acres of gardens & paddock. All rooms, with extra large beds, are attractively furnished with antiques, & have an en-suite bathroom/shower room. Only 3 miles from the New Forest & just over a mile from Romsey - equidistant from the 2 cathedral cities of Winchester & Salisbury. Single supplement.

E-mail: info@ranvilles.com
www.ranvilles.com

Anthea Hughes   Ranvilles Farm House   Romsey SO51 6AA   Hampshire
Tel: (02380) 814481   Fax 02380 814481   Open: ALL YEAR (Excl. Xmas & New Year)   Map Ref No. 15

Highdown

| £22.50 to £27.50 | N | N | N |

Near Rd: M.27, A.32

Highdown is an attractive detached property set in 2 1/2 acres. Offering 2 very comfortable double bedrooms & 1 single/double room. Each room is en-suite & has country views, colour T.V. & tea/coffee-making facilities. Generous breakfasts are served. Highdown is close to the lovely village of Wickham with its 13th-century square housing shops, pubs, wine bars & restaurants. Also, within easy reach are Winchester, Southampton, Portsmouth & Chichester.

E-mail: highdown2000@hotmail.com
www.highdown.net

Carolyn Taylor   Highdown   Twynhams Hill   Shirrell Heath   Southampton SO32 2JL   Hampshire
Tel: (01329) 835876   Fax 01329 835876   Open: ALL YEAR   Map Ref No. 16

Church Farm

| £30.00 to £40.00 | Y | Y | Y |

Near Rd: A.303, A.30

Church Farm is a 15th-century tithe barn with Georgian & modern additions. It features an adjacent coach house & groom's cottage, recently converted, where guests may be totally self-contained, or be welcomed to the log-fired family drawing room & dine on locally produced fresh food. There are 6 beautiful bedrooms for guests, all with a private bathroom, T.V. & tea/coffee-making facilities. Swimming pool & croquet. Tennis court adjacent.

www.bestbandb.co.uk

VISA: M'CARD:

James & Jean Talbot   Church Farm   Bransbury Lane   Barton Stacey   Winchester SO21 3RR
Tel: (01962) 760268   Fax 01962 761825   Open: ALL YEAR   Map Ref No. 17

	rate £ from - to per person	children taken	evening meals	animals taken

Shawlands

Near Rd: A.3090

Shawlands is situated on the edge of Winchester & has a very peaceful location overlooking fields. The bedrooms are bright & attractively decorated, & have colour T.V., hairdryer & welcome tray. A comfortable guest lounge with T.V. Kathy & Bill Pollock ensure a warm welcome & inviting breakfasts include home-made breads & preserves with fruit from the garden. This is an excellent base from which to explore Hampshire. Children over 5. Animals by arrangement.

E-mail: kathy@pollshaw.u-net.com

£22.00 to £27.00	Y	N	Y

VISA: M'CARD:

Mrs Kathy Pollock   Shawlands   46 Kilham Lane   Winchester SO22 5QD   Hampshire
Tel: (01962) 861166 Fax 01962 861166 Open: ALL YEAR (Excl. Xmas & New Year) Map Ref No. 18

All the establishments mentioned in this guide are members of
The Worldwide Bed & Breakfast Association

When booking your accommodation please mention
The Best Bed & Breakfast

Hereford & Worcester

Hereford & Worcester
(Heart of England)

Hereford is a beautiful ancient city standing on the banks of the River Wye, almost a crossing point between England & Wales. It is a market centre for the Marches, the border area which has a very particular history of its own.

Hereford Cathedral has a massive sandstone tower & is a fitting venue for the Three Glories festival which dates from 1727, taking place yearly in one or the other of the three great cathedrals of Hereford, Worcester & Gloucester.

The county is fortunate in having many well preserved historic buildings. Charming "black & white" villages abound here, romantically set in a soft green landscape.

The Royal Forest of Dean spreads its oak & beech trees over 22,000 acres. When people first made their homes in the woodlands it was vaster still. There are rich deposits of coal & iron mined for centuries by the foresters, & the trees have always been felled for charcoal. Ancient courts still exist where forest dwellers can & do claim their rights to use the forest's resources.

The landscape alters dramatically as the land rises to merge with the great Black Mountain range at heights of over 2,600 feet. It is not possible to take cars everywhere but a narrow mountain road, Gospel Pass, takes traffic from Hay-on-Wye to Llanthony with superb views of the upper Wye Valley.

The Pre-Cambrian Malvern Hills form a natural boundary between Herefordshire & Worcestershire & from the highest view points you can see over 14 counties. At their feet nestle pretty little villages such as Eastonor with its 19th century castle in revived Norman style that looks quite mediaeval amongst the parklands & gardens.

There are, in fact, five Malverns. The largest predictably known as Great Malvern was a fashionable 19th century spa & is noted for the purity of the water which is bottled & sold countrywide.

The Priory at Malvern is rich in 15th century stained glass & has a fine collection of mediaeval tiles made locally. William Langland, the 14th century author of "Piers Ploughman" was educated at the Priory & is said to have been sleeping on the Malvern Hills when he had the visionary experience which led to the creation of the poem. Sir Edward Elgar was born, lived & worked here & his "Dream of Gerontius" had its first performance in Hereford Cathedral in 1902.

In Worcestershire another glorious cathedral, with what remains of its monastic buildings, founded in the 11th century, stands beside the River Severn. College Close in Worcester is a lovely group of buildings carefully preserved & very English in character.

The Severn appears to be a very lazy waterway but flood waters can reach astonshing heights, & the "Severn Bore" is a famous phenomenon.

A cruise along the river is a pleasant way to spend a day seeing villages & churches from a different perspective, possibly visiting a riverside inn. To the south of the county lie the undulating Vales of Evesham & Broadway - described as the show village of England.

The Malvern Hills.

Hereford & Worcester

Hereford & Worcester Gazeteer

Areas of outstanding natural beauty.
The Malvern Hills, The Cotswolds, The Wye Valley.

Historic Houses & Castles

Berrington Hall - Leominster
18th century - painted & plastered ceilings. Landscape by Capability Brown.

Brilley - Cwmmau Farmhouse - Whitney-on-Wye
17th century timber-framed & stone tiled farmhouse.

Burton Court - Eardisland
14th century great hall. Exhibition of European & Oriental costume & curios. Model fairground.

Croft Castle - Nr. Leominster
Castle on the Welsh border - inhabited by Croft family for 900 years.

Dinmore Manor - Nr. Hereford
14th century chapel & cloister.

Eastnor Castle - Nr. Ledbury
19th century - Castellated, containing pictures & armour. Arboretum.

Eye Manor - Leominster
17th century Carolean Manor house - excellent plasterwork, paintings, costumes, books, secret passage. Collection of dolls.

Hanbury Hall - Nr. Droitwich
18th century red brick house - only two rooms & painted ceilings on exhibition.

Harvington Hall - Kidderminster
Tudor Manor house with moat, priest's hiding places.

The Greyfriars - Worcester
15th century timber-framed building adjoins Franciscan Priory.

Hellen's - Much Marcle
13th century manorial house of brick & stone. Contains the Great hall with stone table - bedroom of Queen Mary. Much of the original furnishings remain.

Kentchurch Court - Hereford
14th century fortified border Manor house. Paintings & Carvings by Grinling Gibbons.

Moccas Court - Moccas
18th century - designed by Adam - Parklands by Capability Brown - under restoration.

Pembridge Castle - Welsh Newton
17th century moated castle.

Sutton Court - Mordiford
Palladian mansion by Wyatt, watercolours, embroideries, china.

Cathedrals & Churches

Amestry (St. John the Baptist & St.Alkmund)
16th century rood screen.

Abbey Dore (St. Mary & Holy Trinity)
17th century glass & great oak screen - early English architecture.

Brinsop (St. George)
14th century, screen & glass, alabaster reredos, windows in memory of Wordsworth, carved Norman tympanum.

Bredon (St. Giles)
12th century - central tower & spire. Mediaeval heraldic tiles, tombs & early glass.

Brockhampton (St. Eadburgh)
1902. Central tower & thatched roof.

Castle Frome (St. Michael & All Angles)
12th century carved font, 17th century effigies in alabaster.

Chaddesley Corbett (St. Cassian)
14th century monuments, 12th century font.

Elmley (St. Mary)
12th century & 15th century font, tower, gargoyles, mediaeval.

Great Witley (St. Michael)
Baroque - Plasterwork, painted ceiling, painted glass, very fine example.

Hereford (All Saints)
13th-14th centuries, spire, splendid choir stalls, chained library.

Hereford Cathedral
Small cathedral.
Fine central tower c.1325, splendid porch, brasses, early English Lady Chapel with lancet windows. Red sandstone.

Kilpeck (St. Mary & St. David)
Romanesque style - mediaeval windows - fine carvings.

Leominster (St. Peter & St. Paul)
12th century doorway, fine Norman arches, decorated windows.

Much Marcle (St. Bartholomew)
13th century. 14th & 17th century monuments.

Hereford & Worcester

Worcester Cathedral
11th -16th centry. Fine cloisters & crypt.
Tomb of King John
Worcester (St. Swithun)
18th century - furnishings untouched.
Ceiling vaulted in plaster.

Museums& Galleries

Hereford City Museum & Art Gallery
Collections of natural history & archeology,
oootumoo, toxtiloo ombroidrrirn. Irvn
agricultural I bygones.
Paintings by local artists, examples of
applied art, silver, pottery & porcelain.
The Old House - Hereford
Jacobean period museum with furnishings
of time.
Churchill Gardens Museum - Hereford
Extensive costume collection, fine
furniture, work by local artists.
Almony Museum - Evesham
Anglo-British. Roman-British, mediaeval -
monastic remains.

Avoncroft Museum of Buildings -
Stoke Heath.
Open air museum showing buildings of
reconstructed iron-age dwellings to 15th
century merchants homes.
City Museum & Art Gallery
Local History, archaeology, natural history,
environmental studies.
Dyson Perins Museums of Worcester
Porcelain - Worcester
Most comprehensive collection of old
Woroootor in tho world.
The Commandery - Sidbury
15th century timber-framed building, was
originally a hospital. Royalist H.Q. during
battle of Worcester 1651.

Other things to see & do

Three choirs Festival - an annual event,
held in the cathedrals of Hereford,
Worcester & Gloucestershire, alternately.

The River Severn at Bewdley.

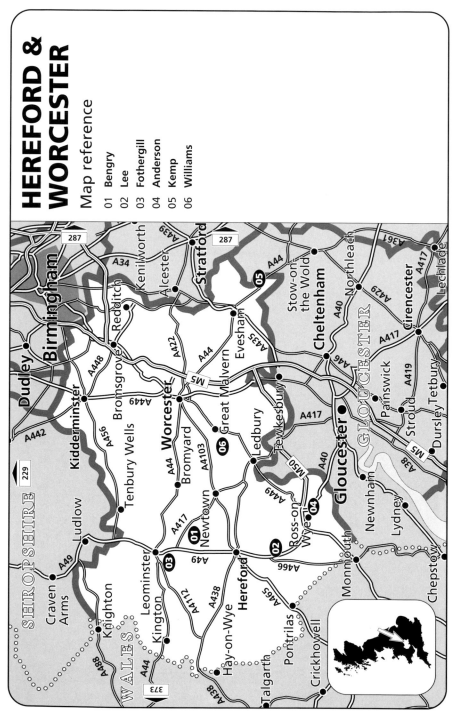

HEREFORD & WORCESTER

Map reference

01 Bengry
02 Lee
03 Fothergill
04 Anderson
05 Kemp
06 Williams

Herefordshire

rate £ from - to per person	children taken	evening meals taken	animals taken		
£25.00 to £35.00	N	Y	N	**The Vauld Farm** Near Rd: A.49 The Vauld Farm is a delightful 16th-century black-&-white former farmhouse, set in a beautiful garden. It retains many period features throughout & affords attractive accommodation. There are 4 charming & elegantly furnished bedrooms, each with an en-suite bathroom, T.V. & tea/coffee-making facilities. (1 with 4-poster.) Hearty breakfasts & delicious evening meals are served in the tastefully decorated dining room. A beautiful home & the perfect location for a relaxing break. www.bestbandb.co.uk	
				Mr & Mrs J. Bengry The Vauld Farm The Vauld Marden Hereford HR1 3HA Herefordshire Tel: (01568) 797898 Open: ALL YEAR Map Ref No. 01	
£19.00 to £19.00	Y	N	N	**Cwm Craig Farm** Near Rd: A.49 Spacious Georgian farmhouse, surrounded by superb unspoilt countryside. Situated between the cathedral city of Hereford & Ross-on-Wye, & just a few mins' drive from the Wye Valley. Ideal base for touring the Forest of Dean. All 3 bedrooms are comfortably furnished & have modern amenities, shaver points, tea/coffee-making facilities & an en-suite bathroom. There is a lounge & separated dining room, both with colour T.V.. A delicious full English breakfast is served. www.bestbandb.co.uk	
				Mrs G. Lee Cwm Craig Farm Little Dewchurch Hereford HR2 6PS Herefordshire Tel: (01432) 840250 Fax 01432 840250 Open: ALL YEAR Map Ref No. 02	
£25.00 to £27.00	N	Y	N	**Highfield** Near Rd: A.44, A.49 Twins Catherine & Marguerite are eager to make you feel welcome & at home in their elegant Edwardian house, set in a rural, tranquil location. You will be very comfortable in any of the 3 attractive bedrooms, all with a bathroom (1 being en-suite) & tea/coffee-making facilities. A large garden & a T.V. lounge with a crackling fire in which guests may relax, & the home-made food is absolutely delicious. Licensed. Reductions for longer stays. E-mail: info@stay-at-highfield.co.uk www.stay-at-highfield.co.uk	
				Catherine & Marguerite Fothergill Highfield Newtown Ivington Road Leominster HR6 8QD Tel: (01568) 613216 Open: ALL YEAR Map Ref No. 03	
£25.00 to £30.00 (no smoking) VISA: M'CARD: AMEX:	Y	Y	Y	**Lea House** Near Rd: A.40 In a small village betwixt the Royal Forest of Dean & the spectacular Wye Valley this 16th-century coaching inn has been prettily refurbished with exposed beams, an inglenook fireplace & imaginative décor - the perfect place to relax. Homemade breads, preserves & fresh squeezed orange juice complement the sumptuous breakfasts & freshly prepared evening meals. 3 individually styled bedrooms (king-size/twin/family) have extra foldaways available & en-suite/private bathrooms. E-mail: enquiries@leahousebandb.com www.leahousebandb.com	
				Mrs Caroline Anderson Lea House Lea Ross-on-Wye HR9 7JZ Herefordshire Tel: (01989) 750652 Fax 01989 750652 Open: ALL YEAR Map Ref No. 04	

Cowley House. Broadway.

rate £ from - to per person	children taken	evening meals	animals taken

Cowley House

| £27.50 to £40.00 | Y | N | N |

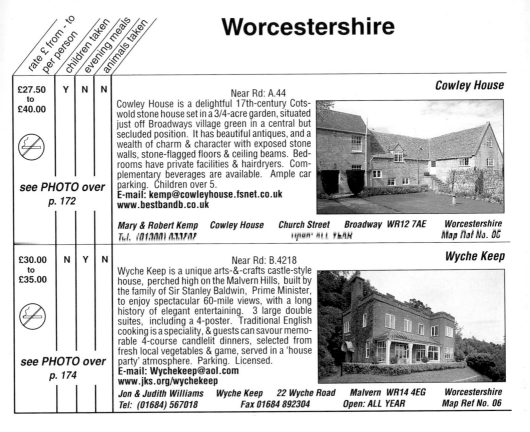

Near Rd: A.44

Cowley House is a delightful 17th-century Cotswold stone house set in a 3/4-acre garden, situated just off Broadways village green in a central but secluded position. It has beautiful antiques, and a wealth of charm & character with exposed stone walls, stone-flagged floors & ceiling beams. Bedrooms have private facilities & hairdryers. Complementary beverages are available. Ample car parking. Children over 5.

E-mail: kemp@cowleyhouse.fsnet.co.uk
www.bestbandb.co.uk

see PHOTO over p. 172

| Mary & Robert Kemp | Cowley House | Church Street | Broadway WR12 7AE | Worcestershire |
| Tel. (01386) 833542 | | Open: ALL YEAR | | Map Ref No. 06 |

Wyche Keep

| £30.00 to £35.00 | N | Y | N |

Near Rd: B.4218

Wyche Keep is a unique arts-&-crafts castle-style house, perched high on the Malvern Hills, built by the family of Sir Stanley Baldwin, Prime Minister, to enjoy spectacular 60-mile views, with a long history of elegant entertaining. 3 large double suites, including a 4-poster. Traditional English cooking is a speciality, & guests can savour memorable 4-course candlelit dinners, selected from fresh local vegetables & game, served in a 'house party' atmosphere. Parking. Licensed.

E-mail: Wychekeep@aol.com
www.jks.org/wychekeep

see PHOTO over p. 174

| Jon & Judith Williams | Wyche Keep | 22 Wyche Road | Malvern WR14 4EG | Worcestershire |
| Tel: (01684) 567018 | Fax 01684 892304 | Open: ALL YEAR | | Map Ref No. 06 |

All the establishments mentioned in this guide are members of
The Worldwide Bed & Breakfast Association

When booking your accommodation please mention
The Best Bed & Breakfast

Wyche Keep. Malvern.

Kent

Kent
(South East)

Kent is best known as "the garden of England". At its heart is a tranquil landscape of apple & cherry orchards, hop-fields & oast-houses, but there are also empty downs, chalk sea-cliffs, rich marshlands, sea ports, castles & the glory of Canterbury Cathedral.

The dramatic chalk ridgeway of the North Downs links the White Cliffs of Dover with the north of the county which extends into the edge of London. It was a trade route in ancient times following the high downs above the Weald, dense forest in those days. It can be followed today & it offers broad views of the now agricultural Weald.

The pilgrims who flocked to Canterbury in the 12th-15th centuries, (colourfully portrayed in Chaucer's Canterbury Tales), probably used the path of the Roman Watling Street rather than the high ridgeway.

Canterbury was the cradle of Christianity in southern England & is by tradition the seat of the Primate of All England. This site, on the River Stour, has been settled since the earliest times & became a Saxon stonghold under King Ethelbert of Kent. He established a church here, but it was in Norman times that the first great building work was carried out, to be continued in stages until the 15th century. The result is a blending of styles with early Norman work, a later Norman choir, a vaulted nave in Gothic style & a great tower of Tudor design. Thomas Becket was murdered on the steps of the Cathedral in 1170. The town retains much of its mediaeval character with half-timbered weavers' cottages, old churches & the twin towers of the west gate.

Two main styles of building give the villages of Kent their special character. The Kentish yeoman's house was the home of the wealthier farmers & is found throughout the county. It is a timber-frame building with white lath & plaster walls & a hipped roof of red tiles. Rather more modest in style is a small weatherboard house, usually painted white or cream. Rolvenden & Groombridge have the typical charm of a Kentish village whilst Tunbridge Wells is an attractive town, with a paved parade known as the Pantiles & excellent antique shops.

There are grand houses & castles throughout the county. Leeds Castle stands in a lake & dates back to the 9th century. It has beautifully landscaped parkland. Knowle House is an impressive Jacobean & Tudor Manor House with rough ragstone walls, & acres of deer-park & woodland.

Kent is easily accessible from the Channel Ports, Gatwick Airport & London.

Leeds Castle.

Kent

Kent Gazeteer

Areas of outstanding natural beauty.
Kent Downs.

Historic Houses & Castles

Aylesford, The Friars - Nr. Maidstone
13th century Friary & shrine of Our Lady,
(much restored), 14th century cloisters -
original.

Allington Castle -Nr. Maidstone
13th century. One time home of Tudor
poet Thomas Wyatt. Restored early 20th
century. Icons & Renaissance paintings.

Black Charles - Nr. Sevenoaks
14th century Hall house - Tudor fireplaces,
beautiful panelling.

Boughton Monchelsea Place - Nr.
Maidstone
Elizabethan Manor House - grey stone
battlements - 18th century landscaped
park, wonderful views of Weald of Kent.

Chartwell - Westerham
Home of Sir Winston Churchill.
Chiddingstone Castle - Nr. Edenbridge
18th century Gothic revival building
encasing old remains of original Manor
House - Royal Stuart & Jacobite
collection.
Ancient Egyptian collection - Japanese
netsuke, etc.

Eyehorne Manor - Hollingbourne
15th century Manor house with 17th
century additions.

Cobham Hall - Cobham
16th century house - Gothic &
Renaissance - Wyatt interior. Now school
for girls.

Fairfield - Eastry, Sandwich
13th-14th centuries - moated castle. Was
home of Anne Boleyn. Beautiful gardens
with unique collection of classical statuary.

Knole - Sevenoaks
15th century - splendid Jacobean interior -
17th & 18th century furniture. One of the
largest private houses in England.

Leeds Castle- Nr. Maidstone
Built in middle of the lake, it was the home
of the mediaeval Queens of England.

Lullingstone Castle - Eynsford
14th century mansion house - frequented
by Henry VIII & Queen Anne.
Still occupied by descendants of the
original owners

Long Barn - Sevenoaks
14th century house - said to be home of
William Caxton. Restored by Edwin
Lutyens; 16th century barn added to
enlarge house. Galleried hall - fine
beaming & fireplaces. Lovely gardens
created by Sir Harold Nicholson & his wife
Vita Sackville-West.

Owletts - Cobham
Carolean house of red brick with
plasterwork ceiling & fine staircase.

Owl House - Lamberhurst
16th century cottage, tile hung; said to be
home of wool smuggler. Charming
gardens.

Penshurst Place - Tonbridge
14th century house with mediaeval Great
Hall perfectly preserved.English Gothic.
Birthplace of Elizabethan poet, Sir Philip
Sidney
Fine staterooms, splendid picture gallery,
famous toy museum. Tudor gardens &
orchards.

Saltwood Castle - Nr. Hythe
Mediaeval - very fine castle & is privately
occupied. Was lived in by Sir Ralph de
Broc, murderer of Thomas a Becket.

Squerreys Court - Westerham
Manor house of William & Mary period,
with furniture, paintings & tapestries of
time. Connections with General Wolfe.

Stoneacre - Otham
15th century yeoman's half-timbered
house.

Cathedrals & Churches

Brook (St. Mary)
11th century paintings in this unaltered
early Norman church.

Brookland (St. Augustine)
13th century & some later part. Crown-
post roofs, detached wooden belfry with
conical cap. 12th century lead font.

Canterbury Cathedral
12th century wall paintings, 12th & 13th
century stained glass. Very fine Norman
crypt. Early perpendicular nave &
cloisters which have heraldic bosses.
Wonderful central tower.

Charing (St. Peter & St. Paul)
13th & 15th century interior with 15th
century tower. 17th century restoration.

Kent

Cobham (St. Mary)
16th century carved & painted tombs - unequalled collection of brasses in county.
Elham (St. Mary the Virgin)
Norman wall with 13th century arcades, perpendicular clerestory. Restored by Eden.
Lullingstone (St. Botolph)
14th century mainly - 16th century wood screen. Painted glass monuments.
Newington-on-the-Street (St. Mary the Virgin)
13th & 14th century - fine tower. 13th century tomb. Wall paintings.
Rochester Cathedral
Norman facade & nave, otherwise early English.
12th century west door. 14th century doorway to Chapter room.
Stone (St. Mary)
13th century - decorated - paintings, 15th century brass, 16th century tomb.
Woodchurch (All Saints)
13th century, having late Norman font & priest's brass of 1320. Arcades alternating octagonal & rounded columns. Triple lancets with banded marble shafting at east end.

Museums & Galleries

Royal Museums - Canterbury
Archaeological, geological, mineralogical exhibits, natural history, pottery & porcelain. Engravings, prints & pictures.
Westgate - Canterbury
Museum of armour, etc. in 14th century gatehouse of city.
Dartford District Museum - Dartford
Roman, Saxon & natural history.
Deal Museum - Deal
Prehistoric & historic antiquities.
Dicken's House Museum - Broadstairs
Personalia of Dickens; prints, costume & Victoriana.
Down House - Downe
The home of Charles Darwin for 40 years, now his memorial & museum.
Dover Museum - Dover
Roman pottery, ceramics, coins, zoology, geology, local history, etc.
Faversham Heritage Society - Faversham
1000 years of history & heritage.
Folkestone Museum & Art Gallery - Folkestone
Archeology, local history & sciences.

Herne Bay Museum - Herne Bay
Stone, Bronze & Early Iron Age specimens. Roman material from Reculver excavations. Items of local & Kentish interest.
Museum & Art Gallery - Maidstone
16th century manor house exhibiting natural history & archaeolgical collections. Costume Gallery, bygones, ceramics, 17th century works by Dutch & Italian painters. Regimental museum

Historic Monuments

Eynsford Castle - Eynsford
12th century castle remains.
Rochester Castle - Rochester
Storied keep - 1126-39
Roman Fort & Anglo-Saxon Church - Reculver
Excavated remains of 3rd century fort & Saxon church.
Little Kit's Coty House - Aylesford
Ruins of burial chambers from 2 long barrows.
Lullingstone Roman Villa - Lullingstone
Roman farmstead excavations.
Roman Fort & Town - Richborough
Roman 'Rutupiae' & fort
Tonbridge Castle - Tonbridge
12th century curtain walls, shell of keep & 14th century gatehouse.
Dover Castle - Dover
Keep built by Henry II in 1180. Outer curtain built 13th century.

Gardens

Chilham Castle Gardens - Nr. Canterbury
25 acre gardens of Jacobean house, laid out by Tradescant.
Lake garden, fine trees & birds of prey. Jousting & mediaeval banquets.
Great Comp Gardens - Nr. Borough Green
Outstanding 7 acre garden with old brick walls.
Owl House Gardens - Lamberhurst
16th century smugglers cottage with beautiful gardens of roses, daffodils & rhododendrons.
Sissinghurst Castle Gardens - Sissinghurst
Famous gardens created by Vita Sackville-West around the remains of an Elizabethan mansion.

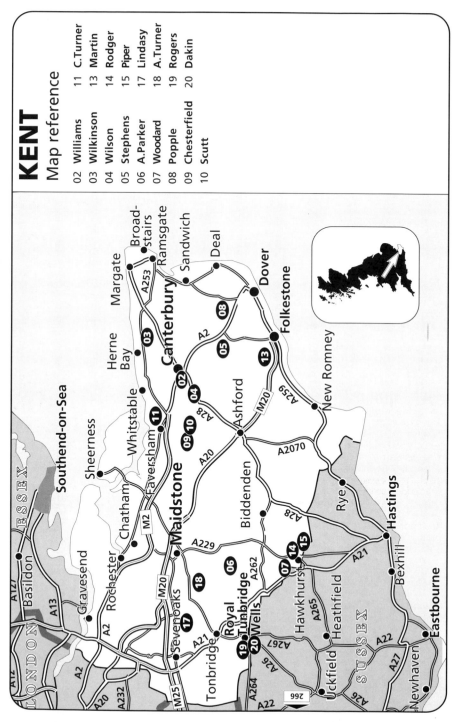

KENT

Map reference

02 Williams	11 C.Turner
03 Wilkinson	13 Martin
04 Wilson	14 Rodger
05 Stephens	15 Piper
06 A.Parker	17 Lindasy
07 Woodard	18 A.Turner
08 Popple	19 Rogers
09 Chesterfield	20 Dakin
10 Scutt	

Kent

rate £ from - to per person	children taken	evening meals	animals taken		

£25.00 to £30.00	Y	N	N	**Clare Ellen Guest House**

Near Rd: A.28

A warm welcome & bed & breakfast in style. Large, elegant en-suite/private rooms, all with colour T.V., clock/radio, hairdryer & tea/coffee-making facilities. Ironing centre with trouser press for guests' convenience. Vegetarians & special diets catered for on request. A cosy residents' lounge. Numerous restaurants/pubs close by. 6 mins' walk to the town centre/cathedral. 4 mins' walk to Canterbury East Station. Private car park & garage available.
E-mail: loraine.williams@clareellenguesthouse.co.uk
www.clareellenguesthouse.co.uk

VISA: M'CARD:

Ms Loraine Williams   **Clare Ellen Guest House**   *9 Victoria Road*   *Canterbury CT1 3SG*   *Kent*
Tel. (01227) 760205   *Fax 01227 784482*   *Open: ALL YEAR*   *Map Ref No. 02*

£30.00 to £35.00	Y	N	N	**Chislet Court Farm**

Near Rd: A.28, A.299

A listed Queen Anne farmhouse, set in mature gardens with views overlooking the surrounding countryside & the ancient village church. There are 2 double en-suite bedrooms, which are large & comfortable with tea/coffee-making facilities & T.V.. Guests are welcome to wander round the garden or relax in the conservatory - where breakfast is served. An ideal base for exploring Canterbury & the Kent countryside. Children over 12.
E-mail: chisletcourtfarm@dial.pipex.com
www.bestbandb.co.uk

Kathy & Mike Wilkinson   **Chislet Court Farm**   *Chislet*   *Canterbury CT3 4DU*   *Kent*
Tel: (01227) 860309   *Fax 01227 860444*   *Open: ALL YEAR (Excl. Xmas)*   *Map Ref No. 03*

£25.00 to £25.00	Y	Y	N	**Stour Farm**

Near Rd: A.28

Stour Farm, overlooking the River Stour on the edge of Chartham village is ideal for visiting Canterbury. Also, convenient for channel ports, castles, gardens, walks & golf courses. 2 attractively furnished en-suite double bedrooms, each with T.V. & tea/coffee-making facilities. Breakfast is served in the guests' own dining room or weather permitting on the sun terrace overlooking the river. Evening meals available on request. Good restaurants & pubs nearby. Parking. Children over 12.
E-mail: info@stourfarm.co.uk
www.stourfarm.co.uk

VISA: M'CARD:

Jeremy & Jane Wilson   **Stour Farm**   *Riverside*   *Chartham*   *Canterbury CT4 7NX*   *Kent*
Tel: (01227) 731977   *Fax 01227 731977*   *Open: ALL YEAR*   *Map Ref No. 04*

£35.00 to £45.00	N	Y	N	**The Manor**

Near Rd: A.2

The Manor, a most impressive house dating from the 18th & early 19th centuries, is set in beautiful gardens extending to over 5 acres. Offering 2 tastefully decorated en-suite rooms with tea/coffee facilities. Heated outdoor pool, tennis court & snooker room available for guests use. Barham is 20 mins' from Dover or the Channel tunnel, but also excellent for visiting Canterbury & the surrounding countryside, which is designated an Area of Outstanding Natural Beauty & special landscape area.
E-mail: lesleyr.stephens@virgin.net

Lesley Stephens   **The Manor**   *Valley Road*   *Barham*   *Canterbury ME20 6SE*   *Kent*
Tel: (01227) 832869   *Fax 01227 832846*   *Open: ALL YEAR*   *Map Ref No. 05*

	rate £ from - to per person	children taken	evening meals	animals taken

West Winchet

Near Rd: A.262

West Winchet is an elegant Victorian house surrounded by parkland in a secluded & peaceful setting. 2 beautifully decorated rooms, 1 double with private bathroom & 1 twin with en-suite shower. Each with T.V., radio & tea/coffee-making facilities. Both rooms are on the ground floor, & the twin-bedded room has French windows onto the terrace & into the garden. A magnificent drawing room for guests' use. An ideal touring centre for Kent & East Sussex. 2 1/2 miles mainline station (London 55 mins). Children over 5.
E-mail: jeremyparker@jpa-ltd.co.uk

| £30.00 to £35.00 | Y | N | Y |

Jeremy & Annie Parker   West Winchet   Winchet Hill   Goudhurst   Cranbrook TN17 1JX   Kent
Tel: (01580) 212024   Fax 01580 212250   Open: ALL YEAR   Map Ref No. 06

Southgate-Little Fowlers

Near Rd: A.268

17th-century historical country house with antique furnishings & a warm, welcoming atmosphere. Beautiful bedrooms, 1 king-size 4-poster, 1 king-size brass bed or a twin, all en-suite with wonderful views & many thoughtful extras. Superb breakfast served in the magnificent Victorian room or original Victorian conservatory housing impressive Muscat vine & collection of plants. 15th-century inns nearby for dinner. Near to Bodiam, Scotney, Rye, Sissinghurst, Battle, & Dixter. Children over 8.
E-mail: Susan.Woodard@southgate.uk.net
www.southgate.uk.net

| £32.00 to £35.00 | Y | N | N |

Susan Woodard   Southgate-Little Fowlers   Rye Road   Hawkhurst   Cranbrook TN18 5DA   Kent
Tel: (01580) 752526   Fax 01580 752526   Open: ALL YEAR (Excl. Xmas)   Map Ref No. 07

Sunshine Cottage

Near Rd: A.2

A 17th-century, Grade II listed cottage, overlooking Shepherdswell village green, with a wealth of beams, an inglenook fireplace & 2 lounges. Tastefully furnished, & with a homely atmosphere. 6 attractive bedrooms. A pretty garden & courtyard. Good home-cooking & home-made preserves. Good food also available at a nearby pub. Shepherdswell is situated halfway between Canterbury & Dover, 25 mins' from the Channel Tunnel. BR station 5 mins' walk away. Children over 12.
E-mail: sunshinecottage@shepherdswell.fsnet.co.uk
www.sunshine-cottage.co.uk

| £25.00 to £29.00 | Y | N | N |

VISA: M'CARD: AMEX:

Lyn Popple   Sunshine Cottage   The Green   Mill Lane   Shepherdswell   Dover CT15 7LQ   Kent
Tel: (01304) 831359   Open: ALL YEAR   Map Ref No. 08

Frith Farm House

Near Rd: A.20

This lovingly restored Georgian farmhouse with orchards, gardens & indoor swimming pool is situated on the North Downs. Extremely peaceful & well-positioned for visiting the historic houses, castles & cathedrals of Kent. Accommodation in beautifully furnished en-suite rooms together with breakfasts that include homemade bread & preserves. Evening meals are by arrangement. 3 nights or more - 10% discount. Self-catering cottage available. Children over 10.
E-mail: enquiries@frithfarmhouse.co.uk
www.frithfarmhouse.co.uk

| £29.00 to £35.00 | Y | Y | N |

see PHOTO over
p. 181

VISA: M'CARD:

Markham & Susan Chesterfield   Frith Farm House   Otterden   Faversham ME13 0DD   Kent
Tel: (01795) 890701   Fax 01795 890009   Open: ALL YEAR   Map Ref No. 09

Frith Farm House.   Otterden.

	rate £ from - to per person	children taken	evening meals	animals taken

Leaveland Court

Near Rd: A.251

Guests are warmly welcomed to this enchanting 15th-century timbered farmhouse, & its delightful gardens with heated swimming pool. Situated in a quiet rural setting, between 13th-century Leaveland church & woodlands, & surrounded by a 300-acre downland farm. All of the attractive bedrooms have en-suite facilities, colour T.V. & tea/coffee tray. Conveniently placed only 5 mins' from M.2 & Faversham, 20 mins' Canterbury & 30 mins' Channel ports. A charming home.
E-mail: info@leavelandcourt.co.uk
www.leavelandcourt.co.uk

£25.00 to £27.50 — Y — N — N
VISA: M'CARD:

Mrs Corrine Scutt   Leaveland Court   Leaveland   Faversham ME13 0NP   Kent
Tel: (01233) 740596   Fax 01233 740015   Open: FEB - NOV   Map Ref No. 10

Preston Lea

Near Rd: A.2

A warm welcome & tea on arrival are guaranteed in this beautiful, elegant private house, set in secluded gardens on the edge of Faversham. Spacious en-suite bedrooms, with garden views, antique furniture & offering every comfort. The lovely drawing-rooms, pannelled dining-room & gardens are available to guests. Help & advice is on hand from your caring hosts. Delicious breakfasts. Good restaurants nearby, beautiful countryside, beaches & places of interest to visit, ensure enjoyable stays.
E-mail: preston.lea@which.net
http://homepages.which.net/~alan.turner10

£27.50 to £30.00 — N — N — N
VISA: M'CARD: AMEX:

Alan & Catherine Turner   Preston Lea   Canterbury Road   Faversham ME13 8XA   Kent
Tel: (01795) 535266   Fax 01795 533388   Open: ALL YEAR   Map Ref No. 11

Pigeonwood House

Near Rd: A.260

Pigeonwood House is the original, 18th-century farmhouse of the surrounding area, positioned in rural tranquillity in chalk downland. The 2 guest bedrooms have beautiful panoramic views over the surrounding countryside & many guests return for the homely, relaxing atmosphere. Pigeonwood House is ideally situated for touring historic Kent as well as having the Channel tunnel & ports close by. Children over 5 years welcome.
E-mail: samandmary@aol.com
www.pigeonwood.com

£22.00 to £25.00 — Y — N — N

Mrs Mary Martin   Pigeonwood House   Arpinge   Folkestone CT18 8AQ   Kent
Tel: (01303) 891111   Open: APR-OCT   Map Ref No. 13

Conghurst Farm

Near Rd: A.268

Set in peaceful, totally unspoilt countryside, Conghurst Farm offers a perfect spot for a restful holiday. Within easy reach of all the marvellous houses & gardens that this part of the country has to offer. 3 very comfortable bedrooms, all with en-suite/private bathrooms. There is a drawing room, a separate T.V. room &, in the summer, a delightful garden for guests to enjoy. Evening meals are available Thursday-Monday inclusive. An ideal base from which to explore Kent. Children over 12.
E-mail: rosa@conghurst.co.uk
www.SmoothHound.co.uk/hotels/conghurst.html

£28.00 to £32.00 — Y — Y — N

see PHOTO over
p. 183

VISA: M'CARD:

Mrs Rosemary Piper   Conghurst Farm   Hawkhurst TN18 4RW   Kent
Tel: (01580) 753331   Fax 01580 754579   Open: FEB - NOV   Map Ref No. 15

Conghurst Farm.   Hawkhurst.

Kent

	rate £ from - to per person	children taken	evening meals	animals taken

The Wren's Nest

Near Rd: A.21
Built in traditional Kentish style, with oak beams & vaulted ceilings, The Wren's Nest suites have been designed specifically for the comfort & pleasure of guests. The suites are spacious & beautifully furnished & are well-equipped with T.V., tea/coffee facilities, tourist information literature, etc. & excellent en-suite bathrooms. The suites are entered via their own front door allowing absolute privacy. Hearty English breakfasts are served in the main house. An idyllic rural setting, well-placed for touring, walking & birdwatching. Children over 10.

£29.50 to £29.50	Y	N	N

Lynne Rodger   The Wren's Nest   Hastings Road   Hawkhurst TN18 4RT   Kent
Tel: (01580) 754919   Fax 01580 754919   Open: MAR - DEC   Map Ref No. 14

Jordans

Near Rd: A.227
Beautiful, picture-postcard, 15th-century Tudor house (awarded a 'Historic Building of Kent' plaque) in the picturesque village of Plaxtol, among orchards & parkland. It has been featured on T.V. & is beautifully furnished, with leaded windows, inglenook fireplaces, oak beams & an enchanting old English garden with rambler roses & espalier trees. Within easy reach are Ightham Mote, Leeds & Hever Castles, Penshurst, Chartwell & Knole. 3 lovely rooms, 2 with en-suite/private facilities. London 35 mins' by train, & easy access to airports. Children over 12.

£30.00 to £35.00	Y	N	N

see PHOTO over
p. 185

Mrs J. Lindsay N.D.D., A.T.D.   Jordans   Sheet Hill   Plaxtol   Sevenoaks TN15 0PU   Kent
Tel: (01732) 810379   Open: Mid JAN - Mid DEC   Map Ref No. 17

Leavers Oast

Near Rd: A.26
A warm, friendly welcome & imaginative cooking is to be found in this beautiful 19th-century oast. An en-suite bedroom in the barn & 2 roundel bedrooms provide comfortable accommodation. The house is furnished with interesting antiques, & the lovely garden overlooks open country. Excellent communications make it an ideal base for visiting many historic houses & gardens. London 40 mins' by rail. Children over 12 years welcome. Evening meals by arrangement.
E-mail: denis@leavers-oast.freeserve.co.uk

£29.00 to £32.50	Y	Y	N

Anne Turner   Leavers Oast   Stanford Lane   Hadlow   Tonbridge TN11 0JN   Kent
Tel: (01732) 850924   Fax 01732 850924   Open: ALL YEAR   Map Ref No. 18

Ash Tree Cottage

Near Rd: A.21
Ash Tree Cottage is situated in a quiet private road just above the famous Pantiles, & within a few mins' walk of the high street & station. There are 2 charming & attractively furnished bedrooms with en-suite bathrooms, radio, T.V., tea/coffee-making facilities & plenty of tourist information. There is an excellent choice of restaurants & country pubs nearby, & many places of interest are within easy reach. Children over 8.
E-mail: rogersashtree@excite.com
www.bestbandb.co.uk

£26.00 to £28.00	Y	N	N

Richard & Sue Rogers   Ash Tree Cottage   7 Eden Road   Tunbridge Wells TN1 1TS   Kent
Tel: (01892) 541317 Fax 01892 616770 Open: ALL YEAR (Excl. Xmas & New Year) Map Ref No. 19

Jordans. Plaxtol.

Kent

	rate £ from - to per person	children taken	evening meals	animals taken
The Old Parsonage Near Rd: A.267 This magnificent award-winning country house, built by Lord Abergavenny 200 years ago, is quietly situated by the church in pretty Frant village with its 2 character pubs close by. It offers superb accommodation in luxury en-suite bedrooms, antique-furnished reception rooms, plus a flower-filled conservatory. Short drive to more than 15 major historic houses, castles & gardens. Gatwick 40 mins. Heathrow 70 mins. London 45 mins by train. Children over 7. Animals by arrangement. E-mail: oldparson@aol.com www.theoldparsonagehotel.co.uk	£39.50 to £49.50 VISA: M'CARD:	Y	N	Y

Mary & Tony Dakin   The Old Parsonage   Church Lane   Frant   Tunbridge Wells TN3 9DX   Kent
Tel: (01892) 750773   Fax 01892 750773   Open: ALL YEAR   Map Ref No. 20

All the establishments mentioned in this guide are members of
The Worldwide Bed & Breakfast Association

When booking your accommodation please mention
The Best Bed & Breakfast

186

Leicestershire, Nottinghamshire & Rutland

Leicestershire
(East Midlands)

Rural Leicestershire is rich in grazing land, a peaceful, undramatic landscape broken up by the waterways that flow through in the south of the county.

The River Avon passes on its way to Stratford running by 17th century Stanford Hall & its motorcycle museum. The Leicester section of the Grand Union Canal was once very important for the transportation of goods from the factories of the Midlands to London Docks. It passes through a fascinating series of multiple locks at Foxton. The decorative barges, the 'narrow boats' are pleasure craft these days rather than the life-blood of the closed community of boat people who lived & worked out their lives on the canals.

Rutland was formerly England's smallest county, but was absorbed into East Leicestershire in the 1970's. Recently, once again, it has become a county in its' own right. Rutland Water, is one of Europe's largest reservoirs & an attractive setting for sailing, fishing or enjoying a trip on the pleasure cruiser. There is also the Rutland Theatre at Tolethorpe Hall, where a summer season of Shakespeare's plays is presented in the open air.

Melton Mowbray is famous for its pork pies & it is also the centre of Stilton cheese country. The "King of Cheeses" is made mainly in the Vale of Belvoir where Leicestershire meets Nottinghamshire, & the battlements & turrets of Belvoir Castle overlook the scene from its hill-top.

To the north-west the Charnwood Forest area is pleasantly wooded & the deer park at Bradgate surrounding the ruined home of Lady Jane Grey, England's nine-day queen, is a popular attraction.

Nottinghamshire
(East Midlands)

Nottinghamshire has a diversity of landscape from forest to farmland, from coal mines to industrial areas.

The north of the county is dominated by the expanse of Sherwood Forest, smaller now than in the time of legendary Robin Hood & his Merry Men but still a lovely old woodland of Oak & Birch.

The Dukeries are so called because of the numerous ducal houses built in the area & there is beautiful parkland on these great estates that can be visited. Clumber Park, for instance has a huge lake & a double avenue of Limes.

Newstead Abbey was a mediaeval priory converted into the Byron family home in the 16th century. It houses the poet Byron's manuscripts & possessions & is set in wonderful gardens.

More modest is the terraced house in Eastwood, where D.H. Lawrence was born into the mining community on which his novels are based.

Nottingham was recorded in the Domesday Book as a thriving community & that tradition continues. It was here that Arkwright perfected his cotton-spinning machinery & went on to develop steam as a power source for industry.

Textiles, shoes, bicycles & tobacco are all famous Nottingham products, & the story of Nottingham Lace can be discovered at the Lace Hall, housed in a former church.

Nottingham Castle, high on Castle Rock, was built & destroyed & rebuilt many times during its history. It now houses the city's Art Gallery & Museum. The Castle towers over the ancient 'Trip to Jerusalem' Inn, said to be so named because crusaders stopped there for a drink on their way to fight in the Holy Land.

Leicestershire, Nottinghamshire & Rutland

Leicestershire Gazeteer

Areas of outstanding natural beauty.
Charnwood Forest, Rutland Water.

Historic Houses & Castles

Belvoir Castle - Nr. Grantham
Overlooking the Vale of Belvoir, castle rebuilt in 1816, with many special events including jousting tournaments. Home of the Duke of Rutland since Henry VIII. Paintings, furniture, historic armoury, military museums, magnificent stateroom.

Belvoir Castle

Belgrave Hall - Leicester
18th century Queen Anne house - furnishing of 18th & 19th centuries.
Langton Hall - Nr. Market Harborough
Privately occupied - perfect English country house from mediaeval times - drawing rooms have 18th century Venetian lace.

Oakham Castle - Oakham
Norman banqueting hall of late 12th C.
Stanford Hall - Nr Lutterworth
17th century William & Mary house - collection of Stuart relics & pictures, antiques & costumes of family from Elizabeth I onward. Motor cycle museum.
Stapleford Park - Nr. Melton Mowbray
Old wing dated 1500, restored 1663. Extended to mansion in 1670. Collection of pictures, tapestries, furniture & Balston's Staffordshire portrait figures of Victorian age.

Cathedrals & Churches

Breedon-on-the-Hill (St. Mary & St. Hardulph)
Norman & 13th century. Jacobean canopied pew, 18th century carvings.
Empingham (St. Peter)
14th century west tower, front & crocketed spire. Early English interior - double piscina, triple sedilla.
Lyddington (St. Andrew)
Perpendicular in the main - mediaeval wall paintings & brasses.
Staunton Harol (Holy Trinity)
17th century - quite unique Cromwellian church - painted ceilings.

Museums & Galleries

Bosworth Battlefield Visitor Centre - Nr Market Bosworth
Exhibitions, models, battlefield trails at site of 1485 Battle of Bosworth where Richard III lost his life & crown to Henry.
Leicestershire Museum of Technology - Leicester
Beam engines, steam shovel, knitting machinery & other aspects of the county's industrial past.
Leicester Museum & Art Gallery - Leicester
Painting collection.
18th & 19th century, watercolours & drawings, 20th century French paintings, Old Master & modern prints.
English silver & ceramics, special exhibitions.
Jewry Wall Museum & Site - Leicester
Roman wall & baths site adjoining museum of archaeology.

Leicestershire, Nottinghamshire & Rutland

Melton Carnegie Museum-Melton Mowbray
Displays of Stilton cheese, pork pies & other
aspects of the past & present life of the
area.
Rutland County Museum - Oakham
Domestic & agricultural life of Rutland,
England's smallest county.
**Donnington Collection of Single-Seater
Racing Cars** - Castle Donington
Large collection of grand prix racing cars
& racing motoroyoloo, adjoining Donington
Park racing circuit..
Wygson's House Museum of Costume -
Leicestershire
Costume, accessories & shop settings in
late mediaeval buildings.
The Bellfoundry Museum -
Loughborough
Moulding, casting, tuning & fitting of bells,
with conducted tours of bellfoundry.

Historic Monuments
The Castle - Ashby-de-la-Zouch
14th century with tower added in 15th
century.
Kirby Muxloe Castle - Kirby Muxloe
15th century fortified manor house with
moat ruins.

Other things to see & do
Rutland Farm Park - Oakham
Rare & commercial breeds of livestock in
18 acres of park & woodland, with early
19th century farm buildings.
Stoughton Farm Park - Nr. Leicester
Shire horses, rare breeds, small animals &
modern 140 dairy herd. Milking
demonstrations, farm museum, woodland
walks. Adventure playground.
Twycross Zoo - Nr. Atherstone
Gorillas, orang-utans, chimpanzees,
gibbons, elephants, giraffes, lions & many
other animals.
The Battlefield Line Nr. Market Bosworth
Steam railway & collection of railway
relics, adjoining Bosworth Battlefield.
Great Central Railway - Loughborough
Steam railway over 5-mile route in
Charnwood Forest area, with steam &
diesel museum.
Rutland Railway Museum - Nr. Oakham
Industrial steam & diesel locomotives.

Nottinghamshire Gazeteer
Historic Houses & Castles
Holme Pierrepont Hall - Nr. Nottingham
Outstanding red brick Tudor manor, in
continuous family ownership, with 19th
century courtyard garden.
Newark Castle - Newark
Dramatic castle ruins on riverside site,
once one of the most important castles of
the north.
Newstead Abbey - Nr. Mansfield
Priory converted to country mansion,
home of poet Lord Byron with many of his
possessions & manuscripts on display.
Beautiful parkland, lakes & gardens.
Nottingham Castle - Nottingham
17th century residence on site of
mediaeval castle.
Fine collections of ceramics, silver,
Nottingham alabaster carvings, local
historical displays. Art gallery. Special
exhibitions & events.
Wollaton Hall - Nottingham
Elizabethan mansion now housing natural
history exhibits. Stands in deer park, with
Industrial Museum in former stables,
illustrating the city's bicycle, hosiery, lace,
pharmaceutical & other industries.

Cathedrals & Churches
Egmanton (St. Mary)
Magnificent interior by Comper. Norman
doorway & font. Canopied rood screen,
17th century altar.
Newark (St. Mary Magdalene)
15th century. 2 painted panels of "Dance
of Death". Reredos by Comper.
Southwell Cathedral
Norman nave, unvaulted, fine early
English choir. Decorated pulpitum, 6
canopied stalls, fine misericords.
Octagonal chapter house..
Terseval (St. Catherine)
12th century - interior 17th century
unrestored.

Museums & Galleries
Castlegate Museum - Nottingham
Row of Georgian terraced houses showing
costume & textile collection.
Lace making equipment & lace collection.

Leicestershire, Nottinghamshire & Rutland

Nottingham Castle Museum - Nottingham
Collections of ceramics, glass & silver. Alabaster carvings.

D.H. Lawrence Birthplace - Eastwood
Home of the novelist & poet, as it would have been at time of his birth, 1885.

Millgate Museum of Social & Folk Life - Newark
Local social & folk life, with craft workshops.

Brewhouse Yard Museum - Nottingham
Daily life in Nottingham, displayed in 17th century cottages & rock-cut cellars.

The Lace Hall - Nottingham
The story of Nottingham Lace audio-visual display & exhibition with lace shops, in fine converted church.

Museum of Costume & Textiles - Nottingham
Costumes, lace & textiles on display in fine Georgian buildings.

Bassetlaw Museum - Retford
Local history of north Nottinghamshire.

Canal Museum - Nottinghamshire
History of the River Trent & canal history, in former canal warehouse.

Ruddington Framework Knitters' Museum - Ruddington
Unique complex of early 19th-century framework knitters' buildings with over 20 hand frames in restored workshop.

Other things to see & do

The Tales of Robin Hood - Nottingham
A 'flight to adventure' from mediaeval Nottingham to Sherwood Forest through the tales of the world's most famous outlaw.

Clumber Park - Nr. Worksop
Landscaped parkland, with double avenue of limes, lake, chapel. One of the Dukeries' estates, though the house no longer remains.

Rufford - Nr. Ollerton
Parkland, lake & gallery with fine crafts, around ruin of Cistercian abbey.

Sherwood Forest Visitor Centre - Nr. Edwinstowe
Robin Hood exhibition. 450 acres of ancient oak woodland associated with the outlaw & his merry men.

Sherwood Forest Farm Park - Nr. Edwinstowe
Rare breeds of cattle, sheep, pigs & goats. Lake with wildfowl.

White Post Farm Centre - Farnsfield, Nr Newark
Working modern farm with crops & many animals, including cows, sheep, pigs, hens, geese, ducks, llamas, horses. Indoor displays & exhibits.

Newark Castle.

LEICESTERSHIRE, NOTTINGHAMSHIRE & RUTLAND

Map reference

01 White
02 Goodwin
04 Hinchley
05 Ibbotson
06 Shipside
07 Morton
08 Kinder

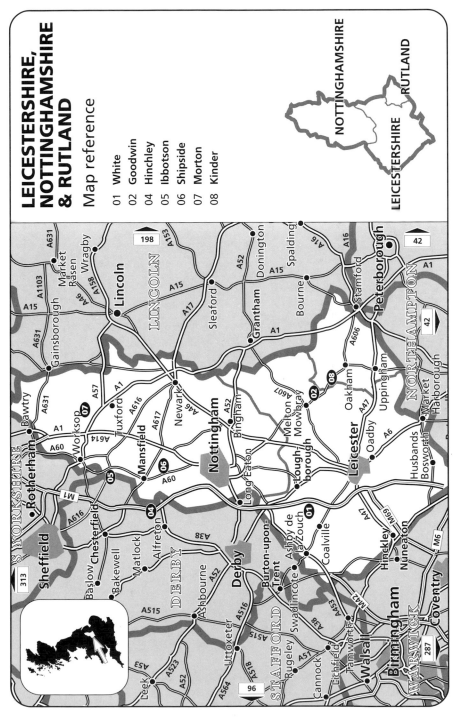

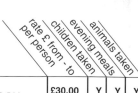

rate £ from - to per person / children taken / evening meals / animals taken

Abbots Oak Country House

Near Rd: A.511
A Grade II listed building with a wealth of oak panelling, & including the staircase reputedly from Nell Gwynn's town house. Set in mature gardens & woodland, with natural granite outcrops. 4 delightful rooms with en-suite/private bathrooms. Open fires create a warm & welcoming atmosphere, & Carolyn's superb dinners are served in the candlelit dining room. Stratford, Belvoir Castle & Rutland Water can all be reached within the hour. Tennis court, billiard room. Children over 6.
www.abbotsoak.com

| | £30.00 to £45.00 | Y | Y | Y |

Mr & Mrs White   Abbots Oak Country House   Warren Hills Road   Coalville LE67 4UY   Leicestershire
Tel: (01530) 832328   Fax 01530 832328   Open: ALL YEAR   Map Ref No. 01

Hillside House

Near Rd: A.606
Charmingly converted farm buildings with superb views over open countryside, in the small village of Burton Lazars. Comfortable accommodation is offered in 1 double & 2 twin-bedded rooms, each with an en-suite/private bathroom. All have tea/coffee facilities & T.V.. A pleasant garden to relax in. Close to Melton Mowbray, famous for its pork pies & Stilton cheese, & with Burghley House, Belvoir Castle & Rutland Water within easy reach. Children over 10. Single supplement.
E-mail: hillhs27@aol.com
www.hillside-house.co.uk

| | £20.00 to £23.00 | Y | N | N |

J. S. Goodwin   Hillside House   27 Melton Road   Burton Lazars   Melton Mowbray LE14 2UR   Leics.
Tel: (01664) 566312   Fax 01664 501819   Open: ALL YEAR (Excl. Xmas & New Year)   Map Ref No. 02

Titchfield House

Near Rd: A.617
This is 2 houses converted into 1 family-run guest house, offering 8 comfortable rooms, a lounge with T.V., a kitchen for guests' use, a bathroom & showers. It also has an adjoining garage. Near to Mansfield, which is a busy market town. Sherwood Forest & the Peak District are both easily accessible. Titchfield Guest House is a very handy location for touring this lovely area, & for onward travel. A warm & friendly welcome is assured at this charming home. Animals by arrangement.
www.bestbandb.co.uk

| | £18.00 to £19.00 | Y | N | Y |

VISA: M'CARD:

Mrs B. Hinchley   Titchfield House   302 Chesterfield Road North   Mansfield NG19 7QU   Notts.
Tel: (01623) 810356/810921   Fax 01623 810356   Open: ALL YEAR   Map Ref No. 04

Blue Barn Farm

Near Rd: A.616
An enjoyable visit is guaranteed at this family-run, 250-acre farm, set in tranquil countryside on the edge of Sherwood Forest (Robin Hood country). 3 guest bedrooms, each with modern amenities including h&c, tea/coffee-making facilities & a guest bathroom with shower. 1 bedroom is en-suite. A colour-T.V. lounge & garden are also available. Guests are very welcome to walk around the farm. Many interesting places, catering for all tastes, only a short journey away.
E-mail: bluebarnfarm@supanet.com
www.bluebarnfarm-notts.co.uk

| | £20.00 to £22.00 | Y | N | N |

June M. Ibbotson   Blue Barn Farm   Langwith   Mansfield NG20 9JD   Nottinghamshire
Tel: (01623) 742248   Fax 01623 742248   Open: ALL YEAR (Excl. Xmas & New Year)   Map Ref No. 05

Holly Lodge. Blidworth.

Nottinghamshire & Rutland

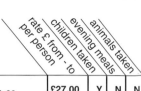

Holly Lodge

Near Rd: A.60

Holly Lodge is situated just off the A.60, 10 miles north of Nottingham. This attractive former hunting lodge stands in 15 acres of grounds. The 4 comfortable & attractive, en-suite guest rooms are housed within the converted stables. There are panoramic countryside views on all sides, with woodland walks, tennis, golf & riding nearby. Ideally situated for a peaceful, rural holiday base with a relaxed & friendly atmosphere.
E-mail: ann.hollylodge@ukonline.co.uk
www.hollylodgenotts.co.uk

	rate £ from - to per person	evening meals	children taken	animals taken
	£27.00 to £30.00	Y	N	N

see PHOTO over
p. 193

VISA: M'CARD: AMEX:

Ann Shipside   Holly Lodge   Ricket Lane   Blidworth   Nottingham NG21 0NQ   Nottinghamshire
Tel: (01623) 793853   Fax 01623 490977   Open: ALL YEAR   Map Ref No. 06

The Barns Country Guest House

Near Rd: A.1

A welcoming & pleasant, relaxed atmosphere awaits you at The Barns. This beautifully converted 18th-century barn, boasts oak beams & pretty bedrooms, all en-suite with full facilities, with a 4-poster room for special occasions. Enjoy a delicious Aga cooked breakfast with vegetarian options, served in a spacious yet comfortable dining room. An interesting base for touring, located at Babworth, home of the Pilgrim Fathers, Robin Hood country & Clumber Park. Children over 8.
E-mail: Peter@thebarns.co.uk
www.thebarns.co.uk

£23.00 to £35.00	Y	N	N

VISA: M'CARD: AMEX:

Mr & Mrs Morton   The Barns Country Guest House   Morton Farm   Babworth   Retford   DN22 8HA Notts.
Tel: (01777) 706336   Fax 01777 709773   Open: ALL YEAR   Map Ref No. 07

Torr Lodge

Near Rd: A.1

A warm welcome awaits you at Torr Lodge, Barrow, in the heart of scenic Rutland, England's smallest county. Belvoir Castle, Burghley House & Geoff Hamilton's famous gardens are all within easy reach, as is Rutland Water. Georgiana has been in the hospitality business for many years & offers tastefully furnished en-suite accommodation, home-cooking on an Aga & hearty breakfasts. Evening meals are available by arrangement. Children over 12 years welocme.
www.bestbandb.co.uk

£25.00 to £28.00	Y	Y	Y

Mrs Georgiana Kinder   Torr Lodge   Main Street   Barrow   Nr. Oakham LE15 7PE   Rutland
Tel: (01572) 813396   Open: ALL YEAR   Map Ref No. 08

Visit our website at:
http://www.bestbandb.co.uk

Lincolnshire

Lincolnshire
(East Midlands)

Lincolnshire is an intriguing mixture of coast & country, of flat fens & gently rising wolds.

There are the popular resorts of Skegness & Mablethorpe as well as quieter coastal regions where flocks of wild birds take food & shelter in the dunes. Gibraltar Point & Saltfleetby are large nature reserves.

Fresh vegetables for much of Britain are produced in the rich soil of the Lincolnshire fens, & windmills punctuate the skyline. There is a unique 8-sailed windmill at Heckington. In spring the fields are ablaze with the red & yellow of tulips. The bulb industry flourishes around Spalding & Holbeach, & in early May tulip flowers in abundance decorate the huge floats of the Spalding Flower Parade.

The city of Lincoln has cobbled streets & ancient buildings & a very beautiful triple-towered Cathedral which shares its hill-top site with the Castle, both dating from the 11th century. There is a 17th century library by Wren in the Cathedral, which has amongst its treasures one of the four original copies of Magna Carta.

Boston has a huge parish church with a distincive octagonal tower which can be seen for miles across the surrounding fenland, & is commonly known as the 'Boston Stump'. The Guildhall Museum displays many aspects of the town's history, including the cells where the early Pilgrim Fathers were imprisioned after their attempt to flee to the Netherlands to find religious freedom. They eventually made the journey & hence to America.

One of England's most outstanding towns is Stamford. It has lovely churches, ancient inns & other fine buildings in a mellow stone.

Sir Isaac Newton was born at Woolsthorpe Manor & educated at nearby Grantham where there is a museum which illustrates his life & work.

The poet Tennyson was born in the village of Somersby, where his father was Rector.

Lincoln Cathedral.

Lincolnshire

Lincolnshire Gazeteer

Areas of outstanding natural beauty.
Lincolnshire Wolds.

Historic Houses & Castles

Auburn House - Nr. Lincoln
16th century house with imposing carved staircase & panelled rooms.
Belton House - Grantham
House built 1684-88 - said to be by Christopher Wren - work by Grinling Gibbons & Wyatt also. Paintings, furniture, porcelain, tapestries, Duke of Windsor mementoes. A great English house with formal gardens & extensive grounds with orangery.
Doddington Hall - Doddington, Nr. Lincoln
16th century Elizabethan mansion with elegant Georgian rooms & gabled Tudor gatehouse. Fine furniture, paintings, porcelain, etc. Formal walled knot gardens, roses & wild gardens.
Burghley House - Stamford
Elizabethan - England's largest & grandest house of the era. Famous for its beautiful painted ceilings, silver fireplaces & art treasures.
Gumby Hall - Burgh-le-Marsh
17th century manor house. Ancient gardens.
Harrington Hall - Spilsby
Mentioned in the Domesday Book - has mediaeval stone base - Carolinean manor house in red brick. Some alterations in 1678 to mullioned windows. Panelling, furnishings of 17th & 18th century.
Marston Hall - Grantham
16th century manor house. Ancient gardens.
The Old Hall - Gainsborough
Fine mediaeval manor house built in 1480's with original kitchen, rebuilt after original hall destroyed during Wars of the Roses. Tower & wings, Great Hall. It was the first meeting place of the "Dissenters", later known as the Pilgrim Fathers.
Woolsthorpe Manor - Grantham
17th century house. Birthplace of Sir Isaac Newton.
Fydell House - Boston
18th century house, now Pilgrim College.

Lincoln Castle - Lincoln
William the Conqueror castle, with complete curtain wall & Norman shell keep. Towers & wall walk. Unique prisoners' chapel.
Tattershall Castle - Tattershall
100 foot high brick keep of 15th century moated castle, with fine views over surrounding country.

Cathedrals & Churches

Addlethorpe (St. Nicholas)
15th century - mediaeval stained glass - original woodwork.
Boston (St. Botolph)
14th century decorated - very large parish church. Beautiful south porch, carved stalls.
Brant Broughton (St. Helens)
13th century arcades - decorated tower & spire - perpendicular clerestory. Exterior decoration.
Ewerby (St. Andrew)
Decorated - splendid example of period - very fine spire. 14th century effigy.
Fleet (St. Mary Magdalene)
14th century - early English arcades - perpendicular windows - detached tower & spire.
Folkingham (St. Andrew)
14th century arcades - 15th century windows - perpendicular tower - early English chancel.
Gedney (St. Mary Magdalene)
Perpendicular spire (unfinished). Early English tower. 13th-14th century monuments, 14th-15th century stained glass.
Grantham (St. Wulfram)
14th century tower & spire - Norman pillars - perpendicular chantry - 14th century vaulted crypt.
Lincoln Cathedral - Lincoln
Magnificent triple-towered Gothic building on fine hill-top site.
Norman west front, 13th century - some 14th century additions. Norman work from 1072. Angel choir - carved & decorated pulpitum - 13th century chapter house - 17th century library by Wren (containing one of the four original copies of Magna Carta).

Lincolnshire

St. Botolph's Church - Boston
Fine parish church, one of the largest in the country, with 272 foot octagonal tower dominating the surrounding fens.
Long Sutton (St. Mary)
15th century south porch, mediaeval brass lectern, very fine early English spire.
Louth (St. James)
Early 16th century - mediaeval Gothic - wonderful spire.
Scotter (St. Peter)
Saxon to perpendicular - early English nave - 15th century rood screen.
Stow (St. Mary)
Norman - very fine example, particularly west door. Wall painting.
Silk Willoughby (St. Denis)
14th century - tower with spire & flying buttresses. 15th-17th century pulpit.
Stainfield (St. Andrew)
Queen Anne - mediaeval armour & early needlework.
Theddlethorpe (All Saints)
14th century - 15th century & reredos of 15th century, 16th century parcloses, 15th century brasses - some mediaeval glass.
Wrangle (St. Mary the Virgin & St. Nicholas)
Early English - decorated - perpendicular - Elizabethan pulpit. 14th century east window & glass.

Museums & Galleries

Alford Manor House - Alford
Tudor manor house - thatched - folk museum. Nearby windmill.
Boston Guildhall Museum - Boston
15th century building with mayor's parlour, court room & cells where Pilgrim Fathers were imprisoned in 1607. Local exhibits.
Lincoln Cathedral Library - Lincoln
Built by Wren housing early printed books & mediaeval manuscripts.
Lincoln Cathedral Treasury - Lincoln
Diocesan gold & silver plate.
Lincoln City & Country Museum - Lincoln
Prehistoric, Roman & mediaeval antiquities with local associations. Armour & local history.
Museum of Lincolnshire Life - Lincoln
Domestic, agricultural, industrial & social history of the county. Edwardian room settings, shop settings, agricultural machinery.

Usher Gallery - Lincoln
Paintings, watches, miniatures, porcelain, silver, coins & medals. Temporary exhibitions. Tennyson collection. Works of English watercolourist Peter de Wint.
Grantham Museum - Grantham
Archeology, prehistoric, Saxon & Roman. Local history with special display about Sir Isaac Newton, born nearby & educated in Grantham.
Church Farm Museum - Skegness
Farmhouse & buildings with local agricultural collections & temporary exhibitions & special events.
Stamford Museum - Stamford
Local history museum, with temporary special exhibitions.
Battle of Britain Memorial Flight - Coningsby
Lancaster bomber, five Spitfires & two Hurricanes with other Battle of Britain memorabilia.
National Cycle Museum - Lincoln
Development of the cycle.
Stamford Steam Brewery Museum - Stamford
Complete Victorian steam brewery with 19th century equipment.

Other things to see & do

Springfield - Spalding
Show gardens of the British bulb industry, & home of the Spalding Flower Parade each May. Summer bedding plants & roses.
Butlins Funcoast World - Skegness
Funsplash Water World with amusements & entertainments
Castle Leisure Park - Tattershall
Windsurfing, water-skiing, sailing, fishing & other sports & leisure facilities.
Long Sutton Butterfly Park - Long Sutton
Walk-through tropical butterfly house with outdoor wildflower meadows & pets corner.
Skegness Natureland Marine Zoo - Skegness
Seal sanctuary with aquaria, tropical house, pets corner & butterfly house.
Windmills - at Lincoln (Ellis Mill - 4 sails), Boston (Maud Foster - 5 sails), Burgh-le-Marsh (5 sails), Alford (5 sails), Sibsey (6 sails), Heckington (8 sails).

LINCOLNSHIRE
Map reference

01 Armstrong
02 Sharman
03 Clarke
04 Honnor
05 Woods

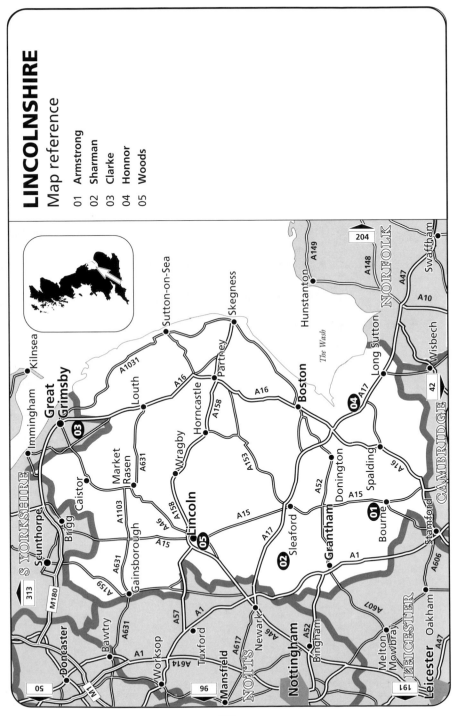

Lincolnshire

rate £ from - to per person	children taken	evening meals taken	animals taken		

| £35.00 to £35.00 | Y | N | Y | | **Cawthorpe Hall** |

Near Rd: A.15

This fine, old, listed house is surrounded by a large pretty garden & fields of roses supplying the rose distillery with fragrant blooms. The rooms are bright, spacious & comfortably furnished & have bathrooms en-suite. A full English breakfast will be served in a family country kitchen. Country lovers can enjoy beautiful woodland walks. Horse riding or golf, Grimsthorpe Castle & Park are all within easy reach. A charming home.
E-mail: chantal@cawthorpebandb.co.uk
www.cawthorpebandb.co.uk

Chantal Armstrong   Cawthorpe Hall   Cawthorpe   Bourne PE10 0AB   Lincolnshire
Tel: (01778) 100000 Fax 01778 400000 Open: ALL YEAR (Excl. Xmas & New Year) Map Ref No. 01

| £22.50 to £50.00 | Y | N | N | | **Gelston Grange Farm** |

Near Rd: A.1, A.17

A warm welcome awaits you at Gelston Grange, a period farmhouse dated 1840, with many original features. Set in a large garden, it overlooks open countryside & has ample parking. All bedrooms are en-suite, designed with comfort in mind & are pleasing to the eye, with many thoughtful extras. Delicious full English breakfasts are served in the dining room, with a log fire on chilly mornings. Approx. 3 miles from A.1 or A.17. Central for Lincoln, Grantham, Stamford & Newark. A home from home. Children over 10 years.

J. Sharman   Gelston Grange Farm   Nr. Marston   Grantham NG32 2AQ   Lincolnshire
Tel: (01400) 250281   Open: Mid JAN - Mid DEC   Map Ref No.02

| £25.00 to £25.00 | Y | N | N | | **The Old Farmhouse** |

Near Rd: A.18

Situated in the Wolds, The Old Farmhouse is an 18th-century treasure recently renovated to a very high standard. Stunning inside & out, & set in a truly peaceful location overlooking a picturesque valley. A large comfortable lounge with inglenook fireplace & old beams is provided for you to relax in. 2 beautifully furnished bedrooms with all amenities. An excellent choice of local pubs. Well-placed for golf, country walks, the coast & horse racing. Parking & horse livery available. Children over 8.
E-mail: nicola@hatcliffe.freeserve.co.uk

Nicola Clarke   The Old Farmhouse   Low Road   Hatcliffe   Grimsby DN37 0SH   Lincolnshire
Tel: (01472) 824455   Open: ALL YEAR (Excl. Xmas & New Year)   Map Ref No.03

| £24.00 to £25.00 | N | N | N | | **Pipwell Manor** |

Near Rd: A.17

Pipwell Manor is a Grade II listed Georgian manor house, built in around 1740, set in paddocks & gardens in a small quiet village in the Lincolnshire Fens, just off the A.17. Beautifully restored & decorated in English-country style, but retaining many original features, this is a delightful place to stay. 3 comfortably furnished & attractive bedrooms, each with an en-suite/private bathroom & tea/coffee. Guests are welcomed with tea & homemade cake. Bicycles available for guests use.
E-mail: honnor@pipwellmanor.freeserve.co.uk
www.smoothhound.co.uk/hotels/pipwell.html

Mrs Lesley Honnor   Pipwell Manor   Washway Road   Saracens Head   Holbeach PE12 8AL   Lincs.
Tel: (01406) 423119   Fax 01406 423119   Open: ALL YEAR   Map Ref No. 04

	rate £ from - to per person	children taken	evening meals	animals taken

Carline Guest House

Near Rd: A.57, A.46

Barrie & Jackie Woods extend a warm welcome. Excellent accommodation, in 6 attractively furnished bedrooms, each with en-suite facilities, T.V., radio, beverage facilities, hairdryers & trouser press. The Carline is a short, pleasant stroll from the Lawns Tourism & Conference Centre, & from the historic Uphill area of Lincoln. There are several restaurants & public houses nearby for your lunch or evening meal. Ask for recommendations.
E-mail: sales@carlineguesthouse.co.uk
www.carlineguesthouse.co.uk

£23.00 to £23.00	Y	N	N

Barrie & Jackie Woods   Carline Guest House   1-3 Carline Road   Lincoln LN1 1HL   Lincolnshire
Tel: (01522) 530422 Fax 01522 530422 Open: ALL YEAR (Excl. Xmas & New Year) Map Ref No. 05

Norfolk

Norfolk
(East Anglia)

One of the largest of the old counties, Norfolk is divided by rivers from neighbouring counties & pushes out into the sea on the north & east sides. This is old East Anglia.

Inland there is great concentration on agriculture where fields are hedged with hawthorn which blossoms like snow in summer. A great deal of land drainage is required & the area is crisscrossed by dykes & ditches - some of them dating back to Roman times.

Holkham Hall.

The Norfolk Broads were formed by the flooding of mediaeval peat diggings to form miles & miles of inland waterways, navigable & safe. On a bright summer's day, on a peaceful backwater bounded by reed & sedge, the Broads seem like paradise. Here are hidden treasures like the Bittern, that shyest of birds, the Swallowtail butterfly & the rare Marsh orchid.

Contrasting with the still inland waters is a lively coastline which takes in a host of towns & villages as it arcs around The Wash. Here are the joys of the seaside at its best, miles of safe & sandy golden beaches to delight children, dunes & salt marshes where bird-life flourishes, & busy ports & fishing villages with pink-washed cottages.

Cromer is a little seaside town with a pier & a prom, cream teas & candy floss, where red, white & blue fishing boats are drawn up on the beach.

Hunstanton is more decorous, with a broad green sweeping down to the cliffs. Great Yarmouth is a boisterous resort. It has a beach that runs for miles, with pony rides & almost every amusement imaginable.

It is possible to take a boat into the heart of Norwich, past warehouses, factories & new penthouses, & under stone & iron bridges. Walking along the riverbank you reach Pulls Ferry where a perfectly proportioned grey flint gateway arcs over what was once a canal dug to transport stone to the cathedral site. Norwich Cathedral is magnificent, with a sharply soaring spire, beautiful cloisters & fine 15th century carving preserved in the choir stalls. Cathedral Close is perfectly preserved, as is Elm Hill, a cobbled street from mediaeval times. There are many little shops & narrow alleys going down to the river.

Norfolk is a county much loved by the Royal family & the Queen has a home at Sandringham. It is no castle, but a solid, comfortable family home with red brick turrets & French windows opening onto the terrace.

Norfolk

Norfolk Gazeteer

Areas of outstanding beauty.
Norfolk coast (part)

Historic Houses & Castles

Anna Sewell House - Great Yarmouth
17th century Tudor frontage. Birthplace of writer Anna Sewell.

Blicking Hall - Aylsham
Great Jacobean house. Fine Russian tapestry, long gallery with exceptional ceiling. Formal garden.

Felbrigg Hall - Nr. Cromer
17th century, good Georgian interior. Set in wooded parklands.

Holkham Hall - Wells
Fine Palladian mansion of 1734. Paintings, statuary, tapestries, furnishings & formal garden by Berry.

Houghton Hall - Wells
18th century mansion. Pictures, china & staterooms.

Oxburgh Hall - Swafftham
Late 15th century moated house. Fine gatehouse tower. Needlework by Mary Queen of Scots.

Wolterton Hall - Nr. Norwich
Built in 1741 contains tapestries, porcelain, furniture.

Trinity Hospital - Castle Rising
17th century, nine brick & tile almshouses, court chapel & treasury.

Cathedrals & Churches

Attleborough (St. Mary)
Norman with late 14th century. Fine rood screen & frescoes.

Barton Turf (St. Michael & All Angles)
Magnificent screen with painting of the Nine Orders of Angles.

Beeston-next-Mileham (St. Mary)
14th century. Perpendicular clerestory tower & spire. Hammer Beam roof, parclose screens, benches, front cover. Tracery in nave & chancel windows.

Cawston (St. Agnes)
Tower faced with freestone. Painted screens, wall paintings, tower, screen & gallery. 15th century angel roof.

East Harding (St. Peter & St. Paul)
14th century, some 15th century alterations. Monuments of 15th-17th century. Splendid mediaeval glass.

Erpingham (St. Mary)
14th century military brass to John de Erpingham, 16th century Rhenish glass. Fine tower.

Gunton (St. Andrew)
18th century. Robert Adam - classical interior in dark wood - gilded.

King's Lynn (St. Margaret)
Norman foundation. Two fine 14th century Flemish brasses, 14th century screens, reredos by Bodley, interesting Georgian pulpit with sounding board.

Norwich Cathedral
Romanesque & late Gothic with 15th century spire. Perpendicular lierne vaults in nave, transeptsand presbytery.

Ranworth (St. Helens)
15th century screen, very fine example. Sarum Antiphoner, 14th century illuminated manuscript - East Anglian work.

Salle (St. Peter & St. Paul)
15th century. Highly decorated west tower & porches. Mediaeval glass, pulpit with 15th century panels & Jacobean tester. Stalls, misericords, brasses & monuments, sacrament font.

Terrington (St. Clement)
Detached perpendicular tower. Western front has fire-light window & canopied niches. Georgian panelling west of nave. 17th century painted font cover. Jacobean commandment boards.

Trunch (St. Botolph)
15th century screen with painted panels, mediaeval glass, famous font canopy with fine carving & painting, ringer's gallery, Elizabethan monument.

Wiggenhall (St. Germans)
17th century pulpit, table, clerk's desk & chair, bench ends 15th century.

Wymondham (St. Mary & St. Thomas of Canterbury)
Norman origins including arcades & triforium windows, 13th century font fragments, complete 15th century font. 15th century clerestory & roof. Comper reredos, famous Corporas Case, rare example of 13th century Opus Anglicanum.

Museums & Galleries

Norwich Castle Museum
Art collection, local & natural history,

Norfolk

Strangers Hall - Norwich
Mediaeval mansion furnished as museum of urban domestic life in 16th-19th centuries.

St. Peter Hungate Church Museum - Norwich
15th century church for the exhibition of ecclesiastical art & East Anglican antiquities.

Sainsbury Centre for Visual Arts - University, Norwich
Collection of modern art, ancient, classical & mediaeval art, Art Nouveau, 20th century constructivist art.

Bridewell Museum of Local Industries - Norwich
Crafts, industries & aspects of city life.

Museum of Social History - King's Lynn
Exhibition of domestic life & dress, etc., noted glass collection.

Bishop Bonner's Cottages
Restored cottages with coloured East Anglia pargetting, c. 1502, museum of archaeological discoveries, exhibition of rural crafts.

The Guildhall - Thetford
Duleep Singh Collection of Norfolk & Suffolk portraits.

Shirehall Museum - Walsingham
18th century court room having original fittings, illustrating Walsingham life.

Historic Monuments

Binham Priory & Cross - Binham
12th century ruins of Benedictine foundation.

Caister Castle - Great Yarmouth
15th century moated castle - ruins. Now motor museum.

The Castle - Burgh Castle
3rd century Saxon fort - walls - ruin.

Mannington Hall - Saxthorpe
Saxon church ruin in gardens of 15th century moated house.

Castle Rising - Castle Rising
Splendid Norman keep & earthworks.

Castle Acre Priory & Castle Gate - Swaffham

Other things to see & do

African Violet Centre - Terrington St. Clements.
60 varieties of African Violets. Talks & Tours.

Norfolk Lavender Centre - Heacham
Open to the public in July & August. Demonstrations of harvesting & distilling the oil.

Thetford Forest
Forest walks, rides & picnic places amongst conifers, oak, beech & birch.

The Broads.

NORFOLK

Map reference

01 Gillam
02 Pugh
03 Douglas
04 Collins

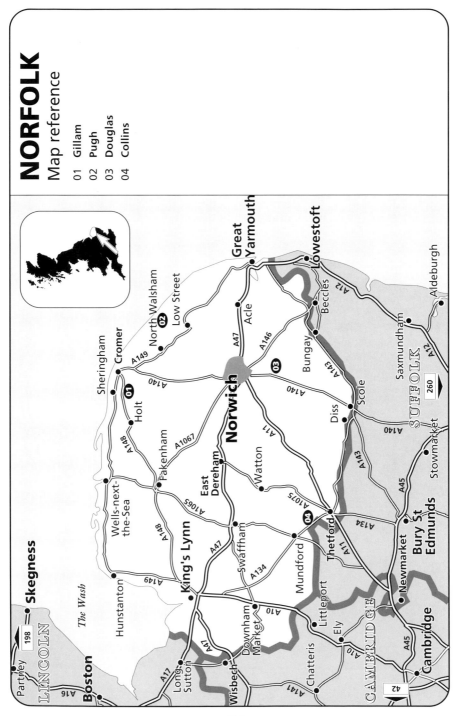

Felbrigg Lodge. Aylmerton.

	rate £ from - to per person	children taken	evening meals	animals taken

Felbrigg Lodge

Near Rd: A.140

Set in beautiful countryside 2 miles from the coast, Felbrigg Lodge is hidden in 8 acres of spectacular woodland gardens. Time has stood still since Edwardian ladies came here in their carriages to take tea & play croquet. Great care has been taken to preserve this atmosphere with comfortable en-suite rooms, luxuriously decorated with every facility. A true haven of peace & tranquillity. A nature lover's paradise. Candlelit dinners & copious breakfasts. Indoor heated pool/gym. Children over 10.
E-mail: info@felbrigglodge.co.uk
www.felbrigglodge.co.uk

£42.00 to £58.00 — Y — Y — N

see PHOTO over p. 205

VISA: M'CARD:

Jill & Ian Gillam   Felbrigg Lodge   Aylmerton   Nr. Holt NR11 8RA   Norfolk
Tel: (01263) 837588   Fax 01263 838012   Open: ALL YEAR   Map Ref No. 01

Mill Common House

Near Rd: A.149

Mill Common House is an elegant Georgian farmhouse set in a rural location, close to the market town of North Walsham & only 1 mile from sandy beaches. Standing in its own grounds, beside the original brick & flint buildings dating back over 200 years. 2 attractive bedrooms, with all amenities, a large conservatory & open log fires on cooler days all add to the relaxed atmosphere & surroundings, typical of comfortable stylish living. Babies & children over 12 years. Animals by arrangement.
E-mail: johnpugh@millcommon.freeserve.co.uk
www.broadland.com/millcommon

£26.00 to £32.00 — Y — Y — Y

Mrs Wendy Pugh   Mill Common House   Mill Common Road   Ridlington   North Walsham NR28 9TY
Tel: (01692) 650792   Fax 01692 651480   Open: ALL YEAR (Excl. Xmas)   Map Ref No. 02

Greenacres Farmhouse

Near Rd: A.140

A period 17th-century farmhouse on a 30-acre common with ponds & wildlife, only 10 miles from Norwich. All of the en-suite/private bedrooms (2 double/1 twin) are tastefully furnished to complement the oak beams & period furniture, with tea/coffee facilities & T.V.. Relax in the beamed sitting room with inglenook fireplace & enjoy a leisurely breakfast in the sunny dining room. Snooker table & tennis court. Therapeutic massage, aromatherapy & reflexology service available.
E-mail: greenacresfarm@tinyworld.co.uk

£22.50 to £27.50 — N — N — N

Joanna Douglas   Greenacres Farmhouse   Woodgreen   Long Stratton   Norwich NR15 2RR   Norfolk
Tel: (01508) 530261   Fax 01508 530261   Open: ALL YEAR   Map Ref No. 03

Cedar Lodge

Near Rd: A.134

A warm welcome awaits you at Cedar Lodge, which stands on the edge of Thetford Forest. There are 2 attractive double rooms overlooking farmland & big log fires in a lovely sitting room. Food is the password - Christine owns a useful catering company & is a member of The Master Chefs of Great Britain & delights in preparing candlelit dinners for her guests. Children over 12 years are welcome. Cedar Lodge is an ideal location for a relaxing break & for exploring Norfolk.
www.bestbandb.co.uk

£26.50 to £26.50 — Y — Y — N

Mrs Christine Collins   Cedar Lodge   West Tofts   Thetford IP26 5DB   Norfolk
Tel: (01842) 878281   Fax 01842 878281   Open: ALL YEAR   Map Ref No. 04

Northumbria

Northumbria

Mountains & moors, hills & fells, coast & country are all to be found in this Northern region which embraces four counties - Northumberland, Durham, Cleveland & Tyne & Wear.

Saxons, Celts, Vikings, Romans & Scots all fought to control what was then a great wasteland between the Humber & Scotland.

Northumberland

Northumberland is England's Border country, a land of history, heritage & breathtaking countryside. Hadrian's Wall, stretching across the county from the mouth of the Tyne in the west to the Solway Firth, was built as the Northern frontier of the Roman Empire in 122 AD. Excavations along the Wall have brought many archaeological treasures to light. To walk along the wall is to discover the genius of Roman building & engineering skill. They left a network of roads, used to transport men & equipment in their attempts to maintain discipline among the wild tribes.

Through the following centuries the Border wars with the Scots led to famous battles such as Otterburn in 1388 & Flodden in 1513, & the construction of great castles including Bamburgh & Lindisfarne. Berwick-on-Tweed, the most northerly town, changed hands between England & Scotland 13 times.

Northumberland's superb countryside includes the Cheviot Hills in the Northumberland National Park, the unforgettable heather moorlands of the Northern Pennines to the west, Kielder Water (Western Europe's largest man-made lake), & 40 miles of glorious coastline.

Holy Island, or Lindisfarne, is reached by a narrow causeway that is covered at every incoming tide. Here St. Aidan of Iona founded a monastery in the 7th century, & with St. Cuthbert set out to Christianise the pagan tribes. The site was destroyed by the Danes, but Lindisfarne Priory was built by the monks of Durham in the 11th century to house a Benedictine community. The ruins are hauntingly beautiful.

Durham

County Durham is the land of the Prince Bishops, who with their armies, nobility, courts & coinage controlled the area for centuries. They ruled as a virtually independent State, holding the first line of defence against the Scots.

In Durham City, the impressive Norman Castle standing proudly over the narrow mediaeval streets was the home of the Prince Bishops for 800 years.

Durham Cathedral, on a wooded peninsula high above the River Wear, was built in the early 12th century & is undoubtably one of the world's finest buildings, long a place of Christian pilgrimage.

The region's turbulent history led to the building of forts & castles. Some like Bowes & Barnard Castle are picturesque ruins whilst others, including Raby, Durham & Lumley still stand complete.

The Durham Dales of Weardale, Teesdale & the Derwent Valley cover about one third of the county & are endowed with some of the highest & wildest scenery. Here are High Force, England's highest waterfall, & the Upper Teesdale National Nature Reserve.

The Bowes Museum at Barnard Castle is a magnificent French-style chateau & houses an important art collection.

In contrast is the award-winning museum at Beamish which imaginatively recreates Northern life at the turn of the century.

Northumbria

Cleveland

Cleveland, the smallest 'shire' in England, has long been famous for its steel, chemical & shipbuilding industries but it is also an area of great beauty. The North Yorkshire National Park lies in the south, & includes the cone-shaped summit of Roseberry Topping, "Cleveland's Matterhorn".

Cleveland means 'land of cliffs', & in places along the magnificent coastline, cliffs tower more than 600 feet above the sea, providing important habitat for wild plants & sea-birds.

Pretty villages such as Hart, Elwick & Staithes are full of steep, narrow alleys. Marton was the birthplace of Captain James Cook & the museum there traces the explorer's early life & forms the start of the 'Cook Heritage Trail'.

The Tees estuary is a paradise for birdwatchers, whilst walkers can follow the Cleveland Way or the 38 miles of the Langbaurgh Loop. There is surfing, windsurfing & sailing at Saltburn, & for the less energetic, the scenic Esk Valley Railway runs from Middlesbrough to Whitby.

Tyne & Wear

Tyne & Wear takes its name from the two rivers running through the area, & includes the large & lively city of Newcastle-on-Tyne.

Weardale lies in a beautiful valley surrounded by wild & bleak fells. Peaceful now, it was the setting for a thriving industry mining coal & silver, zinc & lead. Nature trails & recreation areas have been created among the old village & market towns.

The county was the birthplace of George Stephenson, railway engineer, who pioneered the world's first passenger railway on the Stockton to Darlington Line in 1825.

Durham Cathedral.

Northumbria

Northumbria Gazeeter

Areas of Outstanding Natural Beauty
The Heritage Coast, the Cheviot Hills, the North Pennine chain.

Historic Houses & Castles

Alnwick Castle - Alnwick
A superb mediaeval castle of the 12th century.
Bamburgh Castle-Bamburgh
A restored 12th century castle with Norman keep.
Callaly Castle - Whittingham
A 13th century Pele tower with 17th century mansion. Georgian additions.
Durham Castle - Durham
Part of the University of Durham - a Norman castle.
Lindisfarne Castle - Holy Island
An interesting 14th century castle.
Ormesby Hall - Nr. Middlesbrough
A mid 18th century house.
Raby Castle - Staindrop, Darlington
14th century with some later alteration . Fine art & furniture. Large gardens.
Wallington Hall -Combo
A 17th century house with much alteration & addition.
Washington Old Hall-Washington
Jacobean manor house, parts of which date back to 12th century.

Cathedrals & Churches

Brancepeth (St. Brandon)
12th century with superb 17th century woodwork. Part of 2 mediaeval screens. Flemish carved chest.
Durham Cathedral
A superb Norman cathedral. A unique Galilee chapel & early 12th century vaults.
Escombe
An interesting Saxon Church with sundial.
Hartlepool (St. Hilda)
Early English with fine tower & buttresses.
Hexham (St. Andrews)
Remains of a 17th century church with Roman dressing. A unique night staircase & very early stool. Painted screens.
Jarrow (St. Pauls)
Bede worshipped here. Strange in that it was originally 2 churches until 11th century. Mediaeval chair.

Newcastle (St. Nicholas)
14th century with an interesting lantern tower.
Heraldic font. Roundel of 14th century glass.
Morpeth (St. Mary the Virgin)
Fine mediaeval glass in east window - 14th century.
Pittington (St. Lawrence)
Late Norman nave with wall paintings. Carved tombstone - 13th century.
Skelton (St. Giles)
Early 13th century with notable font, gable crosses, bell-cote & buttresses.
Staindrop (St. Mary)
A fine Saxon window.
Priests dwelling.
Neville tombs & effigies.

Museums & Galleries

Aribea Roman Fort Museum - South Shields
Interesting objects found on site.
Berwick-on-Tweed Museum - Berwick
Special exhibition of interesting local finds.
Bowes Museum - Bernard Castle
European art from mediaeval to 19th century.
Captain Cook Birthplace Museum - Middlesbrough
Cook's life & natural history relating to his travels.
Clayton Collection - Chollerford
A collection of Roman sculpture, weapons & tools from forts.
Corbridge Roman Station - Corbridge
Roman pottery & sculpture.
Dormitory Musuem - Durham Cathedral
Relics of St. Cuthbert.
Mediaeval seats & manuscripts.
Gray Art Gallery - Hartlepool
19th-20th century art & oriental antiquities.
Gulbenkian Museum of Oriental Art - University of Durham
Chinese pottery & porcelain, Chinese jade & stone carvings, Chinese ivories, Chinese textiles, Japenese & Tibetan art. Egyptian & Mesopotamian antiquities.
Jarrow Hall - Jarrow
Excavation finds of Saxon & mediaeval monastery.
Fascinating information room dealing with early Christian sites in England.

Northumbria

Keep Museum - Newcastle-upon-Tyne
Mediaeval collection.
Laing Art Gallery - Newcastle-upon-Tyne
17th-19th century British arts, porcelain,
glass & silver.
National Music Hall Museum -
Sunderland
19th-20th century costume & artefacts
associated with the halls.
Preston Hall Museum - Stockton-on-Tees
Armour & arms, toys, ivory period room
University - New Castle -Upon -Tyne
The Hatton Gallery - housing a fine
collection of Italian paintings.
Museum of Antiquities
Prehistoric, Roman & Saxon collection
with an interesting reconstruction of a
temple.
**Beamish North of England Open Air
Museum** - European Museum of the Year
Chantry Bagpipe Museum - Morpeth
Darlington Museum & Railway Centre.

Historic Monuments

Ariiea Roman Fort - South Shields
Remains which include the gateways &
headquarters.
Barnard Castle - Barnard Castle
17th century ruin with interesting keep.
Bowes Castle - Bowes
Roman Fort with Norman keep.
The Castle & Town Walls - Berwick-on-
Tweed
12th century remains, reconstructed later.
Dunstanburgh Castle - Alnwick
14th century remains.
Egglestone Abbey - Barnard Castle
Remains of a Poor House.
Finchdale Priory - Durham
13 th century church with much
remaining.
Hadrian's Wall - Housesteads
Several miles of the wall including castles
& site museum.
Mithramic Temple - Carrawbrough
Mithraic temple dating back to the 3rd
century.
Norham Castle - Norham
The partial remains of a 12th century
castle.
Prudhoe Castle - Prudhoe
Dating from the 12th century with
additions. Bailey & gatehouse well
preserved.

The Roman Fort - Chesters
Extensive remains of a Roman bath
house.
Tynemouth Priory & Castle - Tynemouth
11th century priory - ruin - with 16th
century towers & keep.
Vindolanda - Barton Mill
Roman fort dating from 3rd century.
Warkworth Castle - Warkworth
Dating from the 11th century with
additions.
A great keep & gatehouse.
Warkworth Hermitage - Warkworth
An interesting 14th century Hermitage.
Lindisfarne Priory - Holy Island
(Lindisfarne)
11th century monastery. Island accessible
only at low tide.

Other things to see & do

Botanical Gardens - Durham University
Bird & Seal Colonies - Farne Islands
Conducted tours by boat
Marine Life Centre & Fishing Museum -
Seahouses
Museum of sealife, & boat trips to the
Farne Islands.
Tower Knowe Visitor Centre - Keilder
Water

Saltburn Victorian Festival.

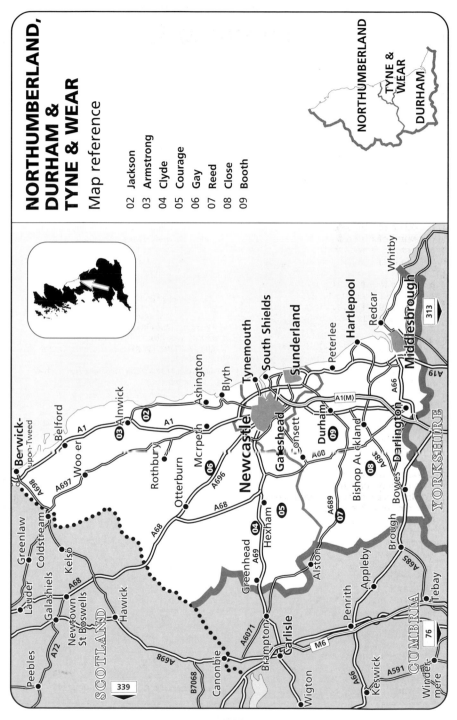

NORTHUMBERLAND, DURHAM & TYNE & WEAR

Map reference

02 Jackson
03 Armstrong
04 Clyde
05 Courage
06 Gay
07 Reed
08 Close
09 Booth

NORTHUMBERLAND

TYNE & WEAR

DURHAM

Northumberland

Bilton Barns Farmhouse

Near Rd: A.1

Dating back to 1715, Bilton Barns has fantastic views over Alnmouth & Warkworth Bay, only 1 1/2 miles away. The spacious & beautifully furnished rooms are all en-suite, centrally heated & with T.V. & tea/coffee-making facilities; or stay in one of the lovely suites, 1 has a 4-poster bed, all have beamed lounges. Choose Craster kippers from the extensive breakfast menu. Dorothy also makes delicious evening meals with a distinctly local flavour, available by arrangement.
E-mail: dorothy@biltonbarns.com
www.biltonbarns.com

| £27.00 to £35.00 | Y | Y | N |

see PHOTO over p. 213

Dorothy Jackson   Bilton Barns Farmhouse   Alnmouth   Alnwick NE66 2TB   Northumberland
Tel: (01665) 830427   Fax 01665 833909   Open: ALL YEAR (Excl. Xmas)   Map Ref No. 02

North Charlton Farm

Near Rd: A.1

Afternoon tea with home-baking is served on arrival in the visitors lounge at North Charlton Farm. The house has just been completely restored & is beautifully furnished with antiques, yet offers every modern comfort in elegant surroundings. Enjoy breakfast in the dining room with views out to the sea (Full English, Craster kippers, home-made preserves & more). The Armstrongs also have a Household & Farming Museum at North Charlton, which is a real 'treasure trove'. Children over 10.
E-mail: ncharlton1@agriplus.net
www.northcharlton.com

| £28.00 to £30.00 | Y | N | N |

Mr & Mrs Charles Armstrong   North Charlton Farm   Chathill   Alnwick NE67 5HP   Northumberland
Tel: (01665) 579407   Fax 01665 579443   Open: ALL YEAR   Map Ref No. 03

Allerwash Farmhouse

Near Rd: A.69

Allerwash is an elegant Regency farm house which is full of character & has secluded gardens surrounded by rolling countryside. Bedrooms are stylishly decorated & include private facilities. Open fires in the 2 drawing rooms add to the warmth of the house & elegant furnishings plus antiques & paintings make this a real house of distinction. Meals are delicious & Angela has many cookery awards to her credit. The Roman Wall, the Lake District, the Northumberland coast & many castles & gardens are within easy reach. Children over 8.

| £42.50 to £42.50 | Y | Y | Y |

Ian & Angela Clyde   Allerwash Farmhouse   Newbrough   Hexham NE47 5AB   Northumberland
Tel: (01434) 674574   Fax 01434 674574   Open: ALL YEAR   Map Ref No. 04

Rye Hill Farm

Near Rd: A.68

Rye Hill Farm dates back some 300 years & is a traditional livestock unit in beautiful countryside just 5 miles south of Hexham. Recently, some of the stone barns adjoining the farmhouse have been converted into superb modern guest accommodation. There are 6 bedrooms, all with private facilities, & all have radio, T.V. & tea/coffee-making facilities. Delicious home-cooked meals. Perfect for a get-away-from-it-all holiday.
E-mail: info@ryehillfarm.co.uk
www.ryehillfarm.co.uk

| £22.50 to £22.50 | Y | Y | Y |

VISA: M'CARD:

Elizabeth Courage   Rye Hill Farm   Slaley   Hexham NE47 OAH   Northumberland
Tel: (01434) 673259   Fax 01434 673259   Open: ALL YEAR   Map Ref No. 05

Bilton Barns Farmhouse.   Alnmouth.

Northumberland & Durham

Shieldhall

Near Rd: A.696

Within acres of well-kept gardens, offering unimpeded views & overlooking the National Trust's Wallington estate, this meticulously restored 18th-century farmhouse is built around a pretty court-yard. All of the 3 en-suite bedrooms are beautifully furnished & have T.V.. Comfortable lounges & an extremely charming inglenooked dining room where home produce is often used for delicious meals which are specially prepared when booked in advance. Children over 12 & animals by arrangement.
E-mail: Robinson.Gay@btinternet.com
www.shieldhallguesthouse.co.uk

£25.00 to £36.00 | Y | Y | Y

VISA: M'CARD:

Stephen & Celia Gay　Shieldhall　Wallington　Morpeth NE61 4AQ　Northumberland
Tel: (01830) 540387　Fax 01830 540490　Open: MAR - NOV　Map Ref No. 06

Lands Farm

Near Rd: A.689

You will be warmly welcomed to Lands Farm, an old stone-built farmhouse within walking distance of Westgate village. A walled garden with stream meandering by. Accommodation is in centrally heated double & family rooms with luxury en-suite facilities, T.V., tea/coffee-making facilities. Full English breakfast or Continental alternative served in an attractive dining room. This is an ideal base for touring (Durham, Hadrian's Wall, Beamish Museum, etc.) & for walking.
E-mail: barbara@landsfarm.fsnet.co.uk

£23.00 to £25.00 | Y | N | N

Mrs Barbara Reed　Lands Farm　Westgate-in-Weardale　Bishop Auckland DL13 1SN　Durham
Tel: (01388) 517210　Fax 01388 517210　Open: ALL YEAR　Map Ref No. 07

Grove House

Near Rd: A.68

Grove House, once an aristocrat's shooting lodge, is tastefully furnished throughout, & is situated in an idyllic setting in the middle of Hamsterley Forest. A spacious lounge with log fire gives a warm & comfortable country-house atmosphere. The gran-deur of the dining room reminds one of an age gone by. (Take note of the door handles!) 3 bedrooms, all en-suite or with private bathrooms. Helene does all the cooking herself to ensure freshness & quality to her evening meals. Children over 10 years.
E-mail: grovehouse@dial.pipex.com
www.grovehouse.biz

£34.00 to £36.00 | Y | Y | N

Helene & Russell Close　Grove House　Hamsterley Forest　Bishop Auckland DL13 3NL　Durham
Tel: (01388) 488203 Fax 01388 488174　Open: ALL YEAR (Excl. Xmas & New Year)　Map Ref No. 08

Ivesley

Near Rd: A.68

Ivesley is an elegantly furnished country house set in 220 acres. Each of the 5 bedrooms is decorated to a high standard. 3 rooms are en-suite. Adjacent to an equestrian centre with first-class facilities. An ideal centre for walking, sightseeing & mountain biking. Collection arranged from Durham Station & Newcastle Airport. Durham 7 miles. Wine cellar. Dogs & horses by arrangement. Babies & children over 8 years welcome.
E-mail: ivesley@msn.com
www.ridingholidays-ivesley.co.uk

£25.00 to £32.00 | Y | Y | Y

VISA: M'CARD:

Roger & Pauline Booth　Ivesley　Waterhouses　Durham DH7 9HB　Durham
Tel: (0191) 3734324　Fax 0191 3734757　Open: ALL YEAR　Map Ref No. 09

**All the establishments mentioned in this guide
are members of the
Worldwide Bed & Breakfast Association.**

**If you have any comments regarding your
accommodation please send them to us
using the form at the back of the book.
We value your comments.**

Oxfordshire

Oxfordshire
(Thames & Chilterns)

Oxfordshire is a county rich in history & delightful countryside. It has prehistoric sites, early Norman churches, 15th century coaching inns, Regency residences, distinctive cottages of black & white chalk flints & lovely Oxford, the city of dreaming spires.

The countryside ranges from lush meadows with willow-edged river banks scattered with small villages of thatched cottages, to the hills of the Oxfordshire Cotswolds in the west, the wooded Chilterns in the east & the distinctive ridge of the Berkshire Downs in the south. "Old Father Thames" meanders gently across the county to Henley, home of the famous regatta.

The ancient track known as the Great Ridgeway runs across the shire, & a walk along its length reveals barrows, hill forts & stone circles. The 2,000 year old Uffington Horse cut into the chalk of the hillside below an ancient hill fort site, is some 360 feet in length & 160 feet high.

The Romans built villas in the county & the remains of one, including a magnificent mosaic can be seen at North Leigh. In later centuries lovely houses were built. Minster Lovell stands beside the Windrush; Rousham house with its William Kent gardens is situated near Steeple Aston & beside the Thames lies Elizabethan Mapledurham House with its working watermill.

At Woodstock is Blenheim Palace, the largest private house in Britain & birthplace of Sir Winston Churchill. King Alfred's statue stands at Wantage, commemorating his birth there, & Banbury has its cross, made famous in the old nursery rhyme.

Oxford is a town of immense atmosphere with fine college buildings around quiet cloisters, & narrow cobbled lanes. It was during the 12th century that Oxford became a meeting place for scholars & grew into the first established centre of learning, outside the monasteries, in England.

The earliest colleges to be founded were University College, Balliol & Merton. Further colleges were added during the reign of the Tudors, as Oxford became a power in the kingdom. There are now 35 university colleges & many other outstanding historic buildings in the city . Christ Church Chapel is now the Cathedral of Oxford, a magnificent building with a deservedly famous choir.

St. Mary's Church.

216

Oxfordshire

Oxfordshire Gazeteer

Areas of Oustanding Natural Beauty
The North Wessex Downs. The Chiltern Hills. The Cotswolds.

Historic Houses & Castles

Ashdown House - Nr. Lambourn
17th century, built for Elizabeth of Bohemia, now contains portraits associated with her. Mansard roof has cupola with golden ball.

Blenheim Palace - Woodstock
Sir John Vanbrugh's classical masterpiece. Garden designed by Vanbrugh & Henry Wise. Further work done by Capability Brown who created the lake. Collection of pictures & tapestries.

Broughton Castle- Banbury.
14th century mansion with moat - interesting plaster work fine panelling & fire places

Chasleton House-Morton in Marsh
17th century,fine examples of plaster work & panelling.Still has original furniture & tapestries. topiary garden from1700.

Grey Court - Henly-on-Thames
16th century house containing 18th century plasterwork & furniture. Mediaeval ruins. Tudor donkey-wheel for raising water from well.

Mapledurham House - Mapledurham
16th century Elizabethan house. Oak staircase, private chapel, paintings, original moulded ceilings. Watermill nearby.

Milton Manor House - Nr. Abingdon
17th century house designed by Inigo Jones - Georgian wings, walled garden, pleasure grounds.

Rousham House - Steeple Ashton
17th century - contains portraits & miniatures.

University of Oxford Colleges

University college ------------------1249
Balliol----------------------------------1263
Merton---------------------------------1264
Hertford-------------------------------1284
Oriel------------------------------------1326
New-------------------------------------1379
All Souls-------------------------------1438
Brasenose-----------------------------1509

Christ Church----------------------1546
St. John's----------------------------1555
Pembroke----------------------------1624
Worcester----------------------------1714
Nuffield ------------------------------1937
St. Edmund Hall-------------------1270
Exeter---------------------------------1314
The Queen's------------------------1340
Lincoln--------------------------------1427
Magdalen ---------------------------1458
Corpus Christi --------------------1516
Trinity--------------------------------1554
Jesus---------------------------------1571
Wadham-----------------------------1610
Keble---------------------------------1868

Cathedrals & Churches

Abingdon (St. Helen)
14th-16th century perpendicular. Painted roof. Georgian stained & enamelled glass.

Burford (St. John the Baptist)
15th century. Sculptured table tombs in churchyard.

Chislehampton (St. Katherine)
18th century. Unspoilt interior of Georgian period. Bellcote.

Dorchester (St. Peter & St. Paul)
13th century knight in stone effigy. Jesse window.

East Hagbourne (St. Andrew)
14th -15th century. Early glass, wooden roofs, 18th century tombs.

North Moreton (All Saints)
13th century with splendid 14th century chantry chapel - tracery.

Oxford Cathedral
Smallest of our English cathedrals. Stone spire form 1230. Norman arcade has double arches, choir vault.

Ryecote (St. Michael & All Angels)
14th century benches & screen base. 17th century altar-piece & communion rails, old clear glass, good ceiling.

Stanton Harcourt (St. Michael)
Early English - old stone & marble floor. Early screen with painting, monuments of 17th -19th century.

Yarnton (St. Bartholomew)
13th century - late perpendicular additions. Jacobean screen. 15th century alabaster reredos.

Oxfordshire

Museums & Galleries

The Ashmolean Museum of Art & Archaeology - Oxford
British ,European ,Mediterranean, Egyptian & Near Eastern archaeology. Oil paintings of Italian, Dutch, Flemish, French & English schools. Old Master watercolours, prints, drawings, ceramics, silver, bronzes & sculptures. Chinese & Japanese porcelain, lacquer & painting, Tibetan, Islamic & Indian art.

Christ Church Picture Gallery - Oxford
Old Master drawings & paintings.

Museum of Modern Art - Oxford
Exhibitiors of contemporary art.

Museum of Oxford
Many exhibits depicting the history of Oxford & its University.

The Rotunda - Oxford
Privately owned collection of dolls' houses 1700-1900, with contents such as furniture, china, silver, dolls, etc.

Oxford University Museum
Entomological, zoological, geological & mineralogical collections.

Pendon Museum of Miniature Landscape & Transport - Abingdon.
Showing in miniature the countryside & its means of transport in the thirties, with trains & thatched village. Railway relics.

Town Museum - Abingdon
17th century building exhibiting fossil, archaeological items & collection of charters & documents.

Tolsey Museum - Burford
Seals, maces, charters & bygones - replica of Regency room with period furnishings & clothing.

Historic Monuments

Uffington Castle & White Horse - Uffington
White horse cut into the chalk - iron age hill fort.

Rollright Stones - Nr. Chipping Norton
77 stones placed in circle - an isolated King's stone & nearby an ancient burial chamber.

Minster Lovell House - Minster Lovell
15th century mediaeval house - ruins.

Deddington Castle - Deddington

Other things to see & do

Didcot railway centre -a large collection of locomotives etc., from Brunel's Great Western Railway.

Filkins -a working wool mill where rugs & garments are woven in traditional way.

Blenheim Palace. Woodstock.

OXFORDSHIRE
Map reference

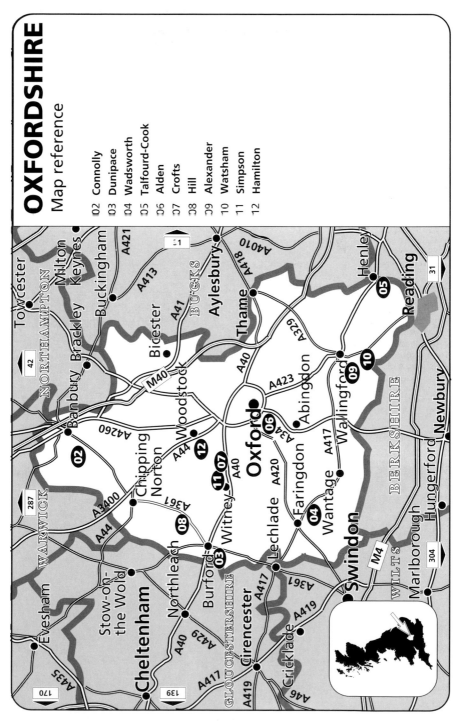

The Craven. Uffington.

| rate £ from - to per person | children taken | evening meals taken | animals taken |

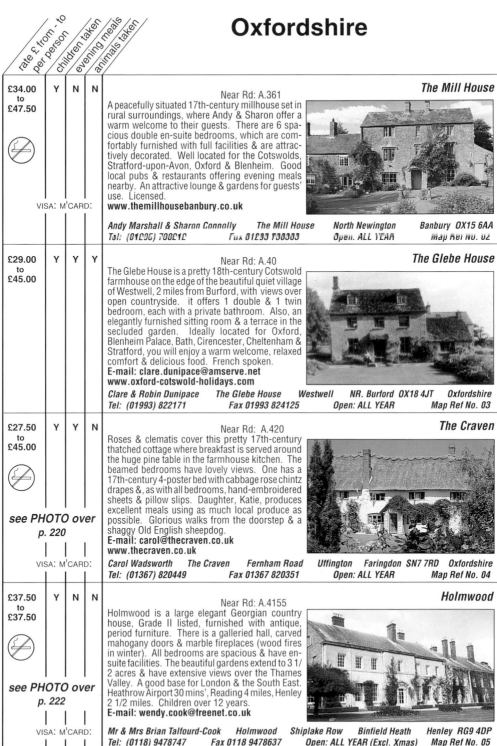

The Mill House

£34.00 to £47.50

Y N N

VISA: M'CARD:

Near Rd: A.361

A peacefully situated 17th-century millhouse set in rural surroundings, where Andy & Sharon offer a warm welcome to their guests. There are 6 spacious double en-suite bedrooms, which are comfortably furnished with full facilities & are attractively decorated. Well located for the Cotswolds, Stratford-upon-Avon, Oxford & Blenheim. Good local pubs & restaurants offering evening meals nearby. An attractive lounge & gardens for guests' use. Licensed.
www.themillhousebanbury.co.uk

Andy Marshall & Sharon Connolly   The Mill House   North Newington   Banbury OX15 6AA
Tel: (01295) 700615   Fax 01295 730033   Open: ALL YEAR   Map Ref No. 02

The Glebe House

£29.00 to £45.00

Y Y Y

Near Rd: A.40

The Glebe House is a pretty 18th-century Cotswold farmhouse on the edge of the beautiful quiet village of Westwell, 2 miles from Burford, with views over open countryside. it offers 1 double & 1 twin bedroom, each with a private bathroom. Also, an elegantly furnished sitting room & a terrace in the secluded garden. Ideally located for Oxford, Blenheim Palace, Bath, Cirencester, Cheltenham & Stratford, you will enjoy a warm welcome, relaxed comfort & delicious food. French spoken.
E-mail: clare.dunipace@amserve.net
www.oxford-cotswold-holidays.com

Clare & Robin Dunipace   The Glebe House   Westwell   NR. Burford OX18 4JT   Oxfordshire
Tel: (01993) 822171   Fax 01993 824125   Open: ALL YEAR   Map Ref No. 03

The Craven

£27.50 to £45.00

Y Y N

see PHOTO over
p. 220

VISA: M'CARD:

Near Rd: A.420

Roses & clematis cover this pretty 17th-century thatched cottage where breakfast is served around the huge pine table in the farmhouse kitchen. The beamed bedrooms have lovely views. One has a 17th-century 4-poster bed with cabbage rose chintz drapes &, as with all bedrooms, hand-embroidered sheets & pillow slips. Daughter, Katie, produces excellent meals using as much local produce as possible. Glorious walks from the doorstep & a shaggy Old English sheepdog.
E-mail: carol@thecraven.co.uk
www.thecraven.co.uk

Carol Wadsworth   The Craven   Fernham Road   Uffington   Faringdon SN7 7RD   Oxfordshire
Tel: (01367) 820449   Fax 01367 820351   Open: ALL YEAR   Map Ref No. 04

Holmwood

£37.50 to £37.50

Y N N

see PHOTO over
p. 222

VISA: M'CARD:

Near Rd: A.4155

Holmwood is a large elegant Georgian country house, Grade II listed, furnished with antique, period furniture. There is a galleried hall, carved mahogany doors & marble fireplaces (wood fires in winter). All bedrooms are spacious & have en-suite facilities. The beautiful gardens extend to 3 1/2 acres & have extensive views over the Thames Valley. A good base for London & the South East. Heathrow Airport 30 mins', Reading 4 miles, Henley 2 1/2 miles. Children over 12 years.
E-mail: wendy.cook@freenet.co.uk

Mr & Mrs Brian Talfourd-Cook   Holmwood   Shiplake Row   Binfield Heath   Henley RG9 4DP
Tel: (0118) 9478747   Fax 0118 9478637   Open: ALL YEAR (Excl. Xmas)   Map Ref No. 05

Holmwood. Binfield Heath.

rate £ from - to per person	children taken	evening meals	animals taken

| £30.00 to £40.00  | Y | N | N |

Near Rd: A.34

Broomhill

Broomhill is a large comfortable family house, set in extensive grounds in a secluded lane & enjoying delightful views over the surrounding countryside. It is situated only 5 mins' between the historic town of Oxford & Abingdon-on-Thames. There are 2 double rooms & 1 single room. Each room is en-suite & has T.V. & tea/coffee-making facilities. Only 45 mins' from London & Heathrow Airport. An excellent base for exploring Oxford & the surrounding region. Children over 10.
E-mail: sara@rralden.force9.co.uk
www.rralden.force9.co.uk

Sara & Richard Alden   *Broomhill*   *Lincombe Lane*   *Boars Hill*   *Oxford OX1 5DZ*   *Oxfordshire*
Tel: (01865) 706009   *Open: ALL YEAR*   *Map Ref No. 06*

| £25.00 to £30.00 | Y | N | N |

Near Rd: A.40

Crofters Guest House

Situated in a lively market town, 10 miles from Oxford, on the edge of the Cotswolds, Blenheim Palace & Burford, & within easy reach of Stratford. Guests are accommodated in comfortable family, double & twin rooms, all with excellent facilities. En-suite & luxury ground-floor garden rooms are available. Your hosts Jean & Peter will make your stay a memorable experience. Arrive as a guest, leave as a friend.
E-mail: crofters.ghouse@virgin.net
www.bestbandb.co.uk

Jean A. Crofts   *Crofters Guest House*   *29 Oxford Hill*   *Witney*   *Oxford OX28 3JU*   *Oxfordshire*
Tel: (01993) 778165   *Fax 01993 778165*   *Open: ALL YEAR*   *Map Ref No. 07*

| £30.00 to £35.00 | Y | N | N |
| see PHOTO over p. 224 | | | |

Near Rd: A.361

Shipton Grange House

A unique conversion of a Georgian coach house & stabling situated in the former grounds of Shipton Court. Secluded in its own walled garden, & approached by a gated archway. There are 3 elegantly furnished guest rooms, each with an en-suite/private bathroom, colour T.V. & beverage facilities. Delicious breakfasts served in the attractive dining room. The friendly hosts are animal lovers & have a number of pet dogs. Shipton Grange is a delightful house, & ideal for visiting Oxford, Blenheim, etc. Children over 12.

Veronica Hill   *Shipton Grange House*   *Shipton-under-Wychwood OX7 6DG*   *Oxfordshire*
Tel: (01993) 831298   *Fax 01993 832082*   *Open: ALL YEAR (Excl. Xmas)*   *Map Ref No. 08*

| £20.00 to £30.00 | Y | N | Y |

Near Rd: A.329

The Well Cottage

The Well Cottage is situated in a pretty garden, close to the River Thames, the historic town of Wallingford, the Berkshire Downs & the Ridgway. The cottage has been extended & now offers a secluded garden flat with 2 double/twin-bedded rooms, each with an en-suite bathroom, T.V. & tea/coffee facilities. Each room has its own private entrance. A charming home for a relaxing break. Within easy reach of Oxford & Henley-on-Thames.
E-mail: joanna@thewellcottage.com
www.thewellcottage.com

Mrs Joanna Alexander   *The Well Cottage*   *Caps Lane*   *Cholsey*   *Wallingford OX10 9HQ*   *Oxfordshire*
Tel: (01491) 651959   *Fax 01491 651675*   *Open: ALL YEAR*   *Map Ref No. 09*

Shipton Grange House. Shipton–under–Wychwood.

rate £ from - to per person	children taken	evening meals taken	animals taken	

| £30.00 to £40.00 | Y | Y | N | **White House** |

Near Rd: A.329

White House is an attractive, detached family home in the picturesque Thameside village of Moulsford on the edge of the Berkshire Downs, close to the Ridgeway & Thames Paths. The accommodation is at ground-floor level with its own separate front door, making access easy for disabled guests. Each room is very comfortable. There is a large garden with croquet lawn, which guests are welcome to enjoy. Delicious evening meals are available by prior arrangement. A delightful home.
E-mail: mwatsham@hotmail.com

Mrs Maria Watsham   White House   Moulsford On Thames   Wallingford OX10 9JD   Oxfordshire
Tel: (01491) 651397 Fax 01491 652560 Open: ALL YEAR (Excl. Xmas & New Year) Map Ref No. 10

| £26.00 to £27.00 | N | N | N | **Field View** |

Near Rd: A.40

An attractive Cotswold stone house set in 2 acres, situated on picturesque Wood Green, mid-way between Oxford University & the Cotswolds. It is an ideal base for touring & yet is only 8 minutes' walk from the centre of this lively Oxfordshire market town. A peaceful setting & a warm, friendly atmosphere await you. The accommodation offered is in 3 comfortable en-suite rooms with all modern amenities, including tea/coffee-making facilities, colour T.V., radio & hairdryer.
E-mail: bandb@fieldview-witney.co.uk
www.fieldview-witney.co.uk

Liz & John Simpson   Field View   Wood Green   Witney OX28 1DE   Oxfordshire
Tel: (01993) 705485   Mobile 07768 614347   Open: ALL YEAR   Map Ref No. 11

| £24.00 to £27.00 | Y | N | Y | **Gorselands Hall** |

VISA: M'CARD:

Near Rd: A.4095

Gorselands Hall is a lovely old Cotswold stone country house with oak beams & flagstone floors in a delightful rural setting, convenient for Oxford (8 miles), Blenheim Palace (4 miles), the Roman Villa at East End & many Cotswold villages. There are 6 attractively furnished en-suite bedrooms, a guest sitting room & a large secluded garden with a grass tennis court. This is good walking country & there is a wide choice of excellent eating places within easy reach. Animals by arrangement.
E-mail: hamilton@gorselandshall.com
www.gorselandshall.com

Mr & Mrs N. Hamilton   Gorselands Hall   Boddington Lane   North Leigh   Witney OX29 6PU
Tel: (01993) 882292   Fax 01993 883629   Open: ALL YEAR   Map Ref No. 12

Visit our website at:
http://www.bestbandb.co.uk

Shropshire

Shropshire
(Heart of England)

Shropshire is a borderland with a very turbulent history. Physically it straddles highlands & lowlands with border mountains to the west, glacial plains, upland, moorland & fertile valleys & the River Severn cutting through. It has been quarrelled & fought over by rulers & kings from earliest times. The English, the Romans & the Welsh all wanted to hold Shropshire because of its unique situation. The ruined castles & fortifications dotted across the county are all reminders of its troubled life. The most impressive of these defences is Offa's Dyke, an enormous undertaking intended to be a permanent frontier between England & Wales.

Shropshire has great natural beauty, countryside where little has changed with the years. Wenlock Edge & Clun Forest, Carding Mill Valley, the Long Mynd, Caer Caradoc, Stiperstones & the trail along Offa's Dyke itself, are lovely walking areas with magnificent scenery.

Shrewsbury was & is a virtual island, almost completely encircled by the Severn River. The castle was built at the only gap, sealing off the town. In this way all comings & goings were strictly controlled. In the 18th century two bridges, the English bridge & the Welsh bridge, were built to carry the increasing traffic to the town but Shrewsbury still remains England's finest Tudor city.

Massive Ludlow Castle was a Royal residence, home of Kings & Queens through the ages, whilst the town is also noted for its Georgian houses.

As order came out of chaos, the county settled to improving itself & became the cradle of the Industrial Revolution. Here Abraham Darby discovered how to use coke (from the locally mined coal) to smelt iron. There was more iron produced here in the 18th century than in any other county. A variety of great industries sprang up as the county's wealth & ingenuity increased. In 1781 the world's first iron bridge opened to traffic.

There are many fine gardens in the county. At Hodnet Hall near Market Drayton, the grounds cover 60 acres & the landscaping includes lakes & pools, trees, shrubs & flowers in profusion. Weston Park has 1,000 acres of parkland, woodland gardens & lakes landscaped by Capability Brown.

The house is Restoration period & has a splendid collection of pictures, furniture, china & tapestries.

Shrewsbury hosts an annual poetry festival & one of England's best flower shows whilst a Festival of Art, Music & Drama is held each year in Ludlow with Shakespeare performed against the castle ruins.

Coalbrookedale Museum.

Shropshire

Shropshire Gazeteer

Areas of Outstanding Natural Beauty
The Shropshire Hills.

Historic Houses & Castles

Stokesay Castle - Craven Arms
13th century fortified manor house. Still occupied - wonderful setting - extremely well preserved. Fine timbered gatehouse.
Weston Park - Nr. Shifnal
17th century - fine example of Restoration period - landscaping by Capability Brown. Superb collection of pictures.
Shrewsbury Castle - Shrewsbury
Built in Norman era - interior decorations - painted boudoir.
Benthall Hall - Much Wenlock
16th century. Stone House - mullioned windows. Fine wooden staircase - splendid plaster ceilings.
Shipton Hall - Much Wenlock
Elizabethan. Manor House - walled garden - mediaeval dovecote.
Upton Cressett Hall - Bridgnorth
Elizabethan. Manor House & Gatehouse. Excellent plaster work. . 14th century great hall.

Cathedrals & Churches

Ludlow (St. Lawrence)
14th century nave & transepts. 15th century pinnacled tower. Restored extensively in 19th century. Carved choir stalls, perpendicular chancel - original glass. Monuments.
Shrewsbury (St. Mary)
14th, 15th, 16th century glass. Norman origins.
Stottesdon (St. Mary)
12th century carvings.Norman font. Fine decorations with columns & tracery.
Lydbury North (St. Michael)
14th century transept, 15th century nave roof, 17th century box pews and altar rails. Norman font.
Longor (St. Mary the Virgin)
13th century having an outer staircase to West gallery.
Cheswardine (St. Swithun)
13th century chapel - largely early English. 19th century glass and old brasses. Fine sculpture.

Tong (St. Mary the Virgin with St. Bartholomew)
15th century. Golden chapel of 1515, stencilled walls, remains of paintings on screens, gilt fan vaulted ceiling. Effigies, fine monuments

Museums & Galleries

Clive House - Shrewsbury
Fine Georgian House - collection of Shropshire ceramics. Regimental museum of 1st Queen's Dragoon Guards.
Rowley's House Museum - Shrewsbury
Roman material from Viroconium and prehistoric collection.
Coleham Pumping Station - Old Coleham
Preserved beam engines
Acton Scott Working Farm Museum - Nr. Church Stretton
Site showing agricultural practice before the advent of mechanization.
Ironbridge Gorge Museum - Telford
Series of industrial sites in the Severn Gorge.
CoalBrookdale Museum & Furnace Site
Showing Abraham Darby's blast furnace history. Ironbridge information centre is next to the world's first iron bridge.
Mortimer Forest Museum - Nr. Ludlow
Forest industries of today and yesterday. Ecology of the forest.
Whitehouse Museum of Buildings & Country life - Aston Munslow
4 houses together in one, drawing from every century 13th to 18th, together with utensils and implements of the time.
The Buttercross Museum - Ludlow
Geology, natural & local history of area.
Reader's House-Ludlow
Splendid example of a 16th century town house. 3 storied porch.
Much Wenlock Museum.-Much Wenlock
Geology, natural & local history.
Clun Town Museum - Clun
Pre-history earthworks, rights of way, commons & photographs.

Historic Monuments

Acton Burnell Castle - Shrewsbury
13th century fortified manor house - ruins only.

Shropshire

Boscobel House - Shifnal
17th century house.
Bear Steps - Shrewsbury
Half timbered buildings. Mediaeval.
Abbot's House - Shrewsbury
15th century half-timbered.
Buildwas Abbey - Nr. Telford
12th century - Savignac Abbey - ruins.
The church is nearly complete with 14
Norman arches.
Haughmond Abbey - Shrewsbury
12th century - remains of house of
Augustinian canons.
Wenlock Priory - Much Wenlock
13th century abbey - ruins.
Roman Town - Wroxeter
2nd century - remains of town of
Viroconium including public baths and
colonnade.
Moreton Corbet Castle - Moreton Corbet
13th century keep, Elizabethan features -

gatehouse altered 1519.
Lilleshall Abbey
12th century - completed 13th century,
West front has notable doorway.
Bridgnorth Castle - Bridgnorth
Ruins of Norman castle whose angle of
incline is greater than Pisa.
Whiteladies Priory - Boscobel
12th century cruciform church - ruins.
Old Oswestry - Oswestry
Iron age hill fort covering 68 acres; five
ramparts and having an elaborate western
portal.

Other things to see & do

Ludlow Festival of Art and Drama -
annual event
Shrewsbury Flower Show - every August
Severn Valley Railway - the longest full
guage steam railway in the country

Kings Head Inn. Shrewsbury.

SHROPSHIRE

Map reference

01 Sanders
02 Prytz
03 Hunter
04 Roberts
05 Mitchell
06 Bebbington

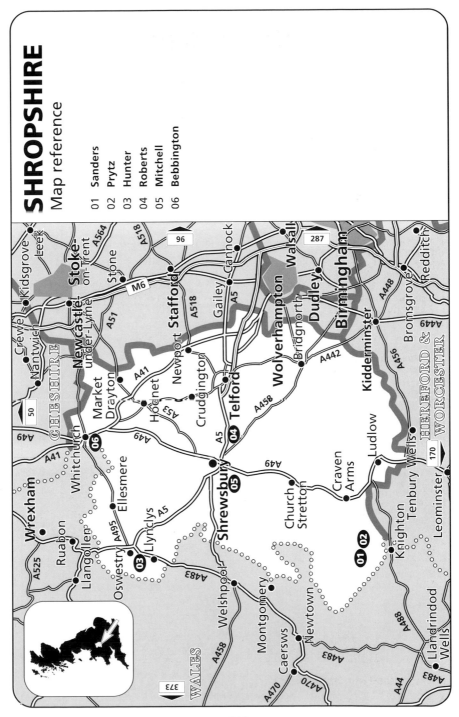

	rate £ from - to per person	children taken	evening meals	animals taken

Cottage Farm

Near Rd: A.49

Clunton is a small village on the B.4368 between Ludlow & Clun in the beautiful Clun Valley, with superb landscapes & numerous public footpaths. Cottage Farm, which dates back 400 years, has many exposed timbers & stonewalls, which, along with roaring log fires in winter, help to create a wonderful ambience. Evening meals by arrangement. 3 bedrooms, each decorated in true country style - 2 doubles (1 en-suite) & a single. A charming home within easy reach of Ludlow & Clun & Stokesay Castles. Children over 12.

£22.50 to £25.00 — Y | Y | N

Mrs Maureen Sanders   Cottage Farm   Clunton   NR. Craven Arms SY7 0HZ   Shropshire
Tel: (01588) 660555   Fax 01588 660666   Open: ALL YEAR (Excl. Xmas)   Map Ref No. 01

Knock Hundred Cottage

Near Rd: A.49

Knock Hundred Cottage is believed to originate from the 16th century & enjoys an open aspect with extensive views. Accommodation is in 1 double bedroom with a private bathroom & 1 en-suite twin-bedded room. Each room is comfortably furnished & has a T.V. Early morning tea/coffee is served in your room & breakfast is provided in the family dining room. Places of interest include Ludlow, the Long Mynd, Offa's Dyke, the beautiful Corve Dale & various National Trust/English Heritage properties & gardens. Single supplement.

£25.00 to £28.00 — N | N | N

Mrs Anne Prytz   Knock Hundred Cottage   Abcott   Clungunford   Craven Arms SY7 0PX   Shropshire
Tel: (01588) 660594   Fax 01588 660594   Open: ALL YEAR   Map Ref No. 02

Pen-Y-Dyffryn Hotel

Near Rd: A.5

Set almost a thousand feet up in the peaceful Shropshire/Wales border hills, this silver-stone Georgian rectory has a real 'away from it all' atmosphere. But the medieval towns of Chester & Shrewsbury are only a short drive, so civilisation is close by. High-quality local food is served in the restaurant, complete with its own log fire. All bedrooms are en-suite, with colour T.V., telephone, etc. & some even have their own private patios & spa baths. Fully licensed. Excellent walking country.
E-mail: stay@peny.co.uk
www.peny.co.uk

£44.00 to £58.00 — Y | Y | Y

see PHOTO over
p. 231

VISA: M'CARD: AMEX:

Miles Hunter   Pen-Y-Dyffryn Hotel   Rhydycroesau   Oswestry SY10 7JD   Shropshire
Tel: (01691) 653700   Fax 01691 650066   Open: ALL YEAR (Excl. 1-24 Jan)   Map Ref No. 03

The White House

Near Rd: A.488, A.5

A lovely, 16th-century, black-and-white, half-timbered home with nearly 2 acres of gardens and river, 3 miles south-west of medieval Shrewsbury. Ironbridge, Mid-Wales and the Long Mynd within a half-hour drive. 6 guest rooms, some en-suite, each with tea/coffee-making facilities. 2 sitting rooms, residents' bar & log fires. Car parking. Your hosts menagerie at the time of going to print consists of chickens, doves, alpacas, bees & one mad duck called Mrs Vlad. Children over 12.
E-mail: mgm@whitehousehanwood.freeserve.co.uk
www.whitehousehanwood.freeserve.co.uk

£27.50 to £32.50 — Y | N | N

Mike & Gill Mitchell   The White House   Hanwood   Shrewsbury SY5 8LP   Shropshire
Tel: (01743) 860414   Open: ALL YEAR   Map Ref No. 05

Pen-Y-Dyffryn Country Hotel . Rhydycroesau.

Shropshire

Upper Brompton Farm

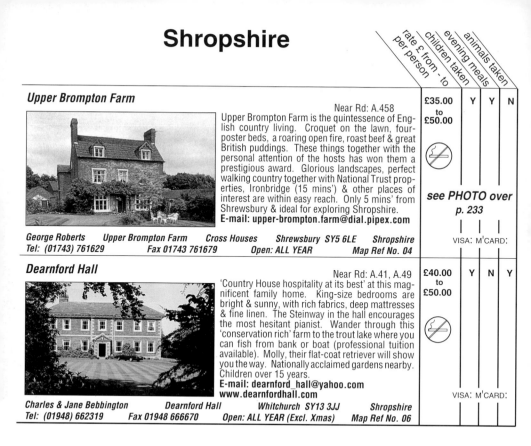

Near Rd: A.458

Upper Brompton Farm is the quintessence of English country living. Croquet on the lawn, four-poster beds, a roaring open fire, roast beef & great British puddings. These things together with the personal attention of the hosts has won them a prestigious award. Glorious landscapes, perfect walking country together with National Trust properties, Ironbridge (15 mins') & other places of interest are within easy reach. Only 5 mins' from Shrewsbury & ideal for exploring Shropshire.

E-mail: upper-brompton.farm@dial.pipex.com

| £35.00 to £50.00 | Y | Y | N |

see PHOTO over p. 233

George Roberts   Upper Brompton Farm   Cross Houses   Shrewsbury SY5 6LE   Shropshire
Tel: (01743) 761629   Fax 01743 761679   Open: ALL YEAR   Map Ref No. 04

VISA: M'CARD:

Dearnford Hall

Near Rd: A.41, A.49

'Country House hospitality at its best' at this magnificent family home. King-size bedrooms are bright & sunny, with rich fabrics, deep mattresses & fine linen. The Steinway in the hall encourages the most hesitant pianist. Wander through this 'conservation rich' farm to the trout lake where you can fish from bank or boat (professional tuition available). Molly, their flat-coat retriever will show you the way. Nationally acclaimed gardens nearby. Children over 15 years.

E-mail: dearnford_hall@yahoo.com
www.dearnfordhall.com

| £40.00 to £50.00 | Y | N | Y |

Charles & Jane Bebbington   Dearnford Hall   Whitchurch SY13 3JJ   Shropshire
Tel: (01948) 662319   Fax 01948 666670   Open: ALL YEAR (Excl. Xmas)   Map Ref No. 06

VISA: M'CARD:

All the establishments mentioned in this guide are members of
The Worldwide Bed & Breakfast Association

![Worldwide Bed & Breakfast Association logo]

When booking your accommodation please mention
The Best Bed & Breakfast

Upper Brompton Farm. Cross Houses.

Somerset, Bath & Bristol

Somerset
(West Country)

Fabulous legends, ancient customs, charming villages, beautiful churches, breathtaking scenery & a glorious cathedral, Somerset has them all, along with a distinctively rich local dialect. The essence of Somerset lies in its history & myth & particularly in the unfolding of the Arthurian tale.

Legend grows from the bringing of the Holy Grail to Glastonbury by Joseph of Arimathea, to King Arthur's castle at Camelot, held by many to be sited at Cadbury, to the image of the dead King's barge moving silently through the mists over the lake to the Isle of Avalon. Archaeological fact lends support to the conjecture that Glastonbury, with its famous Tor, was an island in an ancient lake. Another island story surrounds King Alfred, reputedly sheltering from the Danes on the Isle of Athelney & there burning his cakes.

Historically, Somerset saw the last battle fought on English soil, at Sedgemoor in 1685. The defeat of the Monmouth rebellion resulted in the wrath of James II falling on the West Country in the form of Judge Jeffreys & his "Bloody Assize".

To the west of the county lies part of the Exmoor National Park, with high moorland where deer roam & buzzards soar & a wonderful stretch of cliffs from Minehead to Devon. Dunster is a popular village with its octagonal Yarn market, & its old world cottages, dominated at one end by the castle & at the other by the tower on Conygar Hill.

To the east the woods & moors of the Quantocks are protected as an area of outstanding natural beauty. The Vale of Taunton is famous for its apple orchards & for the golden cider produced from them.

The south of the county is a land of rolling countryside & charming little towns, Chard, Crewkerne, Ilchester & Ilminster amongst others.

To the north the limestone hills of Mendip are honeycombed with spectacular caves & gorges, some with neolithic remains, as at Wookey Hole & Cheddar Gorge.

Wells is nearby, so named because of the multitude of natural springs. Hardly a city, Wells boasts a magnificent cathedral set amongst spacious lawns & trees. The west front is one of the glories of English architecture with its sculptured figures & soaring arches. A spectacular feature is the astronomical clock, the work of 14th century monk Peter Lightfoot. The intricate face tells the hours, minutes, days & phases of the moon. On the hour, four mounted knights charge forth & knock one another from their horses.

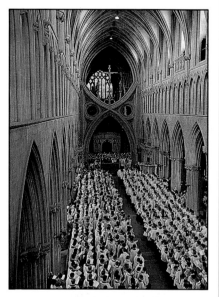

Wells Cathedral Choir.

Somerset, Bath & Bristol

Bath is one of the most loved historic cities in England. It owes its existence to the hot springs which bubble up five hundred thousand gallons of water a day at a temperature of some 120' F. According to legend, King Bladud appreciated the healing qualities of the waters & established his capital here, calling it Aquae Sulis. He built an elaborate healing & entertainment centre around the springs including reservoirs, baths & hypercaust rooms.

The Roman Baths, not uncovered until modern times, are on the lowest of three levels. Above them came the mediaeval city & on the top layer at modern street level is the elegant Georgian Pump Room.

Edward was crowned the first King of all England in 973, in the Saxon Abbey which stood on the site of the present fifteenth century abbey. This building, in the graceful perpendicular style with elegant fan vaulting, is sometimes called the "lantern of the West", on account of its vast clerestories & large areas of glass.

During the Middle Ages the town prospered through Royal patronage & the development of the wool industry. Bath became a city of weavers, the leading industrial town in the West of England.

The 18th century gave us the superb Georgian architecture which is the city's glory. John Wood, an ambitious young architect laid out Queen Anne's Square in the grand Palladian style, & went on to produce his masterpiece, the Royal Crescent. His scheme for the city was continued by his son & a number of other fine architects, using the beautiful Bath stone. Bath was a centre of fashion, with Beau Nash the leader of a glittering society.

In 1497 John & Sebastian Cabot sailed from the Bristol quayside to the land they called Ameryke, in honour of the King's agent in Bristol, Richard Ameryke. Bristol's involvement in the colonisation of the New World & the trade in sugar, tobacco & slaves that followed, made her the second city in the kingdom in the 18th century. John Cabot is commemorated by the Cabot Tower on grassy Brandon Hill - a fine vantage point from which to view the city. On the old docks below are the Bristol Industrial Museum & the SS Great Britain, Brunel's famous iron ship. Another achievement of this master engineer, the Clifton Suspension Bridge, spans Bristol's renowned beauty spot, the Clifton Gorge. For a glimpse of Bristol's elegant past, stroll through Clifton with its stately terraces & spacious Downs.

A short walk from the busy city centre & modern shopping area, the visitor in search of history will find cobbled King Street with its merchant seamen's almhouses & The Theatre Royal, the oldest theatre in continuous use in England, & also Llandoger Trow, an ancient inn associated with Treasure Island & Robinson Crusoe.

Bath Abbey.

Somerset, Bath & Bristol

Somerset, Bath & Bristol Gazeteer

Areas of Outstanding Natural Beauty
Mendip Hills. Quantock Hills. National Park - Exmoor. The Cotswolds.

Historic Houses & Castles

Abbot's Fish House - Meare
14th century house.
Barrington Court - Illminster
16th century house & gardens.
Blaise Castle House - Henbury Nr. Bristol
18th century house - now folk museum, extensive woodlands.
Brympton D'Evercy - Nr. Yeovil
Mansion with 17th century front & Tudor west front. Adjacent is 13th century priest's house & church. Formal gardens & vineyard.
Claverton Manor - Nr. Bath
Greek revival house - furnished with 17th, 18th, 19th century American originals.
Clevedon Court - Clevedon
14th century manor house, 13th century hall, 12th century tower. Lovely garden with rare trees & shrubs. This is where Thackerey wrote much of 'Vanity Fair'.
Dyrham Park - Between Bristol & Bath
17th century house - fine panelled rooms, Dutch paintings, furniture.
Dunster Castle - Dunster
13th century castle with fine 17th century staircase & ceilings.
East Lambrook Manor - South Petherton
15th century house with good panelling.
Gaulden Manor - Tolland
12th century manor. Great Hall having unique plaster ceiling & oak screen. Antique furniture.
Halsway Manor - Crowcombe
14th century house with fine panelling.
Hatch Court - Hatch Beauchamp
Georgian house in the Palladian style with China room.
King John's Hunting Lodge - Axbridge
Early Tudor merchant's house.
Lytes Carry - Somerton
14th & 15th century manor house with a chapel & formal garden.
Montacute House - Yeovil
Elizabethan house with fine examples of Heraldic Glass, tapestries, panelling &

furniture. Portrait gallery of Elizabethan & Jacobean paintings.
Tintinhull House - Yeovil
17th century house with beautiful gardens.
Priory Park College - Bath
18th century Georgian mansion, now Roman Catholic school.
No. 1 Royal Crescent - Bath
An unaltered Georgian house built 1767.
Red Lodge - Bristol
16th century house - period furniture & panelling.
St. Vincent's Priory - Bristol
Gothic revival house, built over caves which were sanctuary for Christians.
St Catherine's Court - Nr. Bath
Small Tudor house - associations with Henry VIII & Elizabeth I.

Cathedrals & Churches

Axbridge (St. John)
1636 plaster ceiling & panelled roofs.
Backwell (St. Andrew)
12th to 17th century, 15th century tower, repaired 17th century. 15th century tomb & chancel, 16th century screen, 18th century brass chandelier.
Bath Abbey
Perpendicular - monastic church, 15th century foundation. Nave finished 17th century, restorations in 1674.
Bishop's Lydeard (St. Mary)
15th century. Notable tower, rood screen & glass.
Bristol Cathedral
Mediaeval. Eastern halfnave Victorian. Chapterhouse richly ornamented. Iron screen, 3 fonts, "fairest parish church in all England".
Bristol (St. Mary Radcliffe)
Bristol (St. Stephens')
Perpendicular - monuments, magnificent tower.
Bruton (St. Mary)
Fine 2 towered 15th century church. Georgian chancel, tie beam roof, Georgian reredos. Jacobean screen. 15th century embroidery.
Chewton Mendip (St. Mary Magdalene)
12th century with later additions. 12th century doorway, 15th century bench ends, magnificent 16th century tower & 17th century lecturn.

Somerset, Bath & Bristol

Crewkerne (St. Bartholomew)
Magnificent west front & roofs, 15th & 16th
century. South doorway dating from 13th
century, wonderful 15th century painted
glass & 18th century chandeliers.
East Brent (St. Mary)
Mainly 15th century. Plaster ceiling,
painted glass & carved bench ends.
Glastonbury (St. John)
One of the finest examples of
perpendicular towers. Tie beam roof, late
mediaeval painted glass, mediaeval
vestment & early 16th century altar tomb.
High Ham (St. Andrew)
Sumptuous roofs & vaulted rood screen.
Carved bench ends. Jacobean lecturn,
mediaeval painted glass. Norman font.
Kingsbury Episcopi (St. Martin)
14th-15th century. Good tower with fan
vaulting. Late mediaeval painted glass.
Long Sutton (Holy Trinity)
15th century with noble tower &
magnificent tie beam roof. 15th century
pulpit & rood screen, tower vaulting.
Martock (All Saints)
13th century chancel. Nave with tie beam
roof, outstanding of its kind. 17th century
paintings of Apostles
North Cadbury (St. Michael)
painted glass.
Pilton (St. John)
12th century with arcades. 15th century
roofs.
Taunton (St. Mary Magdalene)
Highest towers in the county. Five nave
roof, fragments of mediaeval painted
glass.
Trull (All Saints)
15th century with many mediaeval art
treasures & 15th century glass.
Wells Cathedral-Wells
Magnificent west front with carved figures.
Splendid tower. Early English arcade of
nave & transepts. 60 fine misericords
c.1330. Lady chapel with glass & star
vault. Chapter House & Bishop's Palace.
Weston Zoyland (St. Mary)
15th century bench ends. 16th century
heraldic glass. Jacobean pulpit.
Wrington (All Souls)
15th century aisles & nave; font, stone
pulpit, notable screens.

Museums & Galleries

Admiral Blake Museum - Bridgewater
Exhibits relating to Battle of Sedgemoor,
archaeology.
American Museum in Britain - Claverton
Nr. Bath
American decorative arts 17th to 19th
century displayed in series of furnished
rooms & galleries of special exhibits.
Paintings, furniture, glass wood & metal
work, textiles, folk sculpture, etc.
Borough Museum - Hendford Manor Hall,
Yeovil
Archaeology, firearms collections &
Bailward Costume Collection.
Bristol Industrial Museum - Bristol
Collections of transport items of land,
sea & air. Many unique items.
Burdon Manor - Washford
14th century manor house with Saxon
fireplace & cockpit.
City of Bristol Art Gallery - Bristol
Permanent & loan collections of
paintings, English & Oriental ceramics.
Glastonbury Lake Village Museum -
Glastonbury
Late prehistoric antiquities.
Gough's Cave Museum - Cheddar
Upper Paleolithic remains, skeleton,
flints, amber & engraved stones.
Holburne of Menstrie Museum - Bath
Old Master paintings, silver, glass,
porcelain, furniture & miniatures in 18th
century building. Work of 20th century
craftworkers.
Hinton Priory - Hinton Charterhouse
13th century - ruins of Carthusian priory.
Kings Weston Roman Villa - Lawrence
Weston
3rd & 4th centuries - mosaics of villa -
some walls.
Museum of Costume - Bath
Collection of fashion from 17th century
to present day.
Roman Baths - Bath
Roman Museum - Bath
Material from remains of extensive
Roman baths & other Roman sites.
Stoney Littleton Barrow - Nr. Bath
Neolithic burial chamber - restoration
work 1858.
St. Nicholas Church & City Museum -
Bristol
Mediaeval antiquities relating to local

Somerset, Bath & Bristol

history, Church plate & vestments. Altarpiece by Hogarth.

Temple Church - Bristol
14th & 15th century ruins.

Victoria Art Gallery - Bath
Paintings, prints, drawings, glass, ceramics, watches, coins, etc. Bygones - permanent & temporary exhibitions. Geology collections.

Wookey Hole Cave Museum - Wookey Hole
Remains from Pliocene period. Relics of Celtic & Roman civilization. Exhibition of handmade paper-making.

Historic Monuments

Cleeve Abbey - Cleeve
Ruined 13th century house, with timber roof & wall paintings.

Farleigh Castle - Farleigh Hungerford
14th century remains - museums in chapel.

Glastonbury Abbey - Glastonbury
12th & 13th century ruins of St. Joseph's chapel & Abbot's kitchen.

Muchelney Abbey - Muchelney
15th century ruins of Benedictine abbey.

Other things to see & do

Black Rock Nature Reserve - Cheddar
Circular walk through plantation woodland, downland grazing.

Cheddar Caves
Show caves at the foot of beautiful Cheddar Gorge.

Clifton Zoological Gardens - Bristol
Flourishing zoo with many exhibits - beautiful gardens.

Clifton Suspension Bridge - Bristol
Designed by Isambard Kingdom Brunel, opened in 1864. Viewpoint & picnic spot Camera Obscura.

Cricket St. Thomas Wildlife Park - Nr. Chard
Wildlife park, heavy horse centre, countryside museum, etc.

The Pump Room - Bath
18th century neo-classical interior. Spa.

Clifton Suspension Bridge. Bristol.

SOMERSET, BATH & BRISTOL

Map reference

01 Dodd	05 Griffin
01 Greenwood	06 Riley
01 Besley	08 Bale
01 Poole	09 Mott
01 Close	10 Vicary
01 Beckett	11 Redmond
01 Addison	12 Knight
01 Huxley	13 Copeland
01 Kitcher	14 Mitchem
01 Lanz	15 Eyre
01 Metcalf	16 Frost
01 Bryan	17 Nowell
01 Selby	18 Mogford
02 Tiley	19 Thompson
03 Westlake	20 Parsons
04 Graham	21 Durbin
04 Priddle	

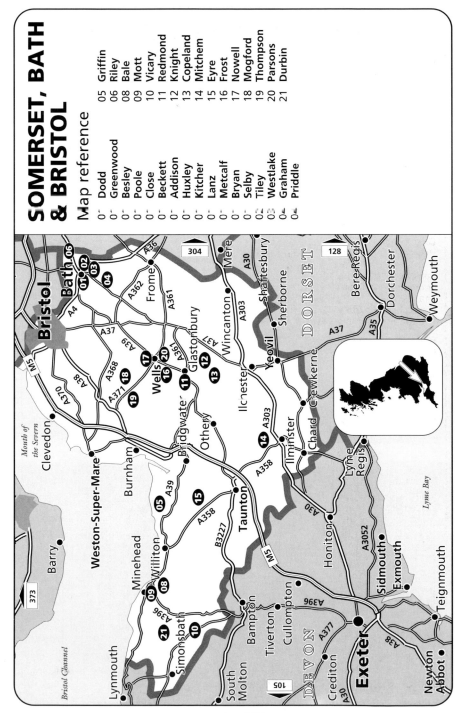

239

Somerset

Brocks

Near Rd: A.4

Brocks is a beautiful Georgian town house built in 1765 by John Wood, situated between the Circus and Royal Crescent. Very close to the Roman Baths, Assembly Rooms, etc. This really is a wonderful part of Bath. This historic house has all modern conveniences, & all of the comfortable bedrooms have en-suite facilities. The aim here is to offer guests the highest standards, and personal attention. A delightful base for exploring Bath.
E-mail: marion@brocksguesthouse.co.uk
www.brocksguesthouse.co.uk

£28.00 to £41.00	Y	N	N

VISA: M'CARD:

Marion Dodd   Brocks   32 Brock Street   Bath BA1 2LN   Somerset
Tel: (01225) 338374   Fax (01225) 334245   Open: ALL YEAR   Map Ref No. 01

Number Thirty

Near Rd: A.36

Number Thirty is a Victorian house situated within 5 mins' level walk of the city centre & Roman Baths, the Pump Room, Circus & Royal Crescent. Number Thirty has been completely refurbished & all rooms are light & airy. The bedrooms all have en-suite bathrooms & are decorated mainly in blue & white. Each one is named after a famous person who has influenced the building or character of this wonderful city. Parking. Children over 12.
E-mail: david.greenwood12@btinternet.com
www.numberthirty.com

£37.50 to £55.00	Y	N	N

VISA: M'CARD:

David & Caroline Greenwood   Number Thirty   30 Crescent Gardens   Bath BA1 2NB   Somerset
Tel: (01225) 337393   Fax 01225 337393   Open: ALL YEAR   Map Ref No. 01

The Old Red House

Near Rd: A.4

This charming Victorian Gingerbread House is colourful, comfortable & warm; full of unexpected touches & intriguing little curiosities. Its leaded & stained glass windows are now double-glazed to ensure a peaceful stay. The extensive breakfast menu, a delight in itself, is served around a large family dining table. Parking. Special rates for 3 or more nights. Dinner available at a local riverside pub. A brochure on request. Children over 5.
E-mail: oldredhouse@amserve.net
www.oldredhouse.co.uk

£25.00 to £35.00	Y	N	N

VISA: M'CARD: AMEX:

Chrissie Besley   The Old Red House   37 Newbridge Road   Bath BA1 3HE   Somerset
Tel: (01225) 330464   Fax 01225 331661   Open: FEB - DEC   Map Ref No. 01

Bailbrook Lodge

Near Rd: A.4, A.46

Bailbrook Lodge is an imposing Grade II listed Georgian house located 1 mile east of Bath. There is a choice of 12 elegantly furnished en-suite bedrooms (some with 4-posters), all with T.V. & hospitality tray. Delicious breakfasts are served. The lounge bar & dining room overlook the garden. Bailbrook Lodge is an ideal base for exploring Bath & touring the beautiful surrounding countryside. Ample car-parking.
E-mail: hotel@bailbrooklodge.co.uk
www.bailbrooklodge.co.uk

£35.00 to £47.50	Y	N	N

see PHOTO over
p. 241

VISA: M'CARD: AMEX:

K. M. Addison   Bailbrook Lodge   35-37 London Road West   Bath BA1 7HZ   Somerset
Tel: (01225) 859090   Fax 01225 852299   Open: ALL YEAR   Map Ref No.01

Ballbrook Lodge. Bath.

Somerset

	rate £ from - to per person	evening meals	children taken	animals taken

Cranleigh

Near Rd: A.431

Situated in a quiet residential area, this comfortable Victorian house has great character, with exceptionally spacious, stylish en-suite bedrooms. Most have lovely views across the Avon Valley. You are welcome to relax in the garden. Breakfast includes such choices as fresh-fruit salad & scrambled eggs with smoked salmon. Easy access to the heart of Bath. Parking. The Pooles have a wealth of information to help you make the most of your stay in Bath. Children over 5 years.
E-mail: cranleigh@btinternet.com
www.cranleighguesthouse.com

£33.00 to £48.00 — Y N N

VISA: M'CARD: AMEX:

Tony & Jan Poole   Cranleigh   159 Newbridge Hill   Bath BA1 3PX   Somerset
Tel: (01225) 310197   Fax 01225 423143   Open: ALL YEAR   Map Ref No. 01

Weston Lawn

Near Rd: A.4

Welcome to this Georgian family house set within its own grounds complete with fossils & Roman remains. Approx. 1 mile from Bath & only yards from the Cotswold Way, this is the base for city visits & magnificent country walks. The 3 bedrooms, all en-suite or with private facilities, have colour T.V, & beverages. Each room is furnished with antiques & decorated in the style of this classic period. Take your breakfast in the conservatory overlooking the lawn.
E-mail: reservations@westonlawn.co.uk
www.westonlawn.co.uk

£23.00 to £40.00 — Y N N

VISA: M'CARD: AMEX:

William & Fiona Close   Weston Lawn   Lucklands Road   Weston   Bath BA1 4AY   Somerset
Tel: (01225) 421362 Mobile 07899 748598   Fax 01225 319106   Open: ALL YEAR   Map Ref No. 01

Cedar Lodge

Near Rd: A.4, A.46

Within easy level walk to the historic city centre, this beautiful, detached Georgian house offers period elegance with modern amenities. 3 lovely bedrooms (1 with 4-poster, 1 half-tester, 1 twin), all with en-suite/private bathrooms. Delightful gardens & comfortable drawing room, with fire, to relax in. Ideally situated for excursions to Avebury, Stonehenge, Salisbury, Longleat, Wells, Cotswolds, Wales & many other attractions. Secure private parking. Children over 10.
www.bestbandb.co.uk

£30.00 to £37.50 — Y N N

Derek & Maria Beckett   Cedar Lodge   13 Lambridge   London Road   Bath BA1 6BJ   Somerset
Tel: (01225) 423468   Open: ALL YEAR   Map Ref No. 01

Bath Oldfields

Near Rd: A.367

Elegant & traditional bed & breakfast at this beautiful Bath stone Victorian house, 8 mins' walk from the city centre. 14 en-suite bedrooms with T.V., 'phone & tea/coffee-making facilities etc. Some rooms have canopied or 4-poster beds. Experience the true ambience of the 19th century: beautiful antique furniture, rich fabrics & warm decor. Enjoy a delicious English breakfast including smoked salmon & scrambled eggs in the elegant dining room overlooking Bath. Children over 12. Car park.
E-mail: info@oldfields.co.uk
www.oldfields.co.uk

£34.50 to £60.00 — Y N N

see PHOTO over
p. 243

VISA: M'CARD: AMEX:

Rod & Alex Kitcher   Bath Oldfields   102 Wells Road   Bath BA2 3AL   Somerset
Tel: (01225) 317984   Open: ALL YEAR   Map Ref No. 01

Oldfields Hotel. Bath.

Somerset

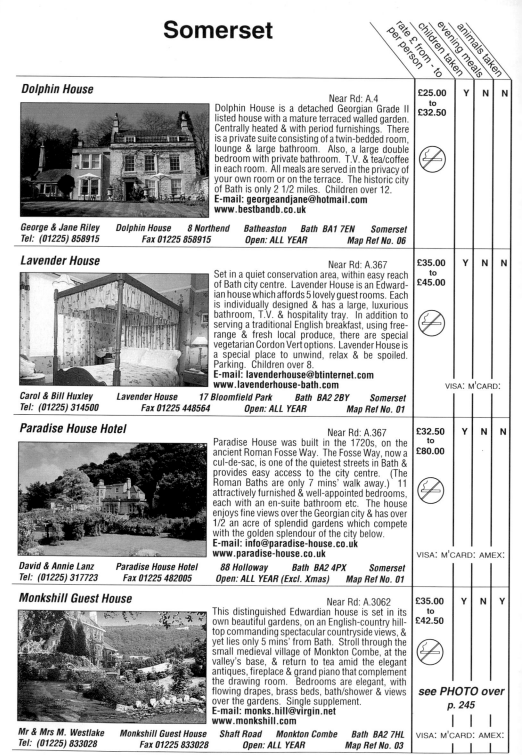

Dolphin House

Near Rd: A.4

Dolphin House is a detached Georgian Grade II listed house with a mature terraced walled garden. Centrally heated & with period furnishings. There is a private suite consisting of a twin-bedded room, lounge & large bathroom. Also, a large double bedroom with private bathroom. T.V. & tea/coffee in each room. All meals are served in the privacy of your own room or on the terrace. The historic city of Bath is only 2 1/2 miles. Children over 12.
E-mail: georgeandjane@hotmail.com
www.bestbandb.co.uk

£25.00 to £32.50 Y N N

George & Jane Riley   Dolphin House   8 Northend   Batheaston   Bath BA1 7EN   Somerset
Tel: (01225) 858915   Fax 01225 858915   Open: ALL YEAR   Map Ref No. 06

Lavender House

Near Rd: A.367

Set in a quiet conservation area, within easy reach of Bath city centre. Lavender House is an Edwardian house which affords 5 lovely guest rooms. Each is individually designed & has a large, luxurious bathroom, T.V. & hospitality tray. In addition to serving a traditional English breakfast, using free-range & fresh local produce, there are special vegetarian Cordon Vert options. Lavender House is a special place to unwind, relax & be spoiled. Parking. Children over 8.
E-mail: lavenderhouse@btinternet.com
www.lavenderhouse-bath.com

£35.00 to £45.00 Y N N

VISA: M'CARD:

Carol & Bill Huxley   Lavender House   17 Bloomfield Park   Bath BA2 2BY   Somerset
Tel: (01225) 314500   Fax 01225 448564   Open: ALL YEAR   Map Ref No. 01

Paradise House Hotel

Near Rd: A.367

Paradise House was built in the 1720s, on the ancient Roman Fosse Way. The Fosse Way, now a cul-de-sac, is one of the quietest streets in Bath & provides easy access to the city centre. (The Roman Baths are only 7 mins' walk away.) 11 attractively furnished & well-appointed bedrooms, each with an en-suite bathroom etc. The house enjoys fine views over the Georgian city & has over 1/2 an acre of splendid gardens which compete with the golden splendour of the city below.
E-mail: info@paradise-house.co.uk
www.paradise-house.co.uk

£32.50 to £80.00 Y N N

VISA: M'CARD: AMEX:

David & Annie Lanz   Paradise House Hotel   88 Holloway   Bath BA2 4PX   Somerset
Tel: (01225) 317723   Fax 01225 482005   Open: ALL YEAR (Excl. Xmas)   Map Ref No. 01

Monkshill Guest House

Near Rd: A.3062

This distinguished Edwardian house is set in its own beautiful gardens, on an English-country hilltop commanding spectacular countryside views, & yet lies only 5 mins' from Bath. Stroll through the small medieval village of Monkton Combe, at the valley's base, & return to tea amid the elegant antiques, fireplace & grand piano that complement the drawing room. Bedrooms are elegant, with flowing drapes, brass beds, bath/shower & views over the gardens. Single supplement.
E-mail: monks.hill@virgin.net
www.monkshill.com

£35.00 to £42.50 Y N Y

see PHOTO over
p. 245

VISA: M'CARD: AMEX:

Mr & Mrs M. Westlake   Monkshill Guest House   Shaft Road   Monkton Combe   Bath BA2 7HL
Tel: (01225) 833028   Fax 01225 833028   Open: ALL YEAR   Map Ref No. 03

Monkshill. Monkton Combe.

Somerset

Northwick House

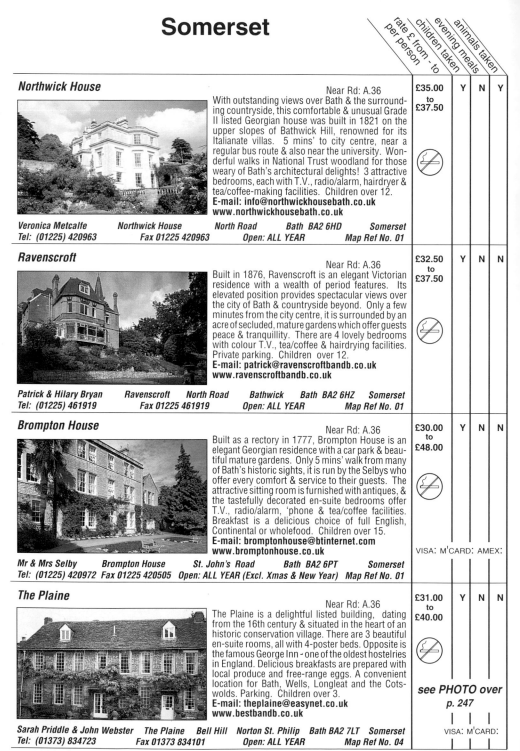

Near Rd: A.36

With outstanding views over Bath & the surrounding countryside, this comfortable & unusual Grade II listed Georgian house was built in 1821 on the upper slopes of Bathwick Hill, renowned for its Italianate villas. 5 mins' to city centre, near a regular bus route & also near the university. Wonderful walks in National Trust woodland for those weary of Bath's architectural delights! 3 attractive bedrooms, each with T.V., radio/alarm, hairdryer & tea/coffee-making facilities. Children over 12.
E-mail: info@northwickhousebath.co.uk
www.northwickhousebath.co.uk

| | £35.00 to £37.50 | Y | N | Y |

Veronica Metcalfe · Northwick House · North Road · Bath BA2 6HD · Somerset
Tel: (01225) 420963 · Fax 01225 420963 · Open: ALL YEAR · Map Ref No. 01

Ravenscroft

Near Rd: A.36

Built in 1876, Ravenscroft is an elegant Victorian residence with a wealth of period features. Its elevated position provides spectacular views over the city of Bath & countryside beyond. Only a few minutes from the city centre, it is surrounded by an acre of secluded, mature gardens which offer guests peace & tranquillity. There are 4 lovely bedrooms with colour T.V., tea/coffee & hairdrying facilities. Private parking. Children over 12.
E-mail: patrick@ravenscroftbandb.co.uk
www.ravenscroftbandb.co.uk

| | £32.50 to £37.50 | Y | N | N |

Patrick & Hilary Bryan · Ravenscroft · North Road · Bathwick · Bath BA2 6HZ · Somerset
Tel: (01225) 461919 · Fax 01225 461919 · Open: ALL YEAR · Map Ref No. 01

Brompton House

Near Rd: A.36

Built as a rectory in 1777, Brompton House is an elegant Georgian residence with a car park & beautiful mature gardens. Only 5 mins' walk from many of Bath's historic sights, it is run by the Selbys who offer every comfort & service to their guests. The attractive sitting room is furnished with antiques, & the tastefully decorated en-suite bedrooms offer T.V., radio/alarm, 'phone & tea/coffee facilities. Breakfast is a delicious choice of full English, Continental or wholefood. Children over 15.
E-mail: bromptonhouse@btinternet.com
www.bromptonhouse.co.uk

| | £30.00 to £48.00 | Y | N | N |

VISA: M'CARD: AMEX:

Mr & Mrs Selby · Brompton House · St. John's Road · Bath BA2 6PT · Somerset
Tel: (01225) 420972 · Fax 01225 420505 · Open: ALL YEAR (Excl. Xmas & New Year) · Map Ref No. 01

The Plaine

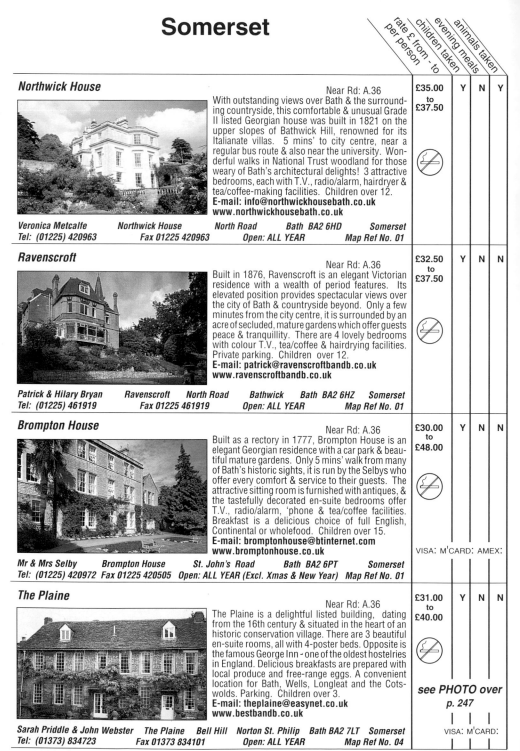

Near Rd: A.36

The Plaine is a delightful listed building, dating from the 16th century & situated in the heart of an historic conservation village. There are 3 beautiful en-suite rooms, all with 4-poster beds. Opposite is the famous George Inn - one of the oldest hostelries in England. Delicious breakfasts are prepared with local produce and free-range eggs. A convenient location for Bath, Wells, Longleat and the Cotswolds. Parking. Children over 3.
E-mail: theplaine@easynet.co.uk
www.bestbandb.co.uk

| | £31.00 to £40.00 | Y | N | N |

see PHOTO over
p. 247

VISA: M'CARD:

Sarah Priddle & John Webster · The Plaine · Bell Hill · Norton St. Philip · Bath BA2 7LT · Somerset
Tel: (01373) 834723 · Fax 01373 834101 · Open: ALL YEAR · Map Ref No. 04

The Plaine. Norton St. Philip.

Header columns: rate £ from - to per person | children taken | evening meals | animals taken

Lindisfarne

Near Rd: A.36
£25.00 to £30.00 — Y | N | N

Just 1 1/2 miles from Bath city centre, Lindisfarne is a lovely home set in attractive gardens, offering comfortable en-suite accommodation with colour T.V. & hospitality tray. A full English breakfast is served in the sunny dining room. The resident proprietors offer a warm welcome, with the local knowledge & personal attention guaranteed to make your stay enjoyable. Car park & frequent bus service to the centre. Historic local pubs & restaurants within walking distance. Children over 8.
E-mail: lindisfarne-bath@talk21.com
www.bath.org/hotel/lindisfarne.htm

VISA: M'CARD: AMEX:

Ian & Carolyn Tiley   Lindisfarne   41a Warminster Road   Bathampton   Bath BA2 6XJ
Tel: (01225) 466342   Open: ALL YEAR   Map Ref No. 02

Monmouth Lodge

Near Rd: B.3110
£33.00 to £40.00 — Y | N | N

Set in an acre of attractive garden, looking on to the Somerset Hills surrounding this historic village. There are 3 attractively furnished ground-floor en-suite bedrooms, with T.V., tea/coffee-making facilities, king-size beds & own patio doors, which offer space & comfort. In the charming sitting room & stylish dining room, there is the same attention to detail & quality, where a good choice of excellent breakfast is served. Ideally situated for Bath, Wells, Stonehenge etc. Private parking. Famous 13th-century pub nearby. Children over 5.
www.bestbandb.co.uk

VISA: M'CARD:

Traudle Graham   Monmouth Lodge   Norton St. Philip   Bath BA2 7LH   Somerset
Tel: (01373) 834367   Open: FEB - DEC   Map Ref No. 04

Winsors Farm

Near Rd: A.39
£25.00 to £25.00 — Y | N | Y

Winsors Farm is a 16th-century Grade II listed Somerset longhouse with exposed beams, flagstone floors & inglenook fireplaces. A relaxed friendly 'home from home'. At the doorway of the Quantock Hills, enjoy gentle walks in unspoilt countryside. There are 2 delightful bedrooms, with views of the hills, an en-suite or private bathroom, colour T.V. & tea/coffee-making facilities. Guest sitting room. Car parking. Use of gardens & paddock. Also, a self-catering cottage.
E-mail: info@winsors-farm.co.uk
www.winsors-farm.co.uk

Jackie & David Griffin   Winsors Farm   Holford   Nr. Bridgwater TA5 1RY   Somerset
Tel: (01278) 741435   Fax 01278 741666   Open: ALL YEAR   Map Ref No. 05

Conygar House

Near Rd: A.39
£26.00 to £28.00 — Y | N | N

Conygar House is situated in a quiet road just off the main street of medieval Dunster village. Restaurants, bars & shops are all within 1 mins' walking distance. Wonderful views of castle & moors. Delightful sunny garden & patio for guests' use. Ideal for exploring Exmoor & coast. All of the rooms are decorated & furnished to a high standard. Personal service & your comfort is guaranteed. Dunster Beach is 1 1/2 miles away, Minehead 2 1/2 miles & Porlock 8 miles.
E-mail: bale.dunster@virgin.net
http://homepage.virgin.net/bale.dunster

Mrs B. Bale   Conygar House   2A The Ball   Dunster TA24 6SD   Somerset
Tel: (01643) 821872   Fax 01643 821872   Open: FEB - NOV   Map Ref No. 08

Number Three Hotel.   Glastonbury.

	rate £ from - to per person	children taken	evening meals	animals taken

Dollons House

Near Rd: A.39

17th-century Grade II listed Dollons House nestles beneath the castle in this delightful medieval village in the Exmoor National Park. 3 attractive & very comfortable en-suite rooms, each with its own character & special decor. 100 years ago, the local pharmacist had his shop in Dollons, & in the back he made marmalade for the Houses of Parliament. Dunster is ideal for touring. Pull up outside the front door to unload & get instructions for parking.
E-mail: jmott@onetel.net.uk
www.bestbandb.co.uk

£27.50 to £27.50	N	N	N

VISA: M'CARD: AMEX:

Mrs Janet Mott Dollons House 10-12 Church Street Dunster TA24 6SH Somerset
Tel: (01643) 821880 Open: ALL YEAR (Excl. Xmas) Map Ref No. 09

Larcombe Foot

Near Rd: A.396

Larcombe Foot, a comfortable old country house set in the beautiful & tranquil Upper Exe Valley, is an ideal base for walking, riding, fishing & touring Exmoor. Guests' comfort is paramount. Accommodation is in 3 bedrooms, 2 with private bathroom, & tea/coffee makers in all rooms. A comfortable sitting room with log fire & T.V., plus a pretty garden to relax in. Evening meals by prior arrangement. Winsford is considered one of the prettiest villages on the moor. Children over 8.
www.bestbandb.co.uk

£24.00 to £24.00	Y	Y	Y

Mrs V. Vicary Larcombe Foot Winsford Exmoor National Park TA24 7HS Somerset
Tel: (01643) 851306 Fax 01643 851306 Open: APR - OCT Map Ref No. 10

Number Three

Near Rd: M.5 Ex. 23

Number Three is a beautiful Georgian town house; once the home of Winston Churchill's mother & also Frederick Bligh Bond. 5 individually designed & refurbished rooms, all with en-suite bathrooms, T.V., telephone & tea/coffee-making facilities. 2 rooms are in the main house & 3 are in the Garden House, set within the large walled garden; with wonderful mature trees, floodlit at night. Car parking. Number Three stands beside Glastonbury Abbey & is a place of peace & tranquillity.
E-mail: info@numberthree.co.uk
www.numberthree.co.uk

£45.00 to £50.00	Y	N	N

see PHOTO over
p. 249

VISA: M'CARD: AMEX:

Patricia Redmond Number Three 3 Magdalene Street Glastonbury BA6 9EW Somerset
Tel: (01458) 832129 Fax 01458 834227 Open: ALL YEAR (Excl. Xmas) Map Ref No. 11

The Lynch Country House

Near Rd: A.303

The Lynch is a charming small hotel, standing in acres of carefully tended, wonderfully mature grounds. Beautifully refurbished & decorated to retain all its Georgian style & elegance, it now offers 8 attractively presented rooms, some with 4-posters, others with Victorian bedsteads, all with thoughtful extras including bathrobes & magazines. Each room has en-suite facilities, 'phone, radio, T.V. & tea/coffee. The elegant dining room overlooks the lawns & lake. Single supplement.
E-mail: the_lynch@talk21.com
www.thelynchcountryhouse.co.uk

£24.50 to £42.50	Y	N	Y

see PHOTO over
p. 251

VISA: M'CARD: AMEX:

Roy Copeland The Lynch Country House 4 Behind Berry Somerton TA11 7PD Somerset
Tel: (01458) 272316 Fax 01458 272590 Open: ALL YEAR (Excl. Xmas & New Year) Map Ref No. 13

The Lynch Country House Hotel.   Somerton.

Somerset

Mill House

Near Rd: A.37, A.303
Ideally situated & beautifully restored, listed Georgian mill house in peaceful garden with mill stream. Close to Glastonbury & Wells with many National Trust properties & classical gardens nearby. Fish without leaving the garden, walk or cycle for miles & enjoy birdwatching on the panoramic Somerset Levels. Beautifully decorated, luxury en-suite bedrooms with wonderful views, an elegant Georgian dining room & delicious Aga breakfasts await you. Children over 10.
E-mail: B&B@MillHouseBarton.co.uk
www.MillHouseBarton.co.uk

| | £26.00 to £30.00 | Y | N | N |

VISA: M'CARD:

Rita & Michael Knight   Mill House   Mill Road   Barton St. David Somerset TA11 6DF Somerset
Tel: (01458) 851215   Fax 01458 851372   Open: ALL YEAR   Map Ref No. 12

Whittles Farm

Near Rd: A.358
Guests at Whittles Farm can be sure of a high standard of accommodation & service. A superior 16th-century farmhouse set in 200 acres of pastureland, it is luxuriously carpeted & furnished in traditional style. Inglenook fireplaces & log-burners. 2 en-suite bedrooms, individually furnished, with T.V. & tea/coffee facilities. Super farmhouse food, using own meat, eggs & vegetables, & local Cheddar cheese & butter. Dinner by arrangement. Table licence. Children over 12 yrs.
E-mail: dj.CM.MITCHEM@themail.co.uk
www.whittlesfarm.co.uk

| | £27.00 to £29.00 | Y | Y | N |

Mrs Claire Mitchem   Whittles Farm   Beercrocombe   Taunton TA3 6AH   Somerset
Tel: (01823) 480301   Fax 01823 480301   Open: FEB - NOV   Map Ref No. 14

Higher House

Near Rd: A.358
Higher House is set 650 feet up on the southern slopes of the Quantock Hills. The views from the house & gardens are exceptional. The principal part of the house is 17th century, built around 2 courtyards, 1 with a heated pool. Each bedroom has its own bathroom, 'phone, T.V., tea/coffee facilities, books, magazines. There is a beautifully presented drawing room. An all-weather tennis court together with 2 well-appointed cottages, are also available. Evening meals by arrangement.
E-mail: eyre@bagborough.u-net.com

| | £30.00 to £30.00 | Y | Y | N |

see PHOTO over
p. 253

Martin & Marise Eyre   Higher House   West Bagborough   Taunton TA4 3EF   Somerset
Tel: (01823) 432996   Fax 01823 433568   Open: ALL YEAR   Map Ref No. 15

Southway Farm

Near Rd: A.39
A friendly welcome is assured at Southway Farm, a Grade II listed Georgian farmhouse, situated half-way between Glastonbury & Wells. Accommodation is in 3 spacious, well-equipped en-suite bedrooms. Delicious quality breakfasts are served using local produce & our free-range eggs, homemade bread & preserves, in the elegant dining room at separate tables. Guests can relax in the cosy lounge with T.V., books, magazines & games or in the pretty gardens.
E-mail: southwayfarm@ukonline.co.uk
www.southwayfarm.co.uk

| | £23.00 to £25.00 | Y | N | N |

Naomi Frost   Southway Farm   Polsham   Wells BA5 1RW   Somerset
Tel: (01749) 673396   Fax 01749 670373   Open: ALL YEAR   Map Ref No. 16

Higher House. West Bagborough.

Somerset

Beryl

Near Rd: A.39

Beryl is a precious gem in a perfect setting, situated 1 mile from the cathedral city of Wells. This striking 19th-century Gothic mansion has beautifully furnished en-suite bedrooms, interesting views & all the accoutrements of luxury living (including a chair lift from ground to first floor). Dinner is available by arrangement & is served in the exquisite dining room. Holly & Mary-Ellen are charming hosts, & your stay is sure to be memorable.
E-mail: stay@beryl-wells.co.uk
www.beryl-wells.co.uk

	rate £ from - to per person	children taken	evening meals	animals taken
Beryl	£35.00 to £52.50	Y	Y	Y

see PHOTO over p. 255

VISA: M'CARD:

Holly & Mary-Ellen Nowell   Beryl   Off Hawkers Lane   Wells BA5 3JP   Somerset
Tel: (01749) 678738   Fax 01749 670508   Open: ALL YEAR (Excl. Xmas)   Map Ref No. 17

The Old Stores

Near Rd: A.371

This charming conversion of The Old Stores is between the church & the pub in the heart of this Mendip village. The en-suite bedrooms, music, open fires & a library provide a high standard of cosy comfort. You will be welcomed with home-made cakes & the use of local organic produce & home-made bread - we cater for all tastes. Malcolm can provide maps & books for visits & walks, including his own book on local footpaths.
E-mail: moglin980@aol.com
www.bestbandb.co.uk

	rate £ from - to per person	children taken	evening meals	animals taken
The Old Stores	£23.00 to £24.00	Y	N	Y

VISA: M'CARD:

Malcolm & Linda Mogford   The Old Stores   Westbury-sub-Mendip   Nr. Wells BA5 1HA   Somerset
Tel: (01749) 870817   Fax 01749 870980   Open: ALL YEAR   Map Ref No. 18

Stoneleigh House

Near Rd: A.371

A beautiful 18th-century farmhouse (flagstone floors, beams, crooked walls) situated between Wells & Cheddar. Wonderful southerly views over unspoilt countryside to Glastonbury Tor from the bedrooms & lounge. Bedrooms are prettily furnished with country antiques & have en-suite bath/shower rooms. Round this off with a delicious breakfast, Wendy's decorative needlework, Tony's classic cars, the old forge, a cottagey garden & friendly cats. Children over 10. Good pubs nearby.
E-mail: stoneleigh@dial.pipex.com
www.stoneleigh.dial.pipex.com

	rate £ from - to per person	children taken	evening meals	animals taken
Stoneleigh House	£27.00 to £30.00	Y	N	N

Wendy & Tony Thompson   Stoneleigh House   Westbury-sub-Mendip   Nr. Wells BA5 1HF   Somerset
Tel: (01749) 870668   Fax 01749 870668   Open: ALL YEAR (Excl. Xmas)   Map Ref No. 19

Tynings House

Near Rd: A.39

Tynings House lies on the edge of a small village, surrounded by 8 acres of garden & meadow, with beautiful views over unspoilt countryside. 3 en-suite bedrooms with T.V. & tea/coffee facilities. Also, a separate guest lounge. The garden is a peaceful place in which to relax after a day's outing. Within easy reach of Glastonbury, Bath, Wookey, Cheddar Gorge & the beautiful Mendip Hills. Tynings is a peaceful retreat from the hustle & bustle of everyday life. Children & animals by arrangement.
E-mail: B+B@tynings.co.uk
www.tynings.co.uk

	rate £ from - to per person	children taken	evening meals	animals taken
Tynings House	£25.00 to £30.00	Y	N	Y

Jill Parsons   Tynings House   Harters Hill Lane   Coxley   Nr. Wells BA5 1RF   Somerset
Tel: (01749) 675368   Open: ALL YEAR   Map Ref No. 20

Beryl.   Wells.

Somerset

Cutthorne

Near Rd: A.396

Tucked away in the heart of Exmoor National Park, Cutthorne offers a quiet & relaxing haven for country lovers. It is situated in an Area of Outstanding Natural Beauty, & walking & riding are unrivalled here, whether by the coast or on the moors. Within easy reach are Lynton & Lynmouth, Tarr Steps & Dunster. The pretty bedrooms all have bathrooms & 1 has a 4-poster bed. The cuisine is traditional or vegetarian, using only the finest local meat & organic vegetables. Licensed.
E-mail: durbin@cutthorne.co.uk
www.cutthorne.co.uk

£29.00 to £38.00

N | Y | Y

VISA: M'CARD: AMEX:

Ann Durbin	Cutthorne	Luckwell Bridge	Wheddon Cross TA24 7EW	Somerset
Tel: (01643) 831255		Fax 01643 831255	Open: ALL YEAR	Map Ref No. 21

**All the establishments mentioned in this guide
are members of
The Worldwide Bed & Breakfast Association**

**When booking your accommodation please
mention
The Best Bed & Breakfast**

Suffolk

Suffolk
(East Anglia)

In July, the lower reaches of the River Orwell hold the essence of Suffolk. Broad fields of green and gold with wooded horizons sweep down to the quiet water. Orwell Bridge spans the wide river where yachts and tan-sailed barges share the water with ocean-going container ships out of Ipswich. Downstream the saltmarshes echo to the cry of the Curlew. The small towns and villages of Suffolk are typical of an area with long seafaring traditions. This is the county of men of vision; like Constable and Gainsborough, Admiral Lord Nelson and Benjamin Britten.

The land is green and fertile and highly productive. The hedgerows shelter some of our prettiest wild flowers, & the narrow country lanes are a pure delight. Most memorable is the ever-changing sky, appearing higher and wider here than elsewhere in England. There is a great deal of heathland, probably the best known being Newmarket where horses have been trained and raced for some hundreds of years. Gorse-covered heath meets sandy cliffs on Suffolks Heritage Coast. Here are bird reserves and the remains of the great mediaeval city of Dunwich, sliding into the sea.

West Suffolk was famous for its wool trade in the Middle Ages, & the merchants gave thanks for their good fortune by building magnificent "Wool Churches". Much-photographed Lavenham has the most perfect black & white timbered houses in Britain, built by the merchants of Tudor times. Ipswich was granted the first charter by King John in 1200, but had long been a trading community of seafarers. Its history can be read from the names of the streets - Buttermarket, Friars Street, Cornhill, Dial Lane & Tavern Street. The latter holds the Great White Horse Hotel mentioned by Charles Dickens in Pickwick Papers. Sadly not many ancient buildings remain, but the mediaeval street pattern and the churches make an interesting trail to follow. The Market town of Bury St. Edmunds is charming, with much of its architectural heritage still surviving, from the Norman Cornhill to a fine Queen Anne House. The great Abbey, now in ruins, was the meeting place of the Barons of England for the creation of the Magna Carta, enshrining the principals of individual freedom, parliamentary democracy and the supremacy of the law. Suffolk has some very fine churches, notably at Mildenhall, Lakenheath, Framlingham, Lavenham & Stoke-by-Nayland, & also a large number of wonderful houses & great halls, evidence of the county's prosperity.

Lavenham.

Suffolk

Suffolk Gazeteer

Areas of Outstanding Natural Beauty
Suffolk Coast. Heathlands. Dedham Vale.

Historic Houses & Castles

Euston Hall - Thetford
18th century house with fine collection of pictures. Gardens & 17th century Parish Church nearby.

Christchurch Mansion - Ipswich
16th century mansion built on site of 12th century Augustinian Priory. Gables & dormers added in 17th century & other alteration & additions made in 17th & 18th centuries.

Gainsborough's House - Sudbury
Birthplace of Gainsborough, well furnished, collection of paintings.

The Guildhall - Hadleigh
15th century.

Glemham Hall - Nr Woodbridge
Elizabethan house of red brick - 18th century alterations. Fine stair, panelled rooms with Queen Anne furniture.

Haughley Park - Nr. Stowmarket
Jacobean manor house.

Heveningham Hall - Nr. Halesworth
Georgian mansion - English Palladian - Interior in Neo-Classical style. Garden by Capability Brown.

Ickworth - Nr. Bury St. Edmunds
Mixed architectural styles - late Regency & 18th century. French furniture, pictures & superb silver. Gardens with orangery.

Kentwell Hall - Long Melford
Elizabethan mansion in red brick, built in E plan, surrounded by moat.

Little Hall - Lavenham
15th century hall house, collection of furniture, pictures, china, etc.

Melford Hall - Nr. Sudbury
16th century - fine pictures, Chinese porcelain, furniture. Garden with gazebo.

Somerleyton Hall - Nr. Lowestoft
Dating from 16th century - additional work in 19th century. Carving by Grinling Gibbons. Tapestries, library, pictures.

Cathedrals & Churches

Bury St. Edmunds (St. Mary)
15th century. Hammer Beam roof in nave, wagon roof in chancel. Boret monument 1467.

Bramfield (St. Andrew)
Early circular tower. Fine screen & vaulting. Renaissance effigy.

Bacton (St. Mary)
15th century timbered roof. East Anglian stone & flintwork.

Dennington (St. Mary)
15th century alabaster monuments & bench ends. Aisle & Parclose screens with lofts & parapets.

Earl Stonhay (St. Mary)
14th century - rebuilt with fine hammer roof & 17th century pulpit with four hour-glasses.

Euston (St. Genevieve)
17th century. Fine panelling, reredos may be Grinling Gibbons.

Framlingham (St. Michael)
15th century nave & west tower, hammer beam roof in false vaulting. Chancel was rebuilt in 16th century for the tombs of the Howard family, monumental art treasures. Thamar organ. 1674.

Fressingfield (St. Peter & St. Paul)
15th century woodwork - very fine.

Lavenham (St. Peter & St. Paul)
15th century. Perpendicular. Fine towers. 14th century chancel screen. 17th century monument in alabaster.

Long Melford (Holy Trinity)
15th century Lady Chapel, splendid brasses. 15th century glass of note. Chantry chapel with fine roof. Like cathedral in proportions.

Stoke-by-Nayland (St. Mary)
16th-17th century library, great tower. Fine nave & arcades. Good brasses & monuments.

Ufford (St. Mary)
Mediaeval font cover - glorious.

Museums & Galleries

Christchurch Mansion - Ipswich
Country house, collection of furniture, pictures, bygones, ceramics of 18th century. Paintings by Gainsborough, Constable & modern artists.

Ipswich Museum - Ipswich
Natural History; prehistory, geology & archaeology to mediaeval period.

Suffolk

Moyse's Hall Musuem - Bury St. Edmunds
12th century dwelling house with local antiquities & natural history.
Abbot's Hall Museum of Rural Life - Stowmarket
Collections describing agriculture, crafts & domestic utensils.
Gershom-Parkington Collection - Bury St. Edmunds
Queen Anne House containing collection of watches & clocks
Dunwich Musuem - Dunwich
Flora & fauna; local history.

Historic Monuments
The Abbey - Bury St. Edmunds
Only west end now standing.

Framlingham Castle
12th & 13th centuries - Tudor almshouses.
Bungay Castle - Bungay
12th century. Restored 13th century drawbridge & gatehouse.
Burgh Castle Roman Fort - Burgh
Coastal defences - 3rd century.
Herringfleet Priory - Herringfleet
13th century - remains of small Augustinian priory.
Leiston Abbey - Leiston
14th century - remains of cloisters, choir & trancepts.
Orford Castle - Orford
12th century - 18-sided keep - three towers.

The House in the Clouds. Thorpeness.

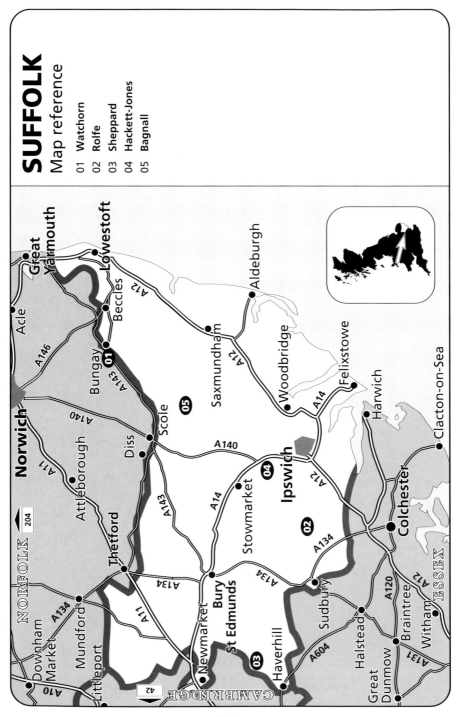

SUFFOLK
Map reference

01 Watchorn
02 Rolfe
03 Sheppard
04 Hackett-Jones
05 Bagnall

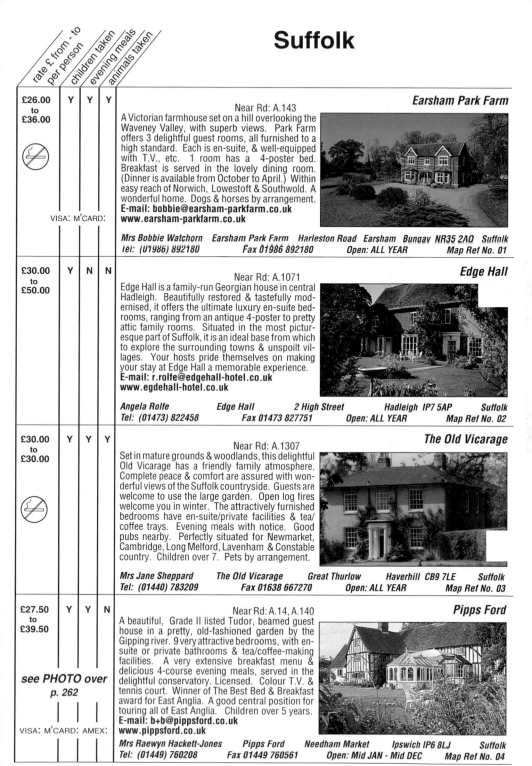

Column headers (rotated):
- rate £ from - to per person
- children taken
- evening meals
- animals taken

£26.00 to £36.00

Y Y Y

(no smoking symbol)

VISA: M'CARD:

Earsham Park Farm

Near Rd: A.143

A Victorian farmhouse set on a hill overlooking the Waveney Valley, with superb views. Park Farm offers 3 delightful guest rooms, all furnished to a high standard. Each is en-suite, & well-equipped with T.V., etc. 1 room has a 4-poster bed. Breakfast is served in the lovely dining room. (Dinner is available from October to April.) Within easy reach of Norwich, Lowestoft & Southwold. A wonderful home. Dogs & horses by arrangement.
E-mail: bobbie@earsham-parkfarm.co.uk
www.earsham-parkfarm.co.uk

Mrs Bobbie Watchorn   Earsham Park Farm   Harleston Road   Earsham   Bungay NR35 2AQ   Suffolk
Tel: (01986) 892180   Fax 01986 892180   Open: ALL YEAR   Map Ref No. 01

£30.00 to £50.00

Y N N

Edge Hall

Near Rd: A.1071

Edge Hall is a family-run Georgian house in central Hadleigh. Beautifully restored & tastefully modernised, it offers the ultimate luxury en-suite bedrooms, ranging from an antique 4-poster to pretty attic family rooms. Situated in the most picturesque part of Suffolk, it is an ideal base from which to explore the surrounding towns & unspoilt villages. Your hosts pride themselves on making your stay at Edge Hall a memorable experience.
E-mail: r.rolfe@edgehall-hotel.co.uk
www.egdehall-hotel.co.uk

Angela Rolfe   Edge Hall   2 High Street   Hadleigh IP7 5AP   Suffolk
Tel: (01473) 822458   Fax 01473 827751   Open: ALL YEAR   Map Ref No. 02

£30.00 to £30.00

Y Y Y

(no smoking symbol)

The Old Vicarage

Near Rd: A.1307

Set in mature grounds & woodlands, this delightful Old Vicarage has a friendly family atmosphere. Complete peace & comfort are assured with wonderful views of the Suffolk countryside. Guests are welcome to use the large garden. Open log fires welcome you in winter. The attractively furnished bedrooms have en-suite/private facilities & tea/coffee trays. Evening meals with notice. Good pubs nearby. Perfectly situated for Newmarket, Cambridge, Long Melford, Lavenham & Constable country. Children over 7. Pets by arrangement.

Mrs Jane Sheppard   The Old Vicarage   Great Thurlow   Haverhill CB9 7LE   Suffolk
Tel: (01440) 783209   Fax 01638 667270   Open: ALL YEAR   Map Ref No. 03

£27.50 to £39.50

Y Y N

see PHOTO over
p. 262

VISA: M'CARD: AMEX:

Pipps Ford

Near Rd: A.14, A.140

A beautiful, Grade II listed Tudor, beamed guest house in a pretty, old-fashioned garden by the Gipping river. 9 very attractive bedrooms, with en-suite or private bathrooms & tea/coffee-making facilities. A very extensive breakfast menu & delicious 4-course evening meals, served in the delightful conservatory. Licensed. Colour T.V. & tennis court. Winner of The Best Bed & Breakfast award for East Anglia. A good central position for touring all of East Anglia. Children over 5 years.
E-mail: b+b@pippsford.co.uk
www.pippsford.co.uk

Mrs Raewyn Hackett-Jones   Pipps Ford   Needham Market   Ipswich IP6 8LJ   Suffolk
Tel: (01449) 760208   Fax 01449 760561   Open: Mid JAN - Mid DEC   Map Ref No. 04

Pipps Ford.   Needham Market.

Suffolk

rate £ from - to per person	children taken	evening meals	animals taken	
£22.50 to £30.00	Y	N	Y	**Abbey House** Near Rd: A.1120 Abbey House is a delightful listed Victorian rectory set in 10 acres of quiet Suffolk countryside. The house is surrounded by secluded gardens with mature trees & several large ponds. Attractively furnished bedrooms, 2 doubles & 1 twin with en-suite or private bathrooms & tea-making facilities. Exclusive use of the dining room & drawing room with T.V. & log fire. Outdoor swimming pool. Central for touring East Anglia, within easy reach of Lavenham, Constable country & the coast. Children over 10. Animals by arrangement.

Sue Bagnall   Abbey House   Monk Soham   Woodbridge IP13 7EN   Suffolk
Tel: (01728) 685225   Open: ALL YEAR (Excl. Xmas & New Year)   Map Ref No. 05

Surrey

Surrey
(South East)

One of the Home Counties, Surrey includes a large area of London, south of the Thames. Communications are good in all directions so it is easy to stay in Surrey & travel either into central London or out to enjoy the lovely countryside which, despite urban development, survives thanks to the 'Green Belt' policy. The county is also very accessible from Gatwick Airport.

The land geographically, is chalk sandwiched in clay, & probably the lack of handy building material was responsible for the area remaining largely uninhabited for centuries. The North Downs were a considerable barrier to cross, but gradually settlements grew along the rivers which were the main routes through. The Romans used the gap created by the River Mole to build Stane Street between London & Chichester, this encouraged the development of small towns. The gap cut by the passage of the River Wey allows the Pilgrims Way to cross the foot of the Downs. Dorking, Reigate & Farnham are small towns along this route, all with attracitve main streets & interesting shops & buildings.

Surrey has very little mention in the Domesday Book, &, although the patronage of the church & of wealthy families established manors which developed over the years, little happened to disturb the rural tranquility of the region. As a county it made little history but rather reflected passing times, although Magna Carta was signed at Egham in 1215.

The heathlands of Surrey were a Royal playground for centuries. The Norman Kings hunted here & horses became part of the landscape & life of the people, as they are today on Epsom Downs.

Nearness to London & Royal patronage began to influence the area, & the buildings of the Tudor period reflect this. Royal palaces were built at Hampton Court & Richmond, & great houses such as Loseley near Guildford often using stone from the monasteries emptied during the Reformation. Huge deer parks were enclosed & stocked. Richmond, described as the "finest village in the British Dominions", is now beset by 20th century traffic but still has a wonderful park with deer, lakes & woodland that was enclosed by Charles I. The terraces & gardens of such buildings as Trumpeters House & Asgill House on the slopes of Richmond overlooking the Thames, have an air of spaciousness & elegance & there are lovely & interesting riverside walks at Richmond.

Polesden Lacey.

Surrey

Surrey Gazeteer

Historic Houses & Castles

Albury Park - Albury, Nr. Guildford
A delightful country mansion designed by Pugin.

Clandon Park - Guildford
A fine house in the Palladian style by Leoni. A good collection of furniture & pictures. The house boasts some fine plasterwork.

Claremont Lohor
A superb Palladian house with interesting interior.

Detillens - Limpsfield
A fine 15th century house with inglenook fireplaces & mediaeval furniture. A large, pleasant garden.

Greathed Manor- Lingfield
An imposing Victorian manor house.

Hatchlands - East Clandon
A National Trust property of the 18th century with a fine Adam interior.

Loseley House - Guildford
A very fine Elizabethan mansion with superb panelling, furniture & paintings.

Polesden Lacy - Dorking
A Regency villa housing the Grevill collection of tapestries, pictures & furnishings. Extensive gardens.

Cathedrals & Churches

Compton (St. Nicholas)
The only surviving 2-storey sanctuary in the country. A fine 17th century pulpit.

Esher (St. George)
A fine altar-piece & marble monument.

Hascombe (St. Peter)
A rich interior with much gilding & painted reredos & roofs.

Lingfield (St. Peter & St. Paul)
15th century. Holding a chained bible.

Ockham (St. Mary & All Saints)
Early church with 13th century east window.

Stoke D'Abernon (St. Mary)
Dating back to Pre-conquest time with additions from the 12th-15th centuries. A fine 13th century painting. Early brasses.

Museums & Galleries

Charterhouse School Museum - Godalming
Peruvian pottery, Greek pottery, archaeology & natural history.

Chertsey Museum - Chertsey
18th-19th century costume & furnishing displayed & local history.

Guildford House - Guildford
The house is 17th century & of architectural interest housing monthly exhibitions.

Guildford Museum - Guildford
A fine needlework collection & plenty on local history.

Old Kiln Agricultural - Tilford
A very interesting collection of old farm implements.

Watermill Museum - Haxted
A restored 17th century mill with working water wheels & machinery.

Weybridge Museum - Weybridge
Good archaeological exhibition plus costume & local history.

The Gardens. Wisley

SURREY

Map reference

01 Franklin-Adams
02 Franks
03 Hill
04 Wallis
05 Grinsted
06 Carmichael
07 Wolf
08 Carey

Surrey

£27.50 to £30.00	Y	N	Y		**High Edser**

🚭

Near Rd: A.25
A large, handsome Grade II listed home, the earliest part built in the 16th century, situated in an Area of Outstanding Natural Beauty. There are three attractively furnished rooms available: two doubles and one twin. Residents' lounge and T.V.. Tennis court in grounds, and golf nearby. 35 minutes to Gatwick and London Airports. Approximately an hour's drive to London. A delightful home, ideal for a relaxing break.
E-mail: franklinadams@highedser.demon.co.uk
www.bestbandb.co.uk

Carol Franklin-Adams   High Edser   Shere Road   Ewhurst   Cranleigh GU6 7PQ   Surrey
Tel: (01483) 278214   Fax 01483 278200   Open: ALL YEAR   Map Ref No. 01

£37.50 to £37.50	Y	Y	N		**Denbies Wine Estate**

🚭

VISA: M'CARD:

Near Rd: A.24, A.25
Denbies is Britain's largest vineyard standing in 265 acres. The B & B is beautifully positioned within the vineyard & it is close to the Visitor Centre, where you can enjoy superb wine tours & lunches. 6 newly refurbished, comfortable double bedrooms with en-suite facilities, beverage tray & T.V. etc. (Single supplement). The historic market town of Dorking is just a short drive or walk away & there is a vineyard train, which (weather-permitting) can take you up to the North Downs Way.
E-mail: info@denbiesvineyard.co.uk
www.denbiesvineyard.co.uk

Mike & Lynda Franks   Denbies Wine Estate   London Road   Dorking RH5 6AA   Surrey
Tel: (01306) 876777   Fax 01306 888930   Open: ALL YEAR   Map Ref No. 02

£29.00 to £40.00	Y	N	N		**Bulmer Farm**

Near Rd: A.25
Enjoy a warm welcome at this delightful 17th-century farmhouse, complete with many beams & an inglenook fireplace. Adjoining the house around a courtyard are 5 attractive & comfortably furnished barn-conversion en-suite bedrooms, for non-smokers. Farm produce & home-made preserves are provided. Situated in a picturesque village, it is convenient for London airports. Children over 12 years. Self-catering also available. A brochure is on request.
www.bestbandb.co.uk

Gill Hill   Bulmer Farm   Pasturewood Road   Holmbury St. Mary   Dorking RH5 6LG   Surrey
Tel: (01306) 730210   Open: ALL YEAR   Map Ref No. 03

£25.00 to £32.50	Y	N	N		**Park House Farm**

🚭

VISA: M'CARD:

Near Rd: A.25
A delightful large family home, tastefully furnished with many antiques. Accommodation is very comfortable with en-suite/private facilities, satellite T.V., tea/coffee-making facilities etc. It is set in 25 acres in an Area of Outstanding Natural Beauty within easy reach of Heathrow & Gatwick Airports, many gardens & National Trust properties. Good train service to London. Ideal walking country, with many village pubs for food. Children over 12.
E-mail: Peterwallis@msn.com
www.smoothhound.co.uk/hotels/parkhous

Ann & Peter Wallis   Park House Farm   Hollow Lane   Abinger Common   Dorking RH5 6LW   Surrey
Tel: (01306) 730101   Fax 01306 730643   Open: ALL YEAR   Map Ref No. 04

	rate £ from - to per person	children taken	evening meals	animals taken

The Lawn Guest House

Near Rd: A.23

A well-appointed Victorian house only 5 mins' from Gatwick Airport & 25 miles to London or Brighton. Very useful as a base for travelling, it is close to the rail station & town centre. 12 en-suite bedrooms, all very comfortable & well decorated, with T.V., hairdryer, 'phone & tea/coffee facilities, etc. A full English breakfast, or a healthy alternative including fruit, yoghurt & muesli, is served in the pleasant dining room. Single supplement. Parking.
E-mail: info@lawnguesthouse.co.uk
www.lawnguesthouse.co.uk

£27.50 to £28.75 | Y | N | Y

VISA: M'CARD: AMEX:

Carole & Adrian Grinsted   The Lawn Guest House   30 Massetts Road   Horley   Gatwick RH6 7DF
Tel: (01293) 775751   Fax 01293 821803   Open: ALL YEAR   Map Ref No. 05

Deerfell

Near Rd: A.286

A warm welcome at a spacious & comfortable stone-built home set in downland countryside, with breathtaking views to the hills & valleys of Surrey/Sussex. 3 pretty rooms with en-suite/private bathrooms, & tea/coffee facilities & T.V.. Wonderful walks right on doorstep. Light suppers available on request. Close by - Haslemere station (4 miles), London (45 mins'), Guildford/Chichester (20 miles), Heathrow/Gatwick Airports 1 hour. Children over 6. Evening meals & animals by arrangement.
E-mail: deerfell@tesco.net

£27.00 to £27.00 | Y | Y | Y

Elizabeth Carmichael   Deerfell   Fernden Lane   Haslemere GU27 3BU   Surrey
Tel: (01428) 653409   Fax 01428 656106   Open: ALL YEAR (Excl. Xmas)   Map Ref No. 06

The Old Farmhouse

Near Rd: A.25

An early 15th-century medieval 4-bay hall house, which is little altered & retains many original features, including the diamond mullions for the hall window & fine panelling. It also has one of the longest unsupported crossing beams in Surrey. 2 of the attractively furnished bedrooms have brass bedsteads, & 1 has an original oak 4-poster bed. A delightful home. The Old Farmhouse is perfect for exploring the south-east of England & many places of historic interest. Children over 10.
E-mail: thecottage@dialstart.net

£30.00 to £30.00 | Y | Y | N

Judie & Philip Wolf   The Old Farmhouse   Wasp Green Lane   Outwood   Nr. Redhill RH1 5QE
Tel: (01342) 842313   Fax 01342 844744   Open: ALL YEAR (Excl. Xmas)   Map Ref No. 07

Swallow Barn

Near Rd: A.3046

Situated in quiet, secluded surroundings on the edge of Chobham, attractively converted outbuildings & stables with outdoor swimming pool. 3 bedrooms with en-suite/private bathrooms, T.V. & tea/coffee. Ideal for Sunningdale, Wentworth & Foxhills golf courses. Also, Wisley & Savill Gardens are within easy reach. Convenient for M.3, M.25, Heathrow Airport, Windsor, Ascot & Hampton Court. Woking station 2 miles - London 25 mins' by train. Single supplement. Children over 8.
E-mail: swallowbarn@web-hq.com
www.swallow-barn.co.uk

£37.50 to £42.50 | Y | N | N

Joan & David Carey   Swallow Barn   Milford Green   Chobham   Woking GU24 8AU   Surrey
Tel: (01276) 856030   Fax 01276 856030   Open: ALL YEAR   Map Ref No. 08

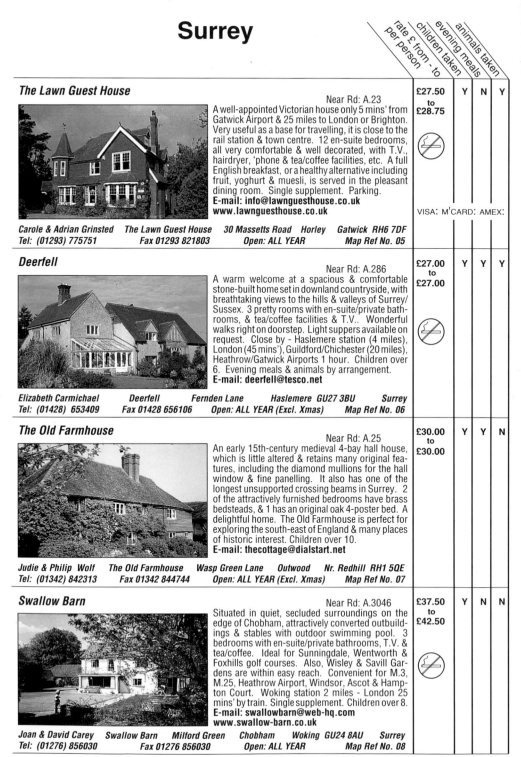

Sussex

Sussex
(South East)

The South Downs of Sussex stretch along the coast, reflecting the expanse of the North Downs of Kent, over the vast stretches of the Weald.

The South Downs extend from dramatic Beachy Head along the coast to Chichester & like the North Downs, they are crossed by an ancient trackway. There is much evidence of prehistoric settlement on the Downs. Mount Caburn, near Lewes, is crowned by an iron age fort, & Cissbury Ring is one of the most important archaeological sites in England. This large earthwork covers 80 acres & must have held a strategic defensive position. Hollingbury Fort carved into the hillside above Brighton, & the Trundle (meaning circle) date from 300-250 B.C., & were constructed on an existing neolithic settlement. The Long Man of Wilmington stands 226 feet high & is believed to be Nordic, possibly representing Woden, the God of War.

Only two towns are located on the Downs but both are of considerable interest. Lewes retains much of its mediaeval past & there is a folk museum in Ann of Cleves' house, which itself is partly 16th century. Arundel has a fascinating mixture of architectural styles, a castle & a superb park with a lake, magnificent beech trees & an unrivalled view of the Arun valley.

The landscape of the inland Weald ranges from bracken-covered heathlands where deer roam, to the deep woodland stretches of the Ashdown Forest, eventually giving way to soft undulating hills & valleys, patterned with hop-fields, meadows, oast houses, windmills & fruit orchards. Originally the whole Weald was dense with forest. Villages like Midhurst & Wadhurst hold the Saxon suffix "hurst" which means wood. As the forests were cleared for agriculture the names of the villages changed & we find Bosham & Stedham whose suffix "ham" means homestead or farm.

Battle, above Hastings, is the site of the famous Norman victory & 16th century Bodiam Castle, built as defence against the French in later times, has a beautiful setting encircled by a lily-covered moat.

Sussex has an extensive coastline, with cliffs near Eastbourne at Beachy Head, & at Hastings. Further east, the great flat Romney Marshes stretch out to sea, & there is considerable variety in the coastal towns.

Chichester has a magnificent cathedral & a harbour reaching deep into the coastal plain that is rich in archaeological remains. The creeks & mudflats make it an excellent place for bird watching.

Brighton is the most famous of the Sussex resorts with its Pier, the Promenade above the beaches, the oriental folly of George IV's Royal Pavilion & its Regency architecture. "The Lanes" are a maze of alleys & small squares full of fascinating shops, a thriving antique trade, & many good pubs & eating places. Hastings to the east preserves its "Old Town" where timbered houses nestle beneath the cliffs & the fishing boats are drawn up on the shingle whilst the nets are hung up to dry in curious tall, thin net stores. Winchelsea stands on a hill where it was rebuilt in the 13th century by Edward I when the original town was engulfed by the sea. It is a beautiful town with a fine Norman church, an excellent museum in the Town Hall, & many pretty houses. Across the Romney Marshes on the next hill stands Rye, its profile dominated by its church. It is a fascinating town with timbered houses & cobbled streets.

Sussex

Sussex Gazeteer

Areas of Outstanding Natural Beauty
The Sussex Downs. Chichester Harbour.

Historic Houses & Castles

Arundel Castle - Arundel
18th century rebuilding of ancient castle, fine portraits, 15th century furniture.
Cuckfield Park - Cuckfield
Elizabethan manor house, gatehouse. Very fine panelling & ceilings.
Danny - Hurstpierpoint
16th century - Elizabethan .
Goodwood House - Chichester
18th century - Jacobean house - Fine Sussex flintwork, paintings by Van Dyck, Canaletto & Stubbs, English & French furniture, tapestries & porcelain.
Newtimber Place - Newtimber
Moated house - Etruscan style wall paintings.
Purham - Pulborough
Elizabethan house containing important collection of Elizabethan, Jacobean & Georgian portraits, also fine furniture.
Petworth House - Petworth
17th century - landscaped by Capability Brown - important paintings - 14th century chapel.
St. Mary's - Bramber
15th century timber framed house - rare panelling.
Tanyard - Sharpthorne
Mediaeval tannery - 16th & 17th century additions.
The Thatched Cottage - Lindfield
Close-studded weald house - reputedly Henry VII hunting lodge.
Uppark - Petersfield
17th century - 18th century interior decorations remain unaltered.
Alfriston Clergy House - Nr. Seaford
14th century parish priest's house - pre-reformation.
Battle Abbey - Battle
Founded by William the Conqueror.
Charleston Manor - Westdean
Norman, Tudor & Georgian architectural styles - Romanesque window in the Norman wing.
Bull House - Lewes
15th century half-timbered house - was home of Tom Paine.

Bateman's - Burwash
17th century - watermill - home of Rudyard Kipling.
Bodiam Castle - Nr. Hawkshurst
14th century - noted example of mediaeval moated military architecture.
Great Dixter - Northiam
15th century half-timbered manor house - great hall - Lutyens gardens
Glynde Place - Nr. Lewes
16th century flint & brick - built around courtyard-collection of paintings by Rubens, Hoppner, Kneller, Lely, Zoffany.
Michelham Priory - Upper Dicker, Nr. Hailsham
13th century Augustinian Priory - became Tudor farmhouse - working watermill, ancient stained glass, etc., enclosed by moat.
Royal Pavilion - Brighton
Built for Prince Regent by Nash upon classical villa by Holland. Exotic Building - has superb original works of art lent by H.M. The Queen. Collections of Regency furniture also Art Nouveau & Art Deco in the Art Gallery & Museum.
Sheffield Park - Nr. Uckfield
Beautiful Tudor House - 18th century alterations - splendid staircase.

Cathedrals & Churches

Alfriston (St. Andrew)
14th century - transition from decorated style to perpendicular, Easter sepulchre.
Boxgrove (St. Mary & St. Blaise)
13th century choir with 16th century painted decoration on vaulting. Relic of Benedictine priory. 16th century chantry. Much decoration.
Chichester Cathedral
Norman & earliest Gothic. Large Romanesque relief sculptures in south choir aisle.
Etchingham (St. Mary & St. Nicholas)
14th century. Old glass, brasses, screen, carved stalls.
Hardham (St. Botolph)
11th century - 12th century wall paintings.
Rotherfield (St. Denys)
16th century font cover, 17th century canopied pulpit, glass by Burne-Jones, wall paintings, Georgian Royal Arms.

Sussex

Sompting (St. Mary)
11th century Saxon tower - Rhenish Helm
Spire - quite unique.
Worth (St. Nicholas)
10th century - chancel arch is the largest
Saxon arch in England. German carved
pulpit c.1500 together with altar rails.
Winchelsea (St. Thomas the Apostle)
14th century - choir & aisles only.
Canopied sedilia & piscina.

Museums & Galleries

Barbican House Museum - Lewes
Collection relating to pre-historic, Romano-
British & , mediaeval antiquities of the
area. Prints & water colours of the area.
Battle Museum-Battle
Remains from archeological sites in area.
Diorama of Battle of Hastings.
Bignor Roman Villa Collection - Bignor
4th century mosaics, Samian pottery,
hypocaust, etc.
Brighton Museum & Art Gallery -
Brighton
Old Master Paintings, watercolours,
ceramics, furniture. Surrealist paintings,
Art Nouveau & Art Deco applied art,
musical instruments & many other
exhibits.

Marlipins Museum - Shoreham
12th century building housing collections
of ship models, photographs, old maps,
geological specimens, etc.
**Royal National Lifeboat Institution
Museum** - Eastbourne
Lifeboats of all types used from earliest
times to present.
Tower 73 - Eastbourne
Martello tower restored to display the
history of these forts. Exhibition of
equipment, uniforms & weapons of the
times.
The Toy Museum - Rottingdean, Brighton
Toys & playthings from many countries -
children's delight.

Other things to see & do

Bewl Water - Nr. Wadhurst
Boat trips, walks, adventure playground
Chichester Festival Theatre - Chichester
Summer season of plays from May to
September.
Goodwood Racecourse

The Royal Pavilion. Brighton.

SUSSEX
Map reference

01	Fuente	13	Cook
02	Earlam	14	Cox
03	Hansell	15	Skinner
04	Birchell	16	Walters
06	Waller	17	Mulcare
06	Reeves	18	Costaras
07	Pyemont	19	Francis
08	Gittoes	20	Brinkhurst
09	Johns	20	Hadfield
11	Cooper	20	Kingsland
12	Kent	21	Woods

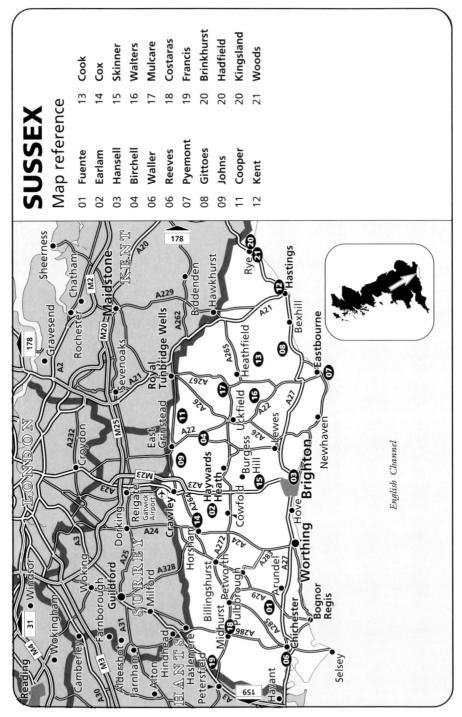

English Channel

rate £ from - to per person	children taken	evening meals	animals taken		

£24.25 to £32.00	Y	N	Y	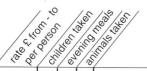 *Mill Lane House*

Near Rd: A.29

Mainly 17th-century house in beautiful National Trust downland village with magnificent views to the coast. There are 5 comfortable en-suite bedrooms, each with T.V.. Superb local hill walking & bird-watching from Pulborough Brooks to Pagham Harbour. Mill Lane House is ithin easy reach of Arundel Castle, Fishbourne Roman Palace, Goodwood & Chichester, the cathedral & the Festival Theatre. Beaches 6 miles. Excellent pubs within easy walking distance.
www.mill-lane-house.com

Jan de la Fuente   Mill Lane House   Slindon Top Road   Slindon   Arundel BN18 0RP   Sussex
Tel: (01243) 814440   Fax 01243 814436   Open: ALL YEAR   Map Ref No. 01

£30.00 to £35.00	N	N	N	*Timbers Edge*

Near Rd: A.272, A.23

This beautiful Sussex country house, set in spacious formal gardens & surrounded by woodlands, is extremely peaceful & quiet. Located within easy reach of Hickstead Showjumping Ground (10 mins), Nymans & Leonardslee Gardens (10 mins), South of England Showground (25 mins), Gatwick Airport (20 mins) & Brighton (30 mins). The attractive bedrooms have a colour T.V., a private bathroom & beverage-making facilities. Breakfast is served in the conservatory overlooking the pool.
E-mail: gearlam@aol.com

Mr & Mrs Earlam Timbers Edge Longhouse Lane Off Spronketts Lane Warninglid Bolney RH17 5TE
Tel: (01444) 461456   Fax 01444 461813   Open: ALL YEAR   Map Ref No. 02

£32.50 to £37.50	Y	N	N	*Trouville Hotel*

Near Rd: A.23

The Trouville is a Regency, Grade II listed townhouse, which has been tastefully restored & furnished throughout. Accommodation is in 8 attractive bedrooms, each with colour T.V. & tea/coffee-making facilities. En-suite & 4-poster bedrooms are available. Situated in a charming seafront square, the Trouville is very convenient for shopping, the Pavilion, the Lanes, Marina & Conference Centre & the many restaurants which are all within walking distance.
www.bestbandb.co.uk

VISA: M'CARD: AMEX:

John & Daphne Hansell   Trouville Hotel   11 New Steine   Brighton BN2 1PB   Sussex
Tel: (01273) 697384   Open: FEB - DEC   Map Ref No. 03

£28.00 to £40.00	Y	Y	Y	*Holly House*

Near Rd: A.275

Holly House, an early-Victorian forest farmhouse with character, offers a warm, friendly welcome to visitors. A 1-acre garden with long views. Situated in an Ashdown Forest village & ideal for touring Sussex, with many National Trust properties nearby. A comfortable lounge is available, & breakfast is taken in the conservatory overlooking the garden. The 5 pleasant rooms, 3 en-suite, have tea-making facilities & T.V.. A small swimming pool heated during the summer. Animals welcome.
E-mail:db@hollyhousebnb.demon.co.uk
www.hollyhousebnb.demon.co.uk

Mrs D. Birchell   Holly House   Beaconsfield Road   Chelwood Gate RH17 7LF   Sussex
Tel: (01825) 740484   Fax 01825 740172   Open: ALL YEAR   Map Ref No. 04

Hatpins. Old Bosham.

Sussex

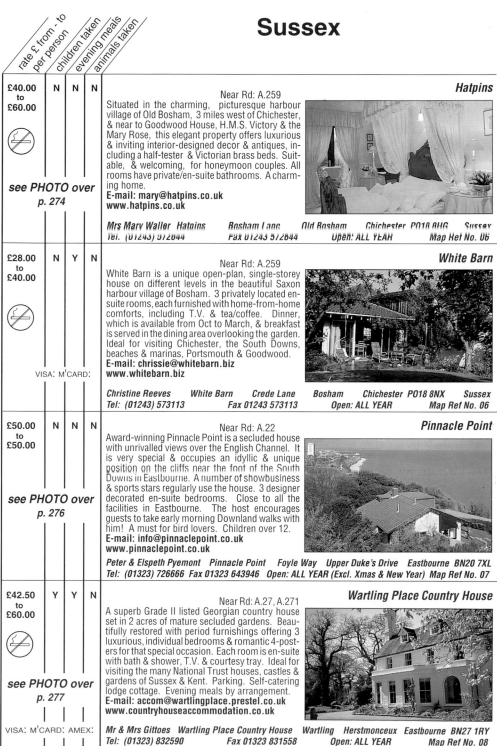

rate £ from - to per person	children taken	evening meals	animals taken		

£40.00 to £60.00

N N N

🚭

see PHOTO over p. 274

Hatpins

Near Rd: A.259

Situated in the charming, picturesque harbour village of Old Bosham, 3 miles west of Chichester, & near to Goodwood House, H.M.S. Victory & the Mary Rose, this elegant property offers luxurious & inviting interior-designed decor & antiques, including a half-tester & Victorian brass beds. Suitable, & welcoming, for honeymoon couples. All rooms have private/en-suite bathrooms. A charming home.
E-mail: mary@hatpins.co.uk
www.hatpins.co.uk

Mrs Mary Waller Hatpins Bosham Lane Old Bosham Chichester PO18 8HG Sussex
Tel. (01243) 572644   Fax 01243 572644   Open: ALL YEAR   Map Ref No. 06

£28.00 to £40.00

N Y N

🚭

VISA: M'CARD:

White Barn

Near Rd: A.259

White Barn is a unique open-plan, single-storey house on different levels in the beautiful Saxon harbour village of Bosham. 3 privately located en-suite rooms, each furnished with home-from-home comforts, including T.V. & tea/coffee. Dinner, which is available from Oct to March, & breakfast is served in the dining area overlooking the garden. Ideal for visiting Chichester, the South Downs, beaches & marinas, Portsmouth & Goodwood.
E-mail: chrissie@whitebarn.biz
www.whitebarn.biz

Christine Reeves   White Barn   Crede Lane   Bosham   Chichester PO18 8NX   Sussex
Tel: (01243) 573113   Fax 01243 573113   Open: ALL YEAR   Map Ref No. 06

£50.00 to £50.00

N N N

see PHOTO over p. 276

Pinnacle Point

Near Rd: A.22

Award-winning Pinnacle Point is a secluded house with unrivalled views over the English Channel. It is very special & occupies an idyllic & unique position on the cliffs near the foot of the South Downs in Eastbourne. A number of showbusiness & sports stars regularly use the house. 3 designer decorated en-suite bedrooms. Close to all the facilities in Eastbourne. The host encourages guests to take early morning Downland walks with him! A must for bird lovers. Children over 12.
E-mail: info@pinnaclepoint.co.uk
www.pinnaclepoint.co.uk

Peter & Elspeth Pyemont   Pinnacle Point   Foyle Way   Upper Duke's Drive   Eastbourne BN20 7XL
Tel: (01323) 726666 Fax 01323 643946 Open: ALL YEAR (Excl. Xmas & New Year) Map Ref No. 07

£42.50 to £60.00

Y Y N

🚭

VISA: M'CARD: AMEX:

see PHOTO over p. 277

Wartling Place Country House

Near Rd: A.27, A.271

A superb Grade II listed Georgian country house set in 2 acres of mature secluded gardens. Beautifully restored with period furnishings offering 3 luxurious, individual bedrooms & romantic 4-posters for that special occasion. Each room is en-suite with bath & shower, T.V. & courtesy tray. Ideal for visiting the many National Trust houses, castles & gardens of Sussex & Kent. Parking. Self-catering lodge cottage. Evening meals by arrangement.
E-mail: accom@wartlingplace.prestel.co.uk
www.countryhouseaccommodation.co.uk

Mr & Mrs Gittoes   Wartling Place Country House   Wartling   Herstmonceux   Eastbourne BN27 1RY
Tel: (01323) 832590   Fax 01323 831558   Open: ALL YEAR   Map Ref No. 08

Pinnacle Point.   Meads Village.

Wartling Place. Wartling.

Sussex

Tiltwood House

Near Rd: A.264

The centre part of an elegant Victorian country house set in tranquil, semi-landscaped gardens. Luxurious, spacious en-suite bedrooms, high ceilings with beautiful mouldings & cornices, king-size beds, T.V./videos, & tea/coffee etc. Full English breakfast, fresh fruits, cold meats & more offer hearty sustenance for visiting National Trust gardens, Hickstead, South Downs, Glynbourne, Lingfield Racecourse, Brighton & London. Gatwick 7 miles, Heathrow 35 miles. Children over 12.
E-mail: vjohnstiltwood@aol.com
www.tiltwood-bedandbreakfast.co.uk

£32.50 to £43.50 | Y | N | N

Mrs Valerie Johns   Tiltwood House   Hophurst Lane   Crawley Down   Gatwick RH10 4LL   Sussex
Tel: (01342) 712942   Open: ALL YEAR   Map Ref No. 09

Bolebroke Watermill

Near Rd: A.264

A magical watermill, first recorded in 1086 A.D., & an Elizabethan miller's barn offer 5 en-suite rooms of genuine, unspoilt rustic charm, set amid woodland, water & pasture, & used as the idyllic setting for the film 'Carrington'. The mill is complete with machinery, trap doors & very steep stairs. The barn has low doors & beamed ceilings, & includes the honeymooners' hayloft with a 4-poster bed. Light supper available, & award-winning breakfasts are served in the mill-house. Children over 8 years.
E-mail: bolebrokemill@btinternet.com
www.bolebrokemillhotel.co.uk

£34.50 to £39.50 | Y | N | N

see PHOTO over
p. 279

VISA: M'CARD: AMEX:

David Cooper   Bolebroke Watermill   Perry Hill   Edenbridge Road   Hartfield TN7 4JP   Sussex
Tel: (01892) 770425   Fax 01892 770425   Open: Mid FEB - DEC 22   Map Ref No. 11

Parkside House

Near Rd: A.21

Located in a quiet residential conservation area, & set in an elevated position opposite a beautiful park. This elegant Victorian house retains all its original features, but with every modern facility. High standards of hospitality, comfort & good home-cooking are provided, creating an informal, friendly & welcoming atmosphere. Bedrooms are en-suite & offer every luxury. The 'Apricot' room has an antique French bed. A quiet location only 15 mins' walk from the town centre & sea front.
E-mail: bkent.parksidehouse@talk21.com
www.bestbandb.co.uk

£27.50 to £30.00 | Y | N | N

VISA: M'CARD:

Brian W. Kent   Parkside House   59 Lower Park Road   Hastings TN34 2LD   Sussex
Tel: (01424) 433096   Fax 01424 421431   Open: ALL YEAR   Map Ref No. 12

The Cottage

Near Rd: A.265

A warm, friendly welcome & elegant, comfortable accommodation await you at The Cottage, a 16th-century family home overlooking the village green in this peaceful hamlet. Beautiful double rooms (one with four-poster) with en-suite facilities, T.V. & courtesy tray. Relax in the pretty drawing room, or the large tranquil garden. Breakfasts include locally grown organic produce wherever possible. (Dinner by arrangement.) Only 200 yards from an award-winning village inn, renowned for fine food.
E-mail: cottageonthegreen@btinternet.com
www.thecottagebandb.com

£35.00 to £45.00 | Y | Y | N

Mrs Karen Cook   The Cottage   Rushlake Green   Heathfield TN21 9QH   Sussex
Tel: (01435) 830348   Fax 01435 830715   Open: ALL YEAR   Map Ref No. 13

Bolebroke Watermill. Hartfield.

Sussex

	rate £ from - to per person	children taken	evening meals	animals taken

Glebe End

Near Rd: A.24

Glebe End is a fascinating medieval house, with a secluded, sunny, walled garden, set in the heart of Warnham village. It retains many original features, including heavy flagstones, curving ships' timbers & an inglenook fireplace. 4 single, twin or king-sized en-suite rooms, charmingly furnished with antiques & each with T.V. & hot-drink trays. Liz Cox is an excellent cook; evening meals (by arrangement) are delicious & include home-grown produce. Tennis, golf & health club nearby. 20 mins' to Gatwick Airport. Animals by arrangement.
E-mail: coxeswarnham@aol.com

£25.00 to £25.00	Y	Y	Y

Liz & Chris Cox   Glebe End   Church Street   Warnham   Nr. Horsham RH12 3QW   Sussex
Tel: (01403) 261711   Fax 01403 257572   Open: ALL YEAR   Map Ref No. 14

Clayton Wickham Farmhouse

Near Rd: A.23

A delightful, secluded 14th-century farmhouse with lovely views, set amidst the beautiful Sussex countryside. The friendly hosts have refurbished their home to a high standard, yet have retained many original features, hence there are a wealth of beams & a huge inglenook fireplace in the drawing room. A variety of tastefully furnished & well-appointed bedrooms, including a super 4-poster en-suite. 4-course candlelit dinner by arrangement. Tennis court. Animals by arrangement.
E-mail: susie@cwfbanb.fsnet.co.uk
www.cwfbandb.co.uk

£35.00 to £45.00	Y	Y	Y

Mike & Susie Skinner   Clayton Wickham Farmhouse   Belmont Lane   Hurstpierpoint BN6 9EP
Tel: (01273) 845698   Fax 01273 841970   Open: ALL YEAR   Map Ref No. 15

Shortgate Manor Farm

Near Rd: A.22

Shortgate Manor Farm is an enchanting 18th-century farmhouse set in 8 acres approached by an avenue of poplars festooned with rambling roses. The 3 charming bedrooms all offer en-suite/private facilities, T.V.'s, courtesy trays, with bathrobes provided for your comfort. The house is surrounded by 2 acres of landscaped gardens which are open under the National Gardens Scheme every June. Glyndebourne 4 miles. A charming home from which to explore Sussex. Children over 10.
E-mail: david@shortgate.co.uk
www.shortgate.co.uk

£30.00 to £35.00	Y	N	N

David & Ethel Walters   Shortgate Manor Farm   Halland   Lewes BN8 6PJ   Sussex
Tel: (01825) 840320   Fax 01825 840320   Open: ALL YEAR   Map Ref No. 16

Huggetts Furnace Farm

Near Rd: A.272

A beautiful medieval farmhouse (Grade II listed) set well off the beaten track in tranquil countryside. 3 attractive bedrooms, all with en-suite/private facilities, radio & tea/coffee. The oak-beamed guests' room has an inglenook fireplace & a T.V.. Super breakfasts & light suppers use the best home-grown & local produce. Heated outdoor swimming pool; 120 acres of grounds. Self-catering cottage (non-smokers). Gatwick 45 mins. 30 mins' coast. Nearby, many N. T. properties. Children over 7.
E-mail: huggettsfurnacefarm@freenet.co.uk
www.huggettsfurnacefarm.co.uk

£30.00 to £40.00	Y	Y	N

Gillian & John Mulcare   Huggetts Furnace Farm   Stonehurst Lane   Five Ashes   Mayfield TN20 6LL
Tel: (01825) 830220   Fax 01825 830722   Open: ALL YEAR (Excl. Xmas)   Map Ref No. 17

rate £ from - to per person	children taken	evening meals	animals taken

---

£30.00 to £35.00

Y | N | N

🚭

Amberfold

Near Rd: A.286

Amberfold is a charming 17th-century listed cottage, situated in quiet, idyllic countryside yet only 5 mins' drive from Midhurst. 2 private self-contained annexes with access all day. 1 is situated on the ground floor. Each annex is comfortably furnished & has private facilities, T.V., clock/radio, fridge, etc. To allow you complete freedom & privacy, a large Continental breakfast is self-service & is taken in your room. An attractive garden in which to relax. An ideal base for exploring Goodwood, Singleton, Chichester & the coast.

Annabelle & Alex Costaras   *Amberfold*   Heyshott   Midhurst GU29 0DA   Sussex
Tel: (01730) 812006   Fax 01730 812042   Open: ALL YEAR   Map Ref No. 18

£31.00 to £37.00

N | N | N

🚭

Mizzards Farm

Near Rd: A.272

This beautifully modernised farmhouse is set in gardens & farmland by the River Rother. All of the bedrooms have en-suite facilities & colour T.V.. There is an elegant drawing room, & breakfast is served in a magnificent vaulted hall dating from the 16th century. There is a covered swimming pool, for guests' use, & beautiful gardens. Situated close to the South Downs, the coast & several National Trust houses. A delightful home.
E-mail: julian.francis@hemscott.net
www.bestbandb.co.uk

Mr & Mrs J. C. Francis   *Mizzards Farm*   Rogate   Petersfield GU31 5HS   Sussex
Tel: (01730) 821656   Fax 01730 821655   Open: ALL YEAR (Excl. Xmas)   Map Ref No. 19

£38.00 to £50.00

Y | N | N

🚭

VISA: M'CARD:

Little Orchard House

Near Rd: A.259

This charming Georgian townhouse, with traditional walled garden & Smuggler's Watchtower, is at the heart of ancient Rye. A perfect touring base, it retains many original features. Open fires, antique furnishings & books ensure a peaceful, relaxed atmosphere. Generous country breakfasts feature organic & free-range local products. The 2 lovely en-suite bedrooms have 4-poster beds & include T.V., VCR, fridge & hot-drinks tray. Children over 12 years welcome.
www.littleorchardhouse.com

Sara Brinkhurst   *Little Orchard House*   3 West Street   Rye TN31 7ES   Sussex
Tel: (01797) 223831   Fax 01797 223831   Open: ALL YEAR   Map Ref No. 20

£42.00 to £58.00

Y | N | Y

see PHOTO over p. 282

VISA: M'CARD:

Jeake's House

Near Rd: A.259

Jeakes House is an outstanding 17th-century Grade II listed building. Retaining original features, including oak beams & wood panelling, & decorated throughout with antiques. 12 bedrooms overlook the gardens, with en-suite/private facilities, T.V. etc. 4-poster available. Dine in the galleried former Baptist chapel, where a choice of full English, wholefood vegetarian or Continental breakfast is served. Located in one of Britain's most picturesque medieval streets. Parking. Children over 12.
E-mail: jeakeshouse@btinternet.com
www.jeakeshouse.com

Jenny Hadfield   *Jeake's House*   Mermaid Street   Rye TN31 7ET   Sussex
Tel: (01797) 222828   Fax 01797 222623   Open: ALL YEAR   Map Ref No. 20

Jeake's House.   Rye.

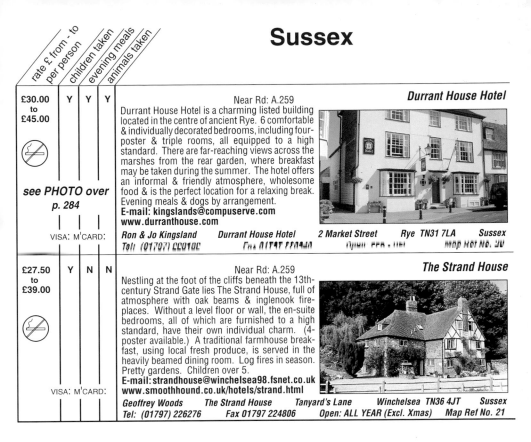

rate £ from - to per person	children taken	evening meals	animals taken		
£30.00 to £45.00 🚭 *see PHOTO over p. 284* VISA: M'CARD:	Y	Y	Y	Near Rd: A.259 Durrant House Hotel is a charming listed building located in the centre of ancient Rye. 6 comfortable & individually decorated bedrooms, including four-poster & triple rooms, all equipped to a high standard. There are far-reaching views across the marshes from the rear garden, where breakfast may be taken during the summer. The hotel offers an informal & friendly atmosphere, wholesome food & is the perfect location for a relaxing break. Evening meals & dogs by arrangement. **E-mail: kingslands@compuserve.com** **www.durranthouse.com** *Ron & Jo Kingsland* *Durrant House Hotel* Tel: (01797) 226064 Fax 01797 224837	**Durrant House Hotel** 2 Market Street Rye TN31 7LA Sussex Open: FEB - DEC Map Ref No. 20
£27.50 to £39.00 🚭 VISA: M'CARD:	Y	N	N	Near Rd: A.259 Nestling at the foot of the cliffs beneath the 13th-century Strand Gate lies The Strand House, full of atmosphere with oak beams & inglenook fire-places. Without a level floor or wall, the en-suite bedrooms, all of which are furnished to a high standard, have their own individual charm. (4-poster available.) A traditional farmhouse break-fast, using local fresh produce, is served in the heavily beamed dining room. Log fires in season. Pretty gardens. Children over 5. **E-mail: strandhouse@winchelsea98.fsnet.co.uk** **www.smoothhound.co.uk/hotels/strand.html** *Geoffrey Woods The Strand House Tanyard's Lane* Tel: (01797) 226276 Fax 01797 224806	**The Strand House** Winchelsea TN36 4JT Sussex Open: ALL YEAR (Excl. Xmas) Map Ref No. 21

All the establishments mentioned in this guide are members of
The Worldwide Bed & Breakfast Association

When booking your accommodation please mention
The Best Bed & Breakfast

Durrant House Hotel.   Rye.

Warwickshire

Warwickshire (Heart of England)

Warwickshire contains much that is thought of as traditional rural England, but it is a county of contradictions. Rural tranquillity surrounds industrial towns, working canals run along with meandering rivers, the mediaeval splendour of Warwick Castle vies with the handsome Regency grace of Leamington Spa.

Of course, Warwickshire is Shakespeare's county, with his birthplace, Stratford-upon-Avon standing at the northern edge of the Cotswolds. You can visit any of half a dozen houses with Shakespearian associations, see his tomb in the lovely Parish church or enjoy a performance by the world famous Royal Shakespeare Company in their theatre on the banks of the River Avon.

Warwickshire was created as the Kingdom of Mercia after the departure of the Romans. King Offa of Mercia left us his own particular mark - a coin which bore the imprint of his likeness known as his "pen" & this became our penny. Lady Godiva was the wife of an Earl of Mercia who pleaded with her husband to lessen the taxation burden on his people. He challenged her to ride naked through the streets of Coventry as the price of her request. She did this knowing that her long hair would cover her nakedness, & the people, who loved her, stayed indoors out of respect. Only Peeping Tom found the temptation irresistible.

The 15th, 16th, & 17th centuries were the heyday of fine building in the county, when many gracious homes were built. Exceptional Compton Wynyates has rosy pink bricks, twisted chimney stacks, battlements & moats & presents an unforgettably romantic picture of a perfect Tudor House.

Coventry has long enjoyed the reputation of a thriving city, noted for its weaving of silks and ribbons, learned from the refugee Huguenots. When progress brought industry, watches, bicycles & cars became the mainstay of the city. Coventry suffered grievously from aerial bombardment in the war & innumerable ancient & treasured buildings were lost.

A magnificent new Cathedral stands besides the shell of the old. Mystery plays enacting the life of Christ are performed in the haunting ruin.

Warwick Castle.

Warwickshire

Warwickshire Gazeteer

Areas of Outstanding Natural Beauty
The Edge Hills

Historic Houses & Castles

Arbury Hall - Nuneaton
18th century Gothic mansion - made famous by George Elliot as Cheverel Manor - paintings, period furnishings, etc.

Compton Wynyates
15th century - famous Tudor house - pink brick, twisted chimneys, battlemented walls. Interior almost untouched - period furnishing.

Coughton Court - Alcester
15th century - Elizabethan half-timbered wings. Holds Jacobite relics.

Harvard House - Stratford-upon-Avon
16th century - home of mother of John Harvard, University founder.

Homington Hall - Shipston-on-Stour
17th century with fine 18th century plasterwork.

Packwood House - Hockley Heath
Tudor timber framed house - with 17th century additions. Famous yew garden.

Ragley Hall - Alcester
17th century Palladian - magnificent house with fine collection of porcelain, paintings, furniture, etc. & a valuable library.

Shakespeare's Birthplace Trust Properties - Stratford-upon-Avon

Anne Hathaway's Cottage - Shottery
The thatched cottage home of Anne Hathaway.

Hall's Croft - Old Town
Tudor house where Shakespeare's daughter Susanna lived.

Mary Arden's House - Wilmcote
Tudor farmhouse with dovecote. Home of Shakespeare's mother.

New Place - Chapel Street
Shakespeare's last home - the foundations of his house are preserved in Elizabethan garden.

Birthplace of Shakespeare - Henley Street
Many rare Shakespeare relics exhibited in this half-timbered house.

Lord Leycester Hospital - Warwick
16th century timber framed group around courtyard - hospital for poor persons in the mediaeval guilds.

Upton House - Edge Hill
Dating from James II reign - contains Brussels tapestries, Sevres porcelain, Chelsea figurines, 18th century furniture & other works of art, including Old Masters.

Warwick Castle - Warwick
Splendid mediaeval castle - site was originally fortified more than a thousand years ago. Present castle 14th century. Armoury.

Cathedrals & Churches

Astley (St. Mary the Virgin)
17th century - has remains of 14th century collegiate church. 15th century painted stalls.

Beaudesert (St. Nicholas)
Norman with fine arches in chancel.

Brailes (St. George)
15th century - decorated nave & aisles - 14th century carved oak chest.

Crompton Wynyates
Church of Restoration period having painted ceiling.

Lapworth (St. Mary)
13th & 14th century - steeple & north aisle connected by passage.

Preston-on-Stour (The Blessed Virgin Mary)
18th century. Gilded ceiling, 17th century glass.

Tredington (St. Gregory)
Saxon walls in nave - largely14th century, 17th century pulpit. Fine spire.

Warwick (St. Mary)
15th century Beauchamp Chapel, vaulted choir, some 17th century Gothic.

Wooten Wawen (St. Peter)
Saxon, with remnants of mediaeval wall painting, 15th century screens & pulpit: small 17th century chained library.

Museums & Galleries

The Royal Shakespeare Theatre Picture Gallery - Stratford-upon-Avon
Original designs & paintings, portraits of famous actors, etc.

Motor Museum - Stratford-upon-Avon
Collection of cars, racing, vintage, exotic, replica of 1930 garage. Fashions, etc. of 1920's era.

WARWICKSHIRE
Map reference

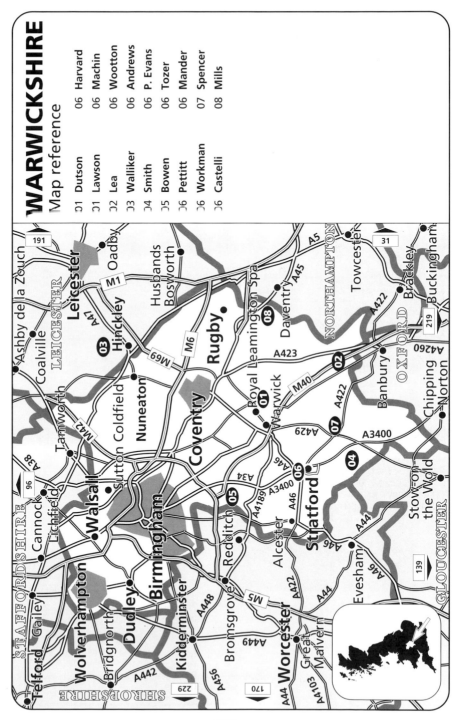

287

8 Clarendon Crescent. Leamington Spa.

rate £ from - to per person | children taken | evening meals taken | animals taken

Wymondley Lodge

| £25.00 to £30.00 | Y | N | N |

Near Rd: A.452

Wymondley Lodge is a newly refurbished Victorian town house relecting the elegance of that era. Situated a few mins' walk from Leamington's shops, restaurants, parks & railway stations. It is an ideal centre for visiting historic Warwick, Kenilworth, Coventry & Stratford-upon-Avon. The NEC & Birmingham's ICC are also easily accessible by car or train. The 2 large double/twin rooms, with spacious en-suite shower rooms, have been individually & tastefully furnished with all facilities. Parking. Children over 5. Dinner by arrangement.

Judith Dutson   Wymondley Lodge   8 Adelaide Road   Leamington Spa CV31 3PW   Warwickshire
Tel: (01926) 882669   Fax 01926 882669   Open: ALL YEAR   Map Ref No. 01

8 Clarendon Crescent

| £30.00 to £30.00 | Y | N | Y |

Near Rd: A.452

A Grade II listed Regency house overlooking a private dell. Situated in a quiet backwater of Leamington. Elegantly furnished with antiques, & offering accommodation in 5 tastefully furnished bedrooms, 4 en-suite. A delicious full English breakfast is served. Only 5 mins' walk from the town centre. Very convenient for Warwick, Stratford, Stoneleigh Agricultural Centre, Warwick University & the N.E.C.. Children over 4 yrs welcome. Animals by arrangement.
E-mail: lawson@lawson71.fsnet.co.uk

see PHOTO over p. 288

Christine Lawson   8 Clarendon Crescent   Leamington Spa CV32 5NR   Warwickshire
Tel: (01926) 429840   Fax 01926 424641   Open: ALL YEAR   Map Ref No. 01

Crandon House

| £23.00 to £28.00 | Y | N | N |

Near Rd: A.423

Crandon House offers an especially warm welcome & exceptionally high standard of accommodation & comfort. Set in 20 acres of beautiful countryside. 5 pretty bedrooms (all non-smoking & 1 on the ground-floor) with en-suite/private bathroom & T.V. etc. Extensive breakfast menu. A tranquil rural retreat, yet within easy reach of Stratford, Warwick, Oxford & the Cotswolds. Located between the M.40 Jts 11 & 12 (4 miles). Children over 8. Single occupancy from £35.00.
E-mail: crandonhouse@talk21.com
www.crandonhouse.co.uk

VISA: M'CARD:

Deborah Lea   Crandon House   Avon Dassett   Nr. Leamington Spa CV47 2AA   Warwickshire
Tel: (01295) 770652   Fax 01295 770632   Open: ALL YEAR   Map Ref No. 02

Ambion Court Hotel

| £30.00 to £35.00 | Y | Y | N |

Near Rd: A.5

Charming, modernised Victorian farmhouse overlooking Dadlington's village green in rolling countryside near Ashby Canal. Rustic character, warm hospitality & exceptional tranquillity abound. All 7 rooms have bathroom, T.V., phone etc; the king-sized Pine Room is particularly imposing. Relax in the comfortable lounge & cocktail bar, savour the excellent cuisine, or amble to good pubs nearby. Well-placed for Coventry, Warwick, Stratford, motorways & airports. Restricted smoking areas.
E-mail: stay@ambionhotel.co.uk
www.ambionhotel.co.uk

VISA: M'CARD: AMEX:

John & Wendy Walliker   Ambion Court Hotel   The Green   Dadlington   Nuneaton CV13 5JB
Tel: (01455) 212292   Fax 01455 213141   Open: ALL YEAR   Map Ref No. 03

Melita Hotel. Stratford-upon-Avon.

Warwickshire

Lower Farm

| £25.00 to £25.00 | Y | N | N |

Near Rd: A.423

On the edge of the Cotswolds, just off the Fosse Way in the pretty, unspoilt hamlet of Darlingscott stands this fine, 18th-century, listed farmhouse. 2 attractive double rooms & 1 twin-bedded room, each with an en-suite bathroom, colour T.V. & tea-making facilities. A perfect location from which to visit Chipping Campden. The magnificent gardens of Hidcote & Kiftsgate are just 5 miles away, & Stratford-upon-Avon only 9 miles. Children over 8.
E-mail: lowerfarmbb@beeb.net
www.cotswoldbandb.co.uk

Jackie Smith   Lower Farm   Darlingscott   Shipston-on-Stour CV36 4PN   Warwickshire
Tel. (01608) 682750   Fax 01608 682750   Open: ALL YEAR   Map Ref No. 04

Grange Farm

| £30.00 to £40.00 | Y | Y | N |

Near Rd: A.435

A warm welcome awaits you at this peaceful 17th-century farmhouse, set in 200 acres of beautiful countryside with footpaths & wildlife pools. Grange Farm has sloping floors, oak beams & log fires. There are 3 very atttractive en-suite bedrooms with colour T.V., tea/coffee-making facilities, clock/radio alarms & hairdryers. The house is centrally located for easy access to the NEC, NAC, Stratford-upon-Avon, the Cotswolds, Warwick & Worcester. Children over 4. Evening meals by arrangement.
www.grange-farm.com

Christine Bowen   Grange Farm   Forde Hall Lane   Tanworth-in-Arden   Solihull B94 5AX   Warks.
Tel: (01564) 742911   Open: ALL YEAR   Map Ref No. 05

Melita Hotel

| £27.00 to £42.00 | Y | N | Y |

Near Rd: A.3400

An extremely friendly family-run hotel. Offering pleasant service, good food & accommodation in 12 excellent bedrooms, with en-suite/private facilities, T.V., tea/coffee & 'phones. A comfortable lounge/bar & pretty, award winning garden for guests' use. Parking is available. A pleasant 5-min. walk to Shakespearian properties/theatres, shopping centre & riverside gardens. Superbly situated for Warwick Castle, Coventry & the Cotswolds.
E-mail: info@melitahotel.co.uk
www.melitahotel.co.uk

see PHOTO over p. 290

VISA: M'CARD: AMEX:

Russell Andrews   Melita Hotel   37 Shipston Road   Stratford-upon-Avon CV37 7LN   Warwickshire
Tel: (01789) 292432 Fax 01789 204867 Open: ALL YEAR (Excl. Xmas & New Year) Map Ref No. 06

Sequoia House

| £32.50 to £47.50 | N | N | N |

Near Rd: A.3400

A beautifully appointed private hotel situated across the River Avon from the Royal Shakespeare Theatre. 23 bedrooms (all en-suite), a cocktail bar, a cottage annex & a fully air-conditioned dining room. The hotel is comfortably furnished, & decorated in a warm & restful style, with many extra thoughtful touches. The garden overlooks the town cricket ground & the old tramway. Pleasant walks along the banks of the River Avon opposite the Theatre & Holy Trinity Church. Children over 5.
E-mail: info@sequoiahotel.co.uk
www.sequoiahotel.co.uk

see PHOTO over p. 292

VISA: M'CARD:

Philip & Jean Evans   Sequoia House   51-53 Shipston Road   Stratford-upon-Avon CV37 7LN   Warks.
Tel: (01789) 268852   Fax 01789 414559   Open: ALL YEAR   Map Ref No. 06

Sequoia House. Stratford-upon-Avon.

rate £ from - to per person	children taken	evening meals taken	animals taken

---

£25.00 to £40.00 Y N N

Minola House

Near Rd: B.439

A comfortable house with a relaxed atmosphere, offering good accommodation in 5 pleasantly furnished bedrooms, 1 with private shower, 3 are ensuite; all have T.V. & tea/coffee-making facilities. Stratford offers a myriad of delights for the visitor, including the Royal Shakespeare Theatre. Set by the River Avon, this makes a lovely place for a picnic lunch or early evening meal before the performance. Children over 10 welcome. Italian & French are spoken.
www.bestbandb.co.uk

Danielle Castelli Minola House 25 Evesham Place Stratford-upon-Avon CV37 6HT Warwickshire
Tel: (01789) 293573 Fax 01789 551626 Open: ALL YEAR Map Ref No. 06

£27.50 to £34.00 N N N

see PHOTO over
p. 294

VISA: M'CARD:

Twelfth Night

Near Rd: B.439

Somewhere special - once owned for almost a quarter of a century by the Royal Shakespeare Company as a pied a terre for actors. Delightfully refurbished, this Victorian villa, built in 1897, has retained its character. Providing modern comforts, it includes central heating, en-suite bedrooms with pocket spring beds, brass bedsteads, canopies & half-testers plus many other personal touches. Centrally placed with private parking. A non-smoking establishment.
www.bestbandb.co.uk

Margaret Harvard Twelfth Night Evesham Place Stratford-upon-Avon CV37 6HT Warwickshire
Tel: (01789) 414595 Open: ALL YEAR Map Ref No. 06

£20.00 to £30.00 Y N Y

Stretton House

Near Rd: A.4390

Stretton House is a 'home from home' where a warm & friendly welcome awaits you. Very comfortable accommodation at reasonable prices. Pretty, full en-suite bedrooms & standard rooms, all having T.V. & tea/coffee facilities. Excellent full English breakfast, vegetarians catered for. Limited car parking. Situated opposite lovely Fir Park, within easy reach of the country, yet only 3 mins' walk from the town centre. Children over 8.
E-mail: skyblues@strettonhouse.co.uk
www.strettonhouse.co.uk

Mr & Mrs M. Machin Stretton House 38 Grove Road Stratford-upon-Avon CV37 6PB
Tel: (01789) 268647 Fax 01789 268647 Open: ALL YEAR Map Ref No. 06

£25.00 to £39.00 Y N N

see PHOTO over
p. 295

VISA: M'CARD: AMEX:

Hardwick Guest House

Near Rd: A.439

Hardwick House is situated in a quiet, residential area of Stratford-upon-Avon, away from main roads yet only a 5-min. walk into the town. All 14 bedrooms are non-smoking, & comfortable, with tea/coffee & T.V. Your hosts ensure a warm welcome & attention to detail. Parking. Directions from M.40: on the A.439, take the first right turn past the 30-mph sign into St. Gregory's Road, & the B & B is 200 yds on the right. Children over 5.
E-mail: hardwick@waverider.co.uk
www.stratford-upon-avon.co.uk/hardwick.htm

Drenagh & Simon Wootton Hardwick Guest House 1 Avenue Road Stratford-upon-Avon CV37 6UY
Tel: (01789) 204307 Fax 01789 296760 Open: ALL YEAR Map Ref No. 06

Twelfth Night. Stratford-upon-Avon.

Hardwick House. Stratford-upon-Avon.

Fulready Manor.   Ettington.

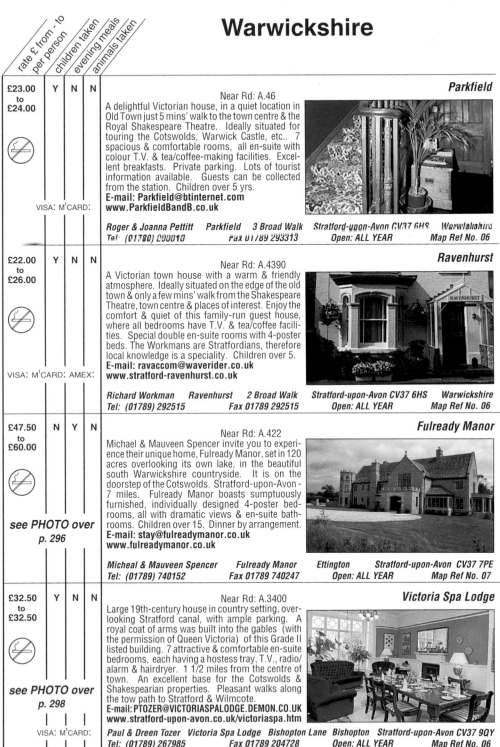

rate £ from - to per person / **children taken** / **evening meals** / **animals taken**

£23.00 to £24.00 Y N N

Parkfield

Near Rd: A.46

A delightful Victorian house, in a quiet location in Old Town just 5 mins' walk to the town centre & the Royal Shakespeare Theatre. Ideally situated for touring the Cotswolds, Warwick Castle, etc.. 7 spacious & comfortable rooms, all en-suite with colour T.V. & tea/coffee-making facilities. Excellent breakfasts. Private parking. Lots of tourist information available. Guests can be collected from the station. Children over 5 yrs.
E-mail: Parkfield@btinternet.com
www.ParkfieldBandB.co.uk

VISA: M'CARD:

Roger & Joanna Pettitt	Parkfield	3 Broad Walk	Stratford-upon-Avon CV37 6HS	Warwickshire
Tel: (01789) 293313		Fax 01789 293313	Open: ALL YEAR	Map Ref No. 06

£22.00 to £26.00 Y N N

Ravenhurst

Near Rd: A.4390

A Victorian town house with a warm & friendly atmosphere. Ideally situated on the edge of the old town & only a few mins' walk from the Shakespeare Theatre, town centre & places of interest. Enjoy the comfort & quiet of this family-run guest house, where all bedrooms have T.V. & tea/coffee facilities. Special double en-suite rooms with 4-poster beds. The Workmans are Stratfordians, therefore local knowledge is a speciality. Children over 5.
E-mail: ravaccom@waverider.co.uk
www.stratford-ravenhurst.co.uk

VISA: M'CARD: AMEX:

Richard Workman	Ravenhurst	2 Broad Walk	Stratford-upon-Avon CV37 6HS	Warwickshire
Tel: (01789) 292515		Fax 01789 292515	Open: ALL YEAR	Map Ref No. 06

£47.50 to £60.00 N Y N

Fulready Manor

Near Rd: A.422

Michael & Mauveen Spencer invite you to experience their unique home, Fulready Manor, set in 120 acres overlooking its own lake, in the beautiful south Warwickshire countryside. It is on the doorstep of the Cotswolds. Stratford-upon-Avon - 7 miles. Fulready Manor boasts sumptuously furnished, individually designed 4-poster bedrooms, all with dramatic views & en-suite bathrooms. Children over 15. Dinner by arrangement.
E-mail: stay@fulreadymanor.co.uk
www.fulreadymanor.co.uk

see PHOTO over p. 296

Micheal & Mauveen Spencer	Fulready Manor	Ettington	Stratford-upon-Avon CV37 7PE
Tel: (01789) 740152	Fax 01789 740247	Open: ALL YEAR	Map Ref No. 07

£32.50 to £32.50 Y N N

Victoria Spa Lodge

Near Rd: A.3400

Large 19th-century house in country setting, overlooking Stratford canal, with ample parking. A royal coat of arms was built into the gables (with the permission of Queen Victoria) of this Grade II listed building. 7 attractive & comfortable en-suite bedrooms, each having a hostess tray, T.V., radio/alarm & hairdryer. 1 1/2 miles from the centre of town. An excellent base for the Cotswolds & Shakespearian properties. Pleasant walks along the tow path to Stratford & Wilmcote.
E-mail: PTOZER@VICTORIASPALODGE.DEMON.CO.UK
www.stratford-upon-avon.co.uk/victoriaspa.htm

see PHOTO over p. 298

VISA: M'CARD:

Paul & Dreen Tozer	Victoria Spa Lodge	Bishopton Lane	Bishopton	Stratford-upon-Avon CV37 9QY
Tel: (01789) 267985	Fax 01789 204728		Open: ALL YEAR	Map Ref No. 06

Victoria Spa Lodge. Stratford-upon-Avon.

rate £ from - to per person	children taken	evening meals taken	animals taken		

Pear Tree Cottage

£28.00 to £28.00 | Y | N | N

🚭 (no smoking)

see PHOTO over p. 300

Near Rd: A.3400

A delightful half-timbered 16th-century house located in the Shakespeare village of Wilmcote. It retains all its original charm & character, with oak beams, flagstone floors, inglenook fireplaces, thick stone walls with deep-set windows & antiques. 5 very comfortable en-suite rooms, all with tea/coffee facilities & T.V.. A delicious breakfast is served each morning in the dining room. A comfortable lounge is also provided. Children over 3.

E-mail: mander@peartreecot.co.uk
www.peartreecot.co.uk

Mrs Margaret Mander Pear Tree Cottage 7 Church Road Wilmcote Stratford-upon-Avon CV37 9UX
Tel: (01789) 205889 Fax 01789 262862 Open: ALL YEAR (Excl. Xmas & New Year) Map Ref No. 06

Tibbits

£30.00 to £30.00 | Y | N | N

Near Rd: A.45, A.425

Retreat along the pretty country lanes on the border of Warwickshire & Northamptonshire to the haven of this totally secluded 17th-century house, beautifully furnished with antiques, where luxury accommodation is offered. The spacious & pretty bedrooms have books, tea/coffee-making facilities, T.V. & en-suite bathroom. Idyllically situated within acres of rolling countryside, providing an ideal base for exploring an area rich in places of historical, scenic & cultural interest

www.bestbandb.co.uk

Mrs C. A. Mills   Tibbits   Nethercote   Rugby CV23 8AS   Warwickshire
Tel: (01788) 890239   Fax 01788 890239   Open: ALL YEAR   Map Ref No. 08

All the establishments mentioned in this guide are members of
The Worldwide Bed & Breakfast Association

When booking your accommodation please mention
The Best Bed & Breakfast

Pear Tree Cottage. Wilmcote.

Wiltshire

Wiltshire
(West Country)

Wiltshire is a county of rolling chalk downs, small towns, delightful villages, fine churches & great country houses. The expanse of Salisbury Plain is divided by the beautiful valleys of Nadder, Wylye, Ebble & Avon. In a county of open landscapes, Savernake Forest, with its stately avenues of trees strikes a note of contrast. In the north west the Cotswolds spill over into Wiltshire from neighbouring Gloucestershire.

No other county is so rich in archaeological sites. Long barrows and ancient hill forts stand on the skylines as evidence of the early habitation of the chalk uplands. Many of these prehistoric sites are at once magnificent and mysterious. The massive stone arches and monoliths of Stonehenge were built over a period of 500 years with stones transported over great distances. At Avebury the small village is completely encircled by standing stones and a massive bank and ditch earthwork. Silbury Hill is a huge, enigmatic man-made mound. England's largest chambered tomb is West Kennet Long Barrow and at Bush Barrow, finds have included fine bronze and gold daggers and a stone sceptre-head similar to one found at Mycenae in Greece.

Some of England's greatest historic houses are in Wiltshire. Longleat is an Elizabethan mansion with priceless collections of paintings, books & furniture. The surrounding park was landscaped by Capability Brown and its great fame in recent years has been its Safari Park, particularly the lions which roam freely around the visiting cars. Stourhead has celebrated 18th century landscaped gardens which are exceptional in spring when rhododendrons bloom.

Two delightful villages are Castle Combe, nestling in a Cotswold valley, & Lacock where the twisting streets hold examples of buildings ranging from mediaeval half-timbered, to Tudor & Georgian. 13th century Lacock Abbey, converted to a house in the 16th century, was the home of Fox Talbot, pioneer of photography.

There are many notable churches in Wiltshire. In Bradford-on-Avon, a fascinating old town, is the church of St. Lawrence, a rare example of an almost perfect Saxon church from around 900. Farley has an unusual brick church thought to have been designed by Sir Christopher Wren, & there is stained glass by William Morris in the church at Rodbourne.

Devizes Castle

Salisbury stands where three rivers join, on a plain of luxuriant water-meadows, where the focal point of the landscape is the soaring spire of the Cathedral; at 404 feet, it is the tallest in England. The 13th century cathedral has a marvellous & rare visual unity. The body of the building was completed in just 38 years, although the spire was added in the next century. Salisbury, or "New Sarum" was founded in 1220 when the Bishop abandoned the original cathedral at Old Sarum, to start the present edifice two miles to the south. At Old Sarum you can see the foundation of the old city including the outline of the first cathedral.

Wiltshire

Wiltshire Gazeteer

Area of Outstanding Natural Beauty
The Costwolds & the North Wessex Downs.

Historic Houses & Castles

Corsham Court - Chippenham
16th & 17th centuries from Elizabethan & Georgian periods. 18th century furniture, British, Flemish & Italian Old Masters. Gardens by Capability Brown.
Great Chalfield Manor - Melksham
15th century manor house - moated.
Church House - Salisbury
15th century house.
Chalcot House - Westbury
17th century small house in Palladian manner.
Lacock Abbey - Nr. Chippenham
13th century abbey. In 1540 converted into house - 18th century alterations. Mediaeval cloisters & brewery.
Longleat House - Warminster
16th century - early Renaissance, alterations in early 1800's. Italian Renaissance decorations. Splendid state rooms, pictures, books, furniture. Victorian kitchens. Game reserve.
Littlecote - Nr. Hungerford
15th century Tudor manor. Panelled rooms, moulded plaster ceilings.
Luckington Court - Luckington
Queen Anne for the most part - fine ancient buildings.
Malmesbury House - Salisbury
Queen Anne house - part 14th century. Rococo plasterwork.
Newhouse - Redlynch
17th century brick Jacobean trinity house - two Georgian wings,
Philips House - Dinton
1816 Classical house.
Sheldon Manor - Chippenham
13th century porch & 15th century chapel in this Plantagenet manor.
Stourhead - Stourton
18th century Palladian house with framed landscape gardens.
Westwood Manor - Bradford-on-Avon
15th century manor house - alterations in 16th & 17th centuries.
Wardour Castle - Tisbury
18th century house in Palladian manner.

Wilton House - Salisbury
17th century - work of Inigo Jones & later of James Wyatt in 1810. Paintings, Kent & Chippendale furniture.
Avebury Manor - Nr Malborough
Elizabethan manor house - beautiful plasterwork, panelling & furniture. Gardens with topiary.
Bowood - Calne
18th century - work of several famous architects. Gardens by Capability Brown - famous beechwoods.
Mompesson House - Salisbury
Queen Anne town house - Georgian plasterwork.

Cathedrals & Churches

Salisbury Cathedral
13th century - decorated tower with stone spire. Part of original stone pulpitum is preserved. Beautiful large decorated cloister. Exterior mostly early English.
Salisbury (St. Thomas of Canterbury)
15th century rebuilding - 12th century font, 14th & 15th century glass, 17th century monuments. 'Doom' painting over chancel & murals in south chapel
Amesbury (St. Mary & St. Melor)
13th century - refashioned 15th & restored in 19th century. Splendid timber roofs, stone vaulting over chapel of north transept, mediaeval painted glass, 15th century screen, Norman font.
Bishops Cannings (St. Mary the Virgin)
13th-15th centuries. Fine arcading in transept - fine porch doorway.
17th century almsbox, Jacobean Holy table.
Bradford-on-Avon (St. Lawrence)
Best known of all Saxon churches in England.
Cricklade (St. Sampson)
12th -16th century. Tudor central tower vault, 15th century chapel.
Inglesham (St. John the Baptist)
Mediaeval wall paintings, high pews, clear glass, remains of painted screens.
Malmesbury (St. Mary)
Norman - 12th century arcades, refashioning in 14th century with clerestory, 15th century stone pulpitum added. Fine sculpture.

Wiltshire

Tisbury (St. John the Baptist)
14th-15th centuries. 15th-17th century
roofing to nave & aisles. Two storeyed
porch & chancel.
Potterne (St. Mary)
13th,14th,15th centuries. Inscribed
Norman tub font. Wooden pulpit.

Museums & Galleries

Salisbury & South Wiltshire Museum -
Salisbury
Collections showing history of the area in
all periods. Models of Stonehenge & Old
Sarum - archaeologically important
collection.
Devizes Museum - Devizes
Unique archaeological & geological
collections, including Sir Richard Colt-
Hoare's Stourhead collection of prehistoric
material.
Alexander Keiller Museum - Avebury
Collection of items from the Neolithic &
Bronze ages & from excavations in
district.
Athelstan Museum - Malmesbury
Collection of articles referring to the town -
household, coin, etc.
Bedwyn Stone Museum - Great Bedwyn
Open-air museum showing where
Stonehenge was carved.
Lydiard Park - Lydiard Tregoze
Parish church of St. Mary & a splendid
Georgian mansion standing in park & also
permanent & travelling exhibitions.

**Borough of Thamesdown Museum &
Art Gallery** - Swindon
Natural History & Geology of Wiltshire,
Bygones, coins, etc. 20th century British
art & ceramic collection.
Great Western Railway Museum -
Swindon
Historic locomotives.

Historic Monuments

Stonehenge - Nr. Amesbury
Prehistoric monument - encircling bank &
ditch & Augrey holes are Neolithic. Stone
circles possibly early Bronze age.
Avebury
Relics of enormous circular gathering
place B.C. 2700-1700.
Old Sarum - Nr. Salisbury
Possibly first Iron Age camp, later Roman
area, then Norman castle.
Silbury Hill - Nr. Avebury
Mound - conical in shape - probably a
memorial c.3000-2000 B.C.
Windmill Hill - Nr. Avebury
Causewayed camp c.3000-2300 B.C.
Bratton Camp & White Horse - Bratton
Hill fort standing above White Horse.
West Kennet Long Barrow
Burial place c.4000-2500 B.C.
Ludgershall Castle - Lugershall
Motte & bailey of Norman castle,
earthworks, also flint walling from
later castle

Castle Combe.

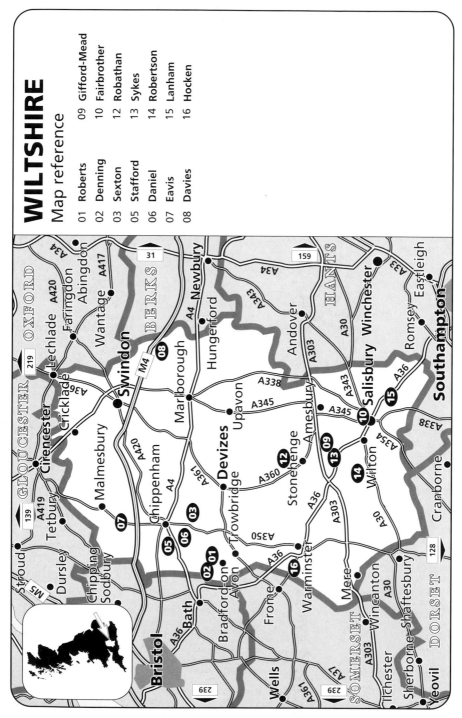

WILTSHIRE
Map reference

01 Roberts	09 Gifford-Mead
02 Denning	10 Fairbrother
03 Sexton	12 Robathan
05 Stafford	13 Sykes
06 Daniel	14 Robertson
07 Eavis	15 Lanham
08 Davies	16 Hocken

rate £ from - to per person	children taken	evening meals	animals taken

£25.00 to £55.00
Y Y N

VISA: M'CARD:

Bradford Old Windmill

Near Rd: A.363

A cosy, relaxed atmosphere greets you at this converted windmill high on the hill above the town. The old stone tower overflows with character, & with the many finds picked up by Peter & Priscilla on their backpacking trips around the world. All of the unusually shaped bedrooms have their own distinctive en-suite bathrooms. Imaginative healthy & unhealthy breakfasts are served beneath the massive grain weighing scales. 5 mins' walk from the town centre. Children over 6 years.
E-mail: bbbw@bradfordoldwindmill.co.uk
www.bradfordoldwindmill.co.uk

Priscilla & Peter Roberts Bradford Old Windmill 4 Masons Lane Bradford-on-Avon Bath BA15 1QN
Tel: (01225) 866048 Fax 01225 866048 Open: MAR - DEC Map Ref No. 01

£42.50 to £50.00
Y N N

VISA: M'CARD: AMEX:

Burghope Manor

Near Rd: A.36

This lovely old home has stood here for 7 centuries overlooking the wonderful valley below - 5 miles from Bath & 1 1/2 miles from Bradford-on-Avon. Although steeped in history, Burghope Manor is first & foremost a living family home, which has been carefully modernised so that the wealth of historical features may complement the present-day comforts. A village pub & restaurant nearby. Evening meals for groups only. Children over 10 years. Single supplement.
E-mail: burghope.manor@virgin.net
www.burghope.co.uk

Elizabeth & John Denning Burghope Manor Winsley Bradford-on-Avon BA15 2LA Wiltshire
Tel: (01225) 723557 Fax 01225 723113 Open: ALL YEAR (Excl. Xmas & New Year) Map Ref No. 02

£25.00 to £32.50
Y N Y

The Old Rectory

Near Rd: A.4

Situated in the medieval village of Lacock, The Old Rectory, built in 1866, is a fine example of Victorian Gothic architecture, with creeper-clad walls & mullioned windows. It stands in 13 acres of its own carefully tended grounds, which include a tennis court & croquet lawn. The Old Rectory offers 6 very attractive bedrooms (1 on the ground floor), all with en-suite/private facilities. An excellent base from which to explore the glorious West Country.
E-mail: sexton@oldrectorylacock.co.uk
www.oldrectorylacock.co.uk

Elaine Sexton The Old Rectory Cantax Hill Lacock Chippenham SN15 2JZ Wiltshire
Tel: (01249) 730335 Fax 01249 730166 Open: ALL YEAR (Excl. Xmas) Map Ref No.03

£25.00 to £28.00
Y N N

Pickwick Lodge Farm

Near Rd: A.4

A delightful 17th-century Cotswold stone farm-house, set in peaceful surroundings. 3 well-appointed & tastefully furnished bedrooms, each with an en-suite/private bathroom, radio, T.V. & tea/coffee-making facilities. Hearty & delicious breakfasts are served. Ideally situated for visiting many sites of historical interest, such as the Wiltshire White Horses, Avebury & Stonehenge; many stately homes & National Trust properties within easy reach. Ample car parking. Children over 12.
E-mail: b&b@pickwickfarm.freeserve.co.uk
www.pickwickfarm.co.uk

Gill Stafford Pickwick Lodge Farm Guyers Lane Corsham SN13 0PS Wiltshire
Tel: (01249) 712207 Fax 01249 701904 Open: ALL YEAR Map Ref No. 05

	rate £ from - to per person	children taken	evening meals	animals taken

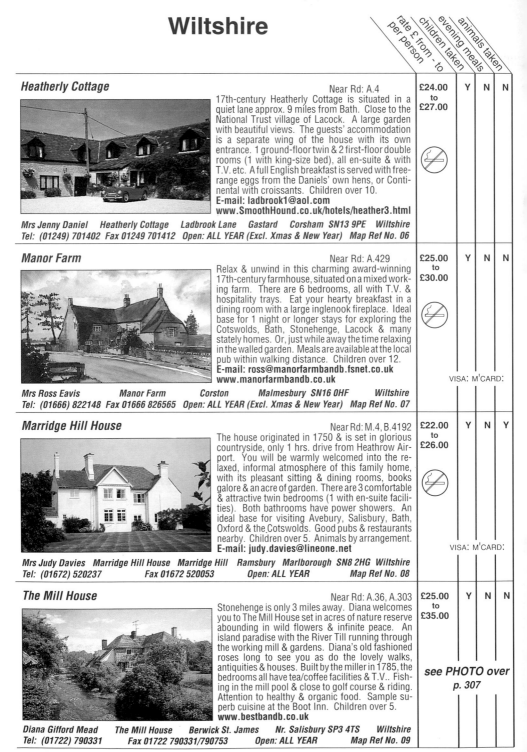

Heatherly Cottage

Near Rd: A.4

17th-century Heatherly Cottage is situated in a quiet lane approx. 9 miles from Bath. Close to the National Trust village of Lacock. A large garden with beautiful views. The guests' accommodation is a separate wing of the house with its own entrance. 1 ground-floor twin & 2 first-floor double rooms (1 with king-size bed), all en-suite & with T.V. etc. A full English breakfast is served with free-range eggs from the Daniels' own hens, or Continental with croissants. Children over 10.
E-mail: ladbrook1@aol.com
www.SmoothHound.co.uk/hotels/heather3.html

£24.00 to £27.00 — Y — N — N

Mrs Jenny Daniel   Heatherly Cottage   Ladbrook Lane   Gastard   Corsham SN13 9PE   Wiltshire
Tel: (01249) 701402 Fax 01249 701412   Open: ALL YEAR (Excl. Xmas & New Year)   Map Ref No. 06

Manor Farm

Near Rd: A.429

Relax & unwind in this charming award-winning 17th-century farmhouse, situated on a mixed working farm. There are 6 bedrooms, all with T.V. & hospitality trays. Eat your hearty breakfast in a dining room with a large inglenook fireplace. Ideal base for 1 night or longer stays for exploring the Cotswolds, Bath, Stonehenge, Lacock & many stately homes. Or, just while away the time relaxing in the walled garden. Meals are available at the local pub within walking distance. Children over 12.
E-mail: ross@manorfarmbandb.fsnet.co.uk
www.manorfarmbandb.co.uk

£25.00 to £30.00 — Y — N — N

VISA: M'CARD:

Mrs Ross Eavis   Manor Farm   Corston   Malmesbury SN16 0HF   Wiltshire
Tel: (01666) 822148 Fax 01666 826565   Open: ALL YEAR (Excl. Xmas & New Year)   Map Ref No. 07

Marridge Hill House

Near Rd: M.4, B.4192

The house originated in 1750 & is set in glorious countryside, only 1 hrs. drive from Heathrow Airport. You will be warmly welcomed into the relaxed, informal atmosphere of this family home, with its pleasant sitting & dining rooms, books galore & an acre of garden. There are 3 comfortable & attractive twin bedrooms (1 with en-suite facilities). Both bathrooms have power showers. An ideal base for visiting Avebury, Salisbury, Bath, Oxford & the Cotswolds. Good pubs & restaurants nearby. Children over 5. Animals by arrangement.
E-mail: judy.davies@lineone.net

£22.00 to £26.00 — Y — N — Y

VISA: M'CARD:

Mrs Judy Davies   Marridge Hill House   Marridge Hill   Ramsbury   Marlborough SN8 2HG   Wiltshire
Tel: (01672) 520237   Fax 01672 520053   Open: ALL YEAR   Map Ref No. 08

The Mill House

Near Rd: A.36, A.303

Stonehenge is only 3 miles away. Diana welcomes you to The Mill House set in acres of nature reserve abounding in wild flowers & infinite peace. An island paradise with the River Till running through the working mill & gardens. Diana's old fashioned roses long to see you as do the lovely walks, antiquities & houses. Built by the miller in 1785, the bedrooms all have tea/coffee facilities & T.V.. Fishing in the mill pool & close to golf course & riding. Attention to healthy & organic food. Sample superb cuisine at the Boot Inn. Children over 5.
www.bestbandb.co.uk

£25.00 to £35.00 — Y — N — N

see PHOTO over
p. 307

Diana Gifford Mead   The Mill House   Berwick St. James   Nr. Salisbury SP3 4TS   Wiltshire
Tel: (01722) 790331   Fax 01722 790331/790753   Open: ALL YEAR   Map Ref No. 09

The Mill House. Berwick St. James

Wiltshire

Glen Lyn House

Near Rd: A.36

Situated in a quiet tree-lined lane, 5 mins' walk from the city centre, Glen Lyn is an elegant Victorian house offering 7 individually appointed bedrooms, 4 en-suite & all with T.V.. Enjoy a great English breakfast & light snacks, then relax in the lounge or listen to birdsong in the beautiful garden. A tranquil base for visiting the cathedral & Stonehenge, & for exploring the New Forest. Parking. Children over 8. Animals by arrangement. Single supplement.
E-mail: glen.lyn@btinternet.com
www.glenlynbandbatsalisbury.co.uk

	rate £ from - to per person	children taken	evening meals	animals taken
	£24.25 to £32.75	Y	N	Y

VISA: M'CARD: AMEX:

Mr Fairbrother & Mrs Watts   Glen Lyn House   6 Bellamy Lane   Milford Hill   Salisbury SP1 2SP
Tel: (01722) 327880   Fax 01722 327880   Open: ALL YEAR   Map Ref No. 10

Maddington House

Near Rd: A.360

Maddington House is the family home of Dick & Joan Robathan. An elegant 17th-century Grade II listed house in the centre of the pretty village of Shrewton - about 2 1/2 miles from Stonehenge & 11 miles from Salisbury. 3 attractive guest rooms, 2 with en-suite facilities. The village has 4 pubs, all within easy walking distance. A delightful home, & the perfect base for a relaxing break. Children over 7 years welcome.
E-mail: rsrobathan@freenet.co.uk
www.bestbandb.co.uk

	rate £ from - to per person	children taken	evening meals	animals taken
	£25.00 to £30.00	Y	N	N

Dick & Joan Robathan   Maddington House   Maddington Street   Shrewton   Salisbury SP3 4JD
Tel: (01980) 620406   Fax 01980 620406   Open: ALL YEAR   Map Ref No. 12

Elm Tree Cottage

Near Rd: A.36, A.303

Elm Tree Cottage is a 17th-century character cottage with inglenook & beams & a lower garden to relax in. The bedrooms, each with an en-suite/ private bathroom, are light & airy, are attractively decorated & have T.V. & tea/coffee. The atmosphere is relaxed & warm, & breakfast is served as required. Situated in a picturesque village, there are views across various valleys, & it is a good centre for Salisbury, Wilton, Longleat, Stonehenge, Avebury, etc. Animals by arrangement.
E-mail: jaw.sykes@virgin.net

	rate £ from - to per person	children taken	evening meals	animals taken
	£26.00 to £27.50	Y	N	Y

Mrs Christine Sykes   Elm Tree Cottage   Chain Hill   Stapleford   Salisbury SP3 4LH   Wiltshire
Tel: (01722) 790507   Open: APR - OCT   Map Ref No. 13

Newton Farmhouse

Near Rd: A.36

This historic listed 16th-century farmhouse, on the borders of the New Forest, was formerly part of the Trafalgar Estate & is situated 8 miles south of Salisbury, convenient for Stonehenge, Romsey, Winchester & Portsmouth. All rooms are en-suite, 3 with genuine period 4-poster beds. The beamed dining room houses a collection of Nelson memorabilia & antiques & has an inglenook fireplace. Breakfast includes home-made breads & preserves. (Dinner by arrangement.) Swimming pool.
E-mail: enquiries@newtonfarmhouse.co.uk
www.newtonfarmhouse.co.uk

	rate £ from - to per person	children taken	evening meals	animals taken
	£28.00 to £38.00	Y	Y	N

John Lanham   Newton Farmhouse   Southampton Road   Whiteparish   Salisbury SP5 2QL   Wilts.
Tel: (01794) 884416   Fax 01794 884416   Open: ALL YEAR   Map Ref No. 15

rate £ from - to per person	children taken	evening meals	animals taken
£32.50 to £32.50	Y	N	N

Bugley Barton

Near Rd: A.36

Ideally placed for trips to Bath, Salisbury, Longleat, Stonehenge & Stourhead; Bugley provides the perfect opportunity to stay in a truly elegant & comfortable Grade II listed Georgian house. Julie & Brian are easy-going & friendly. Home-made cake, delicious breakfasts served in the farmhouse kitchen. The spacious en-suite bedrooms overlook the beautiful garden & have many thoughtful added touches. Good local pubs, parking, train station nearby. Single supplement. Children over 12.
E-mail: bugleybarton@aol.com

Mrs J. Hocken   Bugley Barton   Warminster BA12 8HD   Wiltshire
Tel: (01985) C10009 Fax 01985 000450 Open: ALL YEAR (Excl. Xmas & New Year) Map Ref No. 10

All the establishments mentioned in this guide are members of
The Worldwide Bed & Breakfast Association

When booking your accommodation please mention
The Best Bed & Breakfast

Yorkshire

Yorkshire & Humberside

England's largest county is a region of beautiful landscapes, of hills, peaks, fells, dales & forests with many square miles of National Park. It is a vast area taking in big industrial cities, interesting towns & delightful villages. Yorkshire's broad rivers sweep through the countryside & are an angler's paradise. Cascading waterfalls pour down from hillside & moorland.

The North sea coast can be thrilling, with wild seas & cliff-top walks, or just fun, as at the many resorts where the waves break on long beaches & trickle into green rock-pools. Staithes & Robin Hoods Bay are fascinating old fishing villages. Whitby is an attractive port where, Abbey, the small town tumbles in red-roofed tiers down to the busy harbour from which Captain Cook sailed.

The Yorkshire Dales form one of the finest landscapes in England. From windswept moors to wide green valleys the scenery is incomparable. James Herriot tells of of the effect that the broad vista of Swaledale had on him. "I was captivated", he wrote, "completely spell-bound....". A network of dry stone walls covers the land; some are as old as the stone-built villages but those which climb the valley sides to the high moors are the product of the 18th century enclosures, when a good wall builder would cover seven meters a day.

Each of the Dales has a distinctive character; from the remote upper reaches of Swaledale & Wensleydale, where the air sings with the sound of wind, sheep, & curlew, over to Airedale & the spectacular limestone gorges of Malham Cove & Gordale Scar, & down to the soft meadows & woods of Wharfedale where the ruins of Bolton Priory stand beside the river.

To the east towards Hull with its mighty River Humber crossed by the worlds largest single-span suspension bridge, lie the Yorkshire Wolds. This is lovely countryside where villages have unusual names like Fridaythorpe & Wetwang. Beverley is a picture-postcard town with a fine 13th century Minster.

The North Yorks National Park, where the moors are ablaze with purple fire of heather in the late summer, is exhilarating country. There is moorland to the east also, on the Pennine chain; famous Ilkley Moor with its stone circle known as the twelve apostles, & the Haworth Moors around the plain Yorkshire village where the Bronte sisters lived; "the distant dreamy, dim blue chain of mountains circling every side", which Emily Bronte describes in Wuthering Heights.

The Yorkshire Pennines industrial heritage is being celebrated in fascinating museums, often based in the original Woolen Mills & warehouses, which also provide workshop space for skilled craftspeople.

Yorkshires Monastic past is revealed in the ruins of its once great Abbeys. Rievaulx, Jervaux & Fountains, retain their tranquil beauty in their pastoral settings. The wealth of the county is displayed in many historic houses with glorious gardens, from stately 18th Century Castle Howard of 'Brideshead Revisited' fame to Tudor Shibden Hall, portrayed in Wuthering Heights.

York is the finest mediaeval city in England. It is encircled by its limestone city walls with four Great Gates. Within the walls are the jumbled roof line, dog-leg streets & sudden courtyards of a mediaeval town. Half timbered buildings with over-sailing upper storeys jostle with Georgian brick houses along the network of narrow streets around The Shambles & King Edward Square.

Yorkshire

Yorkshire Gazeteer

Areas of Outstanding Natural Beauty.
The North Yorkshire Moors & The Yorkshire Dales.

Historic Houses & Castles.

Carlton Towers
17th century, remodelled in later centuries. paintings, silver, furniture, pictures. Carved woodwork, painted decorations, examples of Victorian craftmanship.

Castle Howard - nr. York
18th century - celebrated architect, Sir John Vanbrugh - paintings, costumes, furniture by Chippendale, Sheraton, Adam. Not to be missed.

East Riddlesden Hall - Keighley
17th century manor house with fishponds & historic barns, one of which is regarded as very fine example of mediaeval tithe barn.

Newby Hall - Ripon
17th century Wren style extended by Robert Adam. Gobelins tapestry, Chippendale furniture, sculpture galleries with Roman rotunda, statuary. Award-winning gardens.

Nostell Priory - Wakefield
18th century, Georgian mansion, Chippendale furniture, paintings.

Burton Constable Hall - Hull
16th century, Elizabethan, remodelled in Georgian period. Stained glass, Hepplewhite furniture, gardens by Capability Brown.

Ripley Castle - Harrogate
14th century, parts dating during 16th & 18th centuries. Priest hole, armour & weapons, beautiful ceilings.

The Treasurer's House - York
17th & 18th centuries, splendid interiors, furniture, pictures.

Harewood House - Leeds
18th century - Robert Adam design, Chippendale furniture, Italian & English paintings. Sevres & Chinese porcelain.

Benningbrough Hall - York
18th century. Highly decorative woodwork, oak staircase, friezes etc. Splendid hall.

Markenfield Hall - Ripon
14th to 16th century - fine Manor house surrounded by moat.

Heath Hall - Wakefield

18th century, palladian. Fine woodwork & plasterwork, rococo ceilings, excellent furniture, paintings & porcelain

Bishops House - Sheffield
16th century. Only complete timber framed yeoman farmhouse surviving. Vernacular architecture. Superb

Skipton Castle - Skipton
One of the most complete & well preserved mediaeval castles in England.

Cathedral & Churches

York Minster
13th century. Greatest Gothic Cathedral north of the Alps. Imposing grandeur - superb Chapter house, contains half of the mediaeval stained glass of England. Outstandingly beautiful.

York (All Saints, North Street)
15th century roofing in parts - 18th century pulpit wonderful mediaeval glass.

Ripon Cathedral
12th century - though in some parts Saxon in origin. Decorated choir stalls - gables buttresses. Church of 672 preserved in crypt, , Caxton Book, ecclesiastic treasures.

Bolton Percy (All Saints)
15th century.
Maintains original glass in east window. Jacobean font cover. Georgian pulpit. Interesting monuments.

Rievaulx Abbey
12th century, masterpiece of Early English architecture.
One of three great Cistercian Abbeys built in Yorkshire.
Impressive ruins.

Campsall (St. Mary Magdalene)
Fine Norman tower - 15th century rood screen, carved & painted stone altar.

Fountains Abbey - Ripon
Ruins of England's greatest mediaeval abbey - surrounded by wonderful landscaped gardens. Enormous tower, vaulted cellar 300 feet long.

Whitby (St. Mary)
12th century tower & doorway, 18th century remodelling - box pews much interior woodwork painted - galleries. High pulpit. Table tombs.

Yorkshire

Whitby Abbey - Whitby (St. Hilda)
7th century superb ruin - venue of Synod of 664. Destroyed by Vikings, restored 1078 - magnificent north transept.
Halifax (St. John the Baptist)
12th century origins, showing work from each succeeding century - heraldic ceilings. Cromwell glass.
Beverley Minster - Beverley
14th century. Fine Gothic Minster - remarkable mediaeval effigies of musicians playing instruments. Founded as monastery in 700.
Bolton Priory - Nr. Skipton
Nave of Augustinian Priory, now Bolton's Parish Church, amidst ruins of choir & transepts, in beautiful riverside setting.
Selby Abbey - Selby
11th century Benedictine abbey of which the huge church remains. Roof & furnishings are modern after a fire of 1906, but the stonework is intact.

Museums & Galleries

Aldborough Roman Museum - Boroughbridge
Remnants of Roman period of the town - coins, glass, pottery, etc.
Great Ayton
Home of Captain Cook, explorer & seaman. Exhibits of maps, etc.
Art Gallery - City of York
Modern paintings, Old Masters, watercolours, prints, ceramics.
Lotherton Hall - Nr. Leeds
Museum with furniture, paintings, silver, works of art from the Leeds collection & oriental art gallery.
National Railway Museum - York
Devoted to railway engineering & its development.
York Castle Museum
The Kirk Collection of bygones including cobbled streets, shops, costumes, toys, household & farm equipment - fascinating collection.
Cannon Hall Art Gallery - Barnsley
18th century house with fine furniture & glass, etc. Flemish & Dutch paintings. Also houses museum of the 13/18 Royal Hussars.
Mappin Art Gallery - Sheffield
Works from 18th,19th & 20th century.

Graves Art gallery-Sheffield.
British portraiture. European works, & examples of Asian & African art. Loan exhibitions are held there.
Royal Pump Room Museum - Harrogate
Original sulphur well used in the Victorian Spa. Local history costume & pottery.
Bolling Hall - Bradford
A period house with mixture of styles - collections of 17th century oak furniture, domestic utensils, toys & bygones.
Georgian Theatre - Richmond
Oldest theatre in the country - interesting theatrical memorabilia.
Jorvik Viking Centre - York
Recently excavated site in the centre of York showing hundreds of artifacts dating from the Viking period. One of the most important archaeological discoveries this century.
Abbey House Museum - Kirkstall, Leeds
Illustrated past 300 years of Yorkshire life. Shows 3 full streets from 19th century with houses, shops & workplaces.
Piece Hall - Halifax
Remarkable building - constructed around huge quadrangle - now Textile Industrial Museum, Art Gallery & has craft & antique shops.
National Museum of Photography, Film & Television - Bradford
Displays look at art & science of photography, film & T.V. Britain's only IMAX arena.
The Colour Museum - Bradford
Award-winning interactive museum,which allows visitors to explore the world of colour & discover the story of dyeing & textile printing.
Calderdale Industrial Museum - Halifax
Social & industrial Museum of the year 1987
Shibden Hall & Folk Museum of Halifax
Half-timbered house with folk museum, farmland, miniature train & boating lake.
Leeds City Art Gallery & Henry Moore Sculpture Gallery
Yorkshire Sculpture Park - Wakefield
Yorkshire Museum of Farming - Murton
Award-winning museum of farming & the countryside.

YORKSHIRE & HUMBERSIDE

Map reference

01	Williams	18	Schofield
01	Gill	20	Layfield
02	Knox	21	Wood
03	Jillie	22	Chetwynd
04	Greenwood	23	Sugars
05	Oxley	25	Johnson
08	Berry	26	Gordon
09	Kirman	27	Howard-Barker
10	Bateson	29	Watts
10	Evans	30	Goodrum
10	Thomson	31	Bradley
11	Stanton	31	Knibbs
12	Eing	31	Whitbourn-Hammond
13	Banks	31	Blanksby
14	Braithwaite	31	Sluter-Robbins
15	Wells	31	Neighbour
16	Marshall	31	Robinson
17	Murray	31	J. Wood

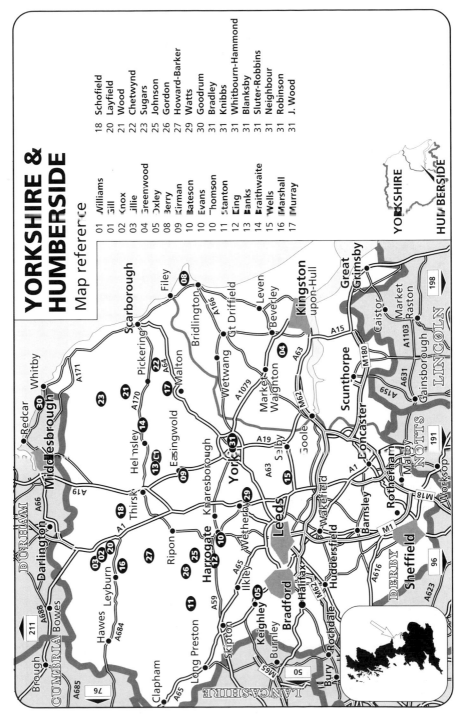

313

Yorkshire

Daleside

Near Rd: A.170

Daleside is listed the oldest house in this charming stone village, with 400-year-old cruck beams & oak panelling. The house has been sympathetically restored, with the 2 en-suite guests' rooms (1 twin, 1 double with half-tester bed) overlooking the garden. There are 2 inns in the village & other good restaurants nearby. Ampleforth is on the edge of the North York Moors National Park, with excellent walks all around. Children from 11.
E-mail: dalesidepaul@hotmail.com
www.bestbandb.co.uk

| | £28.50 to £33.50 | Y | N | N |

Paul & Pat Williams   Daleside   East End   Ampleforth YO62 4DA   Yorkshire
Tel: (01439) 788266   Open: ALL YEAR (Excl. Xmas & New Year)   Map Ref No. 01

Shallowdale House

Near Rd: A.170

This is an outstanding modern country house, with 2 acres of hillside garden, on the southern edge of the North York Moors National Park. All of the spacious rooms enjoy stunning views of unspoilt countryside & are furnished with style & attention to detail. There are 3 guest bedrooms (with bath & shower) & 2 sitting rooms. Meals are imaginatively prepared from fresh seasonal ingredients & there is a drinks licence. A perfect place to unwind when exploring Herriot country & York. Children over 12.
E-mail: stay@shallowdalehouse.co.uk
www.shallowdalehouse.co.uk

| | £37.50 to £45.00 | Y | Y | N |

VISA: M'CARD:

Phillip Gill & Anton Van Der Horst   Shallowdale House   West End   Ampleforth YO62 4DY
Tel: (01439) 788325 Fax 01439 788885 Open: ALL YEAR (Excl. Xmas & New Year) Map Ref No. 01

Mill Close Farm

Near Rd: A.1

17th-century farmhouse at the foothills of the Yorkshire Dales & Herriot country. Very tranquil with exceptional views yet only 3 miles from A.1(M). Luxurious en-suite bedrooms, 1 with jacuzzi, large beds, T.V. & videos, toiletries, tea trays, guest fridges with complimentary fruit, mineral water & chocolates. Walled garden with pond & waterfall. Delicious farmhouse breakfasts. Excellent local pubs. Ideal stopover for Scotland. Animals by arrangement. Children over 12.
E-mail: millclosefarm@btopenworld.com
www.SmoothHound.co.uk/hotels/millclosefarm

| | £30.00 to £32.50 | Y | N | Y |

see PHOTO over p. 315

Mrs Patricia Knox   Mill Close Farm   Patrick Brompton   Bedale DL8 1JY   Yorkshire
Tel: (01677) 450257   Fax 01677 450585   Open: FEB - DEC   Map Ref No. 02

Elmfield Country House

Near Rd: A.684

Located in its own grounds in the country. Enjoy a relaxed, friendly atmosphere in spacious surroundings, with a high standard of furnishings. 9 en-suite bedrooms comprising twin-bedded, double & family rooms. 2 rooms have been adapted for disabled guests & another has a 4-poster bed. All rooms have satellite T.V., 'phone, radio/alarm & tea/coffee makers. A games room & solarium are also available. Excellent farmhouse cooking. Residential licence. A delightful home. Single supplement.
E-mail: stay@elmfieldhouse.freeserve.co.uk
www.elmfieldhouse.co.uk

| | £29.00 to £39.00 | Y | Y | N |

VISA: M'CARD:

Jim & Edith Lillie   Elmfield Country House   Arrathorne   Bedale DL8 1NE   Yorkshire
Tel: (01677) 450558   Fax 01677 450557   Open: ALL YEAR   Map Ref No. 03

Mill Close Farm.   Patrick Brompton.

Yorkshire

Rudstone Walk Country Accommodation

Near Rd: A.1034

Rudstone Walk is renowned for its hospitality & good food. Accommodation is in the very tastefully converted farm buildings, adjacent to the main farmhouse where meals are served. The attractive bedrooms have excellent en-suite facilities, T.V., 'phone, hairdryer & more. Rudstone provides a peaceful retreat after a tiring day. It is ideal for a relaxing break, & is within easy reach of York & many other attractions. Animals by arrangement.
E-mail: office@rudstone-walk.co.uk
www.rudstone-walk.co.uk

£27.50 to £30.00 — Y Y Y

VISA: M'CARD: AMEX:

Charles Greenwood Rudstone Walk Country Accommodation South Cave Beverley HU15 2AH
Tel: (01430) 422230   Fax 01430 424552   Open: ALL YEAR   Map Ref No. 04

Five Rise Locks Hotel & Restaurant

Near Rd: A.650

A Victorian manor house standing in mature terraced gardens overlooking the Aire Valley, minutes walk from Bingley & the Five Rise Locks. Each of the 9 en-suite bedrooms has been individually designed. The award-winning restaurant is open for lunch & dinner & offers imaginative meals complemented by a good selection of wines in elegant surroundings. This is the perfect spot from which to visit Haworth, Saltaire, steam trains, York, Leeds, Mill shopping, Skipton & the glorious Dales.
E-mail: info@five-rise-locks.co.uk
www.five-rise-locks.co.uk

£30.00 to £40.00 — Y Y Y

VISA: M'CARD:

Mr & Mrs Oxley Five Rise Locks Hotel & Restaurant Beck Lane Bingley Bradford BD16 4DD
Tel: (01274) 565296   Fax 01274 568828   Open: ALL YEAR   Map Ref No. 05

The Manor House

Near Rd: A.614

A manor of Flamborough is recorded in the Domesday Book. The current Georgian house is a handsomely proportioned family home offering spacious & comfortable accommodation in well-appointed rooms. Historic Flamborough Head is designated a Heritage Coast, with many interesting walks & a nearby bird reserve. Ideally placed for exploration of North & East Yorkshire. Dinner, by prior arrangement, features local seafood when available. Children over 8 yrs.
E-mail: gm@flamboroughmanor.co.uk
www.flamboroughmanor.co.uk

£35.00 to £40.00 — Y Y N

VISA: M'CARD:

Lesley Berry   The Manor House   Flamborough   Bridlington YO15 1PD   Yorkshire
Tel: (01262) 850943   Fax 01262 850943   Open: ALL YEAR (Excl. Xmas)   Map Ref No. 08

The Old Vicarage

Near Rd: A.19

A listed property of immense character built in the 18th century, thoughtfully brought up to modern standards, & yet still retaining many delightful features. Now offering 5 en-suite rooms with T.V. & tea/coffee makers. Standing in extensive lawned gardens, overlooking the market square, & with a croquet lawn & a walled rose garden, it is an ideal touring centre for York, the Dales, the Yorkshire Moors & 'Herriot' countryside. Parking.
E-mail: kirman@oldvic-easingwold.freeserve.co.uk
www.oldvicarage-easingwold.co.uk

£30.00 to £37.50 — Y N N

Christine & John Kirman   The Old Vicarage   Market Place   Easingwold YO61 3AL   Yorkshire
Tel: (01347) 821015   Fax 01347 823465   Open: FEB - NOV   Map Ref No. 09

Column headers (rotated):
- rate £ from - to / per person
- children taken
- evening meals
- animals taken

£27.50 to £30.00 | Y | N | N | (No smoking)

Ashwood House

Near Rd: A.61

A charming 6-bedroomed Edwardian house retaining many of its original features. Situated in a quiet, residential cul-de-sac mins' from the town centre. The attractive en-suite bedrooms are spacious, some with 4-poster beds, all with hospitality tray, T.V., hairdryer & toiletries. A delicious breakfast is served from lovely Royal Copenhagen china in the elegant dining room. A high standard of service & a warm welcome is assured. Scandinavian languages spoken. Children over 10.
E-mail: ashwoodhouse@aol.com
www.ashwoodhouse.co.uk

Gill & Kristian Bendtson   Ashwood House   7 Spring Grove   Harrogate HG1 2HS   Yorkshire
Tel: (01423) 560081   Fax 01423 527928   Open: ALL YEAR   Map Ref No. 10

£27.50 to £35.00 | Y | Y | N | (No smoking)

VISA: M'CARD: AMEX:

Shannon Court Hotel

Near Rd: A.59

Charming Victorian house hotel, overlooking the 'Stray' in High Harrogate. Enjoy real home cooking in this family-run hotel (evening meals by prior arrangement). 8 delightful bedrooms, all of which are en-suite & have every modern comfort including radio/alarm, T.V. & tea/coffee-making facilities. Licensed for residents & their guests. Close to town centre, railway station & conference centre, with easy parking & direct main routes for moors & dales. An excellent touring base.
E-mail: shannon@courthotel.freeserve.co.uk
www.shannon-court.com

Kath & Bob Evans   Shannon Court Hotel   65 Dragon Avenue   Harrogate HG1 5DS   Yorkshire
Tel: (01423) 509858   Fax 01423 530606   Open: ALL YEAR   Map Ref No. 10

£25.00 to £25.00 | Y | N | N | (No smoking)

Knox Mill House

Near Rd: A.61

Built in 1785, this lovely old millhouse stands on the banks of a stream in a quiet rural setting, & yet is only 1 1/2 miles from the centre of Harrogate. Beautifully renovated, it still retains all its original features: oak beams, an inglenook fireplace & stone arches. There are 3 delightful rooms, attractively & comfortably furnished. 2 are en-suite, & all have tea/coffee makers & views over the stream & fields. A delightful lounge with colour T.V., & a garden for guests' enjoyment. Single supplement. Children over 12 years welcome.
www.bestbandb.co.uk

Peter & Marion Thomson   Knox Mill House   Knox Mill Lane   Killinghall   Harrogate HG3 2AE
Tel: (01423) 560650 Fax 01423 560650 Open: ALL YEAR (Excl. Xmas & New Year) Map Ref No. 10

£26.50 to £30.00 | N | Y | N | (No smoking)

Fountains House

Near Rd: A.61

A charming 18th-century limestone cottage with lovely south-facing garden; situated in the pretty village of Burton Leonard halfway between Harrogate & Ripon, ideally placed for both town & country. There are 2 twin/double rooms with en-suite facilities, T.V. & hospitality tray, which are delightfully furnished & decorated to a high standard. Delicious breakfasts are cooked to order & include homemade preserves & freshly baked bread from the Aga. Evening meals are available by prior arrangement. Parking.
www.bestbandb.co.uk

Clive & Gill King   Fountains House   Burton Leonard   Nr. Harrogate HG3 3RU   Yorkshire
Tel: (01756) 677537   Open: ALL YEAR   Map Ref No. 12

Knottside Farm.   Pateley Bridge.

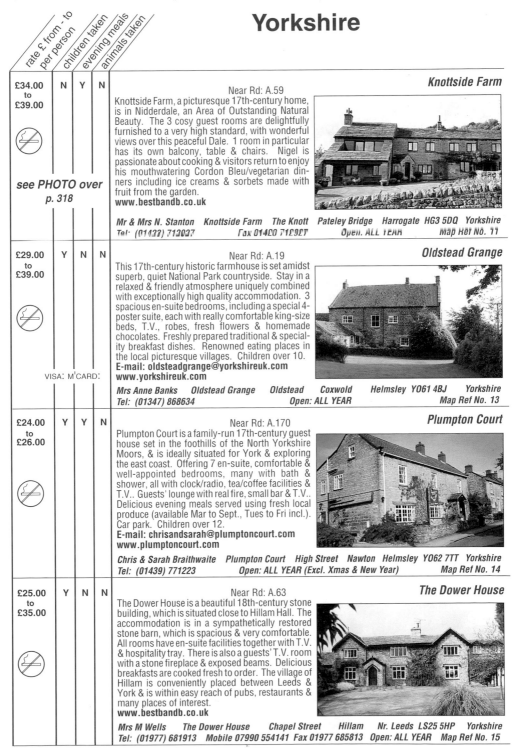

rate £ from - to per person	children taken	evening meals	animals taken		

Knottside Farm

£34.00 to £39.00 — N Y N — (no smoking)

see PHOTO over p. 318

Near Rd: A.59
Knottside Farm, a picturesque 17th-century home, is in Nidderdale, an Area of Outstanding Natural Beauty. The 3 cosy guest rooms are delightfully furnished to a very high standard, with wonderful views over this peaceful Dale. 1 room in particular has its own balcony, table & chairs. Nigel is passionate about cooking & visitors return to enjoy his mouthwatering Cordon Bleu/vegetarian dinners including ice creams & sorbets made with fruit from the garden.
www.bestbandb.co.uk

Mr & Mrs N. Stanton   Knottside Farm   The Knott   Pateley Bridge   Harrogate HG3 5DQ   Yorkshire
Tel: (01423) 712027   Fax 01423 712927   Open: ALL YEAR   Map Ref No. 11

Oldstead Grange

£29.00 to £39.00 — Y N N — (no smoking)
VISA: M'CARD:

Near Rd: A.19
This 17th-century historic farmhouse is set amidst superb, quiet National Park countryside. Stay in a relaxed & friendly atmosphere uniquely combined with exceptionally high quality accommodation. 3 spacious en-suite bedrooms, including a special 4-poster suite, each with really comfortable king-size beds, T.V., robes, fresh flowers & homemade chocolates. Freshly prepared traditional & speciality breakfast dishes. Renowned eating places in the local picturesque villages. Children over 10.
E-mail: oldsteadgrange@yorkshireuk.com
www.yorkshireuk.com

Mrs Anne Banks   Oldstead Grange   Oldstead   Coxwold   Helmsley YO61 4BJ   Yorkshire
Tel: (01347) 868634   Open: ALL YEAR   Map Ref No. 13

Plumpton Court

£24.00 to £26.00 — Y Y N — (no smoking)

Near Rd: A.170
Plumpton Court is a family-run 17th-century guest house set in the foothills of the North Yorkshire Moors, & is ideally situated for York & exploring the east coast. Offering 7 en-suite, comfortable & well-appointed bedrooms, many with bath & shower, all with clock/radio, tea/coffee facilities & T.V.. Guests' lounge with real fire, small bar & T.V.. Delicious evening meals served using fresh local produce (available Mar to Sept., Tues to Fri incl.). Car park. Children over 12.
E-mail: chrisandsarah@plumptoncourt.com
www.plumptoncourt.com

Chris & Sarah Braithwaite   Plumpton Court   High Street   Nawton   Helmsley YO62 7TT   Yorkshire
Tel: (01439) 771223   Open: ALL YEAR (Excl. Xmas & New Year)   Map Ref No. 14

The Dower House

£25.00 to £35.00 — Y N N — (no smoking)

Near Rd: A.63
The Dower House is a beautiful 18th-century stone building, which is situated close to Hillam Hall. The accommodation is in a sympathetically restored stone barn, which is spacious & very comfortable. All rooms have en-suite facilities together with T.V. & hospitality tray. There is also a guests' T.V. room with a stone fireplace & exposed beams. Delicious breakfasts are cooked fresh to order. The village of Hillam is conveniently placed between Leeds & York & is within easy reach of pubs, restaurants & many places of interest.
www.bestbandb.co.uk

Mrs M Wells   The Dower House   Chapel Street   Hillam   Nr. Leeds LS25 5HP   Yorkshire
Tel: (01977) 681913   Mobile 07990 554141   Fax 01977 685813   Open: ALL YEAR   Map Ref No. 15

Yorkshire

Park Gate House

Near Rd: A.684

A warm welcome awaits all guests at this lovely 18th-century house, situated in Lower Wensleydale, an Area of Outstanding Natural Beauty & historical interest. Park Gate House retains its charm with low oak beams, inglenook log fire & cottage gardens. Bedrooms are decorated in country-style old pine furniture, T.V. & private facilities & echo comfort & style. Breakfast is a delight & very high quality. Evening meals by prior arrangement. Single supplement £10. Children over 12.
E-mail: parkgatehouse@freenet.co.uk
www.parkgatehouse.co.uk

rate	children	evening	animals
£30.00 to £35.00	Y	Y	N

VISA: M'CARD:

Terry & Linda Marshall   Park Gate House   Constable Burton   Leyburn DL8 5RG   Yorkshire
Tel: (01677) 450466   Open: ALL YEAR   Map Ref No. 16

Manor Farm

Near Rd: A.169

A charming Georgian manor house set in spacious grounds with hard tennis court, croquet lawn & views to the Howardian Hills. Accommodation is in 3 comfortable & attractively furnished bedrooms, with either an en-suite or a private bathroom. Excellent cooking caters for all tastes. Manor Farm is within easy reach of York, Scarborough, the Moors, Castle Howard & Flamingoland. Dogs & children over 5 are most welcome.
E-mail: cphmurray@compuserve.com
www.bestbandb.co.uk

rate	children	evening	animals
£30.00 to £35.00	Y	Y	Y

Mrs Judith Murray   Manor Farm   Little Barugh   Malton YO17 6UY   Yorkshire
Tel: (01653) 668262   Fax 01653 668600   Open: ALL YEAR   Map Ref No. 17

Elmscott

Near Rd: A.684, A.1

Elmscott is a charming cottage-style property which is set in a delightful landscaped garden. It is situated close to the centre of Northallerton, a thriving market town. Your hosts offer 2 attractively furnished bedrooms, each with an en-suite bathroom, tea/coffee-making facilities & T.V.. A delicious breakfast is served. Elmscott is located mid-way between the North York Moors & the beautiful Yorkshire Dales National Parks, with their famous 'Herriott' connections. A lovely home.
E-mail: elmscott@freenet.co.uk
www.elmscottbedandbreakfast.co.uk

rate	children	evening	animals
£26.00 to £28.00	Y	N	N

Mike & Pauline Schofield   Elmscott   Hatfield Road   Northallerton DL7 8QX   Yorkshire
Tel: (01609) 760575   Open: ALL YEAR   Map Ref No. 18

Little Holtby

Near Rd: A.1

With one foot in the past, but with present day comforts, Little Holtby is the 'somewhere special' in which to relax & unwind. Antiques, beams, polished wood floors & cosy log fires all add to the ambience of a period farmhouse. The 3 guest rooms have wonderful views over rolling countryside to the Dales. En-suite or private facilities are available. Facilities for golf, tennis, riding, fishing & walking are all close by. Children over 12. Come & spoil yourself - other guests do again & again.
E-mail: littleholtby@yahoo.co.uk
www.littleholtby.co.uk

rate	children	evening	animals
£25.00 to £27.50	Y	Y	N

Dorothy Layfield   Little Holtby   Leeming Bar   Northallerton DL7 9LH   Yorkshire
Tel: (01609) 748762   Fax 01609 748822   Open: ALL YEAR (Excl. Xmas)   Map Ref No. 20

Yorkshire

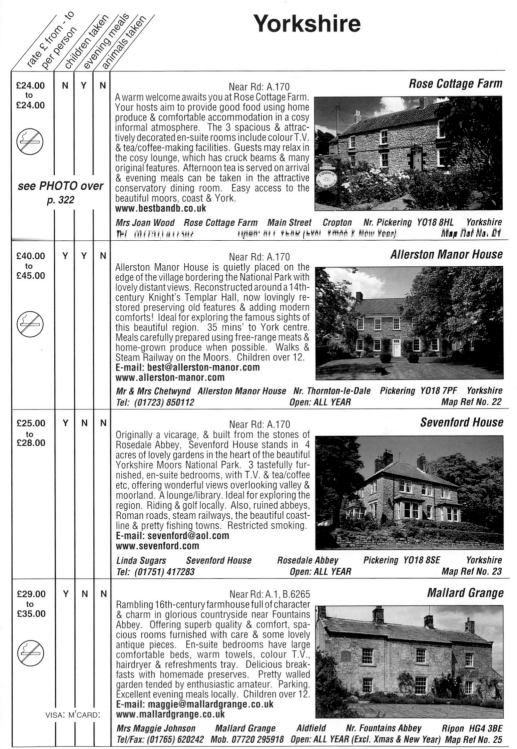

rate £ from - to per person	children taken	evening meals	animals taken		

£24.00 to £24.00 — N Y N

Near Rd: A.170

Rose Cottage Farm

A warm welcome awaits you at Rose Cottage Farm. Your hosts aim to provide good food using home produce & comfortable accommodation in a cosy informal atmosphere. The 3 spacious & attractively decorated en-suite rooms include colour T.V. & tea/coffee-making facilities. Guests may relax in the cosy lounge, which has cruck beams & many original features. Afternoon tea is served on arrival & evening meals can be taken in the attractive conservatory dining room. Easy access to the beautiful moors, coast & York.
www.bestbandb.co.uk

see PHOTO over p. 322

Mrs Joan Wood   Rose Cottage Farm   Main Street   Cropton   Nr. Pickering YO18 8HL   Yorkshire
Tel: (01751) 417592   Open: ALL YEAR (Excl. Xmas & New Year)   Map Ref No. 21

£40.00 to £45.00 — Y Y N

Near Rd: A.170

Allerston Manor House

Allerston Manor House is quietly placed on the edge of the village bordering the National Park with lovely distant views. Reconstructed around a 14th-century Knight's Templar Hall, now lovingly restored preserving old features & adding modern comforts! Ideal for exploring the famous sights of this beautiful region. 35 mins' to York centre. Meals carefully prepared using free-range meats & home-grown produce when possible. Walks & Steam Railway on the Moors. Children over 12.
E-mail: best@allerston-manor.com
www.allerston-manor.com

Mr & Mrs Chetwynd   Allerston Manor House   Nr. Thornton-le-Dale   Pickering YO18 7PF   Yorkshire
Tel: (01723) 850112   Open: ALL YEAR   Map Ref No. 22

£25.00 to £28.00 — Y N N

Near Rd: A.170

Sevenford House

Originally a vicarage, & built from the stones of Rosedale Abbey, Sevenford House stands in 4 acres of lovely gardens in the heart of the beautiful Yorkshire Moors National Park. 3 tastefully furnished, en-suite bedrooms, with T.V. & tea/coffee etc, offering wonderful views overlooking valley & moorland. A lounge/library. Ideal for exploring the region. Riding & golf locally. Also, ruined abbeys, Roman roads, steam railways, the beautiful coastline & pretty fishing towns. Restricted smoking.
E-mail: sevenford@aol.com
www.sevenford.com

Linda Sugars   Sevenford House   Rosedale Abbey   Pickering YO18 8SE   Yorkshire
Tel: (01751) 417283   Open: ALL YEAR   Map Ref No. 23

£29.00 to £35.00 — Y N N

Near Rd: A.1, B.6265

Mallard Grange

Rambling 16th-century farmhouse full of character & charm in glorious countryside near Fountains Abbey. Offering superb quality & comfort, spacious rooms furnished with care & some lovely antique pieces. En-suite bedrooms have large comfortable beds, warm towels, colour T.V., hairdryer & refreshments tray. Delicious breakfasts with homemade preserves. Pretty walled garden tended by enthusiastic amateur. Parking. Excellent evening meals locally. Children over 12.
E-mail: maggie@mallardgrange.co.uk
www.mallardgrange.co.uk

VISA: M'CARD:

Mrs Maggie Johnson   Mallard Grange   Aldfield   Nr. Fountains Abbey   Ripon HG4 3BE
Tel/Fax: (01765) 620242   Mob. 07720 295918   Open: ALL YEAR (Excl. Xmas & New Year) Map Ref No. 25

Rose Cottage Farm. Cropton.

rate £ from - to per person	children taken	evening meals	animals taken

---

£27.50 to £32.50

Y　N　N

🚭 (no smoking)

VISA: M'CARD:

Near Rd: A.1

St. George's Court

St. George's Court is beautifully situated in peaceful countryside & provides comfortable ground-floor rooms in renovated farm buildings. All modern facilities whilst retaining much charm & character. Delicious breakfasts are served in the conservatory dining room, with views, in the delightful listed farmhouse. Peace & tranquillity is the password here. St. George's Court is near Fountains Abbey & Brimham Rocks. Ripon, Harrogate & York are all within easy reach.
E-mail: stgeorgescourt@bronco.co.uk
www.stgeorges-court.co.uk

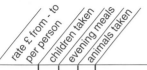

Mrs Sandra Gordon　St. George's Court　Old Home Farm　Grantley　Ripon　HG4 3EU　Yorkshire
Tel: (01765) 620618　Fax 01765 620619　Open: ALL YEAR　Map Ref No. 20

£25.00 to £32.50

Y　Y　N

🚭 (no smoking)

VISA: M'CARD:

Near Rd: A.6108, A.1

Bank Villa

Set in half an acre of terraced garden, this welcoming Grade II listed home has recently been renovated & refurbished to a high standard. It offers guests 2 delightful lounges in which to relax & 6 double bedrooms, each with radio, 4 with en-suite or private facilities, 2 with private shower. Bank Villa is an excellent spot for a relaxing break & it is an ideal base from which to explore the Yorkshire Dales, tour around, walk, horse-ride or fish. Children over 5 years. A warm welcome awaits you.
E-mail: bankvilla@btopenworld.com
www.bankvilla.com

Graham & Liz Howard-Barker　Bank Villa　Masham　Nr. Ripon　HG4 4DB　Yorkshire
Tel: (01765) 689605　Fax 01765 688545　Open: ALL YEAR　Map Ref No. 27

£29.00 to £39.50

Y　N　Y

🚭 (no smoking)

Near Rd: A.659

Four Gables

Visitors will love this special art-and-craft movement house with its wealth of original features, stripped oak & terracotta floors, fireplaces, beautiful ceilings & gardens of over 1/2 an acre which contain many interesting plants & a croquet lawn. Enjoy the peaceful setting, down a private lane, yet only 3 mins' walk from the bussling Georgian stone village of Boston Spa with all its facilities, shops, restaurants, etc. 4 en-suite bedrooms. Log fires in winter. Single supplement. Children over 3.
E-mail: info@fourgables.co.uk
www.fourgables.co.uk

David & Anne Watts　Four Gables　Oaks Lane　Boston Spa　Wetherby　LS23 6DS　Yorkshire
Tel: (01937) 845592　Open: FEB - DEC　Map Ref No. 29

£33.00 to £50.00

Y　Y　Y

VISA: M'CARD:

Near Rd: A.174

Cliffemount Hotel

As the name implies, this privately-run hotel is situated on a clifftop with panoramic views over Runswick Bay. Built in the 1920s with later additions, the hotel is tastefully decorated throughout. There are 20 comfortably furnished bedrooms, all are en-suite, & the majority have spectacular sea views. Cliffemount, with its warm & friendly atmosphere, also enjoys a good reputation for its high standard of food. Fully licensed. Log fires in winter. Animals by arrangement.
E-mail: cliffemount@runswickbay.fsnet.co.uk
www.cliffemounthotel.co.uk

Mrs Ashley Goodrum　Cliffemount Hotel　Runswick Bay　Whitby　TS13 5HU　Yorkshire
Tel: (01947) 840103　Fax 01947 841025　Open: ALL YEAR (Excl. Xmas)　Map Ref No. 30

Barbican House.   York.

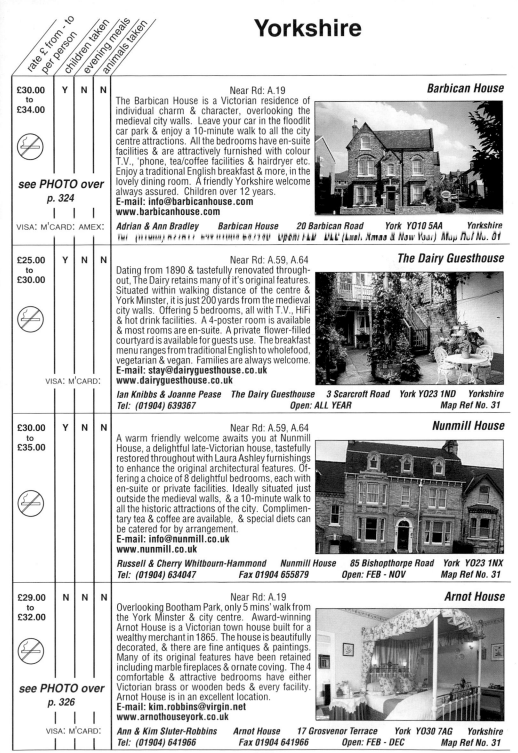

rate £ from - to per person	children taken	evening meals	animals taken

£30.00 to £34.00
Y N N
(non-smoking)

see PHOTO over
p. 324

VISA: M'CARD: AMEX:

Barbican House

Near Rd: A.19

The Barbican House is a Victorian residence of individual charm & character, overlooking the medieval city walls. Leave your car in the floodlit car park & enjoy a 10-minute walk to all the city centre attractions. All the bedrooms have en-suite facilities & are attractively furnished with colour T.V., 'phone, tea/coffee facilities & hairdryer etc. Enjoy a traditional English breakfast & more, in the lovely dining room. A friendly Yorkshire welcome always assured. Children over 12 years.
E-mail: info@barbicanhouse.com
www.barbicanhouse.com

Adrian & Ann Bradley   Barbican House   20 Barbican Road   York YO10 5AA   Yorkshire
Tel: (01904) 627617 Fax 01904 647140 Open: FEB DEC (Excl. Xmas & New Year) Map Ref No. 01

£25.00 to £30.00
Y N N
(non-smoking)

VISA: M'CARD:

The Dairy Guesthouse

Near Rd: A.59, A.64

Dating from 1890 & tastefully renovated throughout, The Dairy retains many of it's original features. Situated within walking distance of the centre & York Minster, it is just 200 yards from the medieval city walls. Offering 5 bedrooms, all with T.V., HiFi & hot drink facilities. A 4-poster room is available & most rooms are en-suite. A private flower-filled courtyard is available for guests use. The breakfast menu ranges from traditional English to wholefood, vegetarian & vegan. Families are always welcome.
E-mail: stay@dairyguesthouse.co.uk
www.dairyguesthouse.co.uk

Ian Knibbs & Joanne Pease   The Dairy Guesthouse   3 Scarcroft Road   York YO23 1ND   Yorkshire
Tel: (01904) 639367   Open: ALL YEAR   Map Ref No. 31

£30.00 to £35.00
Y N N
(non-smoking)

Nunmill House

Near Rd: A.59, A.64

A warm friendly welcome awaits you at Nunmill House, a delightful late-Victorian house, tastefully restored throughout with Laura Ashley furnishings to enhance the original architectural features. Offering a choice of 8 delightful bedrooms, each with en-suite or private facilities. Ideally situated just outside the medieval walls, & a 10-minute walk to all the historic attractions of the city. Complimentary tea & coffee are available, & special diets can be catered for by arrangement.
E-mail: info@nunmill.co.uk
www.nunmill.co.uk

Russell & Cherry Whitbourn-Hammond   Nunmill House   85 Bishopthorpe Road   York YO23 1NX
Tel: (01904) 634047   Fax 01904 655879   Open: FEB - NOV   Map Ref No. 31

£29.00 to £32.00
N N N
(non-smoking)

see PHOTO over
p. 326

VISA: M'CARD:

Arnot House

Near Rd: A.19

Overlooking Bootham Park, only 5 mins' walk from the York Minster & city centre. Award-winning Arnot House is a Victorian town house built for a wealthy merchant in 1865. The house is beautifully decorated, & there are fine antiques & paintings. Many of its original features have been retained including marble fireplaces & ornate coving. The 4 comfortable & attractive bedrooms have either Victorian brass or wooden beds & every facility. Arnot House is in an excellent location.
E-mail: kim.robbins@virgin.net
www.arnothouseyork.co.uk

Ann & Kim Sluter-Robbins   Arnot House   17 Grosvenor Terrace   York YO30 7AG   Yorkshire
Tel: (01904) 641966   Fax 01904 641966   Open: FEB - DEC   Map Ref No. 31

Arnot House.   Bootham.

Yorkshire

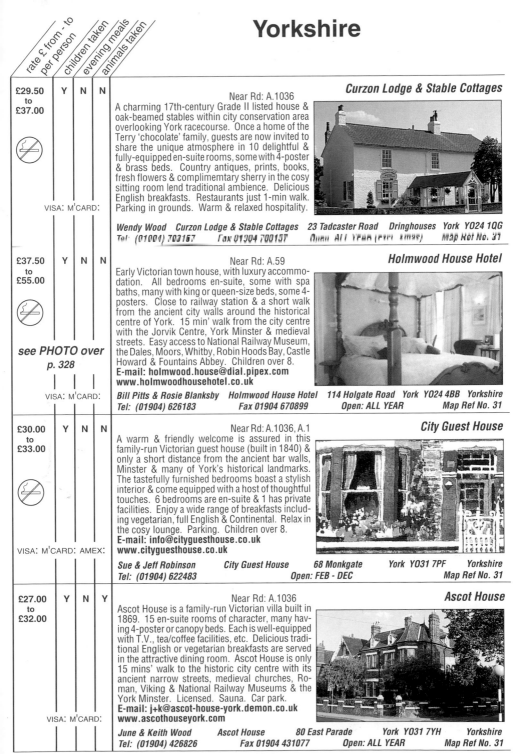

rate £ from - to per person	children taken	evening meals taken	animals taken		

£29.50 to £37.00 Y N N 🚭 VISA: M'CARD:

Curzon Lodge & Stable Cottages

Near Rd: A.1036

A charming 17th-century Grade II listed house & oak-beamed stables within city conservation area overlooking York racecourse. Once a home of the Terry 'chocolate' family, guests are now invited to share the unique atmosphere in 10 delightful & fully-equipped en-suite rooms, some with 4-poster & brass beds. Country antiques, prints, books, fresh flowers & complimemtary sherry in the cosy sitting room lend traditional ambience. Delicious English breakfasts. Restaurants just 1-min walk. Parking in grounds. Warm & relaxed hospitality.

Wendy Wood   *Curzon Lodge & Stable Cottages*   *23 Tadcaster Road*   *Dringhouses*   *York YO24 1QG*
Tel: (01904) 703157   Fax 01904 700157   Open: ALL YEAR (Excl. Xmas)   Map Ref No. 31

£37.50 to £55.00 Y N N 🚭

see PHOTO over p. 328

VISA: M'CARD:

Holmwood House Hotel

Near Rd: A.59

Early Victorian town house, with luxury accommo-dation. All bedrooms en-suite, some with spa baths, many with king or queen-size beds, some 4-posters. Close to railway station & a short walk from the ancient city walls around the historical centre of York. 15 min' walk from the city centre with the Jorvik Centre, York Minster & medieval streets. Easy access to National Railway Museum, the Dales, Moors, Whitby, Robin Hoods Bay, Castle Howard & Fountains Abbey. Children over 8.
E-mail: holmwood.house@dial.pipex.com
www.holmwoodhousehotel.co.uk

Bill Pitts & Rosie Blanksby   *Holmwood House Hotel*   *114 Holgate Road*   *York YO24 4BB*   *Yorkshire*
Tel: (01904) 626183   Fax 01904 670899   Open: ALL YEAR   Map Ref No. 31

£30.00 to £33.00 Y N N 🚭 VISA: M'CARD: AMEX:

City Guest House

Near Rd: A.1036, A.1

A warm & friendly welcome is assured in this family-run Victorian guest house (built in 1840) & only a short distance from the ancient bar walls, Minster & many of York's historical landmarks. The tastefully furnished bedrooms boast a stylish interior & come equipped with a host of thoughtful touches. 6 bedrooms are en-suite & 1 has private facilities. Enjoy a wide range of breakfasts includ-ing vegetarian, full English & Continental. Relax in the cosy lounge. Parking. Children over 8.
E-mail: info@cityguesthouse.co.uk
www.cityguesthouse.co.uk

Sue & Jeff Robinson   *City Guest House*   *68 Monkgate*   *York YO31 7PF*   *Yorkshire*
Tel: (01904) 622483   Open: FEB - DEC   Map Ref No. 31

£27.00 to £32.00 Y N Y 🚭 VISA: M'CARD:

Ascot House

Near Rd: A.1036

Ascot House is a family-run Victorian villa built in 1869. 15 en-suite rooms of character, many hav-ing 4-poster or canopy beds. Each is well-equipped with T.V., tea/coffee facilities, etc. Delicious tradi-tional English or vegetarian breakfasts are served in the attractive dining room. Ascot House is only 15 mins' walk to the historic city centre with its ancient narrow streets, medieval churches, Ro-man, Viking & National Railway Museums & the York Minster. Licensed. Sauna. Car park.
E-mail: j+k@ascot-house-york.demon.co.uk
www.ascothouseyork.com

June & Keith Wood   *Ascot House*   *80 East Parade*   *York YO31 7YH*   *Yorkshire*
Tel: (01904) 426826   Fax 01904 431077   Open: ALL YEAR   Map Ref No. 31

Holmwood House Hotel.   York.

Yorkshire

rate £ from - to / per person	children taken	evening meals	animals taken
£23.00 to £32.00	Y	N	N

see PHOTO over p. 330

VISA: M'CARD: AMEX:

The Bentley Hotel

Near Rd: A.19

The Bentley really is the place to stay if you're looking for the following: an elegant Victorian town house offering en-suite accommodation in rooms furnished with quality, care & comfort in mind; views of York Minster across parkland; delicious breakfasts; guaranteed friendliness, help & courtesy; 8-10 mins' walk into the city centre; parking permits; & above all, the ultimate resting place for horse racing enthusiasts. Children over 10.
E-mail: info@bentleyofyork.co.uk
www.bentleyofyork.co.uk

Andrew & Jennifer Neighbour   The Bentley Hotel   25 Grosvenor Terrace   York YO30 7AG
Tel: (01904) 644313   Fax 01904 644313   Open: FEB - DEC   Map Ref No. 31

All the establishments mentioned in this guide are members of
The Worldwide Bed & Breakfast Association

When booking your accommodation please mention
The Best Bed & Breakfast

The Bentley. York.

Scotland

Scotland

Scotland's culture & traditions, history & literature, languages & accents, its landscape & architecture, even its wildlife set it apart from the rest of Britain. Much of Scotland's history is concerned with the struggle to retain independence from England.

The Romans never conquered the Scottish tribes, but preferred to keep them at bay with Hadrian's Wall stretching across the Border country from Tynemouth to the Solway Firth.

Time lends glamour to events, but from the massacre of Glencoe to the Highland Clearances, much of Scotland's fate has been a harsh one. Robert the Bruce did rout the English enemy at Bannockburn after scaling the heights of Edinburgh Castle to take the city, but in later years Mary, Queen of Scots was to spend much of her life imprisoned by her sister Elizabeth I of England. Bonnie Prince Charlie (Charles Edward Stuart) led the Jacobite rebellion which ended in defeat at Culloden.

These events are recorded in the folklore & songs of Scotland. The Border & Highland Gatherings & the Common Ridings are more than a chance to wear the Tartan, they are reminders of national pride.

Highland Games are held throughout the country where local & national champions compete in events like tossing the caber & in piping contests. There are sword dances & Highland flings, the speciality of young men & boys wearing the full dress tartan of their clan.

Scotland's landscape is rich in variety from the lush green lowlands to the handsome splendour of the mountainous Highlands, from the rounded hills of the Borders to the far-flung islands of the Hebrides, Orkney & Shetland where the sea is ever-present.

There are glens & beautiful lochs deep in the mountains, a spectacular coastline of high cliffs & white sandy beaches, expanses of purple heather moorland where the sparkling water in the burns runs brown with peat, & huge skies bright with cloud & gorgeous sunsets.

Argyll & The Islands

This area has ocean & sea lochs, forests & mountains, 3000 miles of coastline, about 30 inhabited islands, the warming influence of the Gulf Stream & the tallest tree in Britain (in Strone Gardens, near Loch Fyne).

Sites both historic & prehistoric are to be found in plenty. There is a hilltop fort at Dunadd, near Crinan with curious cup-&-ring carvings, & numerous ancient sites surround Kilmartin, from burial cairns to grave slabs.

Kilchurn Castle is a magnificent ruin in contrast to the opulence of Inveraray. Both are associated with the once-powerful Clan Campbell. There are remains of fortresses built by the Lords of the Isles, the proud chieftains who ruled the west after driving out the Norse invaders in the 12th century.

Oban is a small harbour town accessible by road & rail & the point of departure for many of the islands including Mull.

Tobermory. Isle of Mull.

Scotland

Mull is a peaceful island with rugged seascapes, lovely walks & villages, a miniature railway & the famous Mull Little Theatre. It is a short hop from here to the tiny island of Iona & St. Columba's Abbey, cradle of Christianity in Scotland.

Coll & Tiree have lovely beaches & fields of waving barley. The grain grown here was once supplied to the Lords of the Isles but today most goes to Islay & into the whisky. Tiree has superb windsurfing.

Jura is a wilder island famous for its red deer. The Isles of Colonsay & Oronsay are joined at low water.

Gigha, 'God's Isle', is a fertile area of gardens with rare & semitropical plants. The Island of Staffa has Fingal's Cave.

The Borders, Dumfries & Galloway

The borderland with England is a landscape of subtle colours & contours from the round foothills of the Cheviots, purple with heather, to the dark green valley of the Tweed.

The Lammermuir Hills sweep eastwards to a coastline of small harbours & the spectacular cliffs at St. Abbs Head where colonies of seabirds thrive.

The Border towns, set in fine countryside, have distinctive personalities. Hawick, Galashiels, Selkirk & Melrose all played their parts in the various Border skirmishes of this historically turbulent region & then prospered with a textile industry which survives today. They celebrate their traditions in the Common Riding ceremonies.

The years of destructive border warfare have left towers & castles throughout the country. Roxburgh was once a Royal castle & James II was killed here during a seige. Now there are only the shattered remains of the massive stone walls. Hermitage Castle is set amid wild scenery near Hawick & impressive Floors Castle stands above Kelso.

At Jedburgh the Augustine abbey is remarkably complete, & a visitors centre here tells the story of the four great Border Abbeys; Jedburgh itself, Kelso, Dryburgh & Melrose.

The lovely estate of Abbotsford where Sir Walter Scott lived & worked is near Melrose. A prolific poet & novelist, his most famous works are the Waverley novels written around 1800. His house holds many of his possessions, including a collection of armour. Scott's View is one of the best vantage points in the borderlands with a prospect of the silvery Tweed & the three distinctive summits of the Eildon Hills.

Eildon Hills.

There are many gracious stately homes. Manderston is a classical house of great luxury, & Mellerstain is the work of the Adam family. Traquair was originally a Royal hunting lodge. Its main gates were locked in 1745 after a visit from Bonnie Prince Charlie, never to be opened until a Stuart King takes the throne.

Dumfries & Galloway to the southwest is an area of rolling hills with a fine coastline.

Plants flourish in the mild air here & there are palm trees at Ardwell House & the Logan Botanic Garden.

Scotland

The gardens at Castle Kennedy have rhododendrons, azaleas & magnolias & Threave Gardens near Castle Douglas are the National Trust for Scotland's School of gardening.

The Galloway Forest Park covers a vast area of lochs & hills & has views across to offshore Ailsa Craig. At Caerlaveroch Castle, an early Renaissance building near the coast of Dumfries, there is a national nature reserve.

The first church in Scotland was built by St. Ninian at Whithorn in 400 on a site now occupied by the 13th century priory. The spread of Christianity is marked by early memorial stones like the Latinus stone at Whithorn, & the abbeys of Dundrennan, Crossraguel, Glenluce & Sweetheart, named after its founder who carried her husband's heart in a casket & is buried with it in the abbey.

At Dumfries is the poet Burns' house, his mausoleum & the Burns Heritage Centre overlooking the River Nith.

In Upper Nithsdale the Mennock Pass leads to Wanlockhead & Leadhills, once centres of the lead-mining industry. There is a fascinating museum here & the opportunity of an underground trip.

Lowland

The Frith of Clyde & Glascow in the west, & the Firth of Forth with Edinburgh in the east are both areas of rich history, tradition & culture.

Edinburgh is the capital of Scotland & amongst the most visually exciting cities in the world. The New Town is a treasure trove of inspired neo-classical architecture, & below Edinburgh Castle high on the Rock, is the Old Town, a network of courts, closes, wynds & gaunt tenements around the Royal Mile.

The Palace of Holyrood House, home of Mary, Queen of Scots for several years overlooks Holyrood Park & nearby Arthur's Seat, is a popular landmark.

The City's varied art galleries include The Royal Scottish Academy, The National Gallery, Portrait Gallery, Gallery of Modern Art & many other civic & private collections.

The Royal Museum of Scotland displays superb historical & scientific material. The Royal Botanic Gardens are world famous.

Cultural life in Edinburgh peaks at Festival time in August. The official Festival, the Fringe, the Book Festival, Jazz Festival & Film Festival bring together artistes of international reputation.

The gentle hills around the city offer many opportunities for walking. The Pentland Hills are easily reached,

Inverary Castle.

with the Lammermuir Hills a little further south. There are fine beaches at Gullane, Yellowcraigs, North Berwick & at Dunbar.

Tantallon Castle, a 14th century stronghold, stands on the rocky Firth of Forth, & 17th century Hopetoun House, on the outskirts of the city is only one of a number of great houses in the area.

North of Edinburgh across the Firth of Forth lies the ancient Kingdom of Fife. Here is St. Andrews, a pleasant town on the seafront, an old university

Scotland

town & Scotland's ecclesiastical capital, but famous primarily for golf.

Glasgow is the industrial & business capital of Scotland. John Betjeman called it the 'finest Victorian city in Britain' & many buildings are remarkable examples of Victorian splendour, notably the City Chambers.

Many buildings are associated with the architect Charles Rennie MacKintosh; the Glasgow School of Art is one of them. Glasgow Cathedral is a perfect example of pre-Reformation Gothic architecture.

Glasgow is Scotland's largest city with the greatest number of parks & fine Botanic Garden. It is home to both the Scottish Opera & the Scottish Ballet, & has a strong & diverse cultural tradition from theatre to jazz. Its museums include the matchless Burrell Collection, & the Kelvingrove Museum & Art Gallery, which houses one of the best civic collections of paintings in Britain, as well as reflecting the city's engineering & shipbuilding heritage.

The coastal waters of the Clyde are world famous for cruising & sailing, with many harbours & marinas. The long coastline offers many opportunities for sea-angling from Largs to Troon & Prestwick, & right around to Luce Bay on the Solway.

There are many places for birdwatching on the Estuary, whilst the Clyde Valley is famous for its garden centres & nurseries.

Paisley has a mediaeval abbey, an observatory & a museum with a fine display of the famous 'Paisley' pattern shawls.

Further south, Ayr is a large seaside resort with sandy beach, safe bathing & a racecourse. In the Ayrshire valleys there is traditional weaving & lace & bonnet making, & Sorn, in the rolling countryside boasts its 'Best Kept Village' award.

Culzean Castle is one of the finest Adam houses in Scotland & stands in spacious grounds on the Ayrshire cliffs.

Robert Burns is Scotland's best loved poet, & 'Burns night' is widely celebrated. The region of Strathclyde shares with Dumfries & Galloway the title of 'Burns Country'. The son of a peasant farmer, Burns lived in poverty for much of his life. The simple house where he was born is in the village of Alloway. In the town of Ayr is the Auld Kirk where he was baptised & the footbridge of 'The Brigs of Ayr' is still in use. The Tam O'Shanter Inn is now a Burns museum & retains its thatched roof & simple fittings. The Burns Trail leads on to Mauchline where Possie Nansie's Inn remains. At Tarbolton the National Trust now care for the old house where Burns founded the 'Batchelors Club' debating society.

Perthshire, Loch Lomond & The Trossachs

By a happy accident of geology, the Highland Boundary fault which separates the Highlands from the Lowlands runs through Loch Lomond, close to the Trossachs & on through Perthshire, giving rise to marvellous scenery.

In former times Highlanders & Lowlanders raided & fought here. Great castles like Stirling, Huntingtower & Doune were built to protect the routes between the two different cultures.

Stirling was once the seat of Scotland's monarchs & the great Royal castle is set high on a basalt rock. The Guildhall & the Kirk of the Holy Rude are also interesting buildings in the town, with Cambuskenneth Abbey & the Bannockburn Heritage Centre close by.

Perth 'fair city' on the River Tay,

Scotland

has excellent shops & its own repertory theatre. Close by are the Black Watch Museum at Balhousie Castle, & the Branklyn Gardens, which are superb in May & June.

Scone Palace, to the north of Perth was home to the Stone or Scone of Destiny for nearly 500 years until its removal to Westminster. 40 kings of Scotland were crowned here.

Pitlochry sits amid beautiful Highland scenery with forest & hill walks, two nearby distilleries, the famous Festival theatre, Loch Faskally & the Dam Visitor Centre & Fish Ladder.

In the Pass of Killiecrankie, a short drive away, a simple stone marks the spot where the Highlanders charged barefoot to overwhelm the redcoat soldiers of General MacKay.

Queens View.

Famous Queen's View overlooks Loch Tummel beyond Pitlochry with the graceful peak of Schiehallion completing a perfect picture.

Other lochs are picturesque too; Loch Earn, Loch Katrine & bonnie Loch Lomond itself, & they can be enjoyed from a boat on the water. Ospreys nest at the Loch of the Lowes near Dunkeld.

Mountain trails lead through Ben Lawers & the 'Arrocher Alps' beyond Loch Lomond. The Ochils & the Campsie Fells have grassy slopes for walking. Near Callander are the Bracklinn Falls, the Callander Crags & the Falls of Leny.

Wooded areas include the Queen Elizabeth Forest Park & the Black Wood of Rannoch which is a fragment of an ancient Caledonian forest. There are some very tall old trees around Killiecrankie, & the world's tallest beech hedge - 26 metres high - grows at Meikleour near Blairgowrie.

Creiff & Blairgowrie have excellent golf courses set in magnificent scenery

The Grampians, Highlands & Islands

This is spacious countryside with glacier-scarred mountains & deep glens cut through by tumbling rivers. The Grampian Highlands make for fine mountaineering & walking.

There is excellent skiing at Glenshee, & a centre at the Lecht for the less experienced, whilst the broad tops of the giant mountains are ideal for cross-country skiing. The chair-lift at Glenshee is worth a visit at any season.

The Dee, The Spey & The Don flow down to the coastal plain from the heights. Some of the world's finest trout & salmon beats are on these rivers.

Speyside is dotted with famous distilleries from Grantown-on-Spey to Aberdeen, & the unique Malt Whisky Trail can be followed.

Royal Deeside & Donside hold a number of notable castles. Balmoral is the present Royal family's holiday home, & Kildrummy is a romantic ruin in a lovely garden. Fyvie Castle has five dramatic towers & stands in peaceful parkland. Nearby Haddo House, by contrast, is an elegant Georgian home.

There is a 17th century castle at Braemar, but more famous here is the Royal Highland Gathering. There are wonderful walks in the vicinity -

Scotland

Morrone Hill, Glen Quoich & the Linn O'Dee are just a few.

The city of Aberdeen is famed for its sparkling granite buildings, its university, its harbour & fish market & for North Sea Oil. It also has long sandy beaches & lovely year-round flower displays, of roses in particular.

Around the coast are fishing towns & villages. Crovie & Pennan sit below impressive cliffs. Buckie is a typical small port along the picturesque coastline of the Moray Firth.

The Auld Kirk at Cullen has fine architectural features & elegant Elgin has beautiful cathedral ruins. Pluscarden Abbey, Spynie Palace & Duffus Castle are all nearby.

Dunnottar Castle.

Nairn has a long stretch of sandy beach & a golf course with an international reputation. Inland are Cawdor Castle & Culloden Battlefield.

The Northern Highlands are divided from the rest of Scotland by the dramatic valley of the Great Glen. From Fort William to Inverness, sea lochs, canals & the depths of Loch Ness form a chain of waterways linking both coasts.

Here are some of the wildest & most beautiful landscapes in Britain. Far Western Knoydart, the Glens of Cannich & Affric, the mysterious lochs, including Loch Morar, deeper than the North Sea, & the marvellous coastline; all are exceptional.

The glens were once the home of crofting communities, & of the clansmen who supported the Jacobite cause. The wild scenery of Glencoe is a favourite with walkers & climbers, but it has a tragic history. Its name means 'the glen of weeping' & refers to the massacre of the MacDonald clan in 1692, when the Royal troops who had been received as guests treacherously attacked their hosts at dawn.

The valleys are empty today largely as a result of the infamous Highland Clearances in the 19th century when the landowners turned the tenant crofters off the land in order to introduce the more profitable Cheviot sheep. The emigration of many Scots to the U.S.A. & the British Colonies resulted from these events.

South of Inverness lie the majestic Cairngorms. The Aviemore centre provides both summer & winter sports facilities here.

To the north of Loch Ness are the remains of the ancient Caledonian forest where red deer & stags are a common sight on the hills. Rarer are sightings of the Peregrine Falcon, the osprey, the Golden Eagle & the Scottish wildcat. Kincraig has excellent wildlife parks.

Inverness is the last large town in the north, & a natural gateway to the Highlands & to Moray, the Black Isle & the north-east.

The east coast is characterised by the Firths of Moray, Cromarty & Dornoch & by its changing scenery from gentle pastureland, wooded hillsides to sweeping coastal cliffs.

On the Black Isle, which is not a true island but has a causeway & bridge links with the mainland, Fortrose & Rosemarkie in particular have lovely beaches, caves & coastal walks. There is golf on the headland at Rosemarkie & a 13th century cathedral of rosy pink sandstone stands in Fortrose.

Scotland

Scotland Gazeteer

Areas of outstanding natural beauty

It would be invidious, not to say almost impossible, to choose any particular area of Scotland as having a more beautiful aspect than the entire country is a joy to the traveller. The rugged Highlands, the great glens, tumbling waters, tranquil lochs - the deep countryside or the wild coastline - simply come & choose your own piece of paradise.

Historic Houses & Castles

Bowhill - Nr. Selkirk
18th-19th century - home of the Duke of Bucceleugh & Queensberry. Has an outstanding collection of pictures by Canaletto, Claude, Gainsborough, Reynolds & Leonardo da Vinci. Superb silver, porcelain & furniture. 16th & 17th century miniatures.

Traquair House - Innerleithen
A unique & ancient house being the oldest inhabited home in Scotland. It is rich in associations with every form of political history & after Bonnie Prince Charlie passed through its main gates in 1745 no other visitor has been allowed to use them. There are treasures in the house dating from 12th century, & it has an 18th century library & a priest's room with secret stairs

Linlithgow Palace - Linlithgow
The birthplace of Mary, Queen of Scots.

Stirling Castle - Stirling
Royal Castle.

Drumlanrigg Castle - Nr. Thornhill
17th century castle of pale pink stone - romantic & historic - wonderful art treasures including a magnificent Rembrandt & a huge silver chandelier. Beautiful garden setting.

Braemar Castle - Braemar
17th century castle of great historic interest. Has round central tower with spiral staircase giving it a fairy-tale appearance.

Drum Castle - Nr. Aberdeen
Dating in part from 13th century, it has a great square tower.

Cawdor Castle - Nairn
14th century fortress - like castle - has always been the home of the Thanes of Cawdor - background to Shakespeare's Macbeth.

Dunvegan Castle - Isle of Skye
13th century - has always been the home of the Chiefs of McLeod.

Hopetoun House - South Queensferry
Very fine example of Adam architecture & has a fine collection of pictures & furniture. Splendid landscaped grounds.

Inverary Castle - Argyll
Home of the Dukes of Argyll, 18th century - Headquarters of Clan Campbell.

Burn's Cottage - Alloway
Birthplace of Robert Burns - 1659 - thatched cottage - museum of Burns' relics.

Bachelors' Club - Tarbolton
17th century house - thatched - where Burns & friends formed their club - 1780.

Blair Castle - Blair Atholl
Home of the Duke of Atholl, 13th century Baronial mansion - collection of Jacobite relics, armour, paintings, china & many other items.

Glamis Castle - Angus
17th century remodelling in Chateau style - home of the Earl of Strathmore & Kinghorne. Very attractive castle - lovely grounds by Capability Brown.

Scone Palace - Perth
has always been associated with seat of Government of Scotland from earliest times. The Stone of Destiny was removed from the Palace in 1296 & taken to Westminster Abbey. Present palace rebuilt in early 1800's still incorporating parts of the old. Lovely gardens.

Edinburgh Castle
Fortress standing high over the town - famous for military tattoo.

Culzean Castle & Country Park - Maybole
Fine Adam house & spacious gardens perched on Ayrshire cliff.

Dunrobin Castle - Golspie
Ancient seat of the Earls & Dukes of Sutherland.

Eilean Donan Castle - Wester Ross
13th century castle, Jacobite relics.

Manderston - Duns
Great classical house with only silver staircase in the world. Stables, marble dairy, formal gardens.

Scotland

Cathedrals & Churches

Dunfermline Abbey - Dunfermline
Norman remains of beautiful church.
Modern east end & tower.

Edinburgh (Church of the Holy Rood)
15th century - was divided into two in 17th
century & re-united 1938. Here Mary,
Queen of Scots was crowned.

Glasgow (St. Mungo)
12th-15th century cathedral - 19th century
interior. Central tower with spire.

Kirkwall (St. Magnus)
12th century cathedral with very fine nave.

Falkirk Old Parish Church - Falkirk
The spotted appearance (faw) of the
church (kirk) gave the town its name. The
site of the church has been used since 7th
century, with succesive churches built
upon it. The present church was much
rebuilt in 19th century. Interesting
historically.

St Columba's Abbey - Iona

Museums & Galleries

Agnus Folk Museum - Glamis
17th century cottages with stone slab
roofs, restored by the National Trust for
Scotland & houses a fine folk collection.

Mary, Queen of Scots' House - Jedburgh
Life & times of the Queen along with
paintings, etc.

Andrew Carnegie Birthplace -
Dunfermline
The cottage where he was born is now
part of a museum showing his life's work.

Aberdeen Art Gallery & Museum -
Aberdeen
Sculpture, paintings, watercolours, prints
& drawings. Applied arts. Maritime
museum exhibits.

Provost Skene's House - Aberdeen
17th century house now exhibiting local
domestic life, etc.

Highland Folk Museum - Kingussie
Examples of craft work & tools - furnished
cottage with mill.

West Highland Museum - Fort William
Natural & local hsitory. Relics of Jacobites
& exhibition of the '45 Rising.

Clan Macpherson House - Newtonmore
Relics of the Clan.

Glasgow Art Gallery & Museum -
Glasgow
Archaeology, technology, local & natural
history. Old Masters, tapestries, porcelain,
glass & silver, etc. Sculpture.

Scottish National Gallery - Edinburgh
20th century collection - paintings &
sculpture - Arp, Leger, Giacometti,
Matisse, Picasso. Modern Scottish
painting.

**National Museum of Antiquities in
Scotland** - Edinburgh
Collection from Stone Age to modern
times - Relics of Celtic Church, Stuart
relics, Highland weapons, etc.

Gladstone Court - Biggar
Small indoor street of shops, a bank,
schoolroom, library, etc.

Burns' Cottage & Museum - Alloway
Relics of Robert Burns - National Poet.

Inverness Museum & Art Gallery -
Inverness
Social history, archaeology & cultural life
of the Highlands. Display of the Life of the
Clans - good Highland silver - crafts, etc.

Kirkintilloch - Nr. Glasgow
Auld Kirk Museum. Local history,
including archaeological specimens from
the Antonine Wall (Roman). Local
industries, exhibitions, etc

Pollock House & Park - Glasgow
18th century house with collection of
paintings, etc. The park is the home of the
award-winning Burrell Collection
The foregoing are but a few of the many
museums & galleries in Scotland - further
information is always freely available from
the Tourist Information.

Historic Monuments

Aberdour Castle - Aberdour
14th century fortification - part still roofed.

Balvenie Castle - Duffton
15th century castle ruins.

Cambuskenneth Abbey - Nr. Stirling
12th century abbey - seat of Bruce's
Parliament in 1326. Ruins.

Dryburgh Abbey - Dryburgh
Remains of monastery.

Loch Leven Castle - Port Glasgow
15th century ruined stronghold - once lived
in by Mary, Queen of Scots.

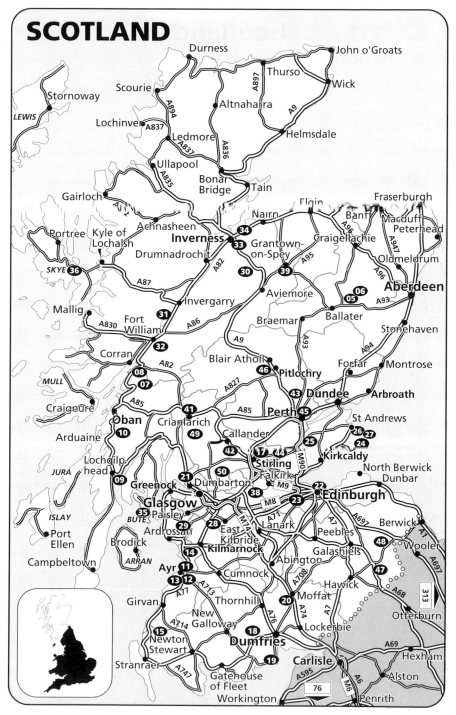

SCOTLAND

SCOTLAND
Map references

05	Chambers	22	Hunt	38	Hunter
06	D. White	22	C.Hamilton	39	M. Stewart
07	Broadbent	22	Robins	41	Gaughan
08	Sutherland	22	Fraser	42	Graham
09	Nicol	22	Drummond	43	Andrew
10	Oatts	22	A.Vidler	44	Lindsay
11	C.McDonald	23	D.Scott	45	Clewley
12	Martin	24	Lawson	46	Maxwell
13	Gemmell	25	Steven	46	Sanderson
14	Payne	26	Fyfe	46	Mathieson
15	Sweeney	27	Erskine	47	Irvine
17	O'Dell	28	Allison	48	B.Smith
18	Dickson	29	Anderson	49	Wilson
19	Fordyce	30	Gardner	50	Haslam
20	Whitsell	31	Cairns		
21	Macdonald	32	Campbell		
22	Sandeman	32	Henderson		
22	Stanley	33	Parsons		
22	McWilliams	34	Pottie		
22	D.Vidler	35	Harrison		
22	Urquhart	36	Wilcken		
22	Redmayne				
22	Walton				
22	Della-Porta				
22	Leishman				
22	Hill				
22	G. Stuart				
22	Virtue				
22	Welch				
22	Stark				

OUTER HEBRIDES
LEWIS
WESTERN ISLES
SKYE
HIGHLANDS
MORAY
INNER HEBRIDES
ABERDEENSHIRE
ABERDEEN
MULL
PERTHSHIRE & KINROSS
ANGUS
JURA
ARGYLL & BUTE
DUNDEE
ISLAY
STIRLING
FIFE
EAST LOTHIAN
NORTH AYRSHIRE
ARRAN
SOUTH LANARKSHIRE
EAST AYRSHIRE
BORDERS
SOUTH AYRSHIRE
DUMFRIES & GALLOWAY

1 INVERCLYDE
2 DUNBARTON & CLYDEBANK
3 RENFREWSHIRE
4 EAST RENFREWSHIRE
5 GLASGOW
6 EAST DUNBARTONSHIRE
7 NORTH LANARKSHIRE
8 FALKIRK
9 CLACKMANNAN
10 WEST LOTHIAN
11 EDINBURGH
12 MID LOTHAIN

rate £ from - to per person	children taken	evening meals	animals taken

---

| £35.00 to £35.00 | Y | Y | Y |

Tigh na Geald

Near Rd: A.93

Tigh na Geald is a beautiful Victorian house overlooking the village green in the centre of Aboyne on Royal Deeside. With Aberdeen & Balmoral only 30 mins' away it is the perfect base for touring. There are 2 large double bedrooms, 1 with en-suite bathroom & the other with private shower room. Guests have exclusive use of a comfortable sitting room & access to the gardens (with croquet). Dinner by arrangement. Fluent French spoken. Animals by arrangement.
E-mail: chambers@planet-talk.co.uk

Mrs Julia Chambers   Tigh na Geald   Ballater Road   Aboyne AB34 5HY   Aberdeenshire
Tel: (013398) 86868   Fax 013398 85808   Open: APR - OCT   Map Ref No. 05

| £30.00 to £40.00 | Y | Y | N |

(no smoking)

Lys-Na-Greyne House

Near Rd: A.93

Lys-Na-Greyne is a beautiful Edwardian mansion situated in idyllic surroundings on the banks of the River Dee on the outskirts of Aboyne in Royal Deeside, in grounds of 3 acres. Ideal for exploring the surrounding countryside where there are many castles & places of historic interest. Golf, riding, fishing, hillwalking & tennis available locally. Shooting available by arrangement. All rooms have en-suite/private bathroom & breathtaking views over the garden or river. Balmoral 30 mins.
E-mail: david@lysnagreyne.freeserve.co.uk
www.aboutscotland.com

David & Meg White   Lys-Na-Greyne House   Rhu-Na-Haven Road   Aboyne AB34 5JD   Aberdeenshire
Tel: (013398) 87397   Fax 013398 86441   Open: ALL YEAR   Map Ref No. 06

| £28.00 to £34.00 | Y | Y | Y |

(no smoking)

Lochside Cottage

Near Rd: A.828

Total peace on the shore of Loch Baile Mhic Chailen, in an idyllic glen of outstanding beauty. There are many walks from the cottage garden; or, visit Fort William, Glencoe & Oban, from where you can board a steamer to explore the Western Isles. At the end of the day, a warm welcome awaits you: delicious home-cooked dinner, a log fire & a perfect night's sleep in one of 3 en-suite bedrooms. Children & animals by arrangement.
E-mail: broadbent@lochsidecottage.fsnet.co.uk
www.lochsidecottage.fsnet.co.uk

Earle & Stella Broadbent   Lochside Cottage   Fasnacloich   Appin PA38 4BJ   Argyll
Tel: (01631) 730216   Fax 01631 730216   Open: ALL YEAR   Map Ref No. 07

| £45.00 to £60.00 | Y | Y | Y |

see PHOTO over
p. 342

VISA: M'CARD: AMEX:

Ardsheal House

Near Rd: A.828

Ardsheal House is spectacularly situated on the shores of Loch Linnhe, in 800 acres of woodlands, fields & gardens. This historic mansion is elegantly furnished throughout with family antiques & pictures, & offers 3 en-suite bedrooms which are attractive & well-appointed. The food at Ardsheal is excellent. It delights the eye & pleases the palate, & includes local fresh produce & home-made bread & preserves. (Dinner is available from Oct. to Apr.) Animals by arrangement.
E-mail: info@ardsheal.co.uk
www.ardsheal.co.uk

Neil & Philippa Sutherland   Ardsheal House   Kentallen of Appin PA38 4BX   Argyll
Tel: (01631) 740227   Fax 01631 740342   Open: ALL YEAR (Excl. Xmas)   Map Ref No. 08

Ardsheal House. Kentallen of Appin.

rate £ from - to per person	children taken	evening meals	animals taken

---

£35.00 to £50.00

Y | Y | Y

VISA: M'CARD:

Allt-na-Craig

Near Rd: A.83

Hamish & Charlotte warmly welcome all their guests to Allt-na-Craig, a lovely old Victorian mansion set in picturesque grounds overlooking Loch Fyne. 5 comfortable en-suite bedrooms with tea/coffee makers, hairdryers & T.V. A guests' drawing room with open fire & dining room is also available. This is a perfect base for outdoor activities, like hillwalking, fishing, golf, riding & windsurfing, or for visiting the islands. Dinner by arrangement.
E-mail: info.allt-na-craig@virgin.net
www.allt-na-craig.co.uk

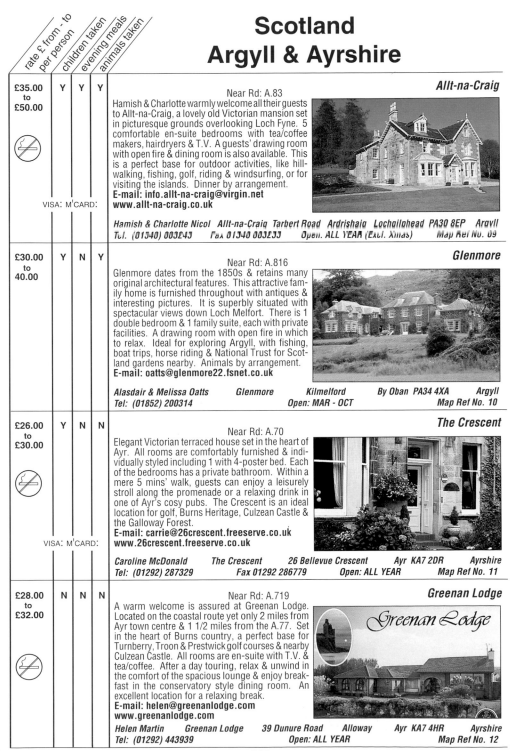

Hamish & Charlotte Nicol   Allt-na-Craig   Tarbert Road   Ardrishaig   Lochgilphead PA30 8EP   Argyll
Tel. (01546) 603245   Fax 01546 603255   Open: ALL YEAR (Excl. Xmas)   Map Ref No. 09

£30.00 to 40.00

Y | N | Y

Glenmore

Near Rd: A.816

Glenmore dates from the 1850s & retains many original architectural features. This attractive family home is furnished throughout with antiques & interesting pictures. It is superbly situated with spectacular views down Loch Melfort. There is 1 double bedroom & 1 family suite, each with private facilities. A drawing room with open fire in which to relax. Ideal for exploring Argyll, with fishing, boat trips, horse riding & National Trust for Scotland gardens nearby. Animals by arrangement.
E-mail: oatts@glenmore22.fsnet.co.uk

Alasdair & Melissa Oatts   Glenmore   Kilmelford   By Oban PA34 4XA   Argyll
Tel: (01852) 200314   Open: MAR - OCT   Map Ref No. 10

£26.00 to £30.00

Y | N | N

VISA: M'CARD:

The Crescent

Near Rd: A.70

Elegant Victorian terraced house set in the heart of Ayr. All rooms are comfortably furnished & individually styled including 1 with 4-poster bed. Each of the bedrooms has a private bathroom. Within a mere 5 mins' walk, guests can enjoy a leisurely stroll along the promenade or a relaxing drink in one of Ayr's cosy pubs. The Crescent is an ideal location for golf, Burns Heritage, Culzean Castle & the Galloway Forest.
E-mail: carrie@26crescent.freeserve.co.uk
www.26crescent.freeserve.co.uk

Caroline McDonald   The Crescent   26 Bellevue Crescent   Ayr KA7 2DR   Ayrshire
Tel: (01292) 287329   Fax 01292 286779   Open: ALL YEAR   Map Ref No. 11

£28.00 to £32.00

N | N | N

Greenan Lodge

Near Rd: A.719

A warm welcome is assured at Greenan Lodge. Located on the coastal route yet only 2 miles from Ayr town centre & 1 1/2 miles from the A.77. Set in the heart of Burns country, a perfect base for Turnberry, Troon & Prestwick golf courses & nearby Culzean Castle. All rooms are en-suite with T.V. & tea/coffee. After a day touring, relax & unwind in the comfort of the spacious lounge & enjoy breakfast in the conservatory style dining room. An excellent location for a relaxing break.
E-mail: helen@greenanlodge.com
www.greenanlodge.com

Greenan Lodge

Helen Martin   Greenan Lodge   39 Dunure Road   Alloway   Ayr KA7 4HR   Ayrshire
Tel: (01292) 443939   Open: ALL YEAR   Map Ref No. 12

	rate £ from - to per person	children taken	evening meals	animals taken

Dunduff House

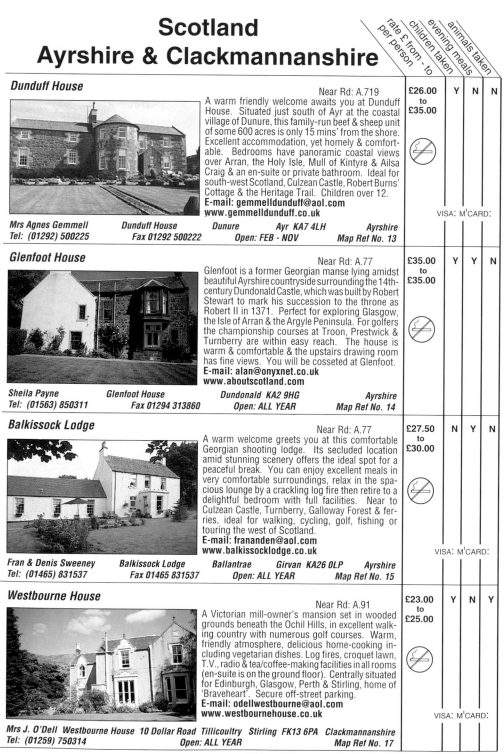

Near Rd: A.719

A warm friendly welcome awaits you at Dunduff House. Situated just south of Ayr at the coastal village of Dunure, this family-run beef & sheep unit of some 600 acres is only 15 mins' from the shore. Excellent accommodation, yet homely & comfortable. Bedrooms have panoramic coastal views over Arran, the Holy Isle, Mull of Kintyre & Ailsa Craig & an en-suite or private bathroom. Ideal for south-west Scotland, Culzean Castle, Robert Burns' Cottage & the Heritage Trail. Children over 12.

E-mail: gemmelldunduff@aol.com
www.gemmelldunduff.co.uk

£26.00 to £35.00 — Y — N — N

VISA: M'CARD:

Mrs Agnes Gemmell   Dunduff House   Dunure   Ayr KA7 4LH   Ayrshire
Tel: (01292) 500225   Fax 01292 500222   Open: FEB - NOV   Map Ref No. 13

Glenfoot House

Near Rd: A.77

Glenfoot is a former Georgian manse lying amidst beautiful Ayrshire countryside surrounding the 14th-century Dundonald Castle, which was built by Robert Stewart to mark his succession to the throne as Robert II in 1371. Perfect for exploring Glasgow, the Isle of Arran & the Argyle Peninsula. For golfers the championship courses at Troon, Prestwick & Turnberry are within easy reach. The house is warm & comfortable & the upstairs drawing room has fine views. You will be cosseted at Glenfoot.

E-mail: alan@onyxnet.co.uk
www.aboutscotland.com

£35.00 to £35.00 — Y — Y — N

Sheila Payne   Glenfoot House   Dundonald KA2 9HG   Ayrshire
Tel: (01563) 850311   Fax 01294 313860   Open: ALL YEAR   Map Ref No. 14

Balkissock Lodge

Near Rd: A.77

A warm welcome greets you at this comfortable Georgian shooting lodge. Its secluded location amid stunning scenery offers the ideal spot for a peaceful break. You can enjoy excellent meals in very comfortable surroundings, relax in the spacious lounge by a crackling log fire then retire to a delightful bedroom with full facilities. Near to Culzean Castle, Turnberry, Galloway Forest & ferries, ideal for walking, cycling, golf, fishing or touring the west of Scotland.

E-mail: frananden@aol.com
www.balkissocklodge.co.uk

£27.50 to £30.00 — N — Y — N

VISA: M'CARD:

Fran & Denis Sweeney   Balkissock Lodge   Ballantrae   Girvan KA26 0LP   Ayrshire
Tel: (01465) 831537   Fax 01465 831537   Open: ALL YEAR   Map Ref No. 15

Westbourne House

Near Rd: A.91

A Victorian mill-owner's mansion set in wooded grounds beneath the Ochil Hills, in excellent walking country with numerous golf courses. Warm, friendly atmosphere, delicious home-cooking including vegetarian dishes. Log fires, croquet lawn, T.V., radio & tea/coffee-making facilities in all rooms (en-suite is on the ground floor). Centrally situated for Edinburgh, Glasgow, Perth & Stirling, home of 'Braveheart'. Secure off-street parking.

E-mail: odellwestbourne@aol.com
www.westbournehouse.co.uk

£23.00 to £25.00 — Y — N — Y

VISA: M'CARD:

Mrs J. O'Dell   Westbourne House   10 Dollar Road   Tillicoultry   Stirling FK13 6PA   Clackmannanshire
Tel: (01259) 750314   Open: ALL YEAR   Map Ref No. 17

rate £ from - to per person	children taken	evening meals	animals taken	

Chipperkyle

£36.00 to £36.00 — Y N N

Near Rd: A.75

Chipperkyle is a beautiful 18th-century Georgian house, without a hint of formality. The Dicksons are both engaging & sociable & will endeavour to make you feel at ease in their elegant home. Bedrooms are light & charming decorated with cast iron beds, excellent furniture & masses of books. An attractive sitting room with feng shui cabinet. 200 acres of grazing land with a dog, cat, donkey & free-ranging hens. Threave & Logan gardens, Drumlanrig & Culzean are within an easy drive.
E-mail: dickson@chipperkyle.freeserve.co.uk

Catriona & Willie Dickson Chipperkyle Kirkpatrick Durham Castle Douglas DG7 3EY Dumfriesshire
Tel: (01556) 650223   Fax (01556) 650223   Open: ALL YEAR   Map Ref No. 18

Cavens House

£50.00 to £70.00 — Y Y N

Near Rd: A.710

Formerly an old mansion with a strong American historical connection, Cavens, now a charming small country house hotel, offers 6 comfortable en-suite bedrooms. 2 lounges with open fires add to the ambience of the house. Standing in 11 acres of gardens & woodland, it is ideal for those wishing to explore the joys of the Solway Coast, with its beautiful scenery & beaches. Sailing, walking, golfing, shooting, fishing & riding by arrangement. A friendly atmosphere. Award-winning cuisine.
E-mail: enquiries@cavens.com
www.cavens.com

VISA: M'CARD: AMEX:

Angus Fordyce   Cavens House   Kirkbean   Dumfries DG2 8AA   Dumfriesshire
Tel: (01387) 880234   Fax 01387 880467   Open: ALL YEAR   Map Ref No. 19

Hartfell House

£25.00 to £30.00 — Y N Y

Near Rd: A.701

Hartfell House is a splendid Victorian manor house located in a rural setting overlooking the hills, yet only a few mins' walk from the town. A listed building known locally for its fine interior woodwork. Accommodation is in 7 spacious & tastefully furnished bedrooms, each with en-suite facilities. Standing in gardens of lawns & trees, & providing an atmosphere of peaceful relaxation. Your hosts speak Japanese & welcome overseas visitors.
E-mail: enquiries@hartfellhouse.co.uk
www.hartfellhouse.co.uk

Mary Whitsell & Peter Sturman Hartfell House Hartfell Crescent Moffat DG10 9AL Dumfriesshire
Tel: (01683) 220153   Open: ALL YEAR (Excl. Xmas & New Year)   Map Ref No. 20

Kirkton House

£29.50 to £39.50 — Y Y Y

Near Rd: A.814

Experience a blend of "olde worlde" charm, modern amenities & superb views at this converted 18/19th-century farmhouse, set in a tranquil location & yet handy for Glasgow Airport (20/25 mins'), Loch Lomond, The Trossachs & most West Highland routes. En-suite bedrooms. A roaring fire on chilly evenings. Enjoy home-cooked food & good wine at dinner by oil lamplight. The dining room has the original stone walls & a fireplace, with the old swee from which the cooking pots were hung.
E-mail: bbiw@kirktonhouse.co.uk
www.kirktonhouse.co.uk

VISA: M'CARD: AMEX:

Mr & Mrs Macdonald Kirkton House Darleith Road Cardross Dumbarton G82 5EZ Dunbartonshire
Tel: (01389) 841951   Fax (01389) 841868   Open: FEB - NOV   Map Ref No. 21

Scotland
Edinburgh

Sandeman House

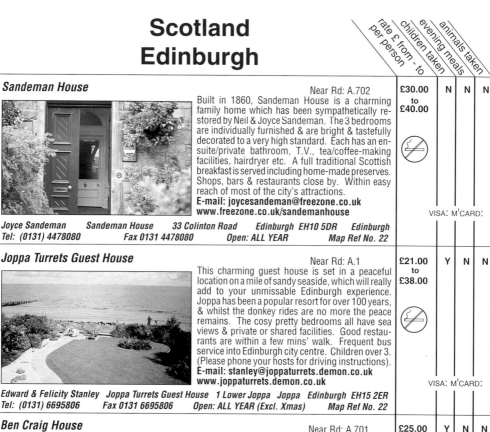

Near Rd: A.702

Built in 1860, Sandeman House is a charming family home which has been sympathetically restored by Neil & Joyce Sandeman. The 3 bedrooms are individually furnished & are bright & tastefully decorated to a very high standard. Each has an en-suite/private bathroom, T.V., tea/coffee-making facilities, hairdryer etc. A full traditional Scottish breakfast is served including home-made preserves. Shops, bars & restaurants close by. Within easy reach of most of the city's attractions.
E-mail: joycesandeman@freezone.co.uk
www.freezone.co.uk/sandemanhouse

£30.00 to £40.00   N   N   N

VISA: M'CARD:

Joyce Sandeman   Sandeman House   33 Colinton Road   Edinburgh EH10 5DR   Edinburgh
Tel: (0131) 4478080   Fax 0131 4478080   Open: ALL YEAR   Map Ref No. 22

Joppa Turrets Guest House

Near Rd: A.1

This charming guest house is set in a peaceful location on a mile of sandy seaside, which will really add to your unmissable Edinburgh experience. Joppa has been a popular resort for over 100 years, & whilst the donkey rides are no more the peace remains. The cosy pretty bedrooms all have sea views & private or shared facilities. Good restaurants are within a few mins' walk. Frequent bus service into Edinburgh city centre. Children over 3. (Please phone your hosts for driving instructions).
E-mail: stanley@joppaturrets.demon.co.uk
www.joppaturrets.demon.co.uk

£21.00 to £38.00   Y   N   N

VISA: M'CARD:

Edward & Felicity Stanley   Joppa Turrets Guest House   1 Lower Joppa   Joppa   Edinburgh EH15 2ER
Tel: (0131) 6695806   Fax 0131 6695806   Open: ALL YEAR (Excl. Xmas)   Map Ref No. 22

Ben Craig House

Near Rd: A.701

Ideally situated close to the city centre, an elegant Victorian villa retaining many period features. Enjoy a delicious Scottish breakfast cooked to order by your chef/proprietor & served in a delightful conservatory overlooking quiet gardens. Each of the bedrooms are en-suite with either bath and/or shower, colour T.V., radio/alarm & welcome tray. Guests are given a complimentary whisky or sherry on arrival. A warm & friendly welcome is assured. Secure private parking. Children over 8.
E-mail: bencraighouse@dial.pipex.com
www.bencraighouse.co.uk

£25.00 to £45.00   Y   N   N

see PHOTO over
p. 347

VISA: M'CARD:

Heather & James McWilliams   Ben Craig House   3 Craigmillar Park   Newington   Edinburgh EH16 3PG
Tel: (0131) 6672593   Fax 0131 6671109   Open: ALL YEAR (Excl. Xmas)   Map Ref No. 22

Kenvie Guest House

Near Rd: A.7, A.68

Kenvie Guest House is charming, comfortable, warm, friendly & inviting. This small Victorian town house is situated in a quiet residential street, 1 small block from the main road, leading to the city centre (an excellent bus service) & the bypass to all routes. Offering, for your comfort, lots of caring touches, including complimentary tea/coffee, colour T.V. & no-smoking rooms. Private facilities available. You are guaranteed a warm welcome from Richard & Dorothy.
E-mail: dorothy@kenvie.co.uk
www.kenvie.co.uk

£28.00 to £35.00   Y   N   N

VISA: M'CARD:

Dorothy Vidler   Kenvie Guest House   16 Kilmaurs Road   Edinburgh EH16 5DA   Edinburgh
Tel: (0131) 6681964   Fax 0131 6681926   Open: ALL YEAR   Map Ref No. 22

Ben Craig House. Edinburgh.

Scotland
Edinburgh

Kildonan Lodge Hotel

Near Rd: A.701

Ideally situated in central Edinburgh, Kildonan Lodge is an outstanding example of Victorian elegance providing the perfect setting for your visit to Scotland's capital. Relax & enjoy a 'dram' at the Honesty bar. Each of the individually designed en-suite bedrooms have T.V., 'phone, radio/alarm & welcome trays. Spa bath & 4-poster beds available in selected rooms. Car park. Dine by candlelight in Potters Fine Dining Restaurant.
E-mail: info@kildonanlodgehotel.co.uk
www.kildonanlodgehotel.co.uk

£39.00 to £65.00 — Y Y N

see PHOTO over
p. 349

VISA: M'CARD: AMEX:

Mrs Maggie Urquhart   Kildonan Lodge Hotel   27 Craigmillar Park   Edinburgh EH16 5PE   Edinburgh
Tel: (0131) 6672793   Fax 0131 6679777   Open: ALL YEAR (Excl. Xmas)   Map Ref No. 22

Kingsley Guest House

Near Rd: A.701

A warm, friendly welcome awaits you at this Victorian terraced villa. Offering 5 comfortably furnished bedrooms, each with either en-suite or private facilities, T.V. & tea/coffee-making facilities. A full English or Continental breakfast is served. Kingsley Guest House is conveniently situated in the south of the city with an excellent bus service at the door to & from the city centre with its many tourist attractions. Private parking.
E-mail: lyn.kingsley@virgin.net
www.kingsleyguesthouse.co.uk

£20.00 to £40.00 — Y N N

Mrs M. B. Redmayne   Kingsley Guest House   30 Craigmillar Park   Edinburgh EH16 5PS   Edinburgh
Tel: (0131) 6673177   Tel/Fax 0131 6678439   Open: ALL YEAR   Map Ref No. 22

Frederick House Hotel

Near Rd: A.8

Frederick House Hotel is perfectly situated in the very heart of Edinburgh's city centre, a stones' throw from Princes Street. All of the 45 newly refurbished & tastefully decorated bedrooms feature en-suite bathrooms (with bath & shower); breakfast is served in your room. Your hosts' aim is to make your stay as comfortable & relaxing as possible, with all modern conveniences combined together with an 'olde worlde' atmosphere.
E-mail: frederickhouse@ednet.co.uk
www.townhousehotels.co.uk

£25.00 to £65.00 — Y N N

VISA: M'CARD: AMEX:

Michael Gilbert   Frederick House Hotel   42 Frederick Street   Edinburgh EH2 1EX   Edinburgh
Tel: (0131) 2261999   Fax 0131 6247064   Open: ALL YEAR   Map Ref No. 22

Ellesmere Guest House

Near Rd: A.702

Guests are made welcome at this very elegant tastefully restored Victorian town house, quietly situated overlooking golf links in the centre of Edinburgh. Bedrooms are en-suite & decorated to a high standard & equipped with every comfort in mind. Delicious breakfasts are served. 'A home away from home.' Convenient for castle, Princes Street, Royal Mile, International Conference Centre, theatres & restaurants. Children over 12.
E-mail: celia@edinburghbandb.co.uk
www.edinburghbandb.co.uk

£30.00 to £40.00 — Y N N

Mrs Cecilia Leishman   Ellesmere Guest House   11 Glengyle Terrace   Edinburgh EH3 9LN   Edinburgh
Tel: (0131) 229 4823   Fax 0131 229 5285   Open: ALL YEAR   Map Ref No. 22

Kildonan Lodge Hotel. Edinburgh.

	rate £ from - to per person	children taken	evening meals	animals taken

Gerald's Place

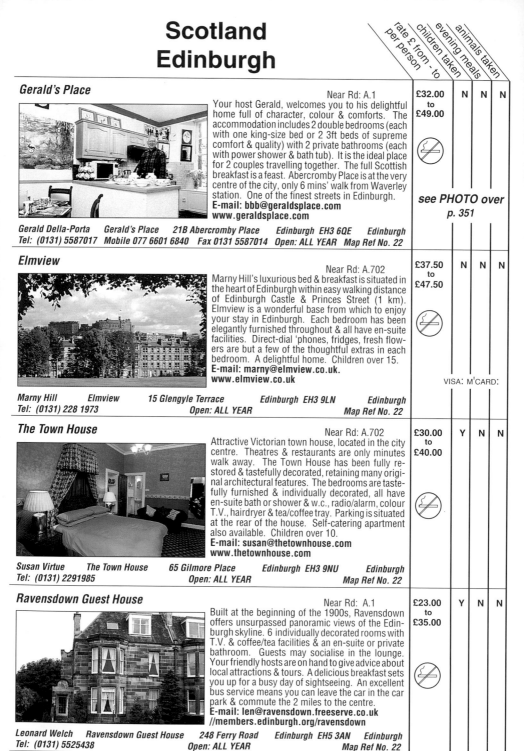

Near Rd: A.1

Your host Gerald, welcomes you to his delightful home full of character, colour & comforts. The accommodation includes 2 double bedrooms (each with one king-size bed or 2 3ft beds of supreme comfort & quality) with 2 private bathrooms (each with power shower & bath tub). It is the ideal place for 2 couples travelling together. The full Scottish breakfast is a feast. Abercromby Place is at the very centre of the city, only 6 mins' walk from Waverley station. One of the finest streets in Edinburgh.
E-mail: bbb@geraldsplace.com
www.geraldsplace.com

£32.00 to £49.00 — N N N

see PHOTO over
p. 351

Gerald Della-Porta   Gerald's Place   21B Abercromby Place   Edinburgh EH3 6QE   Edinburgh
Tel: (0131) 5587017   Mobile 077 6601 6840   Fax 0131 5587014   Open: ALL YEAR   Map Ref No. 22

Elmview

Near Rd: A.702

Marny Hill's luxurious bed & breakfast is situated in the heart of Edinburgh within easy walking distance of Edinburgh Castle & Princes Street (1 km). Elmview is a wonderful base from which to enjoy your stay in Edinburgh. Each bedroom has been elegantly furnished throughout & all have en-suite facilities. Direct-dial 'phones, fridges, fresh flowers are but a few of the thoughtful extras in each bedroom. A delightful home. Children over 15.
E-mail: marny@elmview.co.uk.
www.elmview.co.uk

£37.50 to £47.50 — N N N

VISA: M'CARD:

Marny Hill   Elmview   15 Glengyle Terrace   Edinburgh EH3 9LN   Edinburgh
Tel: (0131) 228 1973   Open: ALL YEAR   Map Ref No. 22

The Town House

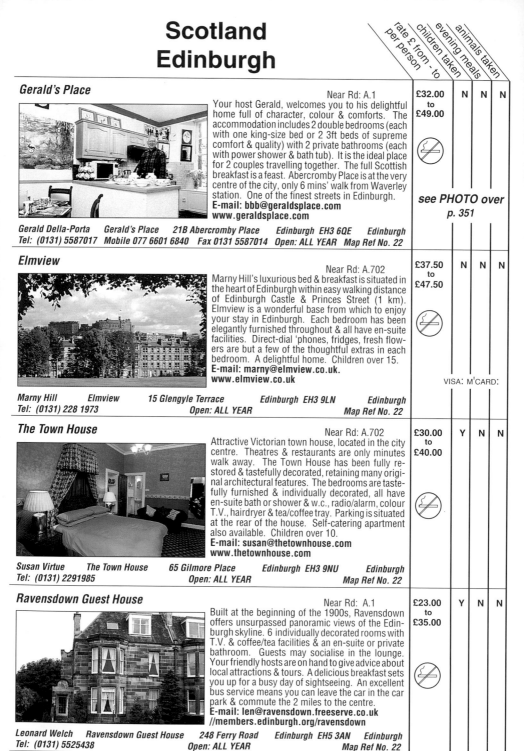

Near Rd: A.702

Attractive Victorian town house, located in the city centre. Theatres & restaurants are only minutes walk away. The Town House has been fully restored & tastefully decorated, retaining many original architectural features. The bedrooms are tastefully furnished & individually decorated, all have en-suite bath or shower & w.c., radio/alarm, colour T.V., hairdryer & tea/coffee tray. Parking is situated at the rear of the house. Self-catering apartment also available. Children over 10.
E-mail: susan@thetownhouse.com
www.thetownhouse.com

£30.00 to £40.00 — Y N N

Susan Virtue   The Town House   65 Gilmore Place   Edinburgh EH3 9NU   Edinburgh
Tel: (0131) 2291985   Open: ALL YEAR   Map Ref No. 22

Ravensdown Guest House

Near Rd: A.1

Built at the beginning of the 1900s, Ravensdown offers unsurpassed panoramic views of the Edinburgh skyline. 6 individually decorated rooms with T.V. & coffee/tea facilities & an en-suite or private bathroom. Guests may socialise in the lounge. Your friendly hosts are on hand to give advice about local attractions & tours. A delicious breakfast sets you up for a busy day of sightseeing. An excellent bus service means you can leave the car in the car park & commute the 2 miles to the centre.
E-mail: len@ravensdown.freeserve.co.uk
//members.edinburgh.org/ravensdown

£23.00 to £35.00 — Y N N

Leonard Welch   Ravensdown Guest House   248 Ferry Road   Edinburgh EH5 3AN   Edinburgh
Tel: (0131) 5525438   Open: ALL YEAR   Map Ref No. 22

Gerald's Place. Edinburgh.

Scotland
Edinburgh

The Stuarts B & B

Near Rd: A.702

25 years talking with guests have enabled the Stuarts to give you all the facilities you want. Their very central location & good-value rates do the rest. Your hosts have thought of everything. The spacious & luxurious bedrooms have comfortable twin beds, which become super king-size doubles. Edinburgh has so much to offer that Jon & Gloria recommend taking advantage of the discount for 3+ consecutive nights (also winter discount).
E-mail: BestBB@the-stuarts.com
www.the-stuarts.com

| | £35.00 to £47.50 | Y | N | N |

see PHOTO over p. 353

VISA: M'CARD: AMEX:

Jon & Gloria Stuart   The Stuarts B & B   17 Glengyle Terrace   Edinburgh EH3 9LN   Edinburgh
Tel: (0131) 2299559   Fax 0131 4776073   Open: ALL YEAR   Map Ref No. 22

Ben Cruachan

Near Rd: A.1

Guests are assured of a warm welcome & a friendly atmosphere at this attractive house, situated 1 km from Princes Street. Offering comfortable & tastefully furnished en-suite bedrooms, well-equipped with every comfort in mind & serving an excellent breakfast. Centrally situated within easy reach of the castle, Royal Mile, Holyrood Palace, shops, theatres & restaurants. Unrestricted parking & on all main bus routes.
E-mail: nan@bencruachan.com
www.bencruachan.com

| | £26.00 to £36.00 | N | N | N |

N. Stark   Ben Cruachan   17 McDonald Road   Edinburgh EH7 4LX   Edinburgh
Tel: (0131) 5563709   Open: APR - OCT   Map Ref No. 22

Ailsa Craig Hotel

Near Rd: A.1

Ailsa Craig Hotel is situated in the heart of Edinburgh near the city centre in one of the most prestigious terraces. This elegant Georgian town house hotel is situated only 10 mins' walk from Princes Street, Waverly Station & many attractions. 16 tastefully furnished & decorated bedrooms, all with en-suite facilities, 'phone, hairdryer, colour T.V. & tea/coffee-making facilities. A delicious breakfast & good evening meals are served.
E-mail: ailsacraighotel@ednet.co.uk
www.townhousehotels.co.uk

| | £25.00 to £50.00 | Y | Y | N |

VISA: M'CARD: AMEX:

Navin Varma   Ailsa Craig Hotel   24 Royal Terrace   Edinburgh EH7 5AB   Edinburgh
Tel: (0131) 5566055/5561022   Fax 0131 5566055   Open: ALL YEAR   Map Ref No. 22

Visit our website at:
http://www.bestbandb.co.uk

The Stuarts. Edinburgh.

	rate £ from - to per person	children taken	evening meals	animals taken

Sonas Guest House

Near Rd: A.701, A.7

Sonas Guest House is a delightful Victorian villa, cira 1876, built for the directors of the railways & quietly situated 1 mile from the city centre. The well-appointed en-suite bedrooms have a T.V., welcome tray & hairdryer. Delicious Scottish breakfasts are served. Parking. Irene & Dennis wish to welcome you to an idyllic base for exploring the attractions of Edinburgh. Many guests favour them with a return visit. 'Sonas' Gaelic for bliss.
E-mail: info@sonasguesthouse.com
www.sonasguesthouse.com

| £20.00 to £40.00 | Y | N | N |

Irene Robins   Sonas Guest House   3 East Mayfield   Newington   Edinburgh EH9 1SD   Edinburgh
Tel: (0131) 6672781   Open: ALL YEAR   Map Ref No. 22

Glenalmond Guest House

Near Rd: A.701

Glenalmond is an attractive family-run guest house, situated only 5 mins' from the city centre. The house is beautifully furnished throughout & offers 10 delightful bedrooms, many with either 4-poster or canopy beds. (5 ground floor rooms.) Each bedroom is spacious & has quality furnishings, T.V. etc. A full Scottish breakfast is served & includes porridge & home-baked scones. An elegant home. Parking. Children over 3.
E-mail: glen@almond25.freeserve.co.uk
www.almond25.freeserve.co.uk

| £25.00 to £50.00 | Y | N | N |

Deborah Fraser   Glenalmond Guest House   25 Mayfield Gardens   Edinburgh EH9 2BX   Edinburgh
Tel: (0131) 6682392   Fax 0131 6682392   Open: ALL YEAR   Map Ref No. 22

Parklands Guest House

Near Rd: A.701

Parklands is an attractive Victorian terraced house conveniently located 1 1/2 miles from Princes Street & all the main tourist attractions. Accommodation is in 6 bedrooms, each is furnished to a high standard & is fully equipped with en-suite/private facilities, colour T.V. & tea/coffee-making facilities. A delicious full Scottish breakfast is served. Nearby are many excellent restaurants. Parklands is family-run with a friendly atmosphere. You are assured of a warm welcome.
E-mail: reservations@parklands-guesthouse.co.uk

| £20.00 to £35.00 | Y | N | N |

Alan Drummond   Parklands Guest House   20 Mayfield Gardens   Edinburgh EH9 2BZ   Edinburgh
Tel: (0131) 6677184   Fax 0131 6672011   Open: ALL YEAR   Map Ref No. 22

Rowan Guest House

Near Rd: A.701, A.7

Elegant Victorian home in one of the city's loveliest areas with free parking & only a 10 min. bus ride to the centre. The castle, Royal Mile, restaurants & other amenities easily reached. The charmingly decorated bedrooms are comfortably & tastefully furnished with complimentary tea/coffee & biscuits. Breakfast, including traditional porridge & freshly baked scones, will keep you going until dinner! Friendly hosts. Restricted smoking.
E-mail: angela@rowan-house.co.uk
www.rowan-house.co.uk

| £24.00 to £37.00 | Y | N | N |

VISA: M'CARD:

Alan & Angela Vidler   Rowan Guest House   13 Glenorchy Terrace   Edinburgh EH9 2DQ   Edinburgh
Tel: (0131) 6672463   Fax 0131 6672463   Open: ALL YEAR   Map Ref No. 22

rate £ from - to per person | **children taken** | **evening meals taken** | **animals taken**

| £35.00 to £35.00 | Y | N | N |

🚭 (no smoking)

VISA: M'CARD: AMEX:

Ashcroft Farm Guest House

Near Rd: A.71

New farmhouse set in beautifully landscaped gardens, enjoying lovely views of the surrounding farmland. 10 miles from Edinburgh, 5 miles from the airport, city bypass, M.8/M.9, Ingliston & Livingston. Parking. Bedrooms, including a 4-poster, are attractively furnished in pine with co-ordinating fabrics. Good bus/train service to city centre (20 mins). Choice of breakfasts with home-made sausage, smoked salmon, kippers & even whisky marmalade. Children over 5.
E-mail: thescotts@ashcroftfarmhouse.com
www.ashcroftfarmhouse.com

Mr & Mrs Scott   Ashcroft Farm Guest House   East Calder   Nr. Edinburgh EH53 0ET   Edinburgh
Tel: (01506) 881810   Fax 01506 884327   Open: ALL YEAR   Map Ref No. 23

| £26.50 to £32.50 | Y | Y | Y |

🚭 (no smoking)

VISA: M'CARD: AMEX:

The Spindrift

Near Rd: A.917

Set in the picturesque fishing village of Anstruther, The Spindrift is an imposing, stone-built Victorian home with many original internal features carefully restored. 8 individually furnished bedrooms with en-suite/private bathrooms, T.V., 'phone, hospitality tray & more. Delicious evening meals are served. A well stocked 'honesty bar'. Only 10 mins' from St. Andrews with its world famous golf courses & excellent beaches. Ideal for central Scotland. Children over 10. Dogs by arrangement.
E-mail: info@thespindrift.co.uk
www.thespindrift.co.uk

Kenneth & Christine Lawson   The Spindrift   Pittenweem Road   Anstruther KY10 3DT   Fifeshire
Tel: (01333) 310573   Fax 01333 310573   Open: ALL YEAR (Excl. Xmas)   Map Ref No. 24

| £30.00 to £35.00 | Y | Y | N |

🚭 (no smoking)

VISA: M'CARD:

Ardchoille Farmhouse

Near Rd: A.91, B.936

Relax & enjoy the warm comfort, delicious Taste of Scotland food & the excellent hospitality at Ardchoille Farmhouse. 3 tastefully furnished twin-bedded rooms, each with an en-suite/private bathroom, colour T.V. A real coffee trays offering home-made butter shortbread. Large comfortable lounge, & elegant dining room with fine china & crystal. Dinner by arrangement. Close by the Royal Palace of Falkland, home of Mary Queen of Scots. 20 mins' from St. Andrews, & 1 hr Edinburgh. Ideal base for golfing & touring. Children over 12.
www.bestbandb.co.uk

Donald & Isobel Steven   Ardchoille Farmhouse   Dunshalt   Auchtermuchty KY14 7EY   Fifeshire
Tel: (01337) 828414   Fax 01337 828414   Open: ALL YEAR   Map Ref No. 25

| £30.00 to £35.00 | Y | Y | Y |

VISA: M'CARD: AMEX:

Kinkell House

Near Rd: A.917

Kinkell is a family home near St. Andrews where Sandy & Frippy Fyfe offer a warm welcome, good food & informal hospitality & are delighted for you to join them for dinner. Accommodation is in 3 very comfortable guest rooms. Kinkell runs down to the sea & has spectacular views of the coast & St. Andrews as well as access to walks on the coast. Some of the attractions of the area include golf, historic buildings, scenic villages, the sea & wonderful beaches. An elegant home.
E-mail: info@kinkell.com
www.kinkell.com

Sandy Fyfe   Kinkell House   St. Andrews KY16 8PN   Fifeshire
Tel: (01334) 472003   Fax 01334 475248   Open: ALL YEAR   Map Ref No. 26

Fifeshire
Glasgow & Inverness-shire

Cambo House

Near Rd: A. 917

The Erskine family home since 1688, this impressive Victorian mansion house, built in 1881, lies at the heart of a 1200-acre estate in one of the most unspoilt areas of Scotland yet is only 1 1/2 hours from Edinburgh & the Highlands. 2 comfortable & elegantly furnished bedrooms (1 with 4-poster) with en-suite/private facilities. The family welcome you to share the comfort of their home, absorb the beauty of the gardens & unwind in the restful atmosphere. Dinner & animals by arrangement.
E-mail: cambo@camboestate.com
www.camboestate.com

| £42.00 to £48.00 | Y | Y | Y |

VISA: M'CARD: AMEX:

Peter & Catherine Erskine   Cambo House   Kingsbarns   St. Andrews KY16 8QD   Fifeshire
Tel: (01333) 450313 Fax 01333 450987 Open: ALL YEAR (Excl. Xmas & New Year) Map Ref No. 27

New Borland B & B

Near Rd: A.726

Near the picturesque village of Eaglesham, yet only 9 miles from Glasgow, a warm Scottish welcome is assured at this converted barn. 2 twin rooms (en-suite) & 2 single rooms sharing a bathroom. All rooms have central heating, colour T.V., radio/alarm & hostess tray, & have recently been refurbished to a high standard. Lounge (log fire) & games room. Hearty Scottish breakfasts are served. Convenient for Glasgow, M.74, Loch Lomond, The Trossachs, Burns Country & the Burrell. Golf & fishing nearby. Children over 12.
E-mail: newborland@dial.pipex.com

| £25.00 to £25.00 | Y | N | N |

Mrs Fiona Allison   New Borland B & B   Glasgow Road   Eaglesham   Glasgow G76 0DN   Glasgow
Tel: (01355) 302051   Fax 01355 302051   Open: ALL YEAR   Map Ref No. 28

East Lochhead

Near Rd: A.760

East Lochhead is a large 100-year-old Scottish farmhouse commanding beautiful views to the south east over Barr Loch & the Renfrewshire hills. 3 beautifully furnished bedrooms with panoramic views, an en-suite/private bathroom, T.V. & tea/coffee facilities. Janet is an enthusiastic cook & the breakfast & dinner are delicious. (Vegetarian & special diets catered for.) An ideal base for visiting Glasgow & touring Ayrshire, the Clyde coast, the Trossachs (Rob Roy country) & Loch Lomond.
E-mail: admin@eastlochhead.co.uk
www.eastlochhead.co.uk

| £35.00 to £40.00 | Y | Y | Y |

VISA: M'CARD: AMEX:

Janet Anderson   East Lochhead   Largs Road   Lochwinnoch PA12 4DX   Glasgow
Tel: (01505) 842610   Fax 01505 842610   Open: ALL YEAR   Map Ref No. 29

Feith Mhor Lodge

Near Rd: A.9

Situated in a peaceful but accessible valley, 25 miles south of Inverness, Feith Mhor Lodge ('Fay Moor') offers bed & breakfast in an elegant Victorian country home with 6 comfortable & tastefully furnished en-suite bedrooms. Your hosts specialise in party bookings for groups enjoying the sporting activities of the area. Shooting, fishing, falconry & golf parties can be exclusively booked on a full-board basis. (Restricted smoking areas). A charming home.
E-mail: feith.mhor@btinternet.com
www.feithmhor.co.uk

| £20.00 to £28.00 | Y | Y | Y |

VISA: M'CARD: AMEX:

John Gardner   Feith Mhor Lodge   Carrbridge   Aviemore PH23 3AP   Inverness-shire
Tel: (01479) 841621   Open: ALL YEAR   Map Ref No. 30

The Grange. Fort William.

	rate £ from - to per person	children taken	evening meals	animals taken

Invergloy House

Near Rd: A.82
A really interesting Scottish coach house, dating back 120 years, offering 2 charming & comfortable rooms (1 double & 1 twin-bedded room), each with modern facilities including an en-suite shower room. 5 miles north of the village of Spean Bridge towards Inverness, it is signposted on the left, along a wooded drive. Guests have use of own sitting room, overlooking Loch Lochy in 50 acres of superb woodland of rhododendron & azaleas. Fishing from the private beach. Children over 8.
E-mail: cairns@invergloy-house.co.uk
www.invergloy-house.co.uk

£26.00 to £26.00 — Y — N — N

Mrs Margaret Cairns   Invergloy House   Spean Bridge   Nr. Fort William PH34 4DY   Inverness-shire
Tel: (01397) 712681   Fax 01397 712681   Open: ALL YEAR   Map Ref No. 31

The Grange

Near Rd: A.82
Tucked away in its own grounds, The Grange sits quietly overlooking Loch Linnhe, yet it is only 10 mins' walk from the town centre & local restaurants. Log fires, crystal, fresh flowers, antiques, loch views, all add to the charm of this luxury B & B in the breathtaking scenery of the Scottish Highlands. One night is not enough to enjoy The Grange or the area surrounding, whether it be walking in famous Glen Nevis, sailing on Loch Linnhe or visiting the distillery.
E-mail: jcampbell@grangefortwilliam.com
www.thegrange-scotland.co.uk

£42.00 to £48.00 — N — N — N

see PHOTO over
p. 357

VISA: M'CARD:

Mrs Joan Campbell   The Grange   Grange Road   Fort William PH33 6JF   Inverness-shire
Tel: (01397) 705516   Fax 01397 701595   Open: MAR - NOV   Map Ref No. 32

Ashburn House

Near Rd: A.82
Ashburn is a splendid Victorian house personally run by Highland hosts. Quietly situated by the shores of Loch Linnhe only 600 yards from the town centre & among others the renowned Crannog Seafood Restaurant. An excellent base for touring the Highlands. Sample an imaginative Highland breakfast, served at your own individual table, complemented with freshly baked scones from the Aga. 7 en-suite bedrooms, 4 with super-king-size beds. Parking. Brochure & weekly rates available.
E-mail: ashburn.house@tinyworld.co.uk
www.highland5star.co.uk

£30.00 to £45.00 — Y — N — N

see PHOTO over
p. 359

VISA: M'CARD: AMEX:

B. B. Henderson   Ashburn House   Achintore Road   Fort William PH33 6RQ   Inverness-shire
Tel: (01397) 706000   Fax 01397 702024   Open: FEB - NOV   Map Ref No. 32

Ballindarroch House

Near Rd: A.9, B.862
Ballindarroch was originally built as a shooting lodge around 1870, & stands in 10 acres of woodland gardens above the Caledonian Canal. Decorated with hand-painted wallpaper & furnished with antiques & an eclectic selection of family pieces, the house offers a totally relaxing & peaceful environment only 10 mins' from Inverness. The generous breakfast includes local specialities, homemade bread & preserves. Lovely river & woodland walks. French, Italian, Spanish & German spoken.
E-mail: ali.phil@ntlworld.com
www.milford.co.uk/go/ballindarroch.html

£25.00 to £35.00 — Y — N — Y

Alison Parsons & Philip Alvy   Ballindarroch House   Aldourie   Inverness IV2 6EL   Inverness-shire
Tel: (01463) 751348   Fax 01463 751372   Open: ALL YEAR   Map Ref No. 33

Ashburn House. Fort William.

Inverness-shire
Isle of Bute & Isle of Skye

Easter Dalziel Farmhouse

Near Rd: A.96

This Scottish farming family offer the visitor a friendly Highland welcome on their 200-acre stock/arable farm. 3 charming bedrooms are available in the delightful early-Victorian farmhouse. The lounge has log fire & T.V.. Delicious home cooking & baking served, including a choice of breakfasts. Dinner by arrangement. Ideal base for exploring the scenic Highlands. Local attractions are Cawdor Castle, Culloden, Fort George, Loch Ness & nearby Castle Stuart. Animals by arrangement.
E-mail: BBB@easterdalzielfarm.co.uk
www.easterdalzielfarm.co.uk

| £20.00 to £23.00 | Y | Y | Y |

VISA: M'CARD:

Mrs Margaret Pottie   Easter Dalziel Farmhouse   Dalcross   Inverness IV2 7JL   Inverness-shire
Tel: (01667) 462213 Fax 01667 462213   Open: ALL YEAR (Excl. Xmas & New Year)   Map Ref No. 34

Balmory Hall

Near Rd: A.844

Experience the delights of this beautifully restored Victorian mansion house, set within its own extensive natural grounds, located on the east coast of the Isle of Bute. Appointed with all modern comforts in mind & with that touch of elegance, which is synonymous with the Victorian age. Enjoy the peaceful serenity of the bright, exceptionally spacious public rooms & the warmth of the cosy bedrooms & bathrooms. Leave all stresses behind; relax & enjoy. A delightful home. Children over 12.
E-mail: enquiries@balmoryhall.com
www.balmoryhall.com

| £45.00 to £70.00 | Y | N | N |

VISA: M'CARD:

Tony & Beryl Harrison   Balmory Hall   Ascog PA20 9LL   Isle of Bute
Tel: (01700) 500669   Fax 01700 500669   Open: ALL YEAR   Map Ref No. 35

Corry Lodge

Near Rd: A.87

Corry Lodge, on the Isle of Skye, is a most attractive period house dating from the late 18th century. It has a fine open outlook over Broadford Bay, but with a sheltered location, & approximately 1,150 metres of unspoilt sea frontage. There are 4 comfortable & tastefully furnished bedrooms, each with en-suite bathroom, radio, colour T.V. & tea/coffee-making facilities. Corry Lodge forms an ideal base from which to tour the island either by car or bicycle, or on foot.
E-mail: jane@corrylodge.freeserve.co.uk
www.corrylodge.co.uk

| £27.50 to £32.50 | Y | N | N |

VISA: M'CARD:

Mrs Jane Wilcken   Corry Lodge   Liveras   Broadford IV49 9AA   Isle of Skye
Tel: (01471) 822235   Fax 01471 822318   Open: APR - OCT   Map Ref No. 36

Visit our website at:
http://www.bestbandb.co.uk

rate £ from - to per person	children taken	evening meals	animals taken		

£21.00 to £25.00 · Y · N · N

VISA: M'CARD:

Near Rd: A.73, B.803

Easter Glentore Farm B & B

Easter Glentore dates back to 1705 & provides quality ground-floor accommodation, with 3 delightful bedrooms with en-suite or private facilities. Great care is taken to ensure guests comfort. Relax & enjoy a homely atmosphere, home-made shortbread, scones, cakes & preserves. A choice of breakfasts. Guests' lounge with panoramic views. A working sheep farm with private woodlands, ideally situated for Stirling, Glasgow & Edinburgh, Falkirk Wheel - 8 miles & M.8, M.74, M.9 & M.80.
E-mail: info@easterglentore.co.uk
www.easterglentore.co.uk

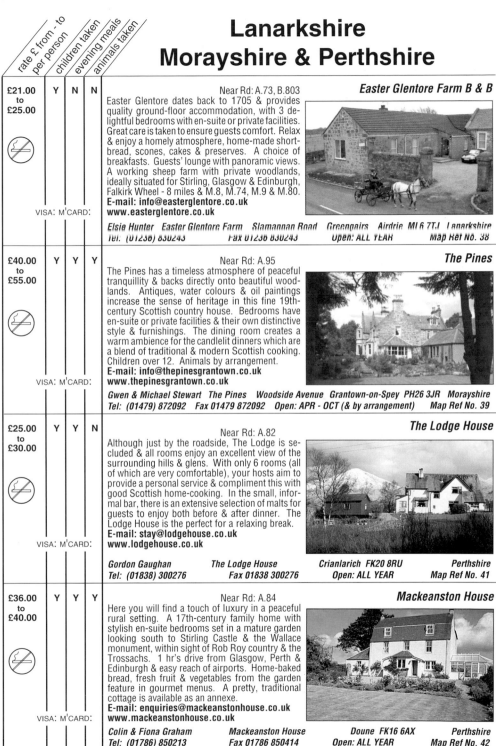

Elsie Hunter Easter Glentore Farm Slamannan Road Greengairs Airdrie ML6 7TJ Lanarkshire
Tel: (01236) 830243   Fax 01236 830243   Open: ALL YEAR   Map Ref No. 38

£40.00 to £55.00 · Y · Y · Y

VISA: M'CARD:

Near Rd: A.95

The Pines

The Pines has a timeless atmosphere of peaceful tranquillity & backs directly onto beautiful woodlands. Antiques, water colours & oil paintings increase the sense of heritage in this fine 19th-century Scottish country house. Bedrooms have en-suite or private facilities & their own distinctive style & furnishings. The dining room creates a warm ambience for the candlelit dinners which are a blend of traditional & modern Scottish cooking. Children over 12. Animals by arrangement.
E-mail: info@thepinesgrantown.co.uk
www.thepinesgrantown.co.uk

Gwen & Michael Stewart The Pines Woodside Avenue Grantown-on-Spey PH26 3JR Morayshire
Tel: (01479) 872092   Fax 01479 872092   Open: APR - OCT (& by arrangement)   Map Ref No. 39

£25.00 to £30.00 · Y · Y · N

VISA: M'CARD:

Near Rd: A.82

The Lodge House

Although just by the roadside, The Lodge is secluded & all rooms enjoy an excellent view of the surrounding hills & glens. With only 6 rooms (all of which are very comfortable), your hosts aim to provide a personal service & compliment this with good Scottish home-cooking. In the small, informal bar, there is an extensive selection of malts for guests to enjoy both before & after dinner. The Lodge House is the perfect for a relaxing break.
E-mail: stay@lodgehouse.co.uk
www.lodgehouse.co.uk

Gordon Gaughan   The Lodge House   Crianlarich FK20 8RU   Perthshire
Tel: (01838) 300276   Fax 01838 300276   Open: ALL YEAR   Map Ref No. 41

£36.00 to £40.00 · Y · Y · Y

VISA: M'CARD:

Near Rd: A.84

Mackeanston House

Here you will find a touch of luxury in a peaceful rural setting. A 17th-century family home with stylish en-suite bedrooms set in a mature garden looking south to Stirling Castle & the Wallace monument, within sight of Rob Roy country & the Trossachs. 1 hr's drive from Glasgow, Perth & Edinburgh & easy reach of airports. Home-baked bread, fresh fruit & vegetables from the garden feature in gourmet menus. A pretty, traditional cottage is available as an annexe.
E-mail: enquiries@mackeanstonhouse.co.uk
www.mackeanstonhouse.co.uk

Colin & Fiona Graham   Mackeanston House   Doune FK16 6AX   Perthshire
Tel: (01786) 850213   Fax 01786 850414   Open: ALL YEAR   Map Ref No. 42

	rate £ from . . to per person	children taken	evening meals	animals taken

Letter Farm

Near Rd: A.923

Situated next to Loch of Lowes Wildlife Reserve, home to nesting osprey, this family-run stock farm is a peaceful haven for guests seeking peace & tranquillity. 3 spacious en-suite bedrooms, 1 ground-floor with king-size bed. A T.V. lounge with log fire. Full breakfast menu with local & homemade produce. Dinner by arrangement. Enjoy afternoon tea on the patio whilst watching the birdlife. Come & treat yourselves to an unforgettable stay.
E-mail: letterlowe@aol.com
www.letterfarm.co.uk

£25.00 to £25.00 — N Y N

VISA: M'CARD:

Mrs Jo Andrew   Letter Farm   Loch of Lowes   Dunkeld PH8 0HH   Perthshire
Tel: (01350) 724254   Fax 01350 724341   Open: Mid JAN - Mid DEC (Excl. Apr.)   Map Ref No. 43

Caplawhead

Near Rd: A.823, A.91

In the beautiful 'Heart of Scotland' lies Caplawhead, a lovingly restored country house & haven to the traveller. On arrival you are given tea in the drawing room with its tower which opens to the garden beyond. Upstairs, the comfortable bedrooms, 1 double & 1 twin, have lovely views & en-suite facilities. Breakfast is a feast with local produce & homemade preserves & a good village pub provides evening meals. Light suppers are available with notice. Children & animals by arrangement.
E-mail: hamish-frances@caplawhead.freeserve.co.uk

£25.00 to £30.00 — Y N Y

Mr & Mrs Lindsay   Caplawhead   By Yett's O'Muckhart   Rumbling Bridge   Kinross KY13 0QD
Perthshire   Tel: (01259) 781556   Open: ALL YEAR (Excl. Xmas)   Map Ref No. 44

Kinnaird Guest House

Near Rd: A.912

Would you like to relax in comfort? Then the warm, friendly atmosphere at Kinnaird is just the place. Mary & Struan aim for high standards & traditional home comforts & cater for individual needs. Beautifully situated overlooking a leafy park to the south, & the charming town centre is within easy walking distance. Buses & trains are also within easy reach. An ideal base for exploring this beautiful region & many historical attractions. Children over 12.
E-mail: usersmac@aol.com
www.kinnaird-guesthouse.co.uk

£28.00 to £32.50 — Y N N

VISA: M'CARD:

Mary Clewley & Struan McIntosh Kinnaird Guest House 5 Marshall Place Perth PH2 8AH Perthshire
Tel: (01738) 628021   Fax 01738 444056   Open: Mid JAN - Mid DEC   Map Ref No. 45

When booking your accommodation please mention
The Best Bed & Breakfast

Easter Dunfallandy Country House. Pitlochry.

Scotland
Perthshire & Roxburghshire

Craigroyston House

Near Rd: A.9
Quietly situated in its own grounds, this fine Victorian villa has direct access from the grounds to the town centre. The spacious en-suite bedrooms, some with 4-poster beds & original antique pieces, are beautifully decorated in keeping with the period. So are the comfortable lounge with seasonal log fire & the dining room with views to the south, where guests can enjoy a traditional Scottish breakfast. Safe off-street parking.
E-mail: reservations@craigroyston.co.uk
www.craigroyston.co.uk

£24.00 to £30.00	Y N N

Gretta & Douglas Maxwell   Craigroyston House   2 Lower Oakfield   Pitlochry   PH16 5HQ   Perthshire
Tel: (01796) 472053   Fax 01796 472053   Open: ALL YEAR   Map Ref No. 46

Tigh Dornie

Near Rd: A.9
Tigh Dornie is situated amid beautiful Perthshire scenery, approx. 5 miles north of Pitlochry. Offering attractive accommodation in 2 very comfortable & tastefully furnished guest bedrooms, each with an en-suite bathroom, T.V. & tea/coffee-making facilities. A warm & friendly welcome is assured from your hosts, who will ensure that your stay is a memorable one. An ideal spot for touring Scotland. Ample car parking. Children over 12.
E-mail: tigh_dornie@btinternet.com
www.btinternet.com/~tigh_dornie/

£25.00 to £27.00	Y N N

Elizabeth Sanderson   Tigh Dornie   Aldclune   Killiecrankie   Pitlochry PH16 5LR   Perthshire
Tel: (01796) 473276   Fax 01796 473276   Open: ALL YEAR   Map Ref No. 46

Easter Dunfallandy House

Near Rd: A.9, A.924
A delightful Victorian country house quietly situated 2 miles south of Pitlochry, off the road to Logierait with wonderful views.   3 twin/double rooms with en-suite bath/shower, T.V. & toiletries. Each room is individually decorated & furnished. Breakfast includes porridge made from local stoneground oats, fresh cream & heather honey & scrambled free-range eggs with cream & smoked salmon - delicious! Dinner by arrangement.
E-mail: sue@dunfallandy.co.uk
www.dunfallandy.co.uk

£30.00 to £35.00	N Y N

see PHOTO over
p. 363

VISA: M'CARD:

Sue Mathieson   Easter Dunfallandy House   Logierait Road   Pitlochry PH16 5NA   Perthshire
Tel: (01796) 474128   Fax 01796 474446   Open: ALL YEAR   Map Ref No. 46

Froylehurst

Near Rd: A.68
An attractive Grade 'B' listed late-Victorian sandstone townhouse retaining most original features, offering 4 comfortable guest bedrooms & residents lounge. All rooms have washbasins with h & c, tea/coffee-making facilities, colour T.V. & radio/alarms. Two shared bathrooms & toilets. Situated in a large garden overlooking the town in a quiet residential area but within 2 mins' walking distance of many good pubs & restaurants. Ample parking. Children over 5 welcome. An ideal base from which to explore this region.

£20.00 to £20.00	Y N N

H. H. Irvine   Froylehurst   Friars   Jedburgh TD8 6BN   Roxburghshire
Tel: (01835) 862477   Fax 01835 862477   Open: MAR - NOV   Map Ref No. 47

Creag-Ard House. Aberfoyle.

rate £ from - to per person / children taken / evening meals / animals taken

Whitehill Farm

	£24.00 to £24.00	Y	N	Y

Near Rd: A.6089

A comfortable & peaceful farmhouse with a large garden standing on a 455 acre, mixed farm 4 miles from Kelso. 4 attractive bedrooms - 2 single & 2 twin, 1 with en-suite shower room - have superb views over rolling countryside. All have central heating & washbasins. A delicious breakfast is served. A sitting room with log fire is available to guests. An ideal base for touring this glorious region; maps available. (Smoking restricted.)
E-mail: besmith@whitehillfarm.freeserve.co.uk
www.whitehillfarm.freeserve.co.uk

Mrs Betty Smith   Whitehill Farm   Nenthorn   Kelso TD5 7RZ   Roxburghshire
Tel: (01573) 470203 Fax 01573 470203 Open: ALL YEAR (Excl. Xmas & New Year) Map Ref No. 48

Creag-Ard House

	£30.00 to £40.00	Y	N	Y

Near Rd: A.81

Nestling in 3 acres of beautiful gardens, Creag-Ard House, a lovely Victorian house, enjoys some of the most magnificent scenery in Scotland; overlooking Loch Ard with superb views of Ben Lomond in a peaceful setting & yet only 1 mile from Aberfoyle. 6 delightful en-suite bedrooms. Enjoy the delicious Scottish breakfast looking out at the views. Private trout fishing & boat hire. Beautiful countryside for walking & cycling. Ideal for the Trossachs.
E-mail: cara@creag-ardhouse.co.uk
www.creag-ardhouse.co.uk

see PHOTO over
p. 365

VISA: M'CARD:

Mrs Cara Wilson   Creag-Ard House   Aberfoyle FK8 3TQ   Stirlingshire
Tel: (01877) 382297   Fax 01877 382297   Open: MAR - OCT   Map Ref No. 49

Culcreuch Castle Hotel & Country Park

	£38.00 to £80.00	Y	Y	Y

Near Rd: A.811, A.81

Retreat to 700 years of history at magical Culcreuch, the ancestral fortalice & clan castle of the Galbraiths, home of the Barons of Culcreuch, & now a country house hotel where the Laird and his family extend an hospitable welcome. Set in 1,600 spectacular acres, yet only 19 miles from central Glasgow & 17 miles from Stirling. 13 bedrooms with en-suite or private facilities, 4-poster supplement. Elegant period-style decor. Animals by arrangement.
E-mail: info@culcreuch.com
www.culcreuch.com

see PHOTO over
p. 367

VISA: M'CARD: AMEX:

Laird Andrew Haslam   Culcreuch Castle Hotel & Country Park   Fintry G63 0LW   Stirlingshire
Tel: (01360) 860555   Fax 01360 860556   Open: ALL YEAR   Map Ref No. 50

Visit our website at:
http://www.bestbandb.co.uk

Culcreuch Castle.   Fintry.

Wales

Wales

Wales is a small country with landscapes of intense beauty. In the north are the massive mountains of the Snowdonia National Park, split by chasms & narrow passes, & bounded by quiet vales & moorland. The Lleyn peninsula & the Isle of Anglesey have lovely remote coastlines.

Forests, hills & lakeland form the scenery of Mid Wales, with the great arc of Cardigan Bay in the west.

To the south there is fertile farming land in the Vale of Glamorgan, mountains & high plateaux in the Brecon Beacons, & also the industrial valleys. The coastline forms two peninsulas, around Pembroke & the Gower.

Welsh, the oldest living language of Europe is spoken & used, most obviously in the north, & is enjoying a resurgence in the number of its speakers.

From Taliesin, the 6th century Celtic poet, to Dylan Thomas, Wales has inspired poetry & song. Every August, at the Royal National Eisteddfod, thousands gather to compete as singers, musicians & poets, or to listen & learn. In the small town of Llangollen, there is an International Music Eisteddfod for a week every July

North Wales.

North Wales is chiefly renowned for the 850 miles of the Snowdonia National Park. It is a land of mountains & lakes, rivers & waterfalls & deep

The Snowdon Mountain Railway.

glacier valleys. The scenery is justly popular with walkers & pony-trekkers, but the Snowdon Mountain Railway provides easy access to the summit of the highest mountain in the range with views over the "roof of Wales".

Within miles of this wild highland landscape is a coastline of smooth beaches & little fishing villages.

Barmouth has mountain scenery on its doorstep & miles of golden sands & estuary walks. Bangor & Llandudno are popular resort towns.

The Lleyn peninsula reaches west & is an area of great charm. Abersoch is a dinghy & windsurfing centre with safe sandy beaches. In the Middle Ages pilgrims would come to visit Bardsey, the Isle of 20,000 saints, just off Aberdaron, at the tip of the peninsula.

The Isle of Anglesey is linked to the mainland by the handsome Menai Straits Suspension Bridge. Beaumaris has a 13th century castle & many other fine buildings in its historic town centre.

Historically North Wales is a fiercely independent land where powerful local lords resisted first the Romans & later the armies of the English Kings.

The coastline is studded with 13th century castles. Dramatically sited Harlech Castle, famed in fable & song, commands the town, & wide sweep of the coastline.

The great citadel of Edward I at Caernarfon comprises the castle & the encircling town walls. In 1969 it was the scene of the investiture of His Royal Highness Prince Charles as Prince of Wales.

There are elegant stately homes like Plas Newydd in Anglesey & Eriddig House near Wrexham, but it is the variety of domestic architecture that is most charming. The timber-frame buildings of the Border country are seen at their best in historic Ruthin set in the

Wales

beautiful Vale of Clwyd. Further west, the stone cottages of Snowdonia are built of large stones & roofed with the distinctive blue & green local slate. The low, snow-white cottages of Anglesey & the Lleyn Peninsula are typical of the "Atlantic Coast" architecture that can be found on all the western coasts of Europe. The houses are constructed of huge boulders with tiny windows & doors.

By contrast there is the marvellous fantasy of Portmeirion village. On a wooded peninsula between Harlech & Porthmadog, Sir Clough Williams Ellis created a perfect Italianate village with pastel coloured buildings, a town hall & luxury hotel.

Mid Wales

Mid Wales is farming country where people are outnumbered three to one by sheep. A flock of ewes, a lone shepherd & a Border Collie are a common sight on these green hills. Country towns like Old Radnor, Knighton & Montgomery with its castle ruin, have a timeless quality. The market towns of Rhyader, Lampeter & Dolgellau have their weekly livestock sales & annual agricultural festivals, the largest of which is the Royal Welsh Show at Builth Wells in July.

This is the background to the craft of weaving practised here for centuries. In the valley of the River Tefi & on an upper tributary of the Wye & the Irfon, there are tiny riverbank mills which produce the colourful Welsh plaid cloth.

Towards the Snowdonia National Park in the North, the land rises to the scale of true mountains. Mighty Cader Idris & the expanses of Plynlimon, once inaccessible to all but the shepherd & the mountaineer, are now popular centres for walking & pony trekking with well-signposted trails.

The line of the border with England is followed by a huge earth work of bank & ditch. This is Offa's Dyke, built by the King of Mercia around 750 A.D. to deter the Welsh from their incessant raids into his kingdom. Later the border was guarded by the castles at Hay-on-Wye, Builth Wells, Welshpool, & Chirk which date from mediaeval times.

North from Rhayader, lies the Dovey estuary & the historic town of Machynlleth. This is where Owain Glyndwr's parliament is thought to have met in 1404, & there is an exhibition about the Welsh leader in the building, believed to have been Parliament House.

Wales lost many fine religious houses during the Dissolution of the Monasteries under Henry VIII. The ruins at Cymer near Dolgellau & at Strata Florida were abbeys of the Cistercian order. However, many remote Parish Churches show evidence of the skills of mediaeval craftsmen with soaring columns & fine rood screens.

The Cambrian Coast (Cardigan Bay) has sand dunes to the north & cliffs to the south with sandy coves & miles of cliff walks.

Llangrannog Headland.

Aberystwyth is the main town of the region with two beaches & a yachting harbour, a Camera Obscura on the cliff top & some fine walks in the area.

Water-skiing, windsurfing &

Wales

sailing are popular at Aberdovey, Aberaeron, New Quay, Tywyn & Barmouth & there are delightful little beaches further south at Aberporth, Tresaith or Llangrannog.

South Wales

South Wales is a region of scenic variety. The Pembrokeshire coastline has sheer cliffs, little coves & lovely beaches. Most of the area is National Park with an 80 mile foot path running along its length, passing pretty harbour villages like Solva & Broad Haven.

A great circle of Norman Castles stands guard over South Pembrokeshire, Roch, Haverfordwest, Tenby, Carew, Pembroke & Manorbier.

The northern headland of Saint

Tenby.

Brides Bay is the most westerly point in the country & at the centre of a tiny village stands the Cathedral of Saint David, the Patron Saint of Wales. At Bosherton near Saint Govans Head, there is a tiny chapel hidden in a cleft in the massive limestone cliffs.

The Preseli Hills hold the vast prehistoric burial chambers of Pentre Ifan, & the same mountains provided the great blue stones used at faraway Stonehenge.

Laugharne is the village where Dylan Thomas lived & worked in what was a boat-house & is now a museum.

In the valleys, towns like Merthyr Tydfil, Ebbw Vale & Treorchy were in the forefront of the boom years of the Industrial Revolution. Now the heavy industries are fast declining & the ravages of the indiscriminate mining & belching smoke of the blast furnaces are disappearing. The famous Male Voice Choirs & the love of rugby football survives.

The Vale of Glamorgan is a rural area with pretty villages. Beyond here the land rises steeply to the high wild moorlands & hill farms of the Brecon Beacons National Park & the Black Mountains, lovely areas for walking & pony trekking.

The Wye Valley leads down to Chepstow & here set amidst the beautiful woodlands is the ruin of the Great Abbey of Tintern, founded in 1131 by the Cistercian Order.

Swansea has a strong sea-faring tradition maintained by its new Marine Quarter - marina, waterfront village, restaurants, art gallery & theatre.

Cardiff, the capital of Wales, is a pleasant city with acres of parkland, the lovely River Taff, & a great castle, as well as a new civic centre, two theatres & the ultra-modern St. David's Concert Hall. It is the home of the Welsh National Opera & here also is the National Stadium where the singing of the rugby crowd on a Saturday afternoon is a treat.

Pony Trekking

Wales

Wales
Gazeteer

Areas of Outstanding Natural Beauty
The Pembrokeshire Coast. The Brecon Beacons. Snowdonia. Gower.'

Historic Houses & Castles

Cardiff Castle - Cardiff
Built on a Roman site in the 11th century.
Caerphilly Castle - Caerphilly
13th century fortress.
Chirk Castle - Nr. Wrexham
14th century Border Castle. Lovely gardens.
Coity Castle - Coity
Mediaeval stronghold - three storied round tower.
Gwydir Castle - Nr. Lanrwst
Royal residence in past days - wonderful Tudor furnishings. Gardens with peacocks.
Penrhyn Castle - Bangor
Neo-Norman architecture 19th century - large grounds with museum & exhibitions. Victorian garden.
Picton Castle - Haverfordwest
12th century - lived in by the same family continuously. Fine gardens.
Caernarfon Castle - Caernarfon
13th century - castle of great importance to Edward I.
Conway Castle - Conwy
13th century - one of Edward I's chain of castles.
Powis Castle - Welshpool
14th century - reconstruction work in 17th century.
Murals, furnishings, tapestries & paintings, terraced gardens.
Pembroke Castle - Pembroke
12th century Norman castle with huge keep & immense walls.
Birthplace of Henry VII.
Plas Newydd - Isle of Anglesey
18th century Gothic style house.
Home of the Marquis of Anglesey.
Stands on the edge of the Menai Strait looking across to the Snowdonia Range. Famous for the Rex Whistler murals.
The Tudor Merchant's House - Tenby
Built in 15th century.
Tretower Court & Castle - Crickhowell
Mediaeval - finest example in Wales.

Cathedrals & Churches

St. Asaph Cathedral
13th century - 19th century restoration. Smallest of Cathedrals in England & Wales.
Holywell (St. Winifred)
15th century well chapel & chamber - fine example.
St. Davids (St. David)
12th century Cathedral - splendid tower - oak roof to nave.
Gwent (St. Woolos)
Norman Cathedral - Gothic additions - 19th century restoration.
Abergavenny (St. Mary)
14th century church of 12th century Benedictine priory.
Llanengan (St. Engan)
Mediaeval church - very large with original roof & stalls 16th century tower.
Esyronen
17th century chapel, much original interior remaining.
Llangdegley (St. Tegla)
18th century Quaker meeting house - thatched roof - simple structure divided into schoolroom & meeting room.
Llandaff Cathedral (St. Peter & St. Paul)
Founded in 6th century - present building began in 12th century. Great damage suffered in bombing during war, restored with Epstein's famous figure of Christ.

Museums & Galleries

National Museum of Wales - Cardiff (also Turner House)
Geology, archaeology, zoology, botany, industry, & art exhibitions.
Welsh Folk Museum - St. Fagans Castle - Cardiff
13th century walls curtaining a 16th century house - now a most interesting & comprehensive folk museum.
County Museum - Carmarthen
Roman jewellery, gold, etc. Romano-British & Stone Age relics.
National Library of Wales - Aberystwyth
Records of Wales & Celtic areas. Great historical interest.
University College of Wales Gallery - AberystwythTravelling exhibitions of painting & sculpture.

Wales

Museum & Art Gallery - Newport
Specialist collection of English
watercolours - natural history, Roman
remains, etc.
Legionary Museum - Caerleon
Roman relics found on the site of
legionary fortress at Risca.
Nelson Museum - Monmouth
Interesting relics of Admiral Lord Nelson &
Lady Hamilton.
Bangor Art Gallery - Bangor
Exhibitions of contemporary paintings &
sculpture.
Bangor Museum of Welsh Antiquities -
Bangor
History of North Wales is shown. Splendid
exhibits of furniture, clothing, domestic
objects, etc. Also Roman antiquities.
Narrow Gauge Railway Museum - Tywyn
Rolling stock & exhibitions of narrow
gauge railways of U.K.
Museum of Childhood - Menai Bridge
Charming museum of dolls & toys &
children's things.

Brecknock Museum - Brecon
Natural history, archaeology, agriculture,
local history, etc.
Glynn Vivian Art Gallery & Museum -
Swansea
Ceramics, old & contemporary, British
paintings & drawings, sculpture, loan
exhibitions.
Stone Museum - Margam
Carved stones & crosses from pre-
historic times.
Plas Mawr - Conwy
A beautiful Elizabethan town mansion
house in its original condition. Now holds
the Royal Cambrain Academy of Art.

Historic Monuments
Rhuddlan Castle - Rhuddlan
13th century castle - interesting diamond
plan.
Valle Crucis Abbey - Llangollen
13th century Cistercian Abbey Church.

Cader Idris.

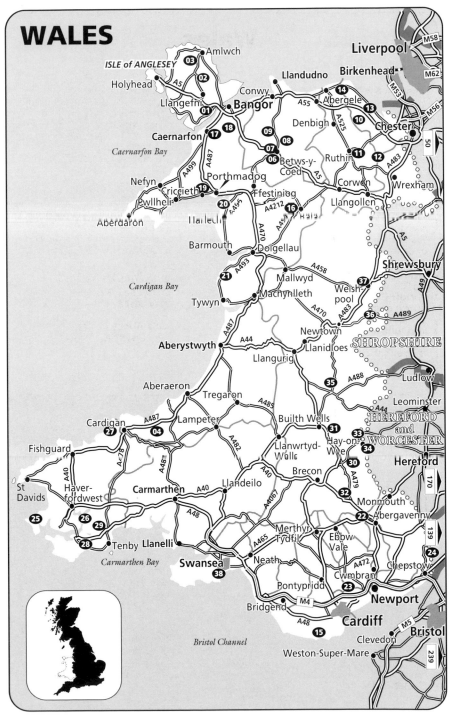

WALES

Liverpool

ISLE of ANGLESEY

Amlwch

Holyhead

Llandudno

Birkenhead

Llangefni

Conwy

Abergele

Bangor

Denbigh

Chester

Caernarfon

Caernarfon Bay

Ruthin

Betws-y-Coed

Corwen

Wrexham

Nefyn

Porthmadog

Criccieth

Ffestiniog

Llangollen

Pwllheli

Harlech

Bala

Aberdaron

Barmouth

Dolgellau

Cardigan Bay

Mallwyd

Shrewsbury

Welsh-pool

Tywyn

Machynlleth

Newtown

SHROPSHIRE

Aberystwyth

Llanidloes

Llangurig

Ludlow

Aberaeron

Tregaron

Leominster

HEREFORD and WORCESTER

Builth Wells

Cardigan

Lampeter

Llanwrtyd-Wells

Hay-on-Wye

Hereford

Fishguard

Brecon

St Davids

Haver-fordwest

Carmarthen

Llandeilo

Monmouth

Abergavenny

Merthyr Tydfil

Ebbw Vale

Tenby

Llanelli

Carmarthen Bay

Swansea

Neath

Cwmbran

Chepstow

Pontypridd

Newport

Bridgend

Cardiff

Bristol Channel

Clevedon

Bristol

Weston-Super-Mare

WALES
Map references

01	Roberts	22	Harris	31	N. Jones
02	Bown	23	Price	32	C. Jackson
03	Hughes	24	Stubbs	33	Newall
04	Lewis	25	Webber	34	P. Roberts
06	Baxter	26	Lort-Phillips	35	Millan
06	Betteney	27	Phillips	36	Bright
07	Bidwell	28	McHugh	37	S. Jones
07	Howard	29	Fielder	38	Maybery
07	K. Jones	30	Meredith		
08	Pitman				
09	Nichols				
10	C. Spencer				
11	J Spencer				
12	Parry				
13	M. Jones				
14	Steele-Mortimer				
15	Farthing				
16	Hind				
17	Bayles				
18	Kettle				
19	Williamson				
20	Williams				
21	Chadwick				

1 BRIDGEND
2 RHONDA CYNON TAFF
3 MERTHYR TYDFIL
4 CAERPHILLY
5 BLAENAU GWENT
6 TORFAEN

Llwydiarth Fawr Farm. Anglesey.

Wales
Isle of Anglesey & Ceredigion

Bodlawen

Near Rd: A.4080

A beautiful large house in a glorious location looking onto Snowdonia & Caernarfon Castle, a short walk to the shore of the tranquil Menai Strait. Ideally based for touring Anglesey & the mainland, its sights & beaches. Close to Plas Newydd (National Trust), the Sea Zoo & the Foel open farm. All bedrooms have en-suite facilities, T.V. etc. The lounge & dining room are exquisitly furnished & there is a grand piano. Snooker table. Marian, a well-known soprano soloist, is Welsh speaking.

E-mail: marion@bodlawen.com
www.bodlawen.com

| £25.00 to £27.00 | Y | N | N |

VISA: M'CARD:

Marian Roberts   Bodlawen   Brynsiencyn   Isle of Anglesey LL61 6TQ   Anglesey
Tel: (01248) 430379   Open: ALL YEAR (Excl. Xmas)   Map Ref No. 01

Drws-Y-Coed

Near Rd: A.5025

Enjoy wonderful panoramic views of Snowdonia & countryside at this beautifully appointed farmhouse on a 550-acre working beef, sheep & arable farm. It is centrally situated to explore the island. Tastefully decorated & furnished, superb en-suite bedrooms with all facilities. An inviting spacious lounge with antiques & log fire. The excellent breakfasts are served in the cosy dining room. Grade II listed farm buildings. Pleasant walks & private fishing. A warm welcome assured.

E-mail: drws.ycoed@virgin.net
www.smoothhound.co.uk/hotels/drwsycoed.html

| £25.00 to £26.00 | Y | N | N |

VISA: M'CARD:

Mrs Jane Bown   Drws-Y-Coed   Llannerch-Y-Medd   Isle of Anglesey LL71 8AD   Anglesey
Tel: (01248) 470473   Open: ALL YEAR   Map Ref No. 02

Llwydiarth Fawr Farm

Near Rd: A.5

Secluded Georgian mansion set in 800 acres of woodland & farmland, with lovely open views. Ideal touring base for the island's coastline, Snowdonia & North Wales coast. 5 delightfully furnished en-suite bedrooms with T.V., & 1 cottage suite. Log fires. Enjoy a taste of Wales with delicious country cooking using farm & local produce. Personal attention & a warm Welsh welcome to guests, who will enjoy the scenic walks & private fishing. Convenient for Holyhead-to-Ireland crossings.

E-mail: llwydiarth@hotmail.com
www.bestbandb.co.uk

| £25.00 to £30.00 | Y | N | N |

see PHOTO over
p. 375

VISA: M'CARD:

Margaret Hughes   Llwydiarth Fawr Farm   Llanerchymedd   Isle of Anglesey LL71 8DF   Anglesey
Tel: (01248) 470321/470540   Open: ALL YEAR (Excl. Xmas)   Map Ref No. 03

Wervil Grange Farm

Near Rd: A.487

A warm welcome awaits you at this superb & luxurious Welsh Georgian farmhouse offering a high standard of accommodation. The comfortable farmhouse is beautifully decorated & furnished, all bedrooms are en-suite. It is a traditional stock-rearing farm with a flock of breeding ewes & a herd of Pedigree Welsh Black cattle. Free fishing on the farm. Only 10 mins' from Llangranog beach in Cardigan Bay, which is home to the only resident population of bottle-nosed dolphins in Welsh waters. Your hosts aim is to provide you with an unforgettable holiday.

| £25.00 to £30.00 | Y | N | Y |

see PHOTO over
p. 377

Mrs Ionwen Lewis   Wervil Grange Farm   Pentregat   Nr. Llangranog SA44 6HW   Ceredigion
Tel: (01239) 654252   Fax 01239 654252   Open: ALL YEAR   Map Ref No. 04

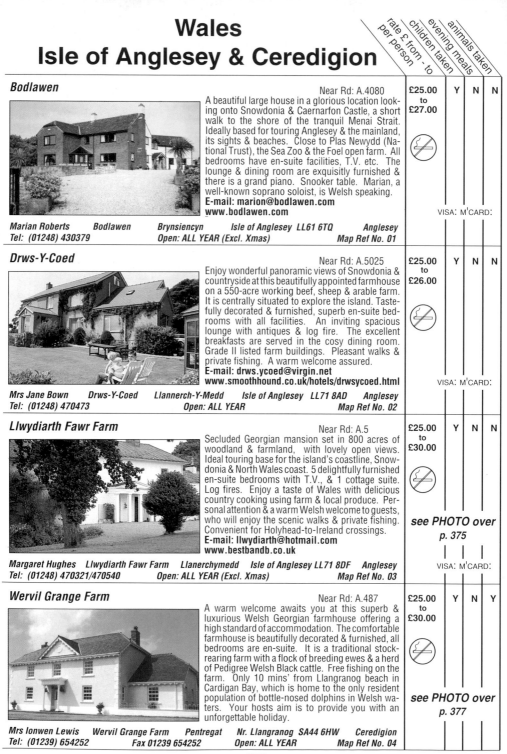

Wervil Grange Farm. Pentregat.

	rate £ from - to per person	children taken	evening meals	animals taken

The Courthouse (Henllys)

Near Rd: A.5

£27.00 to £45.00 — Y — N — N

Charming accommodation is provided in this Victorian property, a former police station & magistrate's court, set in a peaceful riverside garden within the village. Modern comforts include colour T.V.s, hospitality trays & en-suite facilities in every room except the former prison cell, which has its own private bathroom. Breakfast is served in the former court room. Bodnant Gardens, Port Meirion, Snowdon Mountain Railway & the castles of North Wales are nearby.
E-mail: henllys@betws-y-coed.co.uk
www.guesthouse-snowdonia.co.uk

VISA: M'CARD:

Mr & Mrs Bidwell   The Courthouse (Henllys)   Old Church Road   Betws-y-Coed LL24 0AL   Conwy
Tel: (01690) 710534   Fax 01690 710884   Open: ALL YEAR   Map Ref No. 07

The Ferns Guest House

Near Rd: A.5

£22.00 to £25.00 — Y — N — N

A Victorian house, conveniently situated in the village of Betws-y-Coed in the beautiful Snowdonia National Park. 9 attractively furnished bedrooms, all en-suite with T.V. & tea/coffee-making facilities. Ideal base for many local walks, Bodnant Gardens, Conway Castle, Snowdon mountain railway, Portmerion & Carnarfon Castle. Cosy guests' lounge. Hearty British breakfasts. Small garden. Private car parking. Restaurants within easy walking distance. Children over 7.
E-mail: ferns@betws-y-coed.co.uk
www.ferns-guesthouse.co.uk

VISA: M'CARD:

Ian & Deborah Baxter   The Ferns Guest House   Holyhead Road   Betws-y-Coed LL24 0AN   Conwy
Tel: (01690) 710587   Fax 01690 710587   Open: ALL YEAR   Map Ref No. 06

Bryn Afon

Near Rd: A.5

£20.00 to £26.00 — Y — N — N

A Victorian stone-built house situated on the banks of the River Llugwy overlooking the Pont-Y-Pair Bridge & waterfall. Well-appointed bedrooms with comfortable beds ensure a good night's sleep. Central for all tourist attractions & many local walks through the forests. Drying facilities available. Parking for all guests on the premises & a good choice of restaurants within 5-10 mins' walking distance. Children by arrangement.
E-mail: WBETTENEY@aol.com
www.visitwales.com

William & Marion Betteney   Bryn Afon   Pentre Felin   Betws-Y-Coed LL24 0BB   Conwy
Tel: (01690) 710403   Open: ALL YEAR   Map Ref No. 06

Tan Dinas Country House

Near Rd: A.5

£23.00 to £26.00 — Y — N — N

A Victorian country house, offering peace, seclusion & a wonderful view. Surrounded by woodland yet only 500 yds from the village. Start your adventure with a delicious breakfast, coming home to relax in the comfortable lounge or retire with a video or book to an attractive, individually furnished bedroom which is appointed for your comfort. Forest walks from house. An ideal touring centre. Ample parking. A delightful home, perfect for a relaxing break.
www.bestbandb.co.uk

see PHOTO over
p. 379

Ann Howard   Tan Dinas Country House   Coed Cyn Hellier Road   Betws-Y-Coed LL24 0BL   Conwy
Tel: (01690) 710635   Fax 01690 710815   Open: ALL YEAR   Map Ref No. 07

Tan Dinas. Betws-Y-Coed

rate £ from - to per person | children taken | evening meals | animals taken

Aberconwy House

Near Rd: A.470

A high standard of comfort & friendly, helpful hosts await you at Aberconwy. This large Victorian home, located in a lovely position above the picturesque village of Betws-Y-Coed, has panoramic views of the Llugney Valley, mountains & the River Conway. There are 8 very comfortable en-suite bedrooms, with T.V. & tea/coffee makers. Most also have wonderful views. A residents' T.V. lounge & garden are available. This is an ideal centre for touring, walking, fishing & golf. Children over 8.
E-mail: welcome@aberconwy-house.co.uk
www.aberconwy-house.co.uk

£24.00 to £35.00 | Y | N | N

VISA: M'CARD:

Kevin Jones   Aberconwy House   Lon Muriau   Betws-Y-Coed LL24 0HD   Conwy
Tel: (01690) 710202   Fax 01690 710800   Open: ALL YEAR   Map Ref No. 07

Tan-Y-Foel Country House

Near Rd: A.470, A.5

Personally run bijou house built of magnificent Welsh stone. Set away from traffic in secluded gardens with panoramic views of the rolling countryside to the majestic mountains of Snowdonia. Elegant & luxurious, with the ultimate in comfort. This contemporary country house offers every 5-star amenity & has been awarded top accolades for its cuisine. Ideal for relaxing or exploring the many famous castles within the National Park.
E-mail: enquiries@tyfhotel.co.uk
www.tyfhotel.co.uk

£60.00 to £85.00 | Y | Y | N

VISA: M'CARD: AMEX:

Mr & Mrs P.K. Pitman   Tan-Y-Foel Country House   Capel Garmon   Betws-Y-Coed LL26 0RE   Conwy
Tel: (01690) 710507   Fax 01690 710681   Open: JAN - NOV   Map Ref No. 08

Hafod Country House

Near Rd: A.470

Set in the lovely Conwy Valley, on the edge of Snowdonia, Yr Hafod (The Summer Dwelling) is a former 17th-century farmhouse, extensively furnished with antiques. The bedrooms each offer a highly individual sense of style. Warm hospitality at this award-winning hotel is complimented by outstanding food, while drinks can be enjoyed in the oak-panelled bar or in front of a log fire. Children over 11. Animals by arrangement.
E-mail: hafod@breathemail.net
www.hafodhouse.co.uk

£30.00 to £46.00 | Y | Y | Y

VISA: M'CARD: AMEX:

Chris & Rosina Nichols   Hafod Country House   Trefriw   Llanrwst LL27 0RQ   Conwy
Tel: (01492) 640029   Fax 01492 641351   Open: Mid FEB - JAN   Map Ref No. 09

Pentre Cerrig Mawr

Near Rd: A.494

Pheasants & badgers visit the gardens of this peaceful 17th-century country house. Convenient for Chester, Snowdonia, the coast, Holyhead & 50 mins' to Manchester or Liverpool. The principal rooms have beams & open fires. Bedrooms are en-suite with T.V., etc. & magical views across the valley. Country pubs, walks, riding, golf & theatre nearby. The atmosphere is friendly & welcoming. Home-baking & local organic produce. Animals by arrangement. Children over 8. Single supplement.
E-mail: pentre.cerrig@virgin.net
www.pentrecerrigmawr.co.uk

£40.00 to £40.00 | Y | Y | Y

see PHOTO over
p. 381

VISA: M'CARD:

Charmian & Ted Spencer   Pentre Cerrig Mawr   Maeshafn   Nr. Mold CH7 5LU   Denbighshire
Tel: (01352) 810607   Fax 01352 810607   Open: ALL YEAR   Map Ref No. 10

Pentre Cerrig Mawr.   Maeshafn.

Eyarth Station.   Llanfair D.C.

Eyarth Station

rate £ from - to per person	children taken	evening meals	animals taken
£26.00 to £26.00	Y	Y	Y

see PHOTO over p. 382

VISA: M'CARD:

Near Rd: A.525

A warm & friendly reception awaits the visitor to Eyarth Station. A super, converted, former railway station located in the beautiful countryside of the Vale of Clwyd. 6 en-suite bedrooms. T.V. lounge, & guests are welcome to use the garden, sun patio & outdoor heated pool. Conveniently located for many historic towns including Conwy, Caernarfon & Ruthin & their castles, with medieval banquet 2 mins' drive away. Chester is also within driving distance. Best Bed & Breakfast Award winner.
E-mail: stay@eyarthstation.com
www.eyarthstation.co.uk

Jen & Bert Spencer — Eyarth Station — Llanfair D. C. — Ruthin LL15 2EE — Denbighshire
Tel: (01024) 700040 — Fax 01024 707404 — Open: MAN OOT — Map Ref No. 11

Llainwen Ucha

rate £ from - to per person	children taken	evening meals	animals taken
£20.00 to £22.00	Y	Y	N

Near Rd: A.525

A working farm set in 130 acres overlooking the very beautiful Vale of Clwyd. Offering 3 pleasantly decorated rooms with modern amenities, & accommodating up to 6 persons. All rooms are centrally heated. Good home-cooking made with fresh local produce; evening meals & vegetarian options on request. Conveniently situated for visiting Chester, Llangollen, Snowdonia & the coast. Offa's Dyke & fishing nearby. Medieval banquets are held at Ruthin Castle throughout the year.
www.bestbandb.co.uk

Elizabeth A. Parry — Llainwen Ucha — Pentre Celyn — Ruthin LL15 2HL — Denbighshire
Tel: (01978) 790253 — Open: ALL YEAR — Map Ref No. 12

Greenhill Farm

rate £ from - to per person	children taken	evening meals	animals taken
£22.00 to £24.00	Y	Y	N

Near Rd: A.55

A 16th-century working dairy farm, overlooking the Dee Estuary, which retains its old-world charm, with a beamed & panelled interior. Bedrooms are tastefully furnished, some having bathroom/shower en-suite. Relax & enjoy typical farmhouse food in the attractive dining room. (Dinner by prior arrangement.) Children's play area & utility/games room also available. A lovely home, within easy reach of both the coastal & mountain areas of North Wales.
E-mail: mary@greenhillfarm.fsnet.co.uk
www.greenhillfarm.co.uk

Mrs Mary Jones — Greenhill Farm — Bryn Celyn — Holywell CH8 7QF — Flintshire
Tel: (01352) 713270 — Open: FEB - NOV — Map Ref No. 13

Golden Grove

rate £ from - to per person	children taken	evening meals	animals taken
£40.00 to £40.00	Y	Y	N

see PHOTO over p. 384

VISA: M'CARD:

Near Rd: A.5151

Beautiful Elizabethan manor house set in 1,000 acres, close to Chester, Bodnant Gardens & Snowdonia, & en route to Holyhead. The Steele-Mortimer brothers & wives, having returned to the family home from Canada & Ireland, provide a warm welcome for their guests. The menu features home produce, including lamb & game, together with interesting wines & home baking (advance notice required.) The atmosphere is friendly & informal. Children over 12. Licensed.
E-mail: golden.grove@lineone.net

N. & M. Steele-Mortimer — Golden Grove — Llanasa — Nr. Holywell CH8 9NA — Flintshire
Tel: (01745) 854452 — Fax 01745 854547 — Open: FEB - NOV — Map Ref No. 14

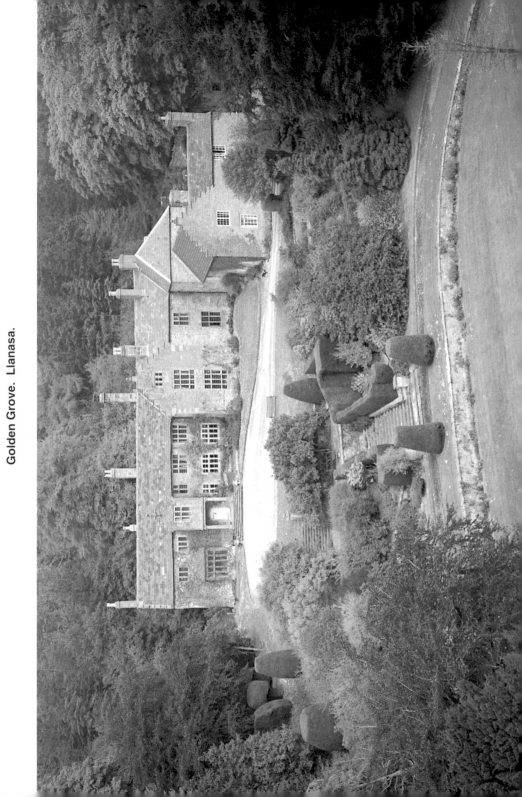

Golden Grove. Llanasa.

rate £ from - to per person	children taken	evening meals	animals taken	

The White House

£25.00 to £25.00

Y N N

Near Rd: A.48

Experience the White House, a Georgian residence 5 mins' walk to the historic town, local pubs & restaurants. 1 mile to the coast, the footpaths start 10 metres from the house. There are 2 gracious bedrooms with en-suite or private bathrooms, easy chairs, T.V., tea/coffee facilities, refrigerator & hairdryer. Neville & Janet with a collection of teddy bears will be delighted to share their home & provide you with a scrumptious & varied breakfast.
E-mail: waleswhitehouse@hotmail.com
www.waleswhitehouse.co.uk

Janet & Neville Farthing   The White House   Flanders Road   Llantwit Major CF61 1RL   Glamorgan
Tel: (01446) 794250   Fax 01446 794250   Open: ALL YEAR   Map Ref No. 15

Abercelyn Country House

£22.50 to £32.00

Y Y N

Near Rd: A.494

Set in landscaped gardens with its own mountain stream running alongside, this Grade II listed former rectory dates back to before 1721. Situated in the Snowdonia National Park, it is ideally located for walking or touring amongst the spectacular scenery. Bright & spacious en-suite bedrooms with views over Bala Lake, evenings relaxing before open log fires. Genuine home cooking a speciality. Dinner by arrangement. Guided walking available.
E-mail: info@abercelyn.co.uk
www.abercelyn.co.uk

Mrs Lindsay Hind   Abercelyn Country House   Llanycil   Bala LL23 7YF   Gwynedd
Tel: (01678) 521109   Fax 01678 520848   Open: ALL YEAR (Excl. Xmas)   Map Ref No. 16

The White House

£21.50 to £23.50

Y N Y

Near Rd: A.487

The White House is a large detached house set in its own grounds, overlooking Foryd Bay, & with the Snowdonia mountains behind. Accommodation is in 4 tastefully decorated bedrooms, all with bath or shower, tea/coffee-making facilities & colour T.V.. Guests are welcome to use the residents' lounge, outdoor pool & gardens. Ideally situated for birdwatching, walking, windsurfing, golf & visiting the historic Welsh castles.
E-mail: RWBAYLES@SJMS.CO.UK
www.bestbandb.co.uk

Richard Bayles   The White House   Llanfaglan   Caernarfon LL54 5RA   Gwynedd
Tel: (01286) 673003   Open: MAR - NOV   Map Ref No. 17

Ty'n Rhos Country Hotel

£40.00 to £50.00

Y Y N

Near Rd: A.487

Ty'n Rhos is a special place, set in a splendid location on the wide-open plain running between Snowdonia & the sea. An elegant country house of great charm & comfort. Each individually designed bedroom has been furnished to the highest of standards. The 3 delightful ground floor rooms, have patio doors opening onto the garden. Award-winning Ty'n Rhos serves excellent meals . Quality allied to exceptional value are the keynotes at Ty'n Rhos. Children over 6.
E-mail: enquiries@tynrhos.co.uk
www.tynrhos.co.uk

VISA: M'CARD: AMEX:

Lynda & Nigel Kettle Ty'n Rhos Country Hotel Seion Llanddeiniolen Caernarfon LL55 3AE Gwynedd
Tel: (01248) 670489   Fax 01248 670079   Open: ALL YEAR   Map Ref No. 18

Wales
Gwynedd & Monmouthshire

Min-Y-Gaer Hotel

Near Rd: A.497

A pleasant, licensed house in a quiet residential area, offering very good accommodation in 10 comfortable rooms, all of which have a bathroom en-suite. All rooms are non-smoking & have colour T.V. & tea/coffee-making facilities. The hotel enjoys commanding views of Criccieth Castle & the scenic Cardigan Bay coastline, & is only 2 mins' walk from the safe, sandy beach. Car parking on the premises. An ideal base for touring Snowdonia.
E-mail: info@minygaer.co.uk
www.minygaer.co.uk

£24.00 to £25.00 | Y | N | N

VISA: M'CARD: AMEX:

Sue Williamson   Min-Y-Gaer Hotel   Porthmadog Road   Criccieth LL52 0HP   Gwynedd
Tel: (01766) 522151   Fax 01766 523540   Open: MAR - OCT   Map Ref No. 19

Gwrach Ynys Country Guest House

Near Rd: A.496

A warm Welsh welcome awaits you at Gwrach Ynys, a 6 bedroom Edwardian country house set in 1 acre of garden, nestled between the sea & the mountains in beautiful Snowdonia National Park. En-suite bedrooms, individually decorated & furnished to a high standard. 2 comfortable guest lounges & a separate dining room. Ideally located for exploring North Wales. Superb area for walkers, birdwatchers & golfers. Children over 3.
E-mail: bestbandb@gwrachynys.co.uk
www.gwrachynys.co.uk

£24.00 to £30.00 | Y | N | N

Deborah Williams   Gwrach Ynys Country Guest House   Talsarnall   Nr. Harlech LL47 6TS   Gwynedd
Tel: (01766) 780742   Fax 01766 781199   Open: MAR - OCT   Map Ref No. 20

Cefn-Coch Country Guest House

Near Rd: A.493

Cefn-Coch is an old coaching inn on the edge of the Snowdonia National Park & is surrounded by over an acre of gardens & paddock. It has been tastefully renovated throughout & now provides quality accommodation. There are 2 attractively furnished bedrooms, each with an en-suite bathroom & tea/coffee-making facilities. Delicious evening meals are served. Guests can enjoy the extensive views of the local countryside. The beautiful Cardigan Bay coast is nearby. A delightful home.
E-mail: Patachadwick@aol.com

£24.00 to £25.00 | N | Y | N

Pat Chadwick   Cefn-Coch Country Guest House   Llanegryn   Tywyn LL36 9SD   Gwynedd
Tel: (01654) 712193   Open: FEB - NOV   Map Ref No. 21

The Wenallt

Near Rd: A.465

A 16th-century Welsh longhouse set in 50 acres of farmland in the Brecon Beacons National Park & commanding magnificent views over the Usk Valley. Retaining all its old charm, with oak beams & inglenook fireplace, yet offering a high standard of accommodation, with en-suite bedrooms, good food & a warm welcome. The Wenallt is an ideal base from which to see glorious Wales & the surrounding areas & attractions. Licensed. Animals by arrangement.
www.bestbandb.co.uk

£19.50 to £24.00 | Y | Y | Y

see PHOTO over p. 387

B. L. Harris   The Wenallt   Gilwern   Abergavenny NP7 0HP   Monmouthshire
Tel: (01873) 830694   Open: ALL YEAR   Map Ref No. 22

The Wenallt. Gilwern.

Monmouthshire & Pembrokeshire

Great House

Near Rd: B.4596

Great House is a pretty 16th-century Grade II listed home on the banks of the River Usk, with clematis garden. Excellent night stopover for those travelling to Wales & Ireland. Retaining much of its original character with beams & inglenook fireplaces. Offering 3 bedrooms with T.V. etc. A drawing room with T.V. & woodburner. Within easy reach of golf course, fishing & forest trails. Caerleon is very near with its amphitheatre, museums & Roman Baths. Good pubs. Children over 10.
E-mail: dinah.price@amserve.net
www.visitgreathouse.co.uk

| £25.00 to £30.00 | Y | N | Y |

| Dinah Price | Great House | Isca Road | Old Village | Caerleon NP18 1QG | Monmouthshire |
| Tel: (01633) 420216 | | Fax 01633 423492 | | Open: ALL YEAR | Map Ref No. 23 |

Parva Farmhouse Hotel

Near Rd: A.466

A delightful 17th-century stone farmhouse situated 50 yards from the River Wye. The quaint en-suite bedrooms, with their designer fabrics, are gorgeous, & some offer breathtaking views over the River Wye & woodland. The beamed lounge, with log fires, leather Chesterfields & 'Honesty Bar', is a tranquil haven in which to unwind. Mouthwatering dishes, served in the intimate, candlelit Inglenook Restaurant, reflect the owner's love of cooking. A perfect home for a relaxing break.
E-mail: parva_hoteltintern@hotmail.com
www.hoteltintern.co.uk

| £35.00 to £38.00 | Y | Y | Y |

see PHOTO over p. 389

VISA: M'CARD:

| Dereck & Vickie Stubbs | Parva Farmhouse Hotel | Tintern NP16 6SQ | Monmouthshire |
| Tel: (01291) 689411 | Fax 01291 689557 | Open: ALL YEAR | Map Ref No. 24 |

Allenbrook

Near Rd: A.40

Allenbrook is a charming country house set in its own grounds. It is adjacent to the beach & situated in the Pembrokeshire National Park on the coastal path. The house is very comfortable with spacious bedrooms fully-equipped with T.V. & tea/coffee-making facilities. All the bedrooms have en-suite or private bathrooms, & there is a large, comfortable guests' sitting room. A delightful home & an ideal spot for a relaxing short break or holiday.
E-mail: elizabeth@allenbrook.freeserve.co.uk
www.ukworld.net/allenbrook

| £30.00 to £30.00 | N | N | N |

| Mrs E. A. Webber | Allenbrook | Dale | Haverfordwest SA62 3RN | Pembrokeshire |
| Tel: (01646) 636254 | | Fax 01646 636954 | Open: ALL YEAR | Map Ref No. 25 |

Knowles Farm

Near Rd: A.4075

Knowles Farm is a lovely old farmhouse which faces south & overlooks organic farmland & ancient hanging woods. The boundary is the Cleddau Estuary & is a delight to discover. Your hosts can arrange river trips; you can leave the car & walk to castles, pubs, woodland. Gardens, galleries, beaches, riding, fishing & ancient monuments are all within a 10-mile radius. Good pubs & restaurants or enjoy a home-cooked organic meal in front of the fire or in the garden (by arrangement).
E-mail: ginilp@lawrenny.org.uk
www.lawrenny.org.uk

| £25.00 to £30.00 | Y | Y | Y |

| Mrs Virginia Lort Phillips | Knowles Farm | Lawrenny SA68 0PX | Pembrokeshire |
| Tel: (01834) 891221 | Fax 01834 891221 | Open: EASTER - OCT | Map Ref No. 26 |

Parva Farmhouse and Restaurant. Tintern.

Wales
Pembrokeshire & Powys

The Old Vicarage

Near Rd: A.487

Patricia & David welcome you to their elegant Edwardian home set in an elevated position with large lawned gardens & glorious views to the sea. Offering 3 comfortably furnished en-suite bedrooms with tea/coffee-making facilities. Situated in Britain's only coastal National Park, 1 mile from one of the most dramatic sections of the Pembrokeshire Coast Path at Ceibwr Bay, with the Preseli Hills & Teifi Valley nearby. Enjoy the timeless & leisurely tranquillity of north Pembrokeshire. Croeso!
E-mail: stay@old-vic.co.uk
www.old-vic.co.uk

	rate	children	evening	animals
	£32.50 to £32.50	N	Y	N

Patricia & David Phillips   The Old Vicarage   Moylegrove SA43 3BN   Pembrokeshire
Tel: (01239) 881231   Open: MAR - OCT   Map Ref No. 27

The Old Vicarage

Near Rd: A.4139

Situated in the coastal village of Manorbier with its beautiful beaches & castle, The Old Vicarage offers gracious accommodation with glimpses of Barafundle Bay. The en-suite bedrooms are furnished with antiques & have tea/coffee-making facilities. Guests may enjoy the mature gardens or sit by a log fire in the drawing room. For the more energetic, the Pembrokeshire Coastal Path passes through the village. Beaches a 5-min. walk. Irish ferries from Pembroke (20 mins') & Fishguard (50 mins'). Children over 7.
E-mail: oldvic_manorbier@yahoo.com

	£25.00 to £30.00	Y	N	N

Mrs Jill McHugh   The Old Vicarage   Manorbier   Nr. Tenby SA70 7TN   Pembrokeshire
Tel: (01834) 871452   Fax 01834 871452   Open: ALL YEAR   Map Ref No. 28

Old Stable Cottage

Near Rd: A.4075

The Cottage (Grade II listed), with inglenook fireplace & original bread oven, was once a stable & carthouse to 13th-century Carew Castle situated near the entrance & the creek of Carew River with its Tidal Mill. A spiral staircase leads to 2 charming, oak beamed en-suite bedrooms with colour T.V., home-baked Welsh cakes & tea/coffee. Delicious breakfasts are prepared in the farmhouse kitchen on the Aga. A conservatory overlooks the garden. Good local pub & restaurant offering evening meals, within walking distance. Children over 10.

	£24.00 to £28.00	Y	N	N

Mrs J. Fielder Old Stable Cottage 3 Picton Terrace Carew Village Tenby SA70 8SL Pembrokeshire
Tel: (01646) 651889   Open: FEB - NOV   Map Ref No. 29

Lodge Farm

Near Rd: A.479

The Merediths welcome you to their 18th-century home, sharing its comfort, old family treasures & warm hospitality. Freshly prepared, interesting meals using home & local produce are a speciality & are served in the attractive dining room with original inglenook fireplace & flagstone floor. Cosy en-suite bedrooms. A lounge with T.V. & literature & local maps etc to help you make the most of your stay. A large garden with mountain views; quietly situated 1 1/2 miles from Talgarth within the Brecon Beacons National Park. Dinner by arrangement.
E-mail: lodgefarm@bushinternet.com

	£23.00 to £26.00	Y	Y	Y

Marion Meredith   Lodge Farm   Talgarth   Brecon LD3 0DP   Powys
Tel: (01874) 711244   Fax 01874 711244   Open: ALL YEAR   Map Ref No. 30

Glangrwyney Court. Crickhowell.

	rate £ from - to per person	children taken	evening meals	animals taken

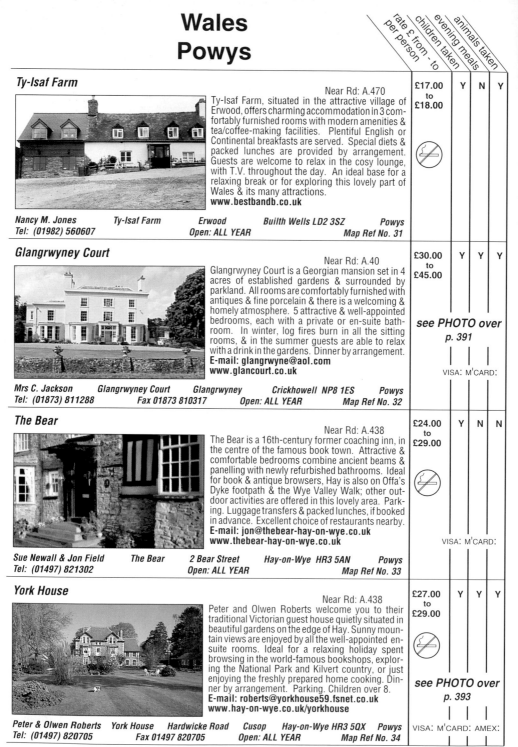

Ty-Isaf Farm

Near Rd: A.470

Ty-Isaf Farm, situated in the attractive village of Erwood, offers charming accommodation in 3 comfortably furnished rooms with modern amenities & tea/coffee-making facilities. Plentiful English or Continental breakfasts are served. Special diets & packed lunches are provided by arrangement. Guests are welcome to relax in the cosy lounge, with T.V. throughout the day. An ideal base for a relaxing break or for exploring this lovely part of Wales & its many attractions.

www.bestbandb.co.uk

£17.00 to £18.00 — Y N Y

Nancy M. Jones   Ty-Isaf Farm   Erwood   Builth Wells LD2 3SZ   Powys
Tel: (01982) 560607   Open: ALL YEAR   Map Ref No. 31

Glangrwyney Court

Near Rd: A.40

Glangrwyney Court is a Georgian mansion set in 4 acres of established gardens & surrounded by parkland. All rooms are comfortably furnished with antiques & fine porcelain & there is a welcoming & homely atmosphere. 5 attractive & well-appointed bedrooms, each with a private or en-suite bathroom. In winter, log fires burn in all the sitting rooms, & in the summer guests are able to relax with a drink in the gardens. Dinner by arrangement.

E-mail: glangrwyne@aol.com
www.glancourt.co.uk

£30.00 to £45.00 — Y Y Y

see PHOTO over p. 391

VISA: M'CARD:

Mrs C. Jackson   Glangrwyney Court   Glangrwyney   Crickhowell NP8 1ES   Powys
Tel: (01873) 811288   Fax 01873 810317   Open: ALL YEAR   Map Ref No. 32

The Bear

Near Rd: A.438

The Bear is a 16th-century former coaching inn, in the centre of the famous book town. Attractive & comfortable bedrooms combine ancient beams & panelling with newly refurbished bathrooms. Ideal for book & antique browsers, Hay is also on Offa's Dyke footpath & the Wye Valley Walk; other outdoor activities are offered in this lovely area. Parking. Luggage transfers & packed lunches, if booked in advance. Excellent choice of restaurants nearby.

E-mail: jon@thebear-hay-on-wye.co.uk
www.thebear-hay-on-wye.co.uk

£24.00 to £29.00 — Y N N

VISA: M'CARD:

Sue Newall & Jon Field   The Bear   2 Bear Street   Hay-on-Wye HR3 5AN   Powys
Tel: (01497) 821302   Open: ALL YEAR   Map Ref No. 33

York House

Near Rd: A.438

Peter and Olwen Roberts welcome you to their traditional Victorian guest house quietly situated in beautiful gardens on the edge of Hay. Sunny mountain views are enjoyed by all the well-appointed en-suite rooms. Ideal for a relaxing holiday spent browsing in the world-famous bookshops, exploring the National Park and Kilvert country, or just enjoying the freshly prepared home cooking. Dinner by arrangement. Parking. Children over 8.

E-mail: roberts@yorkhouse59.fsnet.co.uk
www.hay-on-wye.co.uk/yorkhouse

£27.00 to £29.00 — Y Y Y

see PHOTO over p. 393

VISA: M'CARD: AMEX:

Peter & Olwen Roberts   York House   Hardwicke Road   Cusop   Hay-on-Wye HR3 5QX   Powys
Tel: (01497) 820705   Fax 01497 820705   Open: ALL YEAR   Map Ref No. 34

York House. Cusop.

Wales
Powys & Swansea

Guidfa House

Near Rd: A.483, A.44

Licensed Georgian guest house, situated in an ideal location for touring lakes, mountains, national parks & the coast. The bedrooms are all comfortable, non-smoking & spacious, all are en-suite with colour T.V. & tea/coffee-making facilities. A ground-floor room is also available. Meals are prepared by Anne, who is Cordon-Bleu-trained. Dinner is a set menu, but special diets/requests can always be catered for with prior notice. Children over 10.
E-mail: guidfa@globalnet.co.uk
www.guidfa-house.co.uk

£27.50 to £30.00 | Y | Y | N

VISA: M'CARD:

Tony & Anne Millan   Guidfa House   Crossgates   Llandrindod Wells LD1 6RF   Powys
Tel: (01597) 851241   Fax 01597 851875   Open: ALL YEAR   Map Ref No. 35

Little Brompton Farm

Near Rd: A.489

Robert & Gaynor welcome you to this charming 17th-century farmhouse, situated on this working farm. The house has much original character, with beautiful old oak beams. Pretty en-suite bedrooms, enhanced by quality antiques. T.V.. Offa's Dyke runs through the farm. Situated on the B.4385, 2 miles east of the beautiful Georgian town of Montgomery. Come & be cosseted in old-fashioned comfort in this peaceful countryside.
E-mail: gaynor.brompton@virgin.net
www.littlebromptonfarm.co.uk

£25.00 to £27.00 | Y | N | N

Gaynor Bright   Little Brompton Farm   Montgomery SY15 6HY   Powys
Tel: (01686) 668371   Fax 01686 668371   Open: ALL YEAR   Map Ref No. 36

Lower Trelydan

Near Rd: A.490

Graham & Sue welcome you to their wonderful, award-winning black-&-white farmhouse, set on their working farm & listed for its history & beauty. Tastefully furnished en-suite bedrooms with T.V.. An oak-beamed lounge & a dining room where evening meals are served most nights. Home cooking a speciality. Licensed. Powis Castle & many beauty spots are nearby, also leisure activities & walks. A charming house, steeped in history.
E-mail: stay@lowertrelydan.com
www.lowertrelydan.com

£28.00 to £30.00 | Y | Y | N

see PHOTO over p. 395

Mrs Sue Jones   Lower Trelydan   Guilsfield   Welshpool SY21 9PH   Powys
Tel: (01938) 553105   Fax 01938 553105   Open: ALL YEAR (Excl. Xmas & New Year)   Map Ref No. 37

Tides Reach

Near Rd: A.4067

The warmest of welcomes awaits you at Tides Reach, where you will find a lovingly restored early Victorian town house elegantly furnished with antiques. There are 6 attractive bedrooms, each with private facilities. Well situated on the seafront in the delightful village of Mumbles (the gateway to Gower), only 4 miles from the city centre. An ideal base for business or pleasure & convenient as a stop on your way to Ireland.
E-mail: tidesreachmumbles@yahoo.com
www.tidesreachguesthouse.co.uk

£30.00 to £37.50 | N | N | Y

Jan Maybery   Tides Reach   388 Mumbles Road   Mumbles   Swansea SA3 5TN   Swansea
Tel: (01792) 404877   Fax 01792 404775   Open: FEB - NOV   Map Ref No. 38

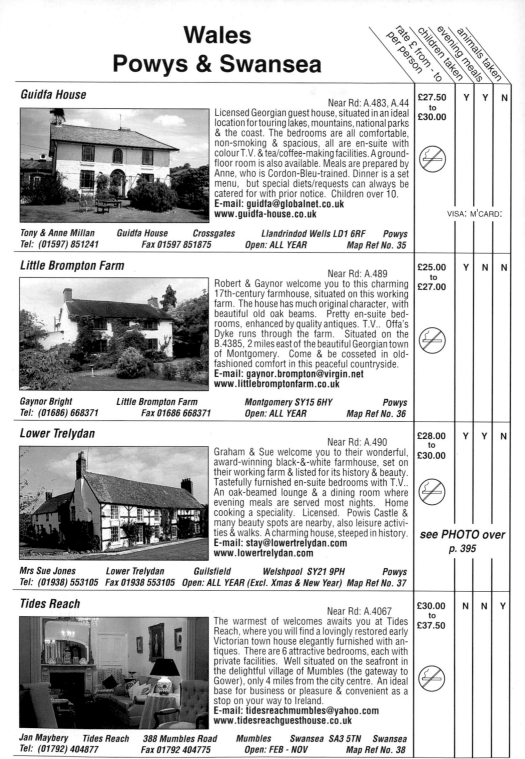

Lower Trelydan Farm. Guilsfield.

Towns & Counties Index

Town	County	Country	Town	County	Country
Aberfoyle	Stirlingshire	Scotland	Chelwood Gate	Sussex	England
Abergavenny	Monmouthshire	Wales	Chester	Cheshire	England
Aboyne	Aberdeenshire	Scotland	Chichester	Sussex	England
Airdrie	Lanarkshire	Scotland	Chippenham	Wiltshire	England
Alnwick	Northumberland	England	Chipping Campden	Gloucestershire	England
Ambleside	Cumbria	England	Christchurch	Hampshire	England
Ampleforth	Yorkshire	England	Cirencester	Gloucestershire	England
Andover	Hampshire	England	Clitheroe	Lancashire	England
Anstruther	Fifeshire	Scotland	Coalville	Leicestershire	England
Appin	Argyll	Scotland	Cockermouth	Cumbria	England
Arundel	Sussex	England	Colyton	Devon	England
Ascog	Isle of Bute	Scotland	Corfe Castle	Dorset	England
Ashbourne	Derbyshire	England	Corsham	Wiltshire	England
Ashby de la Zouche	Derbyshire	England	Crackington Haven	Cornwall	England
Auchtermuchty	Fifeshire	Scotland	Cranbrook	Kent	England
Aviemore	Inverness-shire	Scotland	Cranleigh	Surrey	England
Ayr	Ayrshire	Scotland	Craven Arms	Shropshire	England
Bala	Gwynedd	Wales	Crediton	Devon	England
Banbury	Oxfordshire	England	Crianlarich	Perthshire	Scotland
Barnstaple	Devon	England	Criccieth	Gwynedd	Wales
Bath	Somerset	England	Crickhowell	Powys	Wales
Bath	Wiltshire	England	Dorchester	Dorset	England
Bedale	Yorkshire	England	Dorking	Surrey	England
Bedford	Bedfordshire	England	Doune	Perthshire	Scotland
Berkhamsted	Hertfordshire	England	Dover	Kent	England
Betws-y-Coed	Conwy	Wales	Dumbarton	Dunbartonshire	Scotland
Beverley	Yorkshire	England	Dumfries	Dumfriesshire	Scotland
Bideford	Devon	England	Dundonald	Ayrshire	Scotland
Bishop Auckland	Durham	England	Dunkeld	Perthshire	Scotland
Bolney	Sussex	England	Dunster	Somerset	England
Bolton	Lancashire	England	Durham	Durham	England
Bourne	Lincolnshire	England	Dursley	Gloucestershire	England
Bourton-on-the-Water	Gloucestershire	England	Easingwold	Yorkshire	England
Bradford	Yorkshire	England	Eastbourne	Sussex	England
Bradford-on-Avon	Wiltshire	England	Edinburgh	Edinburgh	Scotland
Brampton	Cumbria	England	Ely	Cambridgeshire	England
Brecon	Powys	Wales	Exeter	Devon	England
Bridgwater	Somerset	England	Exeter	Devon	England
Bridlington	Yorkshire	England	Exmoor National Park	Somerset	England
Bridport	Dorset	England	Exmouth	Devon	England
Brighton	Sussex	England	Eyam	Derbyshire	England
Bristol	Gloucestershire	England	Fairford	Gloucestershire	England
Broadford	Isle of Skye	Scotland	Falmouth	Cornwall	England
Broadway	Worcestershire	England	Faringdon	Oxfordshire	England
Builth Wells	Powys	Wales	Farnham	Hampshire	England
Bungay	Suffolk	England	Faversham	Kent	England
Burford	Oxfordshire	England	Fintry	Stirlingshire	Scotland
Burley	Hampshire	England	Folkestone	Kent	England
Buttermere	Cumbria	England	Fordham	Cambridgeshire	England
Buxton	Derbyshire	England	Fordingbridge	Hampshire	England
Caerleon	Monmouthshire	Wales	Fort William	Inverness-shire	Scotland
Caernarfon	Gwynedd	Wales	Gatwick	Surrey	England
Cambridge	Cambridgeshire	England	Gatwick	Sussex	England
Canterbury	Kent	England	Girvan	Ayrshire	Scotland
Carlisle	Cumbria	England	Glasgow	Glasgow	Scotland
Carnforth	Lancashire	England	Glastonbury	Somerset	England
Castle Douglas	Dumfriesshire	Scotland	Gloucester	Gloucestershire	England
Chagford	Devon	England	Grange-over-Sands	Cumbria	England
Cheltenham	Gloucestershire	England	Grantham	Lincolnshire	England

Towns & Counties Index

Towns & Counties Index